# Criticism
# and the
# Color Line

# Criticism and the Color Line

## Desegregating American Literary Studies

Edited by

HENRY B. WONHAM

Rutgers University Press
New Brunswick, New Jersey

Library of Congress Cataloging-in-Publication Data

Criticism and the color line : desegrating American literary studies / edited by Henry B. Wonham.
   p.  cm.
   Includes bibliographical references (p.   ) and index.
   ISBN 0-8135-2262-5 (cloth : alk. paper).—ISBN 0-8135-2263-3 (pbk. : alk. paper)
   1. American literature—Afro-American authors—History and criticism.  2. American literature—White authors—History and criticism.  3. Afro-Americans in literature.  4. Race relations in literature.  5. Racism in literature.  I. Wonham, Henry B., 1960–.
PS153.N5C78  1996
810.9′896073—dc20                                     95-33062
                                                          CIP

British Cataloging-in-Publication information available

Toni Morrison, "Unspeakable Things Unspoken: The Afro-American Presence in American Literature," from *Michigan Quarterly Review* 28 (Winter 1989); reprinted by permission of International Creative Management, Inc. Copyright © 1989 by Toni Morrison. Eric Lott, "Mr. Clemens and Jim Crow: Twain, Race, and Blackface," from *The Cambridge Companion to Mark Twain*, ed. Forrest G. Robinson (New York: Cambridge University Press, 1995), reprinted with the permission of Cambridge University Press.

*For my parents*

# Contents

# Acknowledgments

Collections of this sort are by definition the result of collaborative effort, but *Criticism and the Color Line* is exceptional for the kind and degree of participation offered by a vast community of scholars. For their indispensable support, I would like to thank first my students and colleagues at St. John's University in New York and the University of Mannheim in Germany, where the concept behind this book first began to take shape in the form of an extended classroom debate. I am also grateful to the tireless correspondents, too numerous to name, who clarified my understanding of the racial landscape in American literary studies, and thus helped me to articulate the collection's aims. I received especially significant input from David Barrow, John W. Crowley, Alice Deck, Laura A. Doyle, Judith Fetterley, Eric Haralson, Susan Harris, Gordon Hutner, Lee Mitchell, Wilson J. Moses, Michael North, Thomas Peyser, Phillip M. Richards, Gary Scharnhorst, David Lionel Smith, Werner Sollors, and Shira Wolosky, all of whom deserve to be listed as contributors to the volume. It would be redundant to thank the essayists individually for the diligence and generosity with which they performed their separate parts in the joint effort, but I would like to acknowledge in particular the extraordinary contributions made by Robert S. Levine and Shelley Fisher Fishkin. Without their constant assistance during more than two years of planning, composing, and compiling, the collection simply would not have been possible. Lastly, I would like to express my indebtedness to Leslie Mitchner of Rutgers University Press, whose good humor and editorial acumen have made my job a pleasure.

Criticism
and the
Color Line

# Introduction

Perhaps the most insidious and least understood form of segregation is that of the word.
—Ralph Ellison, 1946

R alph Ellison launched a remarkably eloquent appeal for desegregation of
America's cultural heritage at a time when the nation's intensely self-conscious literary critical establishment was incapable of heeding him. At the heart
of Ellison's critique was an insight into American cultural identity, an insight
that is as fresh, as relevant, and as controversial today as it must have seemed
irrelevant to the majority of Americans in the years immediately following the
Second World War. "Materially, psychologically, and culturally," Ellison intoned
to a segregated America, "part of the nation's heritage is Negro American, and
whatever it becomes will be shaped in part by the Negro's presence." That which
is "essentially American," he wrote, "springs from the synthesis of our diverse
elements of cultural style." The white American artist or cultural critic shields
himself [sic] from this self-knowledge by enclosing African Americans within
a limiting and dehumanizing stereotype, while "on his side of the joke the Negro
looks at the white man and finds it difficult to believe that [he] . . . can be so
absurdly self-deluded over the true interrelatedness of blackness and whiteness."[1]
   To neglect the shaping effect of "the Negro's presence" upon mainstream
culture, Ellison went on in essay after essay during the forties, fifties, and sixties,
is to misrepresent American identity and to cheat the nation as a whole of its
ethnically dynamic cultural heritage. The price of maintaining a critical illusion
of ethnic purity in American expressive life is simply too high, he argued, for
those who "ignore the Negro . . . distort their own humanity. It is as though we
dread to acknowledge the complex, pluralistic nature of our society, and as a result
we find ourselves stumbling upon our true national identity under circumstances in
which we least expect to do so." To a Cold War critical establishment impervious
to African American culture, Ellison impertinently exclaimed that "the whole of
American life" is "a drama acted out upon the body of a Negro giant, who, lying
trussed up like Gulliver, forms the stage and the scene upon which and within
which the action unfolds." By refusing to acknowledge the "blending and meta-
morphosis" of European and African cultural forms throughout American life,
he concluded, "we misconceive our cultural identity."[2]
   The evasive "dread" Ellison first described on the eve of the Civil Rights
movement was, of course, rooted in historical guilt, for to acknowledge the
presence of African-American culture in shaping American identity would have
been to entertain a devastating affront to the nation's founding principles. From
its beginnings in the late nineteenth century through the period of Ellison's

poignant but lonely appeal, the academic study of American literature had been motivated by the desire not to complicate but to underwrite those principles aesthetically. The national identity, as it was articulated at the turn of the century by a pioneering generation of Americanists, emerged in the uniquely rich political soil of the New World as a consequence of foundational democratic ideals guaranteeing individual freedom. African-American culture, with its many echoes and retentions of the slave regime, posed a standing contradiction to those ideals, and thus Ellison's black Gulliver naturally bore a negative relation to dominant conceptions of American identity, conceptions that were still widely accepted in 1952 when he gave the problem its most memorable expression in *Invisible Man*. A pervasive blindness to "the Negro's presence," in other words, was the necessary condition of a critical establishment determined to legitimate, not to complicate, nativist accounts of America's cultural heritage.

African Americans had challenged the notion of Euro-American ethnocentrism before, none more compellingly than W.E.B. Du Bois. Moving with unprecedented agility between two worlds officially separated by the "veil" of race, Du Bois argued in *The Souls of Black Folk* (1903) that white American culture is unthinkable without black American culture. "Actively we have woven ourselves with the very warp and woof of this nation," he maintained, dramatizing his point by coupling allusions to the sorrow songs with references to classical European texts throughout his masterful book.[3] "Would America have been America without her Negro people?" Du Bois asked rhetorically in 1903, anticipating Ellison's fantasy rejoinder in the 1970 essay, "What America Would Be Like Without Blacks." For both writers, the notion of an America without black culture intended to provoke a rethinking of the national identity; in both cases, white America responded with a collective shrug of the shoulders, implying by its indifference that America without black culture was indeed thinkable, perhaps even desirable, and that such an America would look, sound, and feel very much as it does, only a bit whiter.

Enter Toni Morrison, who challenges Americans to rethink the old question once again in her 1988 lecture "Unspeakable Things Unspoken: The Afro-American Presence in American Literature."[4] The question itself—"Would America have been America without her Negro people?"—has changed very little over time, but Morrison's challenge to traditional figurations of American identity carries a new inflection. "Afro-American culture exists," she asserts unequivocally, abandoning Du Bois's rhetorical gambit, and its presence has inspired remarkable feats of intellectual and artistic evasion on the part of the dominant culture. Like Ellison's black giant, the all-inclusive background against which American life unfolds, Morrison's "Afro-American presence" is often invisible, but in a pervasive way. "Certain absences," she claims, "are so stressed, so ornate, so planned, they call attention to themselves . . . like neighborhoods that are defined by the population held away from them." The greatness of American literature, especially "the founding nineteenth-century works," originates for Morrison in the flight from blackness, from the shadow of a presence that always threatens to envelop the white artist. The act of silencing this presence, she claims, may inspire novelistic invention, or it may lead to "a virtual infantilization of the writer's intellect, his sensibility, his craft." In either case, the founding documents of American culture are shaped by their engagement with blackness, most interestingly and profoundly when those documents strain to exclude overt reference to race.

Morrison challenges students of American culture to reexamine "the American canon . . . for the 'unspeakable things unspoken': for the ways in which the presence of Afro-Americans has shaped the choices, the language, the structure— the meaning of so much American literature. A search, in other words, for the ghost in the machine." Implicit in this call for a reinterpretation of classic American texts is an indictment of the critical establishment that greeted Ralph Ellison's very similar appeal with polite indifference a generation ago, and indeed Morrison's impassioned argument is designed to make another collective shrug of white shoulders highly problematic. The power of canonical works by Poe, Melville, Hawthorne, Twain, and Cather, she contends, lies in their subtle engagement with America's central philosophical, constitutional, moral, and aesthetic dilemma—the dilemma of race—perhaps most characteristically when that engagement entails ingenious novelistic contortions of evasion. A critical practice that neglects the remarkable "intellectual feats" required to perform this hazardous dance with the beast of American ethnicity is guilty of "lobotomizing" the most innovative and important works of American literature, thereby "diminishing both the art and the artist." In its irrational effort to make the canon appear "race-free" and "universal," such a critical practice simplifies and infantilizes a complex body of literature—"like the surgical removal of legs so that the body can remain enthroned, immobile, static." The impression of hegemonic control by a white male cultural elite in American letters, Morrison concludes, may be "the insistent fruit of the scholarship rather than the text." "It only seems that the canon of American literature is 'naturally' or 'inevitably' 'white.' In fact it is studiously so."

Morrison's alternative to a criticism that whitewashes the founding texts of American literature, and trivializes them in the process, is therapeutic in two ways. On one hand, she intends to recover the silenced African-American presence in nineteenth-century works, and to make that presence visible and audible to contemporary sensibilities. On the other hand, in a related gesture, she is interested in "resuscitating" an impoverished canon, restoring to works like *Moby Dick*, *The Narrative of Arthur Gordon Pym*, and *Adventures of Huckleberry Finn* an appreciation for their complex maneuvering around, through, and within racial discourses. Our longstanding habit of neglecting what Ellison called "the true interrelatedness of blackness and whiteness" distorts our understanding of *both* cultural traditions by denying to each a crucial source of its creativity. Morrison never implies that this interrelatedness is cordial, peaceful, or fraternal—to the contrary, transgressions of the color line are apt to entail acts of cultural appropriation, imitation, parody, or evasion. Her point, one that the critics represented in this volume attend to keenly, is that American culture is *produced*, not diluted, by such acts of creative exchange, where the black or white artist wrestles to delineate an image upon a background that always threatens to reabsorb it. Whether the image is that of a white American superimposed on an enveloping black body, as Ellison imagined it, or vice versa, American identity is negotiated along the color line, where clear delineations require an artist's careful, often duplicitous, touch. Morrison asks us to appreciate the dexterity involved in applying this touch to American literature, and to refrain from "disfiguring" the nation's literary heritage by neglecting its most vital field of concern.

Morrison's emphasis in "Unspeakable Things Unspoken" is on the recovery of canonical works by white authors whose engagement with race was overlooked by a generation of critics convinced that great literature must be apolitical, and thus unconcerned with race. Her challenge to critical orthodoxies, however, bears important implications for African-American literature and criticism as well. As the bard of literary desegregation, Ellison warned against the very natural defensive impulse to treat black culture as an ethnocentrically closed field, hermetically shut off from the dominant culture.[5] Yet the tendency persists, and today the notion of dynamic cultural exchange between black and white representational traditions in America is more likely to encounter resistance from an African-American critical establishment understandably sensitive to incursions from the outside than from keepers of the nativist flame.[6] The aggressive appropriation of black cultural forms, these critics maintain, is a process as old as America itself and as demeaning to African Americans as the minstrel show. A truly pluralist literary criticism, they argue, ought to give up the age-old business of cultural appropriation, and dedicate itself instead to recovering the integrity of black cultural life and expression.

The attractiveness of this defensive position is as clear as are its limitations. In the effort to resist further degradation of African-American cultural specificity, critics threaten to impoverish the very tradition they would defend. Morrison's comment on the "sacred texts" of American literature holds equally true for the sacred texts of the African-American tradition, like Frederick Douglass's autobiographies, Harriet Jacobs's *Incidents in the Life of a Slave Girl*, the novels of Charles Chesnutt, Richard Wright, Ellison, and Morrison herself. "The subject of the conflagration," Morrison warns, "is sacrificed, disfigured in the battle" to keep the lines of literary descent artificially pure. These books were written with a pervasive awareness, whether hospitable or not, of "mainstream" literary, cultural, and political life in America, and their power stems in part, like the power of so much American literature, from the creative management of that awareness.

Ellison understood that racial essentialism constituted a necessary critical illusion for members of his generation, for black artists and intellectuals after the Second World War struggled merely to make their voices heard apart from the homogenizing buzz of a dominant culture that failed to acknowledge African-American cultural integrity. A space of "difference," in other words, was essential to the emergence of black voices in artistic, educational, and political life. That space of difference is real, and its constant articulation remains a necessity, especially in the contemporary climate of increasing conservative assaults on the legitimacy of Black Studies programs and multicultural initiatives in academia. Yet in repeating the essentialist gestures that brought institutional legitimacy to the study of American literature one hundred years ago, African-American critics threaten to erect many of the same self-defeating obstacles that their nativist counterparts have been so long in overcoming. As Werner Sollors explains in "A Critique of Pure Pluralism,"

> Literary pluralists of our time would like to construct a mosaic of ethnic stories that relies on the supposed permanence, individuality, and homogeneity of each ancestral tradition and has no space for the syncretistic nature of so much of American literary and cultural life. Ironically . . . literary pluralists share their dislike of mixings and "impurities" with the old nativists who, too, worked very hard at ignoring not only certain ethnic groups but also the polyethnic mixings in American culture.[7]

Is it necessary, Sollors asks, to acknowledge a line of cultural descent stretching from Hemingway to Twain, but not including Ellison, who is supposed—in spite of his own comments on the question of influence—to have learned his art from James Weldon Johnson and Richard Wright? "Can Gertrude Stein be discussed with Richard Wright or only with white women expatriate German-Jewish writers?" Is there an important link between the autobiographies of Benjamin Franklin and Frederick Douglass, or must Douglass be regarded exclusively as "a version of Olaudah Equiano and a precursor to Malcolm X?"[8] Must literary history, we might go on, be organized according to the genetic transfer of biological traits, or do ideas, images, literary and rhetorical forms circulate in interesting ways across racial boundaries? It strikes me as odd that the title of Bernard W. Bell's outstanding book, *The Afro-American Novel and Its Tradition* (1987), alludes to another landmark study, Richard Chase's *The American Novel and Its Tradition* (1957), yet neither book draws the slightest connection between these two presumably discrete literary developments. Morrison has invited students of American literature to reevaluate Chase's romance tradition by asking, "Where . . . in these romances is the shadow of the presence from which the text has fled? Where does it heighten, where does it dislocate, where does it necessitate novelistic invention; what does it release; what does it hobble?" The "white presence" in African-American writing may not be exactly a "ghost in the machine"—that metaphor will have to be revised and Morrison's questions reformulated—but some version of her revisionist inquiry might produce important insight into Bernard Bell's novelistic tradition as well.

It was essential for a generation of African-American critics to search literary works for what Houston Baker ten years ago called "the culturally specific in Afro-American life and expression."[9] Indeed, this collection of essays could not have been conceived without the space of cultural difference so painstakingly marked out by Baker, Stephen Henderson, Amiri Baraka, and other pioneering African-Americanists. But Kenneth Warren strikes a new and very important key in African-American literary criticism when he writes that, "while it remains important, intellectually and politically, to address the multiple factors that have set African Americans apart from the fellow citizens, it is equally worthwhile to attend to the pressures that challenge cultural distinctiveness."[10] Citing Morrison's "Unspeakable Things Unspoken" as his own point of departure in *Black and White Strangers: Race and American Literary Realism*, Warren writes:

> Staring at one another across the void of American identity, African and European Americans have been constructing themselves and each other, each side trying to lay claim to an unchallenged cultural legacy and each failing (to paraphrase Twain) to prove unambiguous title. As each side strives to construct a *sui generis* account of its own heritage, the Other insists upon emerging in unexpected and embarrassing places.[11]

The essays contained in *Criticism and the Color Line* are situated within Warren's provocative "void of American identity," that contested zone where African-American and "mainstream" cultural forms collide, compete, reproduce, and in some cases blend with one another as parts of what Eric Sundquist has recently called "the complex dialectic between 'white' and 'black' cultures that has given rise to some of our most important national literature."[12] The contributors bring a wide range of interests and methodologies to bear on what Du Bois prophetically deemed "the problem of the twentieth century"—"the problem of the color line"—yet they concur in treating racial difference as something more than a problem to be solved by essentialist critical practices.[13] Race in America, according to Warren, "particularly black/white racial difference, emerges not merely as a problem but as part of the discursive building blocks that make expression—political and aesthetic—possible."[14] Significant expression occurs along the color line because it is there that American identity is most at issue, there that the racial "Other," whether black or white, is most insistent and hardest to conceal. The task of criticism, the essayists agree, is to document the "embarrassing" presence of this "Other" in cultural places where one least expects to find it, to historicize rather than to deny the cultural exchanges that *produce* American identity.[15] It would be difficult to guess where any two authors might agree on specific texts, yet they concur in depicting the color line as a site of cultural mutation, and they share the desire to read much of American literature with Sundquist as the product of "two traditions that are always dynamically defining each other."[16]

Those two traditions collide on the racially charged minstrel stage in Eric Lott's "Mr. Clemens and Jim Crow: Twain, Race, and Blackface." Explaining that the origins of blackface performance lie in a peculiar blend of white supremacist fear and identification with African-American culture—an equation that simultaneously insists upon and disavows the common humanity of white and black Americans—Lott contends that "the active exchanges of white self and black Other in blackface performance, however derisive, opened the color line to effacement in the very moment of its construction." Moreover, the contradictoriness of this gesture helps to explain why "one of the nineteenth century's most powerful anti-racist novels," *Adventures of Huckleberry Finn*, is so laden with racist stereotypes and episodes demeaning to African Americans. Twain did not merely lose sight of his anti-racist theme at various points in the novel, according to Lott; rather, the uneven course of Jim's ennoblement and dehumanization betrays the logic of the minstrel stage, in all its contradictory splendor, for Twain's representation of race is "shot through with blackface thinking." Juxtaposing some of the novel's patently racist episodes against Mark Twain's earnest moral observations, the essay demonstrates that *Huckleberry Finn's* "strengths" and "limitations" are *both* "oddly imbricated with strains of thought and feeling that inspired blackface performance." Minstrelsy, according to Lott, "was something like the device or code or signifying system through which Twain worked out his least self-conscious and most sophisticated impulses regarding race in the United States."

Peter Carafiol is also interested in the way American narratives of dissent, both fictional and critical, seem to reinforce the very ethnic boundaries they claim to transgress. Carafiol's argument in " 'Who I Was': Ethnic Identity and American Literary Ethnocentrism" has far-reaching implications for "the critical rhetoric of ethnicity," but his discussion centers on three representative texts: Horatio Alger's *Ragged Dick*, Booker T. Washington's *Up from Slavery*, and Richard Wright's *Native Son*. As classic rags to riches stories, the first two points in this irregular triangle deploy versions of an American myth of self-creation, in which "former identities are sloughed off as if they had never been, leaving essential identities untouched." Alger's novel "works hard to make 'class' look like a permeable boundary," yet the appearance of radical personal growth is deceiving, according to Carafiol, for "change" in *Ragged Dick* really amounts to "the stripping away of the inessential to more fully enact what [Dick] has always been." Washington's autobiographical narrative similarly "pretends that race can be a permeable boundary," yet the upward progress Washington announces in his title, like Dick's journey from poverty to middle-class respectability, is part of a rhetorical equation that "not only displays but insists upon the boundaries between blacks and whites." As texts that epitomize the boomerang logic of American self-creation, *Ragged Dick* and *Up from Slavery* represent for Carafiol an important "genre of revisionist rhetoric," for they "reiterate the terms of the dominant culture in the very process of, and even as a strategy for, dissenting from it." Wright's *Native Son*, a novel that seems to foreclose every possibility for self-creation, ironically emerges as a fictional alternative to this deceptively conservative "American narrative" of personal and cultural transformation. "The figure for the color 'line' in *Native Son*," according to Carafiol, "is a circle, like Pascal's God: its center is everywhere and its circumference nowhere." Thus in different ways all three novels illustrate Carafiol's underlying point that ethnic boundaries, as they are construed in critical and literary discourses of American identity, "cannot be crossed, since as *matters* of definition, they are, *by* definition, impermeable. That is their purpose." The solution is not to give up on change, but to invent new discourses, new vocabularies, new rhetorics for addressing its possibility in social, political, and cultural life.

Like Carafiol, Ashraf H. A. Rushdy is acutely aware of the theoretical and practical difficulties in store for critics who would like to tell a reassuring story about the permeability of racial boundaries, and he warns against allowing the project of envisioning an "integrated American Literature" to degenerate into a "narrative of camaraderie between African-American and European-American authors and literary lineages." A properly historical approach to the integration of American literary traditions, he argues in "Reading Black, White, and Gray in 1968: The Origins of the Contemporary Narrativity of Slavery," would forego the desire for "short-term *rapprochement*" in order to seek out "the deeper meanings of conflict" in literary history. There is no danger of short-term *rapprochement* in Rushdy's account of the heated controversy over William Styron's 1968 novel, *The Confessions of Nat Turner*, a book that inspired African-American intellectuals to speak out forcefully on the issue of cultural appropriation. Yet as so often in American literature, the contested terrain of racial difference is also productive terrain. Indeed, Rushdy maintains that the 1968 debate over Styron's novel produced "a crucial transformation in the intellectual study of slavery—a transformation which has led to a renaissance of African-American literary representations of slavery in the three decades since the conflict." Noting that contemporary narratives by Ernest Gaines, Ishmael Reed, Charles Johnson, Sherley Anne Williams, Toni Morrison, and many other writers "insistently view slavery from the slave's point of view," Rushdy argues that the 1968 controversy set the agenda for future historiographical and fictional representations of slavery. Expanding on the dialectical tensions at work in Thomas Gray's original *Confessions*, he explains that novels like Reed's *Flight to Canada*, Morrison's *Beloved*, and Williams's *Dessa Rose* "all represent that same struggle between a form of writing that would master and the practice of orality that would free the slave."

In "The Politics of Mourning: Cultural Grief-Work from Frederick Douglass to Fanny Fern," Jeffrey Steele offers compelling evidence that certain rhetorical and representational strategies *do*, in fact, bridge racial and cultural differences. "Sentimentalized images of mourning" in writings by nineteenth-century women and African Americans offer one such bridge by making available a range of subjective emotions that were denied to women and blacks. Steele contends that nineteenth-century Americans regarded the iconographic figure of the female mourner as "the natural signifier of grief," and that women writers of the century learned to employ this officially sanctioned figure to signify an unsanctioned awareness of feminine injury and loss "within a culture that inhibited the full expression of their being." The female mourner, in other words, mourns not only for the loss of a family member or loved one, but for the loss "structured into [her] being" by the dominant culture. Opportunities for the expression of deep subjective emotion, Steele contends, were severely limited for both women and African Americans, and thus a "politics of mourning" emerged on both sides of the color line as a subversive means of managing the "ontological liability" imposed on women and blacks alike. To betray rage over existing power relations, Steele explains, would have been—for either women or black Americans— "to violate conventional categories of being." The image of the mourner thus emerged as a means of encoding dissent within terms acceptable to the dominant culture's highly restrictive discourses of gender and race. Incorporating an astounding range of works by Frederick Douglass, Harriet Jacobs, Margaret Fuller, Pauline

Hopkins, Harriet Beecher Stowe, Harriet Wilson, Louisa May Alcott, Fanny Fern, Richard Wright, Toni Morrison, and others, Steele constructs a convincing theoretical bridge between African-American and nineteenth-century white women's writing by demonstrating that each of these authors positions "central characters as mourners, whose grief extends beyond specific losses to a consideration of the cultural conditions that make mourning a fit emblem" for black or female existence in America.

In "Black and White Voices in an Early African-American Colonization Narrative: Problems of Genre and Emergence," Dickson D. Bruce, Jr., reminds readers that a complicated interplay of voices permeates American culture generally, raising more than literary questions. Bruce focuses on an obscure colonizationist pamphlet written in 1826, ostensibly by a group of free blacks in Baltimore. The pamphlet's publication was arranged by a group of influential whites who favored removal of free African Americans to the west coast of Africa, and, in order to win support from potential white patrons for the colonizationist cause, wished to demonstrate unified black support. The pamphlet, then, which begins with an introduction by members of the white-led American Colonization Society, is a tangle of differently situated and differently motivated voices that rivals Nat Turner's many-layered confessions in complexity. Bruce shows that the black colonizationists *did* have a voice in the pamphlet's composition—the very project of colonization, he notes, emerged among African Americans—but that this voice is never entirely distinct from the authenticating presence of the pamphlet's sponsors, who give the document their own inflection in numerous places. The sponsors, in turn, were relying on the pamphlet's ostensible black authors to validate *their* social agenda, so that "the process of authentication in the memorial's production was . . . reciprocal." This reciprocal action has the paradoxical effect of blurring rather than fixing lines of textual difference, so that questions of voice (who is speaking to whom?) become far more complicated than the pamphlet's deceptively simple use of pronouns ("we" for blacks, "you" for whites) would suggest. The "inseparability of 'black' and 'white' voices" in the pamphlet is finally instructive, because it helps us to understand the ways in which these voices constitute each other throughout American cultural life, ironically even in a document that argues for the most radical form of segregation. Taking the Baltimore pamphlet as a representative text, Bruce concludes that in profound cultural contradictions, "rather than in any irreducible distinctions among Americans themselves, lie the deepest sources for the differing 'voices' in American thought and letters."

If Bruce's essay can be understood as an attempt to make sense of a tangled web of black and white voices, Henry B. Wonham's contribution might be described as an effort to tangle voices that are generally assumed to be distinct. His essay, "Howells, Du Bois, and the Effect of 'Common-Sense': Race, Realism, and Nervousness in *An Imperative Duty* and *The Souls of Black Folk*," argues that W.E.B. Du Bois learned something important about the representation of African-American identity from an unlikely source, namely William Dean Howells's little-appreciated novel about racial miscegenation. The critical consensus

in Howells's time, as in our own, was that on matters of race, as Anna Julia
Cooper put it in 1892, "Mr. Howells does not know what he is talking about."
Yet Howells's representation of an identity crisis that befalls his mulatta heroine
contained an important key to what Eric Sundquist has called Du Bois's emerging
"theory of diasporic consciousness." "Rhoda Aldgate's racial 'two-ness'," Wonham contends, "while clearly Jamesian in conception, translates the medical and
romantic discourses of double consciousness into the murky language of racial
identity, a gesture that is magnificently completed in *The Souls of Black Folk*."
Moreover, Wonham argues that Du Bois did much more than simply mimic
Howells's racial application of the concept of double consciousness. In fact,
he stood the racialist logic of Howells's novel on its head by appropriating
"nervousness" as African-American cultural property. *An Imperative Duty* and
*The Souls of Black Folk* thus become, in Wonham's reading, sites of "dynamic
cultural exchange, with Howells and Du Bois positioned beside one another on
the richly contested psychological terrain of double consciousness."

Carla L. Peterson's essay, "The Remaking of Americans: Gertrude Stein's
'Melanctha' and African-American Musical Traditions," takes up Toni Morrison's call for a more profound critical awareness of the imaginative uses to
which blackness has been put in American literature. Noting that critics usually
dismiss the African-American presence in Stein's "Melanctha," preferring to
emphasize the story's experimental style, or disparage her representation of
African-American culture as "racist stereotyping," Peterson suggests that Stein's
engagement with black cultural forms served complex and important purposes.
Situating Stein within Raymond Williams's concept of modernism, Peterson
argues that Stein turned to African-American musical traditions in "Melanctha"
not only to assert her Americanness and her opposition to the culture of the
hegemony, but also to work out her sense of her Jewishness, from which she
was increasingly dissociating herself, and her lesbianism, which she was slowly
coming to acknowledge. The African-American presence in Stein's work, "ser-
viceable to the last," as Toni Morrison might explain, is part of a meditation on
the self, a device which "makes it possible to say and not say, to inscribe and
erase, to escape and engage" fundamental insecurities about the author's culture
and personality. Stein's appropriation of black musical culture, including coon
songs, ragtime, and early blues, according to Peterson, is finally a "complex and
ambivalent" gesture, "permitting both identification and rejection."

While Peterson discloses the cultural resonance of black musical traditions
in high modernist writing, Todd Vogel's essay describes an African-American
woman's subtle assimilation and radical deployment of a classical tradition of
rhetoric. In "The Master's Tools Revisited: Foundation Work in Anna Julia
Cooper," Vogel takes issue with critics who have questioned the radicalism of
Cooper's *A Voice from the South* on the grounds that her arguments issue from
a perspective *inside* the elite power structure she ostensibly critiques. While
conceding that activists like Ida B. Wells practiced a more confrontational form of
protest, Vogel maintains that Cooper adopted predominately white-male rhetorical
forms *not* as a concession to patriarchal values, but as an audacious and effective

strategy for overturning them. "Cooper understood that hard figures poured into a biased mind will go nowhere," and so she adopted an argumentative style designed to "attack the problem at its root—at the basic cognitive level that whites use to understand African Americans." Eschewing the more dramatic strategies of emotional appeal and anecdotal evidence, Cooper deployed the tools of classical rhetoric to argue for comprehensive social change. Her challenge to patriarchal values, according to Vogel, is all the *more* radical precisely because she so deftly breaches the color line in arguing her case, deploying the master's favorite tools in defiance of the master's ideology. As Vogel explains, "Cooper might have been inside the master's house instead of seeking its destruction from outside, but she was quietly placing a new dictionary into the master's library, one that could change forever how the master read his own books."

Noting that modern criticism usually dismisses Harriet Beecher Stowe's engagement with African-American culture as rooted in paternalism and benevolent racialism, Robert S. Levine proposes that a careful reading of Stowe's "'other' antislavery novel" will reveal her "complex and contradictory racial politics *in evolution*." In "The African-American Presence in Stowe's *Dred*," Levine argues that Stowe's often overlooked 1856 novel "can be regarded as an African-American–inspired revision of *Uncle Tom's Cabin*"—a revision provoked by black responses to her sensationally popular 1852 novel. In the years immediately following the appearance of *Uncle Tom's Cabin*, Levine contends, Stowe carefully attended to reactions from Martin Delany, Frederick Douglass, Sojourner Truth, William C. Nell, and other prominent African Americans, who, in some cases, openly challenged her representation of Uncle Tom's Christian passivity and the novel's colonizationist solution to America's racial dilemma. These encounters inspired Stowe to rethink the Christian imperatives that underlie Tom's martyrdom in the earlier novel, with the result that *Dred* projects a "syncretic Afro-Christian vision" as the basis for "a legitimately revolutionary antislavery perspective." The centrality of *Uncle Tom's Cabin* to Stowe's canon, Levine argues, has supported the impression that she valorized "only one black response to slavery: the pacifist religiosity of Uncle Tom." But African-American "interventions," like Douglass's 1853 story "The Heroic Slave," "ultimately impelled Stowe to rethink and revise her view of black heroism." *Dred* deserves attention from readers interested in Stowe's literary achievement, Levine concludes, because the novel "explodes critical myths about her purported blindness to African American realities" and, more than *Uncle Tom's Cabin*, underscores her "unusually brave engagements" with black voices and perspectives in antebellum culture.

Whereas Levine is interested in recuperating an important novel by revealing Stowe's sensitivity to African-American voices, including perhaps most importantly that of Frederick Douglass, Gabrielle Foreman intends to enrich our understanding of Douglass's own literary and political development by reminding readers of his ongoing engagement with sentimental discourses in nineteenth-century America. In "Sentimental Abolition in Douglass's Decade: Revision, Erotic Conversion, and the Politics of Witnessing in 'The Heroic Slave' and *My*

*Bondage and My Freedom*," Foreman explains that between 1845 and 1855 Douglass's prose became increasingly sentimental, even as he abandoned Garrisonian "moral suasion" in favor of a more stridently political position on abolition. Taking this paradoxical development as her point of departure, Foreman explores the relation between sentimental discourse and political abolition, arguing that Douglass "revised" the terms of sentimentality to suit his own political purposes in two crucial works, "The Heroic Slave" and *My Bondage and My Freedom*. Noting that "sympathetic witnessing is necessary to any abolitionist project," Foreman maintains that Douglass translated sentimental bonds of sympathy and affection into a "homoerotic" realm, where sentiment potentially bears a direct relation to political agency. Douglass, in short, intended to convert readers who could vote. Thus, while he encoded "his political intervention within the language of domestic affection," "women's voices" were "written out" of this language in Douglass's effort to translate sentimentality into a homoerotic discourse centering on political and judicial rights. Stowe and the "scribbling women" to whom Hawthorne famously objected finally performed an important role in Douglass's move from Garrisonian moral suasion to political abolition, even as he consciously worked to position himself in opposition to the "feminine" politics of *Uncle Tom's Cabin*.

"The Heroic Slave" is also an important text for Herman Beavers, whose essay, "The Blind Leading the Blind: The Racial Gaze as Plot Dilemma in 'Benito Cereno' and 'The Heroic Slave,' " teases out an important affinity between antislavery writings by Melville and Douglass. According to Beavers, nineteenth-century artists and writers, including abolitionists, typically situated African Americans within a "visual sphere" that served to confirm and reinforce black social, political, and intellectual inferiority. "Benito Cereno" and "The Heroic Slave" are parallel texts for Beavers because both deploy a strikingly profound variety of abolitionist rhetoric, one that effectively subverts not only the institution of slavery, but the authority of the visual sphere itself. Amasa Delano, the American ship captain who stumbles onto a slave insurrection in Melville's tale, is so thoroughly enchanted by visual tokens of white superiority aboard a Spanish slave-trader that he fails to notice the violent revolution occurring in his midst. If Melville critiques the "racial gaze" by revealing its catastrophic interpretive limitations, Douglass achieves a parallel effect by substituting "aural" for visual evidence of Madison Washington's heroic character. Washington's voice, not his Herculean body or arresting visual image, constitutes "the unfailing index" of his soul. His heroic stature is an attempt, Beavers convincingly argues, not to revise the visual sphere but to subvert its authority over the representation and interpretation of African-American character. Melville and Douglass are finally up to very different narrative games, yet both deploy "an alternative iconography" to challenge the complacency of dominant versions of anti-slavery rhetoric that insisted on a neatly visible color line between black and white.

Teresa Goddu's essay, "The Ghost of Race: Edgar Allan Poe and the Southern Gothic," begins by echoing Toni Morrison's call for a more rigorously historicist understanding of the American gothic, whose "blackness," according to Goddu, "needs to be examined in terms of slavery and, more generally, ideologies of race." Poe is the natural candidate for such a historicist project, but Goddu maintains that critics have traditionally resisted social readings of Poe's gothic fiction, preferring to dismiss him as a psychological eccentric or to bracket him as a Southerner whose social consciousness was shaped by aberrant and regionally specific historical conditions. Thus, instead of "reducing Poe's gothic tales to Southern stories or his meditations on the problem of racial identity to 'racial phobia,'" Goddu proposes to show how "the gothic offers Poe a complex and complementary notation to explore the racial discourse of his period." That discourse, according to Goddu, hinged on the debate between "monogenism," or "the belief in the original sameness of men," and an emerging theory of "polygenism," which argued for innate differences between races. Situating Poe's *The Narrative of Arthur Gordon Pym* squarely at the center of this debate, Goddu remarks that traditional readings of the novel either bury its historical context in psychological details or, if they acknowledge a historical referent, "reduce Poe's complex meditation on race to proslavery cant." For Goddu, the novel's obsessive juxtaposition of white and black is neither pure psychology nor mere race-baiting; rather, "*Pym*'s color symbolism seems constantly to create difference [even as] it elides that difference by articulating a discourse of racial identity that is constucted and, hence, vulnerable to change." In other words, Goddu's Poe is a monogenist, a believer in the constructedness and mutability of racial difference, whose ostensible proslavery allegory finally does more to complicate notions of "perfect whiteness" and "total darkness" than to support them.

In closing with Shelley Fisher Fishkin's essay, "Interrogating 'Whiteness,' Complicating 'Blackness': Remapping American Culture," this book ends where it began, for it was Fishkin's pathbreaking 1993 study of Mark Twain, *Was Huck Black?: Mark Twain and African-American Voices*, that opened my eyes to the importance of cultural exchanges in American literary history and culture. In that book she observed that:

> We may no longer segregate trains, schools, water fountains, waiting rooms, bibles for witnesses in courtrooms, parks, residences, textbooks, telephone booths, ticket windows, ambulances, hospitals, orphanages, prisons, morgues, and cemeteries. But segregation is alive and well among literary historians, who persist in affirming that white writers come from white literary ancestors, and black writers from black ones.[17]

A glance at Fishkin's overview of more than one hundred books and articles written between 1990 and 1995 is likely to cast doubt on this statement, for it seems that scholars in fields from literary criticism to dance history have begun actively to challenge the traditionally segregated understanding of American culture. Nevertheless, as an indispensable guide to further research on the historical and theoretical implications of cultural exchange between African-American and "mainstream" expressive traditions, Fishkin's essay participates in what she calls "a defining moment in the study of American culture." What defines this moment is a growing scholarly consensus that, as Henry Louis Gates, Jr., puts it, "the world we live in is multicultural already. Mixing and hybridity are the rule, not the exception."[18] This is a fact that, according to Fishkin, "we can no longer bury or deny," for to do so—as Ralph Ellison and Toni Morrison have so eloquently charged—is to misconceive our cultural identity and to impoverish our literary past. "It is by understanding and celebrating the hybridity of mainstream American culture," Fishkin concludes, that we can collectively forge a truly pluralistic interpretation of our rich and dynamic heritage.

In daring to celebrate transgressions of the color line in American creative life, these essays willingly enter a highly contentious area of academic discourse. Arguments about canons and "sacred texts" inevitably raise related questions about institutional legitimacy, questions that are politically and emotionally charged. Morrison prefaces her own entrance into the culture wars in "Unspeakable Things Unspoken" by admonishing that "the guns are very big; the trigger-fingers quick," and thus it would seem prudent to conclude these introductory remarks by reiterating a concern that is implicit throughout the collection. It might fairly be asked if, in highlighting the sometimes fluid, sometimes turbulent, sometimes illusory exchange of cultural practices across the color line, the critical perspective celebrated in these essays works to cancel or neutralize black difference, thereby confirming the dominant culture's right to define black identity according to its own ideological purposes.

This is a very important concern, and one to which the collection as a whole cannot provide a theoretically definitive answer. Morrison's program *can* be directed toward reactionary ends if she is misrepresented as saying, "everything important you need to know about black culture is contained (though hidden) in texts by famous white authors." Of course, she is saying nothing of this kind, and only the most cynical reader would accuse either Morrison or the contributors to this collection of wishing to erode the institutional integrity of African-American studies by blurring the frontiers of black/white cultural difference. In calling for an end to the segregation of American literary studies, the scholars assembled here do not invite a return to the assimilationist ideal of a "race-blind" American literature. Rather, they dispense with essentialist conceptions of race in order to chart the literary historical effects of dynamic cultural difference. The point, in other words, is not to erase the color line, but to historicize a mutually constitutive relationship between African and European cultures in America.

## Notes

1. Ralph Ellison, "Twentieth-Century Fiction and the Black Mask of Humanity," in *Shadow and Act* (New York: Random House, 1964), 24; "What America Would Be Like Without Blacks," in *Going to the Territory* (New York: Random House, 1987), 111; "Going to the Territory," in *Territory*, 142; "Change the Joke and Slip the Yoke," in *Shadow*, 55.

2. Ellison, "Twentieth-Century Fiction and the Black Mask of Humanity," 44; "Going to the Territory," 125; "Twentieth-Century Fiction and the Black Mask of Humanity," 28; "Going to the Territory," 125.

3. W.E.B. Du Bois, *The Souls of Black Folk* (1903; rpt. New York: Penguin, 1989), 214–215.

4. Morrison's Tanner Lecture on Human Values, delivered at the University of Michigan on October 7, 1988, appeared in *Michigan Quarterly Review* 28 (Winter 1989): 1–34. The excerpt reprinted in this volume constitutes approximately two-thirds, or pages 1–19, of the *Michigan Quarterly Review* text.

5. Ellison, "Blues People," in *Shadow*, 247–258.

6. Werner Sollors, "A Critique of Pure Pluralism," in *Reconstructing American Literary History*, ed. Sacvan Bercovitch (Cambridge, Mass.: Harvard University Press, 1986), 274–275.

7. Ibid., 257.

8. Houston A. Baker, Jr., *Blues, Ideology, and Afro-American Literature: A Vernacular Theory* (Chicago: University of Chicago Press, 1984), 200.

9. Kenneth W. Warren, *Black and White Strangers: Race and American Literary Realism* (Chicago: University of Chicago Press, 1993), 10. It should be pointed out in fairness that Baker and other pioneering African Americanists are currently leading the way toward a desegregated vision of American literature and culture. See, for example, Baker's "Introduction" to the MLA "Presidential Forum on Multiculturalism: The Task of Literary Representation in the Twenty-First Century," *Profession 93* (1993): 5.

10. Warren, *Strangers*, 10.

11. Ibid.

12. Eric J. Sundquist, *To Wake the Nations: Race in the Making of American Literature* (Cambridge, Mass.: Harvard University Press, 1993), 2.

13. Du Bois, *Souls*, 1.

14. Warren, *Strangers*, 10.

15. For all the variety of subject matter covered in the essays that follow, readers will undoubtedly notice several glaring omissions. It might fairly be pointed out that, given the collection's aims, William Faulkner, Charles Chesnutt, James Baldwin, and any number of other writers neglected here deserve extensive consideration, whereas Frederick Douglass—who is the subject of one essay and figures importantly in three others—might reasonably have occupied a more peripheral role. That is an understandable objection, but one that fails to register the collection's primary aim, which has been to suggest the contours of one important new direction in American literary and cultural studies.

16. Sundquist, *Nations*, 8.

17. Shelley Fisher Fishkin, *Was Huck Black?: Mark Twain and African-American Voices* (New York: Oxford University Press, 1993), 142.

18. Henry Louis Gates, Jr., *Loose Canons: Notes on the Culture Wars* (New York: Oxford University Press, 1992), xvi.

# Unspeakable Things Unspoken:
# The Afro-American Presence in
# American Literature

I

I planned to call this paper "Canon Fodder," because the terms put me in mind of a kind of trained muscular response that appears to be on display in some areas of the recent canon debate. But I changed my mind (so many have used the phrase) and hope to make clear the appropriateness of the title I settled on.

My purpose here is to observe the panoply of this most recent and most anxious series of questions concerning what should or does constitute a literary canon in order to suggest ways of addressing the Afro-American presence in American Literature that require neither slaughter nor reification—views that may spring the whole literature of an entire nation from the solitude into which it has been locked. There is something called American literature that, according to conventional wisdom, is certainly not Chicano literature, or Afro-American literature, or Asian-American, or Native American, or . . . it is somehow separate from them and they from it, and in spite of the efforts of recent literary histories, restructured curricula and anthologies, this separate confinement, be it breached or endorsed, is the subject of a large part of these debates. Although the terms used, like the vocabulary of earlier canon debates, refer to literary and/or humanistic value, aesthetic criteria, value-free or socially anchored readings, the contemporary battle plain is most often understood to be the claims of others against the white male origins and definitions of those values; whether those definitions reflect an eternal, universal and transcending paradigm or whether they constitute a disguise for a temporal, political and culturally specific program.

Part of the history of this particular debate is located in the successful assault that the feminist scholarship of men and women (black and white) made and continues to make on traditional literary discourse. The male part of the whitemale equation is already deeply engaged, and no one believes the body of literature and its criticism will ever again be what it was in 1965: the protected preserve of the thoughts and works and analytical strategies of whitemen.

It is, however, the "white" part of the question that this paper focuses on, and it is to my great relief that such terms as "white" and "race" can enter serious discussion of literature. Although still a swift and swiftly obeyed call to arms, their use is no longer forbidden.[1] It may appear churlish to doubt the sincerity, or question the proclaimed well-intentioned self-lessness of a 900-year-old academy struggling through decades of chaos to "maintain standards." Yet of what use is it to go on about "quality" being the only criterion for greatness knowing that the definition of quality is itself the subject of much rage and is seldom universally agreed upon by everyone at all times? Is it to appropriate the term for reasons of state; to be in the position to distribute greatness or withhold it? Or to actively pursue the ways and places in which quality surfaces and stuns us into silence or into language worthy enough to describe it? What is possible is to try to recognize, identify and applaud the fight for and triumph of quality when it is revealed to us and to let go the notion that only the dominant culture or gender can make those judgments, identify that quality or produce it.

Those who claim the superiority of Western culture are entitled to that claim only when Western civilization is measured thoroughly against other civilizations and not found wanting, and when Western civilization owns up to its own sources in the cultures that preceded it.

A large part of the satisfaction I have always received from reading Greek tragedy, for example, is in its similarity to Afro-American communal structures (the function of song and chorus, the heroic struggle between the claims of community and individual hubris) and African religion and philosophy. In other words, that is part of the reason it has quality for me—I feel intellectually at home there. But that could hardly be so for those unfamiliar with my "home," and hardly a requisite for the pleasure they take. The point is, the form (Greek tragedy) makes available these varieties of provocative love because *it* is masterly—not because the civilization that is its referent was flawless or superior to all others.

One has the feeling that nights are becoming sleepless in some quarters, and it seems to me obvious that the recoil of traditional "humanists" and some postmodern theorists to this particular aspect of the debate, the "race" aspect, is as severe as it is because the claims for attention come from that segment of scholarly and artistic labor in which the mention of "race" is either inevitable or elaborately, painstakingly masked; and if all of the ramifications that the term demands are taken seriously, the bases of Western civilization will require re-thinking. Thus, in spite of its implicit and explicit acknowledgment, "race" is still a virtually unspeakable thing, as can be seen in the apologies, notes of "special use" and circumscribed definitions that accompany it[2]—not least of which is my own deference in surrounding it with quotation marks. Suddenly (for our purposes, suddenly) "race" does not exist. For three hundred years black Americans insisted that "race" was no usefully distinguishing factor in human relationships. During those same three centuries every academic discipline, including theology, history, and natural science, insisted "race" was *the* determining factor in human development. When blacks discovered they had shaped or become a culturally formed race, and that it had specific and revered difference, suddenly they were told there is no such thing as "race," biological or cultural, that matters and that genuinely intellectual exchange cannot accommodate it.[3] In trying to come to some terms about "race" and writing, I am tempted to throw my hands up. It always seemed to me that the people who invented the hierarchy of "race" when it was convenient for them ought not to be the ones to explain it away, now that it does not suit their purposes for it to exist. But there *is* culture and both gender and "race" inform and are informed by it. Afro-American culture exists and though it is clear (and becoming clearer) how it has responded to Western culture, the instances where and means by which it has shaped Western culture are poorly recognized or understood.

I want to address ways in which the presence of Afro-American literature and the awareness of its culture both resuscitate the study of literature in the United States and raise that study's standards. In pursuit of that goal, it will suit my purposes to contextualize the route canon debates have taken in Western literary criticism.

I do not believe this current anxiety can be attributed solely to the routine, even cyclical arguments within literary communities reflecting unpredictable yet inevitable shifts in taste, relevance or perception. Shifts in which an enthusiasm for and official endorsement of William Dean Howells, for example, withered; or in which the legalization of Mark Twain in critical court rose and fell like the fathoming of a sounding line (for which he may or may not have named himself); or even the slow, delayed but steady swell of attention and devotion on which Emily Dickinson soared to what is now, surely, a permanent crest of respect. No. Those were discoveries, reappraisals of individual artists. Serious but not destabilizing. Such accommodations were simple because the questions they posed were simple: Are there one hundred sterling examples of high literary art in American literature and no more? One hundred and six? If one or two fall into disrepute, is there space, then, for one or two others in the vestibule, waiting like girls for bells chimed by future husbands who alone can promise them security, legitimacy—and in whose hands alone rests the gift of critical longevity? Interesting questions, but, as I say, not endangering.

Nor is this detectable academic sleeplessness the consequence of a much more radical shift, such as the mid-nineteenth century one heralding the authenticity of American literature itself. Or an even earlier upheaval—receding now into the distant past—in which theology, and thereby Latin, was displaced for the equally rigorous study of the classics and Greek to be followed by what was considered a strangely arrogant and upstart proposal: that English literature was a suitable course of study for an aristocratic education, and not simply morally instructive fodder designed for the working classes. (The Chaucer Society was founded in 1848, four hundred years after Chaucer died.) No. This exchange seems unusual somehow, keener. It has a more strenuously argued (and felt) defense and a more vigorously insistent attack. And both defenses and attacks have spilled out of the academy into the popular press. Why? Resistance to displacement within or expansion of a canon is not, after all, surprising or unwarranted. That's what canonization is for. (And the question of whether there should be a canon or not seems disingenuous to me—there always is one whether there should be or not—for it is in the interests of the professional critical community to have one.) Certainly a sharp alertness as to *why* a work is or is not worthy of study is the legitimate occupation of the critic, the pedagogue and the artist. What is astonishing in the contemporary debate is not the resistance to displacement of works or to the expansion of genre within it, but the virulent passion that accompanies this resistance and, more importantly, the quality of its defense weaponry. The guns are very big; the trigger-fingers quick. But I am convinced the mechanism of the defenders of the flame is faulty. Not only may the hands of the gun-slinging cowboy-scholars be blown off, not only may the target be missed, but the subject of the conflagration (the sacred texts) is sacrificed, disfigured in the battle. This canon fodder may kill the canon. And I, at least, do not intend to live without Aeschylus or William Shakespeare, or James or Twain or Hawthorne, or Melville, etc., etc., etc. There must be some way to enhance canon readings without enshrining them.

When Milan Kundera, in *The Art of the Novel*, identified the historical territory of the novel by saying "The novel is Europe's creation" and that "The only context for grasping a novel's worth is the history of the European novel," the *New Yorker* reviewer stiffened. Kundera's "personal 'idea of the novel,'" he wrote, "is so profoundly Eurocentric that it's likely to seem exotic, even perverse, to American readers . . . . *The Art of the Novel* gives off the occasional (but pungent) whiff of cultural arrogance, and we may feel that Kundera's discourse . . . reveals an aspect of his character that we'd rather not have known about. . . . In order to become the artist he now is, the Czech novelist had to discover himself a second time, as a European. But what if that second, grander possibility hadn't been there to be discovered? What if Broch, Kafka, Musil—all that reading—had never been a part of his education, or had entered it only as exotic, alien presence? Kundera's polemical fervor in *The Art of the Novel* annoys us, as American readers, because we feel defensive, excluded from the transcendent 'idea of the novel' that for him seems simply to have been there for the taking. (If only he had cited, in his redeeming version of the novel's history, a few more heroes from the New World's culture.) Our novelists don't discover cultural values within themselves; they invent them."[4]

Kundera's views, obliterating American writers (with the exception of William Faulkner) from his own canon, are relegated to a "smugness" that Terrence Rafferty disassociates from Kundera's imaginative work and applies to the "sublime confidence" of his critical prose. The confidence of an exile who has the sentimental education of, and the choice to become, a European.

I was refreshed by Rafferty's comments. With the substitution of certain phrases, his observations and the justifiable umbrage he takes can be appropriated entirely by Afro-American writers regarding their own exclusion from the "transcendent 'idea of the novel.'"

For the present turbulence seems not to be about the flexibility of a canon, its range among and between Western countries, but about its miscegenation. The word is informative here and I do mean its use. A powerful ingredient in this debate concerns the incursion of third-world or so-called minority literature into a Eurocentric stronghold. When the topic of third world culture is raised, unlike the topic of Scandinavian culture, for example, a possible threat to and implicit criticism of the reigning equilibrium is seen to be raised as well. From the seventeenth century to the twentieth, the arguments resisting that incursion have marched in predictable sequence: 1) there is no Afro-American (or third world) art. 2) it exists but is inferior. 3) it exists and is superior when it measures up to the "universal" criteria of Western art. 4) it is not so much "art" as ore—rich ore—that requires a Western or Eurocentric smith to refine it from its "natural" state into an aesthetically complex form.

A few comments on a larger, older, but no less telling academic struggle—an extremely successful one—may be helpful here. It is telling because it sheds light on certain aspects of this current debate and may locate its sources. I made reference above to the radical upheaval in canon-building that took place at the inauguration of classical studies and Greek. This canonical re-routing from scholasticism to humanism was not merely radical, it must have been (may I say it?) savage. And it took some seventy years to accomplish. Seventy years to eliminate Egypt as the cradle of civilization *and* its model and replace it with Greece. The triumph of that process was that Greece lost its own origins and became itself original. A number of scholars in various disciplines (history, anthropology, ethnobotany, etc.) have put forward their research into cross-cultural and inter-cultural transmissions with varying degrees of success in the reception of their work. I am reminded of the curious publishing history of Ivan van Sertima's work, *They Came Before Columbus*, which researches the African presence in Ancient America. I am reminded of Edward Said's *Orientalism*, and especially the work of Martin Bernal, a linguist, trained in Chinese history, who has defined himself as an interloper in the field of classical civilization but who has offered, in *Black Athena*, a stunning investigation of the field. According to Bernal, there are two "models" of Greek history: one views Greece as Aryan or European (the Aryan Model); the other sees it as Levantine—absorbed by Egyptian and Semitic culture (the Ancient Model). "If I am right," writes Professor Bernal, "in urging the overthrow of the Aryan Model and its replacement by the Revised Ancient one, it will be necessary not only to rethink the fundamental bases of 'Western Civilization' but also to recognize the penetration of racism and 'continental chauvinism' into all our historiography, or philosophy of writing history. The Ancient Model had no major 'internal' deficiencies or weaknesses in explanatory power. It was overthrown for external reasons. For eighteenth- and nineteenth-century Romantics and racists it was simply intolerable for Greece, which was seen not merely as the epitome of Europe but also as its pure childhood, to have been the result of the mixture of native Europeans and *colonizing* Africans and Semites. Therefore the Ancient Model had to be overthrown and replaced by something more acceptable."[5]

It is difficult not to be persuaded by the weight of documentation Martin Bernal brings to his task and his rather dazzling analytical insights. What struck me in his analysis were the *process* of the fabrication of Ancient Greece and the *motives* for the fabrication. The latter (motive) involved the concept of purity of progress. The former (process) required mis-reading, pre-determined selectivity of authentic sources, and—silence. From the Christian theological appropriation of Israel (the Levant), to the early nineteenth-century work of the prodigious Karl Miller, work that effectively dismissed the Greeks' own record of their influences and origins as their "Egyptomania," their tendency to be "wonderstruck" by Egyptian culture, a tendency "manifested in the 'delusion' that Egyptians and other non-European 'barbarians' had possessed superior cultures, from which the Greeks had borrowed massively,"[6] on through the Romantic response to the Enlightenment, and the decline into disfavor of the Phoenicians, "the essential force behind the rejection of the tradition of massive Phoenician influence on early Greece was the rise of racial—as opposed to religious—anti-semitism. This was because the Phoenicians were correctly perceived to have been culturally very close to the Jews."[7]

I have quoted at perhaps too great a length from Bernal's text because *motive*, so seldom an element brought to bear on the history of history, is located, delineated and confronted in Bernal's research, and has helped my own thinking about the process and motives of scholarly attention to and an appraisal of Afro-American presence in the literature of the United States.

Canon building is Empire building. Canon defense is national defense. Canon debate, whatever the terrain, nature and range (of criticism, of history, of the history of knowledge, of the definition of language, the universality of aesthetic principles, the sociology of art, the humanistic imagination), is the clash of cultures. And *all* of the interests are vested.

In such a melee as this one—a provocative, healthy, explosive melee—extraordinarily profound work is being done. Some of the controversy, however, has degenerated into *ad hominem* and unwarranted speculation on the personal habits of artists, specious and silly arguments about politics (the destabilizing forces are dismissed as merely political; the status quo sees itself as not—as though the term "*a*political" were only its prefix and not the most obviously political stance imaginable since one of the functions of political ideology is to pass itself off as immutable, natural and "innocent"), and covert expressions of critical inquiry designed to neutralize and disguise the political interests of the discourse. Yet much of the research and analysis has rendered speakable what was formerly unspoken and has made humanistic studies, once again, the place where one has to go to find out what's going on. Cultures, whether silenced or monologistic, whether repressed or repressing, seek meaning in the language and images available to them.

Silences are being broken, lost things have been found and at least two generations of scholars are disentangling received knowledge from the apparatus of control, most notably those who are engaged in investigations of French and British Colonialist Literature, American slave narratives, and the delineation of the Afro-American literary tradition.

Now that Afro-American artistic presence has been "discovered" actually to exist, now that serious scholarship has moved from silencing the witnesses and erasing their meaningful place in and contribution to American culture, it is no longer acceptable merely to imagine us and imagine for us. We have always been imagining ourselves. We are not Isak Dinesen's "aspects of nature," nor Conrad's unspeaking. We are the subjects of our own narrative, witnesses to and participants in our own experience, and, in no way coincidentally, in the experience of those with whom we have come in contact. We are not, in fact, "other." We are choices. And to read imaginative literature by and about us is to choose to examine centers of the self and to have the opportunity to compare these centers with the "raceless" one with which we are, all of us, most familiar.

## II

Recent approaches to the reading of Afro-American literature have come some distance; have addressed those arguments, mentioned earlier (which are not arguments, but attitudes) that have, since the seventeenth century, effectively silenced the autonomy of that literature. As for the charge that "there is no Afro-American art," contemporary critical analysis of the literature and the recent surge of reprints and re-discoveries have buried it, and are pressing on to expand the traditional canon to include classic Afro-American works where generically and chronologically appropriate, and to devise strategies for reading and thinking about these texts.

As to the second silencing charge, "Afro-American art exists, but is inferior," again, close readings and careful research into the culture out of which the art is born have addressed and still address the labels that once passed for stringent analysis but can no more: that it is imitative, excessive, sensational, mimetic (merely), and unintellectual, though very often "moving," "passionate," "naturalistic," "realistic" or sociologically "revealing." These labels may be construed as compliments or pejoratives and if valid, and shown as such, so much the better. More often than not, however, they are the lazy, easy brand-name applications when the hard work of analysis is deemed too hard, or when the critic does not have access to the scope the work demands. Strategies designed to counter this lazy labeling include the application of recent literary theories to Afro-American literature so that non-canonical texts can be incorporated into existing and forming critical discourse.

The third charge, that "Afro-American art exists, but is superior only when it measures up to the 'universal' criteria of Western art," produces the most seductive form of analysis, for both writer and critic, because comparisons are a major form of knowledge and flattery. The risks, nevertheless, are twofold: 1) the gathering of a culture's difference into the skirts of the Queen is a neutralization designed and constituted to elevate and maintain hegemony. 2) circumscribing and limiting the literature to a mere reaction to or denial of the Queen, judging the work solely in terms of its referents to Eurocentric criteria, or its sociological accuracy, political correctness or its pretense of having no politics at all, cripple the literature and infantilize the serious work of imaginative writing. This response-oriented concept of Afro-American literature contains the seeds of the next (fourth) charge: that when

Afro-American art is worthy, it is because it is "raw" and "rich," like ore, and like ore needs refining by Western intelligences. Finding or imposing Western influences in/on Afro-American literature has value, but when its sole purpose is to *place* value only where that influence is located it is pernicious.

My unease stems from the possible, probable, consequences these approaches may have upon the work itself. They can lead to an incipient orphanization of the work in order to issue its adoption papers. They can confine the discourse to the advocacy of diversification within the canon and/or a kind of benign co-existence near or within reach of the already sacred texts. Either of these two positions can quickly become another kind of silencing if permitted to ignore the indigenous created qualities of the writing. So many questions surface and irritate. What have these critiques made of the work's own canvas? Its paint, its frame, its framelessness, its spaces? Another list of approved subjects? Of approved treatments? More self-censoring, more exclusion of the specificity of the culture, the gender, the language? Is there perhaps an alternative utility in these studies? To advance power or locate its fissures? To oppose elitist interests in order to enthrone egalitarian effacement? or is it merely to rank and grade the readable product as distinct from the writeable production? Can this criticism reveal ways in which the author combats and confronts received prejudices and even creates *other terms* in which to rethink one's attachment to or intolerance of the material of these works? What is important in all of this is that the critic not be engaged in laying claim on behalf of the text to his or her own dominance and power. Nor to exchange his or her professional anxieties for the imagined turbulence of the text. "The text should become a problem of passion, not a pretext for it."

There are at least three focuses that seem to me to be neither reactionary nor simple pluralism, nor the even simpler methods by which the study of Afro-American literature remains the helpful doorman into the halls of sociology. Each of them, however, requires wakefulness.

One is the development of a theory of literature that truly accommodates Afro-American literature: one that is based on its culture, its history, and the artistic strategies the works employ to negotiate the world it inhabits.

Another is the examination and re-interpretation of the American canon, the founding nineteenth-century works, for the "unspeakable things unspoken"; for the ways in which the presence of Afro-Americans has shaped the choices, the language, the structure—the meaning of so much American literature. A search, in other words, for the ghost in the machine.

A third is the examination of contemporary and/or non-canonical literature for this presence, regardless of its category as mainstream, minority, or what you will. I am always amazed by the resonances, the structural gear-shifts, and the *uses* to which Afro-American narrative, persona and idiom are put in contemporary "white" literature. And in Afro-American literature itself the question of difference, of essence, is critical. What makes a work "Black"? The most valuable point of entry into the question of cultural (or racial) distinction, the one most fraught, is its language—its unpoliced, seditious, confrontational, manipulative, inventive, disruptive, masked and unmasking language. Such a penetration will entail the most careful study, one in which the impact of Afro-American presence on modernity becomes clear and is no longer a well-kept secret.

I would like to touch, for just a moment, on focuses two and three.

We can agree, I think, that invisible things are not necessarily "not-there"; that a void may be empty, but is not a vacuum. In addition, certain absences are so stressed, so ornate, so planned, they call attention to themselves; arrest us with intentionality and purpose, like neighborhoods that are defined by the population held away from them. Looking at the scope of American literature, I can't help thinking that the question should never have been "Why am I, an Afro-American, absent from it?" It is not a particularly interesting query anyway. The spectacularly interesting question is "What intellectual feats had to be performed by the author or his critic to erase me from a society seething with my presence, and what effect has that performance had on the work?" What are the strategies of escape from knowledge? Of willful oblivion? I am not recommending an inquiry into the obvious impulse that overtakes a soldier sitting in a World War I trench to think of salmon fishing. That kind of pointed "turning from," deliberate escapism or transcendence may be life-saving in a circumstance of immediate duress. The exploration I am suggesting is, how does one sit in the audience observing, watching the performance of Young America, say, in the nineteenth century, say, and reconstruct the play, its director, its plot and its cast in such a manner that its very point never surfaces? Not why. How? Ten years after Tocqueville's prediction in 1840 that " 'Finding no stuff for the ideal in what is real and true, poets would flee to imaginary regions' ... in 1850 at the height of slavery and burgeoning abolitionism, American writers chose romance."[8] Where, I wonder, in these romances is the shadow of the presence from which the text has fled? Where does it heighten, where does it dislocate, where does it necessitate novelistic invention; what does it release; what does it hobble?

The device (or arsenal) that serves the purpose of flight can be Romanticism versus verisimilitude; new criticism versus shabbily disguised and questionably sanctioned "moral uplift"; the "complex series of evasions," that is sometimes believed to be the essence of modernism; the perception of the evolution of art; the cultivation of irony, parody; the nostalgia for "literary language"; the rhetorically unconstrained textuality versus socially anchored textuality, and the undoing of textuality altogether. These critical strategies can (but need not) be put into service to reconstruct the historical world to suit specific cultural and political purposes. Many of these strategies have produced powerfully creative work. Whatever *uses* to which Romanticism is put, however suspicious its origins, it has produced an incontestably wonderful body of work. In other instances these strategies have succeeded in paralyzing both the work and its criticism. In still others they have led to a virtual infantilization of the writer's intellect, his sensibility, his craft. They have reduced the meditations on theory into a "power struggle among sects" reading unauthored and unauthorable material, rather than an outcome of reading *with* the author the text both construct.

In other words, the critical process has made wonderful work of some wonderful work, and recently the means of access to the old debates have altered. The problem now is putting the question. Is the nineteenth-century flight from blackness, for example, successful in mainstream American literature? Beautiful? Artistically problematic? Is the text sabotaged by its own proclamations of "universality"? Are there ghosts in the machine? Active but unsummoned presences that can distort the workings of the machine and can also *make* it work? These kinds of questions have been consistently put by critics of Colonial Literature vis-à-vis Africa and India and other third-world countries. American literature would benefit from similar critiques. I am made melancholy when I consider that the act of defending the Eurocentric Western posture in literature as not only "universal" but also "race-free" may have resulted in lobotomizing that literature, and in diminishing both the art and the artist. Like the surgical removal of legs so that the body can remain enthroned, immobile, static—under house arrest, so to speak. It may be, of course, that contemporary writers deliberately exclude from their conscious writerly world the subjective appraisal of groups perceived as "other," and whitemale writers frequently abjure and deny the excitement of framing or locating their literature in the political world. Nineteenth-century writers, however, would never have given it a thought. Mainstream writers in Young America understood their competition to be national, cultural, but only in relationship to the Old World, certainly not vis-à-vis an ancient race (whether Native American or African) that was stripped of articulateness and intellectual thought, rendered, in D. H. Lawrence's term, "uncreate." For these early American writers, how could there be competition with nations or peoples who were presumed unable to handle or uninterested in handling the written word? One could write about them, but there was never the danger of their "writing back." Just as one could speak to them without fear of their "talking back." One could even observe them, hold them in prolonged gaze, without encountering the risk of being observed, viewed, or judged in return. And if, on occasion, they were themselves viewed and judged, it was out of a political necessity and, for the purposes of art, could not matter. Or so thought Young America. It could never have occurred to Edgar Allan Poe in 1848 that I, for example, might read *The Gold Bug* and watch his efforts to render my grandfather's speech to something as close to braying as possible, an effort so intense you can see the perspiration—and the stupidity—when Jupiter says "I knows," and Mr. Poe spells the verb "nose."*

Yet in spite or because of this monologism there is a great, ornamental, prescribed absence in early American literature and, I submit, it is instructive. It only seems that the canon of American literature is "naturally" or "inevitably" "white." In fact it is studiously so. In fact these absences of vital presences in Young American literature may be the insistent fruit of the scholarship rather

---

*Author's Note: Older America is not always distinguishable from its infancy. We may pardon Edgar Allan Poe in 1848 but it should have occurred to Kenneth Lynn in 1986 that some young Native American might read his Hemingway biography and see herself described as "squaw" by this respected scholar, and that some young men might shudder reading the words "buck" and "half-breed" so casually included in his scholarly speculations.

than the text. Perhaps some of these writers, although under current house arrest, have much more to say than had been realized. Perhaps some were not so much transcending politics, or escaping blackness, as they were transforming it into intelligible, accessible, yet artistic modes of discourse. To ignore this possibility by never questioning the strategies of transformation is to disenfranchise the writer, diminish the text and render the bulk of the literature aesthetically and historically incoherent—an exorbitant price for cultural (whitemale) purity, and, I believe, a spendthrift one. The re-examination of founding literature of the United States for the unspeakable unspoken may reveal those texts to have deeper and other meanings, deeper and other power, deeper and other significances.

One such writer, in particular, it has been almost impossible to keep under lock and key is Herman Melville.

Among several astute scholars, Michael Rogin has done one of the most exhaustive studies of how deeply Melville's social thought is woven into his writing. He calls our attention to the connection Melville made between American slavery and American freedom, how heightened the one rendered the other. And he has provided evidence of the impact on the work of Melville's family, milieu, and, most importantly, the raging, all-encompassing conflict of the time: slavery. He has reminded us that it was Melville's father-in-law who had, as judge, decided the case that made the Fugitive Slave Law law, and that "other evidence in Moby Dick also suggests the impact of Shaw's ruling on the climax of Melville's tale. Melville conceived the final confrontation between Ahab and the white whale some time in the first half of 1851, He may well have written his last chapters only after returning from a trip to New York in June." [Judge Shaw's decision was handed down in April, 1851.] When New York anti-slavery leaders William Seward and John van Buren wrote public letters protesting the *Sims* ruling, the New York *Herald* responded. Its attack on "The Anti-Slavery Agitators" began: "Did you ever see a whale? Did you ever see a mighty whale struggling?". . .[9]

Rogin also traces the chronology of the whale from its "birth in a state of nature" to its final end as commodity.[10] Central to his argument is that Melville in *Moby Dick* was being allegorically and insistently political in his choice of the whale. But within his chronology, one singular whale transcends all others, goes beyond nature, adventure, politics and commodity to an abstraction. What is this abstraction? This "wicked idea"? Interpretation has been varied. It has been viewed as an allegory of the state in which Ahab is Calhoun, or Daniel Webster; an allegory of capitalism and corruption, God and man, the individual and fate, and most commonly, the single allegorical meaning of the white whale is understood to be brute, indifferent Nature, and Ahab the madman who challenges that Nature.

But let us consider, again, the principal actor, Ahab, created by an author who calls himself Typee, signed himself Tawney, identified himself as Ishmael, and, who had written several books before *Moby Dick* criticizing missionary forays into various paradises.

Ahab loses sight of the commercial value of his ship's voyage, its point, and pursues an idea in order to destroy it. His intention, revenge, "an audacious, immitigable and supernatural revenge," develops stature—maturity—when we realize that he is not a man mourning his lost leg or a scar on his face. However intense and dislocating his fever and recovery had been after his encounter with the white whale, however satisfactorily "male" this vengeance is read, the vanity of it is almost adolescent. But if the whale is more than blind, indifferent Nature unsubduable by masculine aggression, if it is as much its adjective as it is its noun, we can consider the possibility that Melville's "truth" was his recognition of the moment in America when whiteness became ideology. And if the white whale is the ideology of race, what Ahab has lost to it is personal dismemberment and family and society and his own place as a human in the world. The trauma of racism is, for the racist and victim, the severe fragmentation of the self, and has always seemed to me a cause (not a symptom) of psychosis—strangely of no interest to psychiatry. Ahab, then, is navigating between an idea of civilization that he renounces and an idea of savagery he must annihilate, because the two cannot co-exist. The former is based on the latter. What is terrible in its complexity is that the idea of savagery is not the missionary one: it is white racial ideology that is savage and if, indeed, a white, nineteenth-century, American male took on not abolition, not the amelioration of racist institutions or their laws, but the very concept of whiteness as an inhuman idea, he would be very alone, very desperate, and very doomed. Madness would be the only appropriate description of such audacity, and "he heaves me," the most succinct and appropriate description of that obsession.

I would not like to be understood to argue that Melville was engaged in some simple and simple-minded black/white didacticism, or that he was satanizing white people. Nothing like that. What I am suggesting is that he was overwhelmed by the philosophical and metaphysical inconsistencies of an extraordinary and unprecedented idea that had its fullest manifestation in his own time in his own country, and that that idea was the successful assertion of whiteness as ideology.

On the *Pequod* the multiracial, mainly foreign, proletariat is at work to produce a commodity, but it is diverted and converted from that labor to Ahab's more significant intellectual quest. We leave whale as commerce and confront whale as metaphor. With that interpretation in place, two of the most famous chapters of the book become luminous in a completely new way. One is Chapter 9, The Sermon. In Father Mapple's thrilling rendition of Jonah's trials, emphasis is given to the purpose of Jonah's salvation. He is saved from the fish's belly for one single purpose, "To preach the Truth to the face of Falsehood! That was it!" Only then the reward "Delight"—which strongly calls to mind Ahab's lonely necessity. "Delight is to him . . . who against the proud gods and commodores of this earth, ever stands forth his own inexorable self. Delight is to him whose strong arms yet support him, when the ship of this base treacherous world has gone down beneath him. Delight is to him, who gives no quarter in the truth, and kills, burns, and destroys all *sin* though he pluck it out from under the robes of Senators and Judges. Delight,—top-gallant delight is to him, who acknowledges no law or lord, but the Lord his God, and is only a *patriot to heaven*" [italics mine]. No one, I think, has denied that the sermon is designed to be prophetic, but it seems unremarked what the nature of the sin is—the sin that must be destroyed, regardless. Nature? A sin? The terms do not apply. Capitalism? Perhaps. Capitalism fed greed, lent itself inexorably to corruption, but probably was not in and of itself sinful to Melville. Sin suggests a moral outrage within the bounds of man to repair. The concept of racial superiority would fit seamlessly. It is difficult to read those words ("destruction of sin," "patriot to heaven") and not hear in them the description of a different Ahab. Not an adolescent male in adult clothing, a maniacal egocentric, or the "exotic plant" that V. S. Parrington thought Melville was. Not even a morally fine liberal voice adjusting, balancing, compromising with racial institutions. But another Ahab: the only white male American heroic enough to try to slay the monster that was devouring the world as he knew it.

Another chapter that seems freshly lit by this reading is Chapter 42, The Whiteness of the Whale. Melville points to the do-or-die significance of his effort to say something unsayable in this chapter. "I almost despair," he writes, "of putting it in a comprehensive form. It was the whiteness of the whale that above all things appalled me. But how can I hope to explain myself here; and yet in some dim, random way, explain myself I must, *else all these chapters might be naught*" [italics mine]. The language of this chapter ranges between benevolent, beautiful images of whiteness and whiteness as sinister and shocking. After dissecting the ineffable, he concludes: "Therefore . . . symbolize whatever grand or gracious he will by whiteness, no man can deny that in its profoundest *idealized significance* it calls up a peculiar apparition to the soul." I stress "idealized significance" to emphasize and make clear (if such clarity needs stating) that Melville is not exploring white *people*, but whiteness idealized. Then, after informing the reader of his "hope to light upon some chance clue to conduct us to the hidden course we seek," he tries to nail it. To provide the key to the "hidden course." His struggle to do so is gigantic. He cannot. Nor can we. But in nonfigurative language, he identifies the imaginative tools needed to solve the problem: "subtlety appeals to subtlety, and without imagination no man can follow another into these halls." And his final observation reverberates with personal trauma. "This visible [colored] world seems formed in love, the invisible [white] spheres were formed in fright." The necessity for whiteness as privileged "natural" state, the invention of it, was indeed formed in fright.

"Slavery," writes Rogin, "confirmed Melville's isolation, decisively established in *Moby Dick*, from the dominant consciousness of his time." I differ on this point and submit that Melville's hostility and repugnance for slavery would have found company. There were many white Americans of his acquaintance who felt repelled by slavery, wrote journalism about it, spoke about it, legislated on it and were active in abolishing it. His attitude to slavery alone would not have condemned him to the almost autistic separation visited upon him. And if he felt convinced that blacks were worthy of being treated like whites, or that capitalism was dangerous—he had company or could have found it. But to question the very notion of white progress, the very idea of racial superiority, of whiteness as privileged place in the evolutionary ladder of humankind, and to meditate on the fraudulent, self-destroying philosophy of that superiority, to "pluck it out from under the robes of Senators and Judges," to drag the "judge himself to the bar,"—that was dangerous, solitary, radical work. Especially then. Especially now. To be "only a patriot to heaven" is no mean aspiration in Young America for a writer—or the captain of a whaling ship.

A complex, heaving, disorderly, profound text is *Moby Dick*, and among its several meanings it seems to me this "unspeakable" one has remained the "hidden course," the "truth in the Face of Falsehood." To this day no novelist has so wrestled with its subject. To this day literary analyses of canonical texts have shied away from that perspective: the informing and determining Afro-American presence in traditional American literature. The chapters I have made reference to are only a fraction of the instances where the text surrenders such insights, and points a helpful finger toward the ways in which the ghost drives the machine.

Melville is not the only author whose works double their fascination and their power when scoured for this presence and the writerly strategies taken to address or deny it. Edgar Allan Poe will sustain such a reading. So will Nathaniel Hawthorne and Mark Twain; and in the twentieth century, Willa Cather, Ernest Hemingway, F. Scott Fitzgerald, and William Faulkner, to name a few. Canonical American literature is begging for such attention.

It seems to me a more than fruitful project to produce some cogent analysis showing instances where early American literature identifies itself, risks itself, to assert its antithesis to blackness. How its linguistic gestures prove the intimate relationship to what is being nulled by implying a full descriptive apparatus (identity) to a presence-that-is-assumed-not-to-exist. Afro-American critical inquiry can do this work.

## Notes

1. See *"Race," Writing, and Difference*, ed. Henry Louis Gates (Chicago: University of Chicago Press, 1986).

2. Among many examples, *They Came Before Columbus, The African Presence in Ancient America* by Ivan van Sertima (New York: Random House, 1976), xvi–xvii.

3. Tzvetan Todorov, " 'Race,' Writing, and Culture," trans. Loulou Mack, in *"Race,"* ed. Gates, 370–380.

4. Terrence Rafferty, "Articles of Faith," *The New Yorker*, 16 May 1988, 100–118.

5. Martin Bernal, *Black Athena: The Afroasiatic Roots of Classical Civilization, volume I: The Fabrication of Ancient Greece 1785–1985* (New Brunswick, N.J.: Rutgers University Press, 1987), 2.

6. Ibid., 310.

7. Ibid., 337.

8. See Michael Paul Rogin, *Subversive Genealogy: The Politics and Art of Herman Melville* (Berkeley and Los Angeles: University of California Press, 1985), 15.

9. Ibid., 107 and 142.

10. Ibid., 112.

# Mr. Clemens and Jim Crow:
# Twain, Race, and Blackface

Soon after leaving Hannibal for New York in 1853, Sam Clemens wrote home to his mother: "I reckon I had better black my face, for in these Eastern States niggers are considerably better than white people."[1] As the youth who would be Mark Twain wrote these words, Christy's Minstrels were at the peak of their extraordinary eight-year run (1846–1854) at New York City's Mechanics' Hall, and many other blackface troupes battled them for public attention. Meanwhile, the whole new phenomenon of the "Tom show"—dramatic blackface productions of Harriet Beecher Stowe's *Uncle Tom's Cabin*, published the year before—was emerging to (briefly) displace and reorient the minstrel tradition; by 1854 there were several such shows running in New York alone. Probably the prominence of blackface in New York only clinched Clemens's love of minstrelsy, which extended back to his Hannibal childhood.

Blackface minstrelsy—"the genuine nigger show, the extravagant nigger show," Twain calls it in the autobiography he dictated in his last years—had burst upon the unwitting town in the early 1840s as a "glad and stunning surprise."[2] Usually involving a small band of white men armed with banjo, fiddle, tambourine, and bone castanets and arrayed in blackface makeup and ludicrous dress, the minstrel show, from the 1830s to the early years of the twentieth century, offered white travesties and imitations of black humor, dance, speech, and music. It most often opened with assorted songs, breakdowns, and gags, followed by an "olio" portion of novelty acts such as malapropistic "stump speeches" or parodic "lectures," and concluded with a burlesque skit set in the South. In his *Autobiography* Twain averred: "If I could have the nigger show back again in its pristine purity and perfection I should have but little further use for opera" (64). This quite unguarded attraction to "blacking up" perhaps made it inevitable that in a letter to his mother Twain would reach for the blackface mask to finesse his response to racial difference in the northern city. For the rest of his life, Twain's imaginative encounters with race would be unavoidably bound up with blackface minstrelsy.

If Sam Clemens's class- and race-conscious recoil from free blacks sounds a lot like Huck Finn's Pap—"And to see the cool way of that nigger—why, he wouldn't a give me the road if I hadn't shoved him out o' the way"[3]—it also reminds us that such consciousness, as in minstrelsy, often acknowledged the lure to *be* black ("I reckon I had better black my face"), to inhabit the cool, virility, humility, abandon, degradation, or *gaite de coeur* that were the prime components of white fantasies of black manhood. Pap himself, in Twain's sly depiction of his rage against the black professor, is actually as black as the hated "mulatter," since he is, as Huck says, "just all mud" after a drunken night lying in the gutter (26). These subterranean links between black and lower-class white men called forth in the minstrel show, as in Mark Twain's work, interracial recognitions and identifications no less than the imperative to disavow them. Certainly nineteenth-century blackface acts sought to deny the idea that blacks and whites shared a common humanity. Their racist gibes and pastoral gambols asserted that slavery was amusing, right, and natural; their racial portrayals turned blacks into simps, dupes, and docile tunesmiths.

> Come listen all you galls and boys
> I'se jist from Tuckyhoe,
> I'm goin to sing a little song,
> My name's Jim Crow.
>
> Weel about and turn about
> And do jis so,
> Eb'ry time I weel about
> And jump Jim Crow.[4]

Exhibited before tradesmen, teamsters, and shopkeepers (and, in the 1850s and after, their female counterparts) in northern entertainment venues such as New York City's Mechanics' Hall, minstrel shows were in part the cultural flank of a generalized working-class hostility to blacks. This hostility was evinced in public slurs and violent acts—the casual racial policing that produced innumerable brawls and forced indignities, as well as the organized racial panic that fomented New York's terrible 1834 antiabolitionist race riots.

Yet the minstrel show very often twinned black and white, equating as much as differentiating them. The sources of this equation lay in exactly the same social conditions that gave rise to racist violence. One glimpses in the violence a severe white insecurity about the status of whiteness. To be lower class and white in the early nineteenth century, as the industrial revolution began to grind into high gear, was to be subject to remorseless assaults on one's independence and livelihood. The terms and conditions of work were steadily and alarmingly deteriorating; the status and character of white manhood struck masculinist workingmen as increasingly like that of women and blacks. The term "wage slave" came into being to denote this social drift, implying a defiant, "manly" outrage about the common condition of slaves and workingmen, as well as a primacy of concern for the status of white wage workers. Blackface minstrelsy was founded on this social antinomy. On one hand it basked in what one historian has called the "wages of whiteness"; on the other it revelled in the identifications between white men and slaves.[5] As for the latter, the very form of blackface acts—an inhabitance of black bodies, clothing, and gesture—records the literal white "investment" in black culture and an implicit desire to cross the color line. Blackface burlesque skits such as T. D. Rice's *O Hush! or, The Virginny Cupids* (1834) assumed, however contradictorily, a white audience alliance with "'spectable" black mechanics onstage even as they ridiculed supercilious black "dandies"—a racist designation that nonetheless reveals the class animus fueling much of the minstrel show's racial disdain.[6] The interracial recognition on which minstrelsy often called was visible in the artisan abolitionism that competed with artisan racism for the hearts and minds of workingmen; working-class antislavery feeling was intermittently strong in the antebellum years and may have aided blackface minstrelsy's turn toward a liberating sentimentalism in the late 1840s.[7] Stephen Foster's "Old Folks at Home" (1851) or "My Old Kentucky Home, Good-Night!" (1853), sung from behind the blackface mask, unquestionably evoked sympathy for separated slave families and generally implied the feeling humanity of slaves, though in doing so it relied on the old racial stereotypes. As Ralph Ellison has remarked, even when the intentions of minstrel performers were least palatable, still "these fellows had to go and listen, they had to open their ears to (black) speech even if their purpose was to make it comic."[8] The complex and active exchanges of white self and black Other in blackface performance, however derisive, opened the color line to effacement in the very moment of its construction.[9]

Twain's own response to blackface minstrelsy illustrates the ambivalence of lower-class white racial feeling, which suffuses his greatest novelistic treatments of race and slavery. Said Twain of the minstrel show:

> The minstrels appeared with coal-black hands and faces and their clothing was a loud and extravagant burlesque of the clothing worn by the plantation slave of the time; not that the rags of the poor slave were burlesqued, for that would not have been possible; burlesque could have added nothing in the way of extravagance to the sorrowful accumulation of rags and patches which constituted his costume; it was the form and color of his dress that was burlesqued.

Twain proceeds here with some caution and not a little sympathy for the slave; he senses, perhaps uncomfortably, that the pleasures of stage burlesque have been wrought out of the quotidian violence of slavery. He even observes that blackface minstrels had "buttons as big as a blacking box," collapsing blackface masquerade, the means of its artifice, and an echo of one of its literal models— Negro bootblacks—in a single self-conscious figure. But Twain easily abandons such self-consciousness, as his reference to the slave's "costume," a clearly aestheticizing gesture, might lead us to expect:

> The minstrel used a very broad negro dialect; he used it competently and with easy facility and it was funny—delightfully and satisfyingly funny. . . . [Minstrels'] lips were thickened and lengthened with bright red paint to such a degree that their mouths resembled slices cut in a ripe watermelon. . . . The minstrel troupes had good voices and both their solos and their choruses were a delight to me as long as the negro show continued in existence. (64–66)

Twain is undeniably attracted to and celebratory of black culture. Yet just what that culture *is* to him is not altogether easy to make out, distorted and filtered as it is by white fantasy, desire, and delight. When views like Twain's do not simply fall into ridicule they are certainly the patronizing flip-side of it, suggesting Twain's ability to lose sight of the sorry circumstances that underlie his mirth and his continued and unexamined interest in racial exoticism. Ralph Ellison once observed that *Huckleberry Finn*'s Jim rarely emerges from behind the minstrel mask; Twain's remarks on the minstrel show lend a great deal of force to that observation.[10]

Already in *Tom Sawyer* (1876), Twain had called on the pleasures of minstrelsy in his portrayal of Jim; in chapter 2 Jim comes "skipping out at the gate" singing "Buffalo Gals"—a blackface tune previously known as "Lubly Fan" (1844):

> Den lubly Fan will you cum out to night,
> > will you cum out to night,
> > will you cum out to night,
> Den lubly Fan will you cum out to night,
> An dance by de lite ob de moon.
>
> I stopt her an I had some talk,
> > Had some talk,
> > Had some talk,
> But her foot covered up de whole side-walk
> An left no room for me.
> . . . . . . . . .
> Her lips are like de oyster plant,
> > De oyster plant,
> > De oyster plant,
> I try to kiss dem but I cant
> Dey am so berry large.[11]

It may well be that blacks picked up even outrageously untoward songs from the blackface theater and adapted them to their own uses, as the long history of black "signifying" on such white productions, and the rowdy misogyny of much black oral culture, both suggest.[12] Conversely, Twain's own intent might have been irony rather than realism: for Jim, a black man, sings this blackface ditty as Tom whitewashes his aunt's fence in punishmenl for his truancy, the heightening of racial markers working up a certain self-consciousness here. There may even be an implied equation between Tom and Jim, since Tom's frequent disappearances mimic the escapes of fugitive slaves (which Jim would soon become in *Huckleberry Finn*) and require a constant whitening or chastening in order to distinguish Tom from such a status. Or perhaps Aunt Polly is merely the "lubly" object of a veiled blackface joke on Twain's part (if so, this puts Twain himself in blackface). Just as surely as all of these conjectures, however, Twain saw the character of Jim through lenses the minstrel show had afforded— he let a racist song go out of Jim's heart. The minstrel show's influence on Twain oddly redoubled over the next eight years, the years of *Huckleberry Finn*'s composition.

Blackface minstrelsy indeed underwrote one of the nineteenth century's most powerful antiracist novels—a tribute to the political fractures of minstrelsy and

*Huckleberry Finn* both. This is no simple matter of minstrel-show "trappings" or "residues" in Twain's novel (as we often hurry to say), an issue of unfortunate, merely historical formal qualities in the portrayal of Jim disrupting Twain's liberal thematic intentions. The text is shot through with blackface thinking. Written as well as situated in the minstrel show's boom years, *Huckleberry Finn*, as Anthony J. Berret has argued, relies on comic dialogues between Huck and Jim (much of the humor at Jim's expense), many and various novelty acts (the king and the duke's scams, the circus, and so forth), and riotous burlesques of social and cultural matters (Emmeline Grangerford's sentimental poetry, the final setting-free of an already-free Jim). The whole book may thus conform to a tripartite minstrel-show structure of comic dialogues, olio, and southern burlesque.[13] And circumstances surrounding *Huckleberry Finn*'s writing only clarify its indebtedness to the minstrel tradition.

In 1882 Twain got the idea for a lecture tour (which he termed a circus or menagerie) to include himself, William Dean Howells, Thomas Bailey Aldrich, George Washington Cable, and Joel Chandler Harris. This authorial circus seems hardly more than the variety acts of a minstrel show, and the reading tour that came out of the idea, featuring Cable's straight man and Twain's clown, was in a sense precisely one, since both authors read the roles of black characters onstage, Cable even singing black songs.[14] This was the tour during which Twain first read parts of *Huckleberry Finn*, significantly the "King Sollermun" and "How come a Frenchman doan' talk like a man?" passages, whose blackface resonances are very clear. These passages may in fact have been written to be so performed after *Huckleberry Finn* was already completed.[15] The political complexity of this affair is compounded by Cable's having published, mid-tour, "The Freedman's Case in Equity," a forthright attack on southern racism that appeared in the same issue of *Century Magazine* that ran an excerpt from *Huckleberry Finn*. Somehow the authors' views did not arrest the blackface tones of their readings, nor Twain's naming of one of his selections "Can't Learn a Nigger to Argue," a title he changed only when Cable requested it.[16] These events no doubt put a highly ambiguous spin on *Huckleberry Finn*, but they indicate as well that the contradiction between the book's overt politics and its indebtedness to the minstrel show was less cumbrous in the nineteenth century. Even the most enlightened nineteenth-century political thinkers, for example, adhered to "romantic racialism," as historian George Fredrickson has termed it, which celebrated the supposedly greater emotional depth and spiritual resources of black people even as it postulated innate differences between the races, just as the minstrel show seemed to do.[17] *Huckleberry Finn*'s limitations can surely be laid at the minstrel show's doorstep, but its strengths are oddly imbricated with strains of thought and feeling that inspired blackface performance.

We are thus led to a rather scandalous conclusion. The liberatory coupling of Huck and Jim *and* the gruesome blackface sources of Jim's character are the unseparate and equal results of minstrelsy's influence on the work of Mark Twain. Writers who have rightly denounced the minstrel-show aura of *Huckleberry Finn* miss the extent to which even the best moments have a blackface cast.[18] True enough Twain's lapses are easy to spot, and we ought to remark a few of these. There is, for instance, the slave down on the Phelps farm who at the end of *Huckleberry Finn* tends to Jim in his reenslavement. Named Nat in what one can only assume is jocular homage to Nat Turner, this character is so reminiscent of Jim's portrayal at the novel's beginning that he undermines the steady commitment Jim exhibits in the final chapters; the blackface aspersions against him taint Jim as well. Possessed of what Huck/Twain calls a "good-natured, chuckle-headed face," obsessed with fending off the witches he says have been haunting him, Nat is a sort of hysterical paranoiac (186). (The reference to Nat Turner's obsessive, visionary Christianity works to discredit both men.) Nat observes that Jim sings out when he first sees Huck and Tom, and says so; but the boys flatly deny having heard it, pushing Nat to resort to mystical explanations. " 'Oh, it's de dad-blame' witches, sah, en I wisht I was dead, I do. Dey's awluz at it, sah, en dey do mos' kill me, dey sk'yers me so' " (187). Even if we remark that Nat is forced to this conclusion by the boys' denial, his squirms are rendered with infantilizing exactitude. Shortly after, amid one of Tom's strategems in the digressive freeing of Jim, some hounds rush into the hut and Nat is again afrighted: "you'll say I's a fool, but if I didn't b'lieve I see most a million dogs, er devils, er some'n, I wisht I may die right heah in dese tracks. I did, mos' sholy" (196). Tom offers to make Nat a witch pie to ward them off, to which Nat responds: "Will you do it, honey?—will you? I'll wusshup de groun' und' yo' foot, I will!" (197). Twain may have intended us to pick up on Tom's callousness in fanning the flames of Nat's fear: we note, for instance, that Nat has never heard of the now-implanted idea of a witch pie, and indeed that Nat promises not to disregard Tom's request that he let alone the witch preparations, "not f'r ten hund'd thous'n' billion dollars" (197)—a sum that would probably free Nat from his fetters. But the very uncertainty of Twain's intentions, together with his seemingly happy blackface depiction of Nat's self-abasement, undercuts all but racist meanings from the scene.

At the same time, moments very like this one may reveal more sympathetic dimensions. At the beginning of *Huckleberry Finn* Tom Sawyer can't help playing a trick on Jim while he sleeps; he puts his hat on a branch above his head. Jim believes he's been bewitched and put in a trance and ridden by witches. Huck says Jim tells demonstrably self-serving tales of his adventures:

> Jim was monstrous proud about it, and he got so he wouldn't hardly notice the other niggers. Niggers would come miles to hear Jim tell about it, and he was more looked up to than any nigger in that country. Strange niggers would stand with their mouths open and look him all over, same as if he was a wonder. . . . Jim was most ruined, for a servant, because he got so stuck up on account of having seen the devil and been rode by witches. (11)

In one sense this is standard "darky" fare. Huck even supplies the proper white exasperation with such charlatanism. Yet as several scholars have shown, this moment of apparent blackface foolishness is in fact an occasion in which Jim seizes rhetorical and perhaps actual power. Despite Huck's rather harsh judgement of Jim's self-investment, the fact is that he becomes a "wonder" within the black community and is "most ruined" for a servant—unsuited for slavery—in the wake of his tales. The superstition to which we are encouraged by Huck to condescend has actual and potentially subverting results in the world of the novel. One notes that Jim's actual words are not rendered here, which in the orthographic hierarchy of white dialect writing might have had the effect of reducing their impact. This is a moment when Jim, as he does in other ways throughout *Huckleberry Finn*, uses tricks and deceits to his advantage.[19] We may call this a kind of blackface antiracism, of whose political duplicity and indeed variability Twain was not always the complete master.

This may even be a moment, as Shelley Fisher Fishkin has argued, that reveals Twain's intimacy with black life. For beliefs and stories such as Jim's were present and alive within black culture, which coded terrifying "night rides" by patrolling whites or Ku Klux Klan brigades as those of ghouls and spirits. Tales of such night rides, says Gladys-Marie Fry, duly suffered and survived by resiliant blacks, allowed the heroic exploits of a subject people free expression.[20] Yet Twain leaves his white readers to divine for themselves the pressing uses of such tales as Jim tells, and in doing so steps again into the uncharmed circle of blackface—for it is, after all, Twain who is deploying black lore for his own ambiguous uses. Ambiguity arises also in scenes where racialist assumptions seem to be under the novelist's scrutinizing gaze. Soon after Huck and Tom arrive on the Phelps farm, with Jim still to be located, Tom suddenly realizes that the dinners the boys see regularly transported to a certain hut seem suspicious:

> "Looky here, Huck, what fools we are, to not think of it before! I bet I know where Jim is."
>
> "No! Where?"
>
> "In that hut down by the ash-hopper. Why, looky here. When we was at dinner, didn't you see a nigger man go in there with some vittles?"
>
> "Yes."
>
> "What did you think the vittles was for?"
>
> "For a dog."
>
> "So'd I. Well, it wasn't for a dog."
>
> "Why?"
>
> "Because part of it was watermelon."
>
> "So it was—I noticed it. Well, it does beat all, that I never thought about a dog not eating watermelon. It shows how a body can see and don't see at the same time." (183)

Working on the assumption that, as Tom puts it, "Watermelon shows man," Huck and Tom detect Jim's whereabouts. This is a craftily constructed scene, one that makes some of Twain's largest political points. Huck's recognition that one can see and not see simultaneously is perhaps the aptest self-description in his whole twisted history of antislavery antiabolitionism. The scene pointedly distinguishes man from dog. And yet the means of this distinction is the clichéd watermelon reference, as though that stereotypical food in particular were the one to best locate Jim. It is true that Tom's words only suggest that dogs do not eat watermelon, not that black people do; and even if this latter is implied, it is Tom and Huck, not Twain, speaking. But Twain is joking around here even in the midst of one of his most earnest moral observations. I think we are justified in concluding that the closer Twain got to black cultural practices and to racially subversive meanings the more, paradoxically, his blackface debts multiplied. Blackface was something like the device or code or signifying system through which Twain worked out his least self-conscious and most sophisticated impulses regarding race in the United States. Jim's triumphs and Twain's ironies have to be as elaborately deciphered as Huck's future through Jim's hair-ball, so self-evident are their minstrel roots.

What is more, scenes we always take as Twain's most enlightened strokes suggest a surprising complicity with the minstrel show. Jim's emotionalism, and the fugitives' several joyous reunions on the raft, call on the romantic racialism that underwrote minstrelsy's sentimental strain—its broken-family nostalgia and long-suffered separations. Stephen Foster's "Old Folks at Home" (1851), for instance, depends for its effect on the pathos culled from black families forced to split up:

> Way down upon de Swanee ribber,
> Far, far away,
> Dere's wha my heart is turning ebber,
> Dere's wha de old folks stay.
>
> All up and down de whole creation,
> Sadly I roam,
> Still longing for de old plantation,
> And for de old folks at home.

Foster's "Oh! Susanna" (1848) exploits the poignance of black attempts to reunite:

> I came from Alabama wid
> my banjo on my knee,
> I'm g'wan to Lousiana
> My true love for to see,
> It rain'd all night the day I left,
> The weather it was dry,
> The sun so hot I frose to death;
> Susanna, dont you cry.
>
> Oh! Susanna,
> Oh! dont you cry for me,
> I've come from Alabama,
> wid my banjo on my knee.[21]

Twain's novel relies on similar familial predicaments whose resonance derives from the slave's stereotyped emotionality, his deeper well of feeling. Jim does not ache for the old plantation but he does miss his children, from whom he has been separated: "He was often moaning and mourning that way, nights, when he judged I was asleep, and saying, 'Po' little 'Lizabeth! po' little Johnny! its

mighty hard; I spec' I ain't ever gwyne to see you no mo', no mo'!' He was a
mighty good nigger, Jim was" (125). This moment demonstrates to Huck that
Jim "cared just as much for his people as white folks does for their'n" (125),
one of Twain's heavier-handed interventions, but in calling on the black types
evident in minstrelsy the scene qualifies the very point it wants to make. Investing
black people with human feeling, in the minstrel show or in *Huckleberry Finn*,
was no doubt an advance over other less charitable views. Yet doing it by way
of the postulated inequality of romantic racialism troubled the commitment to
American freedom.

In their flight down the river, Jim and Huck are themselves occasionally
separated, whereupon the two are placed in the longing position of "Oh! Susanna" 's lovers (as Leslie Fiedler somewhat anxiously suspicioned long ago).[22] The
most famous of their reunions, after Huck and Jim lose each other in a fog, is
an aesthetic and political triumph. Adrift in a canoe on the foggy river with no
idea as to Jim's and the raft's whereabouts, Huck falls into uneasy sleep. When
he wakes up, it takes him a moment to recall his dilemma. The fog is gone, and
in no time Huck has made it to the raft. Jim is asleep, the raft littered with
evidence of its difficult passage in the fog. Huck decides to play a trick on
Jim–shades of Tom Sawyer—by telling him that he dreamt the whole thing. Jim
rouses: " 'Goodness gracious, is dat you, Huck? En you ain' dead—you ain'
drowned—you's back agin? It's too good for true, honey, it's too good for true.
Lemme look at you, chile, lemme feel o' you. No, you ain' dead! you's back
agin, 'live en soun', jis de same ole Huck—de same ole Huck, thanks to goodness!" (70). Huck mutes Jim's gladness as he gets him to adopt the theory that
the fog was all a dream. Once convinced, Jim sets out to interpret the dream, to
Huck's considerable derision. Huck lets on that it was a joke after all, and Jim's
response to Huck's prank apportions most of the humanity on the raft to himself:

> "When I got all wore out wid work, en wid de callin' for you, en went to sleep,
> my heart wuz mos' broke bekase you wuz los', en I didn' k'yer no mo' what become
> er me en de raf'. En when I wake up en fine you back agin', all safe en soun', de
> tears come en I could a got down on my knees en kiss' yo' foot I's so thankful. En
> all you wuz thinkin' 'bout wuz how you could make a fool uv ole Jim wid a lie.
> Dat truck dah is *trash*; en trash is what people is dat puts dirt on de head er dey
> fren's en makes 'em ashamed." (72)

Jim gets to call Huck white trash. Jim's concern for Huck transcends mere
worry over his own safety as a fugitive; it is a concern that is not visibly
reciprocated by Huck. Indeed Huck, whose experience of the fog curiously
resembles that of Jim—he is lost and lonely, falls asleep and feels like he is
dreaming, then is glad to see Jim—denies his vulnerability by projecting it onto
the slave. Unable to deal with his own experience, to treat him like a human
being, or to express his feelings, Huck concocts a trick that makes Jim do all
the work—first of articulating Huck's joy at reuniting, then of experiencing
Huck's puzzlement and frustration. The "solid white fog" (68), that apt metaphor
for white supremacy, which separated Huck and Jim even from the sight of each

other, now dissolves only to find Huck reerecting racial barriers. It takes Jim's speech to make Huck "humble myself to a nigger" (72). We might remark, however, that Twain himself is leaning heavily on Jim in this scene to do his work for him. Even as he exposes Huck's racist failings he needs the pathos that minstrel shows in the 1840s and 1850s had begun to pin to the slaves to make his case. Not only does Jim's joy reiterate the steadfast urge to reunion of "Oh! Susanna," but his delivery of Huck's comeuppance is swelled by its air of broken-hearted disappointment. Twain knew well the aggregated sources of racial guilt, racial desire, and racial longing that make just the kind of emotional strategy Jim uses irresistably effective to whites, whether Huck, Twain himself, or his white readers; and his working of the white audience through his manipulations of Jim's character is not the least of *Huckleberry Finn*'s convergences with the minstrel tradition. That Twain may have come to know the appeal of racial emotionalism from the minstrel show itself only shows how variable the political work of minstrelsy could be. If, in other words, some of *Huckleberry Finn*'s best scenes come close to blackface minstrelsy, this hardly cancels their impact (though it does show how little literature transcends its cultural moment). The duplicity of these scenes simply evidences how implicated we remain in the contradictions of North American racial life.

Perhaps Twain was remarking on the absurd consequences of this fundamental cultural fact when he put Jim in what can only be called Arabface. In order to free the fugitive slave from being tied up all day while the king, the duke, and Huck go ashore, the duke disguises Jim as an Arab to keep the curious at bay. Attired in a King Lear outfit and horse-hair wig and whiskers, and his face and hands theater-painted a dead dull solid blue (126), Jim's appearance surely recalls the art of blackface at the same time that it explodes the very idea of racial performance. Twain no doubt means to lampoon the racial thinking behind forms such as blackface when he has the duke tell Jim that, should anyone draw near the raft, Jim must "hop out of the wigwam, and carry on a little, and fetch a howl or two like a wild beast" (126). Savage injuns and niggers and A-rabs too are invoked here as figments of the white-supremacist imagination. The effect of Jim's costuming, we note, is to make him look, as Huck puts it, "like a man that's been drownded nine days" and "like he was dead" (126–127)—racist caricature is itself a kind of death.

Despite Twain's self-consciousness, though, the evidence suggests we take Huck's admiring remark about Jim in Chapter 40—that he "knowed" Jim was "white inside"—as the crowning statement on the centrality of blackface's contra-dictions to Twain's imagination. The remark is a perfect specimen of the imperial psychological orientation Homi Bhabha calls "ambivalence."[23] Convinced of the humanity and identity of American blacks, Twain seems nonetheless to have been haunted by their difference. Hence he returned over and over to the actual practice and literary trope of blackface, which hedges by imagining the Other as black only in exterior, still white inside. A delicate balance must be maintained here. To think of blacks as altogether the same—as all white—threatens white supremacist identity; to think of them as altogether different—as all black—raises the specter of white annihilation and superfluity. As in many societies with subject populations at home or abroad, the Other must be rendered not quite black and yet not white. "They" must be versions of "us," caught in a cycle of mimicry (usually construed as "civilizing" or benevolent rule), and yet perennially unable to make the grade. Racist ideologies, even the relatively gentle ones Twain deploys, insert the boundaries that ever threaten to evaporate between the kinds of human beings stuck in such a hierarchical relationship. Why should it surprise us that, even in a dissenter like Twain, the colonial mentality, so routinely unsettled by an anxiety of otherness, produced a need to preserve the differentness of blacks through blackface gestures, even as it nervously asserted that "they" were like "us" after all?

Exploring as well as enacting this logic, Twain anticipated Antonio Gramsci's remarks on "national-popular" literature—that it emerges out of extant popular materials rather than artificially refined or imposed ideas.[24] Twain took up the American dilemma not by avoiding popular racial representations but by inhabiting them so forcefully that he produced an immanent criticism of them. It is not just that Huck more or less fulfills Twain's intention of making nonsense of America's racial strictures (including those of Twain's readers) by living up to them the best anyone can; Twain himself pushed his blackface devices so far that they turned back on themselves, revealing the contradictory character of white racial feeling.[25] It is this simultaneous inhabitance and critique that makes *Huckleberry Finn* so scabrous, unassimilable, and perhaps unteachable to our own time. I don't think Twain chose to work within the popular racial codes of his day out of calculation, as a way of exploiting racist entertainment for antiracist uses, though that often turns out to be *Huckleberry Finn*'s effect. He did it with an odd relish, out of a sense of inwardness and intimacy with the mass audience who shared his love of minstrelsy—the "mighty mass of the uncultivated" he said he wanted to reach with his novel (sold door to door by canvassing agents) and with whom he felt the greatest kinship.[26] It is worth noting here Twain's own willingness in effect to put on the blackface mask. After dinner one night at an 1874 Twain dinner party in Hartford, Twain dropped into his version of several slave spirituals, which had begun to be disseminated by black university singing groups in the early 1870s. Later, an overimbibed Twain mimicked a black man at a hoedown, dancing black dances for his guests in his drawing room.[27] Out of this sensibility came writing based on Twain's immersion in lower- or working-class racial feeling: writing that still resists attempts to tame down or clean up its engagements with race and class in America, and that is as partial, flawed, and disturbing as it is penetrating, emblematic, and current.

## Notes

1. Mark Twain, *Mark Twain's Letters*, ed. Edgar Marquess Branch et al. (Berkeley: University of California Press, 1988), 4.

2. Mark Twain, *The Autobiography of Mark Twain*, ed. Charles Neider (New York: Harper and Row, 1959), 63–64.

3. Samuel Langhorne Clemens, *Adventures of Huckleberry Finn* (1884; rpt. New York: Norton, 1977), 27.

4. "Jim Crow" (New York: E. Riley, early 1830s); for this song and some of its variations, see Sam Dennison, *Scandalize My Name: Black Imagery in American Popular Music* (New York: Garland, 1982), 51–57.

5. David Roediger, *The Wages of Whiteness: Race and the Making of the American Working Class* (London: Verso, 1991).

6. For the text of *O Hush!* see Gary Engle, ed., *This Grotesque Essence: Plays from the American Minstrel Stage* (Baton Rouge: Louisiana State University Press, 1978), 1–12.

7. John B. Jentz, "The Anti-Slavery Constituency in Jacksonian New York City," *Civil War History* 27.2 (1981): 101–122; Williston Lofton, "Abolition and Labor," *Journal of Negro History* 33.3 (1948): 249–283; Joseph G. Rayback, "The American Workingman and the Antislavery Crusade," *Journal of Economic History* 3.2 (1943): 152–163; Eric Foner, "Abolitionism and the Labor Movement in Ante-Bellum America," *Politics and Ideology in the Age of the Civil War* (New York: Oxford University Press, 1980), 57–76; Herbert Shapiro, "Labor and Antislavery: Reflections on the Literature," *Nature, Society, and Thought* 2.4 (1989): 471–490.

8. Interview with Ralph Ellison, quoted in Shelley Fisher Fishkin, *Was Huck Black?: Mark Twain and African-American Voices* (New York: Oxford University Press, 1993), 90.

9. For more on the minstrel show, see Eric Lott, *Love and Theft: Blackface Minstrelsy and the American Working Class* (New York: Oxford University Press, 1993).

10. Ralph Ellison, *Shadow and Act* (1964; rpt. New York: Vintage, 1972), 50.

11. "Lubly Fan," in S. Foster Damon, comp., *Series of Old American Songs* (Providence: Brown University Library, 1936), no. 39.

12. For examples of each tendency see Lawrence Levine, *Black Culture and Black Consciousness: Afro-American Folk Thought From Slavery to Freedom* (New York: Oxford University Press, 1977), 190–366.

13. Anthony J. Berret, "*Huckleberry Finn* and the Minstrel Show," *American Studies* 27.2 (1986): 37–49.

14. Paul Fatout, *Mark Twain on the Lecture Circuit* (Carbondale and Edwardsville: Southern Illinois University Press, 1960), 204–231.

15. Fredrick Woodard and Donnarae MacCann, "*Huckleberry Finn* and the Traditions of Blackface Minstrelsy," *Interracial Books for Children Bulletin* 15 (1984): 5.

16. Guy Cardwell, *Twins of Genius* (East Lansing: Michigan State College Press, 1953), 105; Steven Mailloux, *Rhetorical Power* (Ithaca: Cornell University Press, 1989), 57–99; Forrest Robinson, *In Bad Faith: The Dynamics of Deception in Mark Twain's America* (Cambridge: Harvard University Press, 1986), 111–211.

17. George M. Fredrickson, *The Black Image in the White Mind: The Debate on Afro-American Character and Destiny 1817–1914* (New York: Harper and Row, 1971), 101–102.

18. Woodard and MacCann, "*Huckleberry Finn* and the Traditions of Blackface Minstrelsy"; Woodard and MacCann, "Minstrel Shackles and Nineteenth-Century 'Liberality' in *Huckleberry Finn*," in James S. Leonard, Thomas A. Tenney, and Thadious M. Davis, ed., *Satire or Evasion? Black Perspectives on Huckleberry Finn* (Durham and London: Duke University Press, 1991), 141–153; Bernard Bell, "Twain's 'Nigger' Jim: The Tragic Face Behind the Minstrel Mask," *Mark Twain Journal* 23.1 (1985): 10–17.

19. David L. Smith, "Huck, Jim, and American Racial Discourse," in James S. Leonard et al., eds., *Satire or Evasion?*, 103–120; James M. Cox, "A Hard Book to Take," in Robert Sattelmeyer and J. Donald Crowley, eds., *One Hundred Years of Huckleberry Finn* (Columbia: University of Missouri Press, 1985), 386–403.

20. Gladys-Marie Fry, *Night Riders in Black Folk History* (1975; rpt., Athens: University of Georgia Press, 1991), 9–10.

21. Richard Jackson, ed., *Stephen Foster Song Book* (New York: Dover, 1974), 101–102, 89–91.

22. Leslie Fiedler, "Come Back to the Raft Ag'in, Huck Honey!" *The Collected Essays of Leslie Fiedler* (New York: Stein and Day, 1971), vol. 1, 142–151.

23. Homi Bhabha, "The Other Question: The Stereotype and Colonial Discourse," *Screen* 24 (1983): 18–36.

24. Antonio Gramsci, *Selections from Cultural Writings*, ed. David Forgacs and Geoffrey Nowell-Smith, trans. William Boelhower (London: Lawrence and Wishart, 1985), 207, 209–211.

25. On immanent criticism see Theodor Adorno, "Cultural Criticism and Society," *Prisms*, trans. Samuel and Shierry Weber (Cambridge: MIT Press, 1967), 32.

26. Justin Kaplan, *Mr. Clemens and Mark Twain* (New York: Simon and Schuster, 1966), 270.

27. Ibid., 174.

# "Who I Was":
# Ethnic Identity and
# American Literary Ethnocentrism

I want to start by recounting two far-flung moments in American ethnic history. The second is from Booker T. Washington—the first is more recent. It comes from the *New York Times News Service*, February 2, 1994, the day after Deval Patrick was appointed assistant attorney general for civil rights. I offer it as a pointedly concentrated rendering of a familiar piece of the cultural liturgy. "Patrick's entire life," the *Times* intones, "has been one of overcoming obstacles. His rise from poverty to success is the kind of story that even some conservatives would cheer."[1] The significance of this formula is precisely in its brevity. Its short-hand and unselfconscious reference to terms that are elaborated in countless texts, and its deliberate association of those terms with "conservative," which is to say self-consciously "American," identities suggest how thoroughly settled these terms are, by now, in our vocabularies. Only the barest hint is necessary since the operative language is so deeply embedded in the cultural code.

The generic story of self creation in America condensed by the *Times* is a simple and familiar one. A boy is born into obscure poverty.[2] But, taking full advantage of such opportunities as life offers, and by dint of native abilities, hard work, and good character, he leaves his low past behind and achieves the solid American success he had barely dreamed for himself. The potency of this script is reflected in its broad use—so common as to seem almost natural, a cultural habit, a routine. As the official organizing interpretation and shaping ideal for numberless American narratives from Franklin's fragmented "Memoirs" to Nixon's, it has remained so powerful in our culture—even long after it had been made an object of parody by the militantly disillusioned like Nathaniel West—precisely because it embodies in individual terms the past and future of the nation. Patrick's appointment is so resonant because it encourages us to associate that promise of personal success and fufillment with a "civil right."

The second incident, from near the end of Booker T. Washington's work of automythography, *Up from Slavery*, relates what I take to be the defining moment of the book.[3] Traveling by train in Georgia, Washington is invited to sit with two white Bostonian women of his acquaintance in a car full of white Georgia men. To Washington's discomfort and the obvious dismay of the Georgians, one of the women orders a meal, and, unable to get away, Washington rushes through his dinner under the glare of Southern eyes. Afterwards, Washington moves apprehensively to the smoking car to find out how things stand. But, once there, he is surprised to be greeted cordially all round because, in the interim, it had become known, as he says, "who I was."

This triumphant moment comes, as triumph must in these ritual dramatizations of cultural progress, near the end not just of the book, but of years of struggle and suffering during most of which the world was indifferent to Washington's presence. And it comes just before the narrative turns away from personal struggle to recite a litany of public accomplishment and (especially) recognition represented most prominently by the text of his speech at the Atlanta Exposition, which the account presents in full as documentary evidence of the "recognition" dramatized in the railroad car encounter.

It is the point of such key narrative moments to seem definitive—brief, bold assertions of unqualified personal identity, marking as they do the relationship between, in this case, Washington and the surrounding culture. This apparent simplicity, however, only covers up conflicts inevitable to communication around and about ethnic boundary lines, conflicts that could be said to define such boundaries through the formative intersection of rhetorical forms, linguistic and social. Huck Finn's famous "I'll go to Hell," for example, presents itself as subversive, but as James Cox has persuasively argued, Huck's repudiation of his own culture's values actually reinforces the ethical assumptions of Twain's post–Civil War audience and thus demonstrates both the futility of Huck's quest for "freedom," and the speciousness of the idealized notion of "freedom" he seeks. The doubleness of this ostensibly definitive statement receives its fullest and fully appropriate expression in what has often been seen as the Phelps Farm "farce" that follows. Washington's moment, as I shall suggest below, conceals a similarly convoluted dance of desire for and dissent from larger cultural norms.

In this essay, I want to look briefly at the composition of individual identity and of a specifically "ethnic" identity in Horatio Alger's *Ragged Dick*, Booker T. Washington's *Up from Slavery*, and Richard Wright's *Native Son*. Each of these works has been a model for the nature and construction of ethnic identity in America. Each has been a springboard for generalizations about the conditions of an American "Character"—and it is that connection between "ethnic" and "American" identities I want to focus on here. I am interested in what these texts have to say about narratives that take ethnos for a subject in the American context, including the critical narratives of ethnicity produced by literary scholars. I want to use them to suggest some of the interrelationships between critiques of the subject and the problems posed by ethnic boundaries as writers draw and redraw them. Read both in and against the context of revisionist discourses, these works yield problematic and even ideologically uncomfortable understandings of the interplay of self and culture, of individual and ethnos. Among other things, they prompt us to ask what the construction of the ethnic self within a larger hegemonic culture suggests about the integrity or the "otherness" of our own cultural identities and the institutions we construct around them with our fictive and critical accounts.

Their ambiguous relations to American cultural ideals implicate these narratives of personal identity in the influential narrative strategies that have defined America and its writing in an equally ambivalent opposition to the European tradition. The story of America, in its numerous manifestations and as told for various purposes, has been an effort to represent original identity against the background of an established authoritative tradition. This is its particular importance to the construction of narratives that play on self-discovery, self-creation, and self-development, like those I am dealing with here. American literary studies offers a particularly instructive study in critical versions of such narratives since American literary studies has always depended on at once defining and effacing ethnic identity. In *The American Ideal*, I argued that the idea of "America" has—particularly in literary studies—been a strategy for asserting difference without having to explain it.[4] As "America" subsumes particulars within its overarching and literally unquestionable unity, it has represented an "other" world within worldly experience, an analog of, and a temporal substitute for, the divine order toward which Christian history aspired.

Perched awkwardly and self-consciously on the outskirts of British culture, all American literature has been regional literature, by which I also mean that it is literature from the margin, alienated from yet unavoidably supplicant to an established dominant literary tradition, the product of a colonial culture and people, and thus a literature of ethnos. In short, American literature is ethnic literature. It is ethnic not because its authors are members of a repressed minority, but because its narrative forms and rhetorical strategies speak to and from its marginal position, and are the same as, could even be said to have provided the models for, the narratives we more typically think of as ethnic that followed. In their zeal to distinguish American texts from British, American cultural rhetoricians imagined a powerful model for ethnocentric self-creation, and set the terms that subsequent ethnic narratives have worked with and against.

The tradition of critical writing that comprises American literary scholarship, both before and after its professional institutionalization in the last quarter of the nineteenth century, constructed a coherent literary tradition to incarnate and legitimate the national identity, and at the same time justify its own professional existence. From its first exemplars in nineteenth-century literary scholarship, the "American" tradition of literary study can be seen as an early instance of what has become, in more recent academic discourse, a ritualistic invocation of "change." Like the Lutheran dissent from Catholicism, the secession of American literature from the British tradition was only the first step toward unbounded future fracturing. In that sense, monolithic as American literary scholarship may seem to its modern dissenters, its initiation into the institution of literary studies more than a century ago prefigured and paved the way for what modern revisionist critics usually identify as characteristically "post-modernist" programs of canonical revision and diversity. In the realm of scholarship, American literary studies opened new rhetorical territory. The embryonic narrative of "America" appeared at the end of the fifteenth century as a necessarily ambivalent early strategy for dealing with the authority of historical experience.[5] The historiography incarnated in that narrative reimagined apocalyptic or revolutionary change as the fulfillment of received values, and on earth in the New Eden rather than in heaven. On that Christian model, the stories of American identity have dramatized a crossing from the European past to the New World American future in which former identities are sloughed off as if they had never been, leaving essential identities untouched. Four hundred years later, in the developing field of American literary scholarship, that meant accommodating while claiming to abandon the past and making the new tolerable by bringing it within the existing horizon of critical understanding and social desire—specifically, at the time, the desire for national unity and security after the Civil War, a longing that seemed particularly acute amidst the crushing world-wide depression of the 1870s and after.

The idea of "America" has been a way of *assuming* cultural, historical, and narrative coherence, and in the process, of constraining the interpretation of facts and of texts. In scholarship, it has produced a tradition of critical writing that I have described elsewhere as the Rhetoric of Revisionism.[6] In faithful imitation of the New World settlers' claims to have left the Old behind, each initiative in American literary scholarship repudiates its own professional past in this way, and in that same gesture reiterates it. Even at their most conventional, they are narratives of dissent; at their most rebellious, aspirants to the tradition. Each has depended on forgetting the central fact that its revolutionary posture is a rhetorical *norm* in the field. The remarkable persistence of the narrative of America as a strategy for assuming a double position vis à vis tradition reappears in the place "America" takes in contemporary academic conversations about ethnicity, where it represents—Janus-like—both the repressive and failed past and the idealized all-embracing future. In this period of what Umberto Eco might call Hypercritique, it is not surprising that traditional narratives of American identity and the estab- lished assumptions of American literary scholarship have all, finally, begun to quiver under critical scrutiny. Such is the pace of critical turnover that, in the past few years, even the next generation of dissent, the exclusivist notion of ethnicity that justified the early inroads of ethnic writing into the tradition, has already been subjected to same critique that's being directed at exclusivist models of literary nationalism. Yet it is still a powerful, an essential question whether the critique of ethnicity will take a form as superficial and cosmetic as it so far has in American literary studies while more fundamental questions are ignored or short-circuited.

Both the conflicts and the progress of critical accounts among prominent scholars of ethnic literature reenact problems faced by others in the attempt to tell an ethnic story against the all-absorbing background of American narratives that have, in effect, already covered and thus occupied the same ground. Debates among scholars of ethnic literature echo venerable debates among Americanists about the unity in diversity of American cultural and literary traditions. My point here is not that there is something "wrong" with the critical rhetoric of ethnicity. On the contrary, I take its features simply as examples of the way critical arguments depend on dominant and pervasive surrounding rhetorics, professional or cultural. The movements performed by the criticism of ethnicity mark both developmental stages in its own professional initiation and the reiterated forms of revisionist rhetoric. The contradictions implicit in particular formulations reflect the doubleness of American literary discourse and of the genres of critical writing–Ethnic, Feminist, New Historicist—that huddle, however awkwardly, under that rubric. These genres of critical dissent shuttle nervously between stasis and change, eternity and history–performing an increasingly strenuous dance under conditions such as our own, when the *desire* for change coexists with cynicism about any particular effort to realize it.

Alger's and Washington's books promise social change and the willed production of a better world. They present themselves as stories of boundaries and of the crossing of boundaries, of new identities achieved and old ones abandoned. The boundaries they describe define the conditions of ethnos, laying out the values by which one ethnic group distinguishes itself from its "other" and thus, implicitly, the terms required for a successful initiation into membership. These fables of crossing model the resolution of social divisions, imply the flexibility of ethnos, and affirm the desirability of new membership and of change itself at the same time that they reaffirm existing values and beliefs. The new identity achieved by an individual figures the character of the repeatedly renewed ethnic order. As stories of ethnic identity, *Ragged Dick* and *Up from Slavery* recapitulate and legitimate, in their different ways, the rhetoric of American national identity. Of course, just as the official interpretation of Franklin's *Autobiography* depends on ignoring most of his text—and indeed, just as the official understanding of American literature depends on ignoring most of the texts in the United States, or by American citizens, much less those written in "America"—the embracing description of the American success story has for the most part ignored the complexities of Alger's and Washington's works, complexities that make them more interesting and provoking than propaganda tracts for the American dream. As these works reveal the fractured boundaries of the multi-layered American social structure, they interrogate not just traditional notions of American cultural coherence (by now, one hopes, that move has lost its power to startle), but also the particular arrangement of ethnic boundaries that have composed the social order and formulated debate about ethnic difference in America.

As Alger's work shows, these conflicts are not restricted to narratives of race, but characterize rhetorics of ethnos, of crossing and power, of social construction in general. *Ragged Dick* tells its story of ethnos from the inside rather than from the margin, and thus is bent on affirming its own middle-class identity. Thus, contrary to the usual "rags to riches" characterizations of the Alger tales, Dick is not seeking admission to the capitalist aristocracy. Modeling an appropriate personal modesty and the democratic instincts that define a truly American spirit, even while he is still Ragged Dick in fact, the grimy shoeshine boy who sleeps in cardboard boxes longs only to be respectable, worthy of induction into the middling class that (for the purposes of the book) defines the nation. He stars in a reassuringly ritualistic drama of self-discovery composed in the conventional terms of the established culture. There is nothing threatening or subversive about this initiation across social classes. And the fact that Dick is helped along at every stage by agents of the ethnos he wants to join—barely concealed avatars of his own future self—simply reflects the unspeakable importance of his progress to the cultural self-image.[7]

*Ragged Dick* works hard to make "class" look like a permeable boundary. And it is obviously in the interest of the middle-class ethnos to present it that way. According to the tale, all Dick needs to achieve respectability are a bath, a new suit of clothes, a certain refinement of manners, a modicum of education, and a clearer understanding that he might actually achieve these things by throwing off his old ways. This emphasis on the superficial is possible precisely because "character," an essential trait, is at the heart of Dick's ability to move into the respectable classes, as it was at the heart of the discourse surrounding American national identity in the third quarter of the nineteenth century. Dick's movement from shoeshine boy to respectable citizen requires only superficial fine tuning because he possessed the only really essential and intrinsic trait all along. From the first page of the text, when Dick is rousted out of his flimsy cardboard abode by a passing porter who recognizes right away that "there's some good in you, Dick, after all," there was, the narrator adds, "something about Dick that made him attractive."[8] It is this appearance, rather than the heroic deeds that are popularly associated with the success of Alger heroes, that gets Dick his first break—the responsibility of showing a respectable middle-class youth around New York. "He looks honest," the Father says. "He has an open face, and I think can be depended upon."[9] And repeatedly in moments of crisis—when Dick is accused of trying to pass a bad bill, or of robbing a "middle-aged woman" on the trolley—his honest expression reassures those in authority that he could not be guilty. The point here is not just that Dick's initiation among the respectable depends on this innate character unrelated to background or experience (although it does), and, therefore could not really, as the book promises, simply be imitated by those with similar aspirations. The point is that this essential, this inner, trait must *manifest* itself on the outside as well. Dick's face *advertises* his worthiness for membership. There is no need to fear a mistake. In the commercial ethos of this book, unifying Spirit must become material, a motif the American and the Christian stories (by no coincidence) share. No longer a marker of strictly otherworldly worth, it is a worldly form of social currency.

The desirability of these changes is never in doubt. There is no hint that Dick might be losing anything by leaving his old associations behind, since it is hard to image poverty, as Dick initially embodies it, as a desirable state, or the poor as a group with which even its own members are particularly eager to identify.[10] His friend Frank's obligatory democratic assertion that "you are none the worse for being a bootblack" is belied by the narrative's pervasive disdain for the lower classes.[11] Nothing in the narrative is allowed to impede or cloud Dick's deliberate ascent from poverty, a change that Dick unaccountably says "reminds me of Cinderella . . . when she was changed into a fairy princess."[12] This fairy-tale analogy is unaccountable simply because there is absolutely nothing magical about what Dick does, and the materiality of it, as accumulation and work— core middle-class values—is both means and end in one. Dick's apparent ethnocentric fear, in the midst of his transformation, that he might be seen by his old crowd as putting on airs is less an expression of class solidarity than one of middle-class distaste for aristocratic snobbery. His assimilation into the group of respectable adults—older versions of Dick who made their own way over the ground he is traveling and who help him out as he later helps out others in his old place—portrays society as a spiritual rather than a worldly order, one produced not by contingent experience, acts in the world, but by spiritual identities independent of worldly circumstances. Dick's experience redefines "middle-class culture" as, in effect, a latter day "gathered church" of the respectable. As in the gathered churches of seventeenth-century New England, members are brought together by the common spirit (now of honesty and uprightness) they share, although in a nineteenth-century spirit of enterprise, they turn their energies toward expanding their numbers by helping new initiates along the material path to full membership. In this narrative of self revision, Dick both changes and does not change. Becoming a member of the new ethnos is the process of stripping away the inessential to more fully enact what he has always been.

As Dick marches toward the inevitably successful end of this cultural self-celebration, there lingers the question of what he gives up, the "value" of the past that is scapegoated in this narrative as it always is in revisionist accounts, and of the character he has had to sacrifice to join the "respectable" club. Like Twain's vernacular characters, Dick wields an ironic humor and his own characteristic idiom to puncture the posing and pretension that have taken on particularly threatening implications in an increasingly anonymous and predatory urban commercial culture. In this nineteenth-century American version of the venerable debate between country and town, the terms have gotten mixed. The town is still sophisticated and experienced, but now lowclass and unrefined, while the country embodies both upper-class refinement and a bumpkin-like naiveté. As middle-class America's new urban hero, Dick must have, in effect, two identities at once. The officially sanctioned one is "essential" but also undistinguishing. Its "character" is like that ascribed to the nation as its principle of coherence rather than an expression of personal uniqueness, and (as we see it in the other boys), it is helpless. The other, described from the dominant perspective as "superficial" and changeable, is nevertheless the more attractive and effective. This personality, rather than the proper little clerk he becomes, is the reason Dick is so appealing a character, one worth building a story around.

More than anything else, it is Dick's language that identifies and "otherizes" him. It locates Dick in a different ethnos as the speaker of a foreign language. That language articulates a unique personal identity, distinct from the honest "Character" that identifies him as a candidate for conversion, and not, like that "Character," an abstract principle that can span apparent lines of ethnos precisely because it is shared universally by all the "respectable" alike. Dick's anti-formal speech, his personal linguistic style, distinguishes him even from his own lower-class companions, and makes him, literally, incomprehensible to his new middle-class friends. Because of his peculiar individual style, he is variously called "a queer boy," "a character," a "queer chap." "What a chap you are," says his friend Frank, and little Ida Greyson (Dick's symbolic love interest) calls him a "droll boy"—"What a funny boy you are."[13] By which, of course, they all mean that he is really very "strange," very "other," though in the nicest possible way.

Yet, Dick's "drollery" is more than merely entertaining. However inessential and hence disposable traits associated with his lower-class self might seem on the high road to the middle class, as tools for surviving in nineteenth-century society they are not, functionally speaking, merely superficial. On the contrary, they are essential not just to the interest of his character and of the narrative, but to the very social promise that is the book's premise and aim, a promise embodied in Dick's "democratic" union of the "common" and the respectable. Articulated in that "droll" language, Dick's lower-class traits make him both a source of strength to lower-class youths who share his ambition, but not his characteristically positive humor, and a champion of less experienced middle-class youths whose greater refinement leaves them prey to urban frauds. And, combined with the new character that he has put on with his new clothes, Dick's street smarts give him almost magical power to turn aside threats from pickpockets, swindlers, and sharp business practitioners that would have made easy victims of his well-bred middle-class companions. In effect, his lower-class experience puts him in a position to save the middle-class characters who are busy saving him from the lower class. This power is central to the issue that, after the promise of progress, most preoccupies *Ragged Dick*: the terrifying increase in the possibilities for unethical and predatory, even criminal, business practices in the alienating and confusing life of the big city, a society so large that personal relationships cannot possibly provide the security associated with smaller rural communities. The power to provide that sort of security for city life is what Dick gives up when he shucks his old identity.

Whatever their uses, however, vernacular characters are, typically, subversive of the very middle-class values Dick longs to assume. So, along with his "new life," Dick puts on a new identity and a new language, keeping the old one only as a humorous style, a sort of vernacular joke that condescendingly insists on the distance between classes rather than bridging it. In the process, he gives up the most characteristic, the most interesting, entertaining, and powerful part of himself. Consequently, however unambiguously desirable the transformation may have seemed at the start, by the time Alger works his way to the conclusion of *Ragged Dick*, the social success that had provided the narrative with its reason for being also demands the silent sacrifice of personal distinction to a commercial standard. Gaining official acceptance, Ragged Dick fades away into "Richard Hunter, Esq., a young gentleman on the way to fame and fortune," and thus into the common values of a commodity culture that substitutes dollars for style. More importantly, this transformation jettisons the only powers in the book that have successfully opposed the divisive and exploitative energies of urban capitalism—that dark underbelly of nineteenth-century progress and the great implicit obsession of Alger's work.

Alger's "American success" storyline reappears relatively unchanged in Booker T. Washington's *Up from Slavery*. But, unlike Alger's story, Washington's work has not (and not accidentally), for all its centrality and influence, been taken as a paradigm of American experience. Although criticism has often seen Washington as dupe or shill, he ought also to be viewed as a consummate rhetorician, one who knew his audience and its attitudes all too well. On that view, the repression of identity and of feeling (anger and bitterness) that could be said not just to characterize, but very nearly to constitute the text looks very much like the self-discipline Washington exercised throughout his life. From one end of the book to the other, Washington describes his willingness to do anything to get what he wants. In the context of late nineteenth-century racism and its social consequences, ignoring or denying his own feelings and self-respect can reasonably be considered *trivial* prices to pay, and it seems inevitable that the *composition* of his "life" would inscribe those same traits.

Responding to the overwhelming racial repressions of the time, *Up from Slavery* sets modest goals. It seeks only to allay white racial paranoia and elicit a benign neglect so that the negro might ultimately "lift himself up" to equality, though (pointedly) not social integration, with whites. With this end in view, the true national evil is not racism but blame, all trace of which must be eradicated. The resulting social dynamic is more rigorously naturalistic than anything in Norris or Dreiser. Slaves and slave owners are all alike "victims of the system of slavery" that "the Nation unhappily [and in the passive voice] had engrafted on it at that time."[14] Amidst such universal yet agentless victimage, blame, however improbably, is impossible, and thus neither Washington nor, as we are told, any other black has ever felt any anger or bitterness toward whites.

Washington's narrative unfolds spasmodically between his desire to elicit sympathy by presenting the poverty and deprivation of southern negroes and his desire to avoid offense. He wants, in short, to induce sympathy without inducing guilt. That conflict leads to the retractions that end so many of his chapters. What might be called the abstract governing principles expressed in the final paragraphs of these chapters oddly deny the particular facts that make up both the substance of the narrative and the (pasteurized) reality of life in the South. For example, having described the appalling conditions of "colored" life around Tuskegee, Washington leaves his readers with the reassurance that "in giving all these descriptions . . . I wish my readers to keep in mind the fact that there were many encouraging exceptions [though they are never presented] to the conditions which I have described," and he justifies even relating these distressing facts as an effort to highlight "the encouraging changes that have taken place" since the time he describes.[15] Even when pain *must* be assigned to slavery and its consequences, Washington does so according to an inverse economy of the spirit rather than to one of the body—an almost perverse appropriation of familiar Christian rhetoric. Injustices perpetrated on negroes by whites redound upon the perpetrators, Washington argues. "The most harmful effect of the practice to which the people in certain sections of the South have felt themselves compelled to resort, in order to get rid of the force of the negroes' ballot, is not wholly in the wrong done to the negro, but in the permanent injury to the morals of the white man. The wrong to the negro is temporary, but to the morals of the white man the injury is permanent." This piece of revisionist moral history is the more extreme since Washington is describing the consequences here not just of restrictive voting laws, "cheating," and perjury, but of lynching. These passages engage the narrative in an odd self-canceling dance typical of the revisionist rhetoric of ethnicity, one that is performed in similar ways by *Ragged Dick* and *Native Son*.

However it may appear to modern eyes, in its own terms Washington's outlook is optimistic—earnest effort, we are repeatedly told, will bring its reward. Despite the burdens imposed by the history of slavery and the episodic determinism of his own account, Washington's world is plastic. The instrument of change, however, is not revolutionary or economic—it is a matter of character, of discipline. The attitude of whites toward blacks can be changed, but only if blacks violate white expectations through a superhuman conformity to their values, and those values define the limits of the world's plasticity. This plea for a place within the existing order is both the aim and the success of the work. *Up from Slavery* encourages whites to reimagine blacks in a beneficial (though not redemptive) way. And in 1900, that, Washington suggests, was the best that could be hoped.

In the process, Washington's rigorous rhetoric not only displays but insists on the boundaries between blacks and whites, rather than trying to cross them. While Dick's struggles earn him the right to disappear into the middle-class norm, Washington's success has made him stick out, not just from society at large but even and especially from other blacks. Washington's final persona, the public figure who has earned "recognition," and can therefore eat in a railroad dining car with whites, reveals no connection to the still unregenerate earlier versions of his self (uneducated negroes) he claims to represent. Like St. Augustine, he has miraculously undergone an apocalyptic change, the very apocalypse he cannot imagine for society at large, one that transubstantiates and thus abandons his own history, his ethnic past, by inscribing it in a revisionist narrative.

Not only is Washington unique rather than representative, but from the first he does not actually cross the boundaries that divide the races and enter, as Dick does, a new ethnos. He takes on, instead, a special status—recognition—*of* but not *in* the white world, and that status depends not on his individual personality, but on a persona that is only nominally "his." Even his ultimate recognition comes exclusively in white terms. The fact that white strangers on a train knew "who I was" begs just the question *Up from Slavery* most represses: just who might that actually be? One unexamined implication of the line is that, as regards his "recognition," who he *was* is more important than who he *is*. It is his past identity as a slave, rather than his current character, that makes him remarkable and the object of public notice. Incarnating his own prescription, he has achieved social recognition as that negro who has so excelled in conformity to white values, and thus is so unlike the rest of the race, as to be admissible to the forms of the white world. He is the official negro, the representative of his race to the white world precisely because, like other mythic American figures (Franklin, Whitman, Lincoln), he's at once so exceptional and so ordinary. The distance he repeatedly measures between himself and other blacks—by his disdain for their less refined manners, his accounts of his own extraordinary trials, his inability to explain his success apart from intrinsic character traits that might be unique to *him*—confirms white views of the negro by presenting Washington's experience as inimitable. His special status *and* his narrative speak to the inferiority of other members of the race as much as to their potential, and in fact might be seen as enabling their continued exclusion–that, after all, being the historical work of tokenism.

Like other narratives of ethnos, *Up from Slavery* pretends that race can be a permeable boundary akin to class in Alger. For Washington, however, the superficial traits that worked to Dick's advantage are the insurmountable problem, the definer of boundaries. In effect, while in the revisionist discourse of class the essential becomes superficial—Dick's essential character shows in his face—in the revisionist discourse of race, the superficial becomes the most essential. It is perhaps the most inescapable feature of Washington's condition that he can never be (mis)taken for the paradigmatic American. Washington's status as "representative" is necessary if the narrative is to claim a larger cultural, rather than a merely personal, significance. But, especially in light of his "essential" uniqueness from the first, it can only be attributed to a biological similarity that really substantial change, a genuine crossing of boundaries, would somehow have to erase. Unlike Dick, Washington is necessarily "alone," a unique to be "recognized," rather than to be embraced by a new ethnos. The alienation Washington's uniqueness creates from "his" people also mirrors his unbridgable distance from the whites whose culture he has acquired. He is not, cannot be, in either world. In contrast to Dick, the Washington of *Up from Slavery* is and must always be a show piece. His identity does not depend on reputation, it *is* a reputation. In the rhetoric of crossing offered by that book, it is unthinkable for Washington to be made part of the white ethnos—he travels there on the visa of his notoriety.

The American narrative, in its ambivalence to its own European past, articulated American identity as both hermetic and (in a subtext that seems clearer to us than to its original authors) an extension of the dominant European culture. Like this revisionist American narrative, the work of ethnic narrative is double—to define both the self and the other. But, more importantly, texts seeking inclusion from the margin, like Washington's, define the self *as* other. To gain entry into the dominant discourse, these narratives must "otherize" the marginal self to make it fit into that "other" world to which they aspire. These two works, *Ragged Dick* and *Up from Slavery* seem so conservative, so familiar, because they reiterate the terms of the dominant culture in the very process of, and even as a strategy for, dissenting from it. This self-effacement in order to assume dominant values is the most remarkably alienating characteristic of this genre of revisionist rhetoric. Characters like Booker T. Washington and Ragged Dick echo each other as they reflect the powerful transubstantiation upon which the American narrative depends–the faith that the common present harbors a transcendent destiny, the perfected future of mankind–a faith that finds continuing voice among Americanist culture critics.

Narratives of ethnos typically present the appearance of crossing in order to bolster social optimism and place the narrative (and the society it constructs) in the modern world of progress, the world of "America," figuring themselves as vehicles of ethnic aspiration in a hospitable and sympathetic world. But, whatever else they may be—and despite their own promises–these narratives of ethnicity are not models for *crossing* ethnic boundaries. Despite their claims to foster social progress in the spirit of an American culture not shackled to and by social strata, no crossing occurs in these works. On the contrary, *Ragged Dick* and *Up from Slavery* ethnocentrically insist on the taking of sides, and reinforce the necessity of boundaries. That conflict between the need to represent and the need to cross characterizes both Washington's condition and revisionist narrative in general—in this respect, his own narrative conditions make him a particularly forceful expression of the rhetoric of ethnicity in general, poised between an irretrievable past and an unattainable future. In that position, they must do double duty in a second, and still more important, sense. Representing change, but unable to embrace it, they advertise the mythic *promise* of change in a system that makes change impossible. Most crucially, they domesticate the very idea of change by reading it as the ideal fulfillment of existing assumptions.

I want to turn now to *Native Son*, which seems to me to provoke change of a different sort and in a different way.[16] From the first, this book has been drafted into any number of available interpretive frames. I'd like to suggest that it is a subversive recruit, one that breaks those frames down and then leaves itself open, as a book of ethnos that can't be comfortably fitted with any ready ethnic "moral." Unlike Washington's, Bigger's world is not plastic, not open, not even to the possibility of fulfilling white expectations—intentionally at least. It is a world not even of obstacles, but of an unremitting, a crushing poverty of options. Bigger's inarticulate longing for purposeful action that would define his "being" in the world can have no expression. Denied the ability to act, he stares heavenward toward the plane that represents, at once, his desire for a place in the world through action and his desire to transcend it. Even Bigger's desire for self-defining action is precisely matched by an overwhelming fear of any action that might strip him of his protective anonymity, thrust him into vulnerable relief, burden him with a responsibility that, personally void, he cannot possibly sustain. Consequently, Bigger hates and fears everything, not just the forces that prevent action, but also those (like his family) that he cannot act *for*. Fear of action: fear of no action. Living this hopeless conflict, Bigger is left with only hysteria and a sort of spontaneous explosion as behaviors, involuntary responses to what Wright calls the "rhythms of his life: indifference and violence"—sweeping the pool balls dramatically but ineffectually around the table, leaping at Gus because he reflects Bigger's own fear of the white man—actions unreasoned, unmotivated, more cathartic than practical.[17] He rigorously denies even his own existence, for if he were to acknowledge it, he would either have to destroy the world that gives him existence but denies him expression or, alternatively, destroy himself. Constantly confronted with impossible situations in which he must do what he fears, must act but cannot, Bigger's universal hatred turns to spasmodic violence. Permitted no acceptable action, all Bigger can do is rebel against action itself ("The moment a situation became so that it exacted something of him, he rebelled").[18] Crushed under universal prohibitions, the only behaviors open to him are criminal or accidental, or both.

Hating the rules that subjugate him, Bigger cannot imagine any others. When Jan and Mary ignore the taboos against egalitarian black/white social relations, he can only assume it must be some kind of joke at his expense, or worse, a trap. Their clumsy and inevitably condescending attempts at kindness only return Bigger to the end of all his ventures into life: "He felt he had no physical existence at all right then; he was something he hated. . . . At that moment he felt toward Jan and Mary a dumb, cold, inarticulate hate."[19] Mindless, dead, speechless, bodiless—all Bigger knows is that he lacks something, that he feels incomplete. A gun, a knife, a car complete him, and violence makes him forget his hate, which is also his fear.

These conditions place Bigger so far outside the game of "recognition" Washington plays, that he can only count as an ironic commentary on it. Of course, on one hand, insofar as the boundaries of his identity are defined by white culture, the Washington of *Up from Slavery* is incongruously kin to the various characters attributed to Bigger Thomas. Yet apart from the stereotyped identities created for him by whites, Bigger is simply void, and in that sense he could be said to express the view of self that is left out in Washington's account. Bigger is the black experience Washington's myth of the self leaves behind and can never really represent, the black self that isn't Washington's unique exemplary negro. The conditions of crossing are altered here. A major consequence of white capitalist hegemony is to make everything "black" undesirable in the same terms that "poor" is undesirable for Alger. Bigger cannot stop being black by exercising intrinsic virtues and learning good grammar like Dick, or by exercising discipline and assuming white values like Washington. That he can't cross racial boundaries is a statement not just about extrinsic social barriers or about his character, but also about the terms of his existence. Bigger cannot *make* himself anything any more than he can do anything. Unlike Dick and Washington, he isn't special from the first. There are no successful versions of himself to help him; instead, his would-be "benefactors" are clearly slumming, and in Bigger's world, being "recognized" is not fulfillment, it is death.

To Bigger's imagination, killing looks like a way to make a place for himself in the world, and he brandishes his vaunted willingness to kill as a way of dominating others. But, when killing is a reality rather than a fantasy like the movies that shape his impossible desires, when Bigger actually kills Mary, it is just another spasmodic and unconscious act imposed on him by his own terror of the "white." Mary's death is the natural result of Bigger's fear in the face of white power, produced by an unconscious contraction of the muscles in terror at the possibility of being discovered in a white girl's bedroom. But, however similar in its causes to his earlier acts of reflex violence, the consequences are crucially different. Mary's corpse is material testimony that, for the first time, he has done something the white world must notice. And in a sense that might seem still more bizarre had we not just seen Washington's example, that possibility of recognition (however skewed) looks, to Bigger's eye, something like an identity. The recognition his acts bring to him in white newspapers gives him the same satisfaction it gave Washington (a fact that represents the perversity of Bigger's position). As far as the world (and he) is concerned, Bigger is alive for the first time, alive to the only world that counts—the white world of action, and he assumes for himself a new character befitting his new residence. As a naturalized citizen in that world, he imagines, he has to "do better," and is bothered that he should have gotten more money out of it; "he should have *planned* it."[20]

As the subsequent action inexorably shows, Bigger's life, even in this moment of personal triumph, is self-canceling. With one act, Bigger both gives himself life and declares himself dead, gives himself a place in the world for the first time and goes out of it entirely, kills and commits suicide. All his longing, after the fact, for purposeful action is a gross self-deception, not to mention a capitulation to the assumptions of the white world he hates and that now wants to kill him. In the first place, he was not, as I have suggested, even *responsible* for Mary's murder. He just did it. And his wish that he had planned it better is a pathetic illusion. As it turns out, he was actually relatively safe as long as he stuck to *purposeless* action, partly because purposeless action makes no sense to a society that gives scope to motives. But the purposeful action into which his new sense of "self" lures him assures his destruction. When he tries to act intentionally, tries actually to do something for himself, first to cover up and then to profit from his crime, he calls his own doom down upon him. It is essential to Bigger's particular act of self-expression, that he cannot and must not express it. In his contradictory efforts to render his acts inconsequential by destroying Mary's body and to profit from her death, he rouses the sleeping beast—the one to which Washington spent a lifetime singing lullabies—and its eye is upon him.[21]

When it finally comes, his capture only dramatizes externally and explicitly the internal and implicit imprisonment that has been the defining experience of Bigger's life. Despite Bigger's newly coined but specious self-respect, his actual crime does not even exist in that white view. The world refuses even to *misconstrue* his actions as murder, much less as what they were, or to hate and kill him for himself, since that would require some acknowledgment of his self-lessness. Instead, it casts him in an old, familiar, and in its way, comfortably racist story, making him embody stereotyped fears of black sexual threat. It appears there not as murder, but as a "sex crime" that "excludes him from the world" and pronounces his "death sentence." This misreading of his defining act "meant a wiping out of his life even before his capture." And it will kill him for that, for what he did not do (rape) rather than for what he (sort of) did.

Worse still, those on the other side, those who want to help him—Max, Jan—don't understand him any better than anyone else. Each tries to cast Bigger in his own pet moral or political drama. Sympathy and hatred alike, it seems, reflect ideological preconceptions. But worst of all, amidst all this dehumanization, Bigger himself is no different from the rest, and ends up adopting their views as his own. Following Jan's lead, Bigger justifies his own actions by assuming they must have had a purpose—or, more accurately, he assumes that he had a purpose, a direction, an organizing self, *because* he acted. In a world without meaning or purpose, a world where the concentrated essence and meaning of his life has been its essential meaninglessness, he buys into the reassuring white view that actions are securely connected to purpose—that the world is a coherent place. Like Dick (unself-consciously) and Washington (with great determination), all Bigger's efforts to imagine a "self" for himself echo assumptions that are alien to him. Even his imaginary selves are imagined by others. Bigger Thomas doesn't know "who I was," and efforts to answer that question are always and only efforts to answer it for him, and thus demonstrate its unanswerability in the traditional terms the attempts assume. Apart from these impositions, there is nothing to see, and Bigger subjects himself even to death in terms composed on cliché models, rather than imagining (as he could not do) his exteriority to all available terms.

Bigger's starkly self-contradictory experience embodies Wright's paradoxical efforts to write a book that both is and is not about black life, an effort that generates a text that exceeds the conventional categories of ethnicity. "Bigger was not black all the time, he was white too," Wright wrote.[22] Wright wanted to stress "that part of him which is part of all Negroes and all whites." "Neither Bigger nor I resided fully in either camp," he says.[23] Bigger's problem is not simply a matter of race. It is not just being a "black" self in a white world, but being any self at all. His stake is not so much in black ethnos as in his own fear. Inside and outside in the novel have lost clear meaning amidst universal emptiness and blindness. Bigger Thomas does not learn, and if he did, it would do no good. But neither does anyone else. *Native Son* portrays a cultural blindness, an impermeability so absolute that it amounts to fixity for all its characters. In this book, none dwell free, and thus the text rewrites the ethnic rhetoric of oppositions. I'm not suggesting by this that Wright's blacks and whites are "equal" in *power*, and all equally victims (as Washington would have it), even of blindness. Such quietist claims, like their revisionist alternatives, miss the sense in which *Native Son* revises the conventional models of identity and agency that drive traditional narratives of ethnicity, confusing, in the process, the boundaries that parcel out power.

As a result, Wright's text is subversive in a still broader sense than opposition to prevailing social arrangements of power would entail. Wright refuses to fulfill revisionist expectations by offering any viable substitute for blindness, imposed identities, and emptiness. *Native Son* will not move a step from the inhuman initial conditions it posits. It carries the naturalist subordination of individuals to culture beyond the conservatively determinist implications writers like Norris were prepared to envision, displaying not only the hopeless progress toward disaster of a character victimized by vast forces far beyond his meager capacities, like McTeague, but also the pitiful self-deception of Bigger Thomas in accepting that disaster, explaining his own fate in the very terms that doomed him, and using that explanation as a source of pathetic comfort.

For Bigger, being black is unacceptable, being white is impossible. *Native Son* discomposes the cultural categories, the ideological vocabularies, that made Alger's and Washington's works possible, refusing the available vocabularies of revision along with those of oppression. *Native Son* explodes the pretense not just of permeability, but of received vocabularies of ethnic boundary. Its world would seem to be the most radical *expression* of boundaries, but actually it dissolves them. The figure for the color "line" in *Native Son* is a circle, like Pascal's God: its center is everywhere and its circumference nowhere. Not less pervasive or powerful, but less binary, oppositional, neatly definable—less congruent with lines of personal identity.

By diffusing the idealist center of revisionist narratives, Wright's example speaks to contemporary critical questions about the role of texts in cultural change. Conventional tales of social change like *Ragged Dick* and *Up from Slavery* make "crossing" possible by assuming intrinsic and eternal traits, a spiritual identity, shared universally by community members. These narratives portray abandonment—of old identities, of history—as essential to progress. The spiritual model of social identity they feature both justifies that abandonment and drowns out unreconciled voices even as it assures that the old world will appear essentially unchanged in the new. Wright, however, cannot imagine an easy transition between antiseptically opposed worlds. Bigger lacks the spirit—individual and cultural—that made social order imaginable for Alger and Washington, with the catastrophic results for him that we see. His life is made meaningful to others only as they impose their own universalizing assumptions to domesticate his otherness. And Bigger's challenge to these traditional models of social progress also challenges those who would compose a contemporary narrative of social progress—fictive or critical.

His disaster opens questions about the imagining of new social orders, the reimagining of cultural coherence consistent with a rigorous critique of totalizing narratives that have had growing prominence in recent critical discussions, but have their foundation in "American" discourse. The contemporary criticism of diversity, of which American Literary Scholarship was an ancestor, has unquestionably contributed to the breakdown of faith in idealist critical models. Yet that same focus continues, as it has throughout the long history of the "America" debate, to frustrate the coherence that supports collective action. Americans have, understandably enough, been preoccupied, as they tried to construct their nation, with ethnos, with understanding themselves as a community, rather than as a ragtag collection of races, creeds, and opinions. In literary studies, American ethnocentrism has represented itself as a way of defining and collecting works under a corporate identity. It has, in fact, been the triumph of the eternally revisionist narrative of America that it has done this successfully for so long, bringing alien groups under its umbrella and making them glad to be there. This inclusiveness, however, depended on idealist models of personal and corporate identity that now seem to many more destructive than creative, and thus no longer useful either for society or, more narrowly, for new critical projects.

Yet in repudiating oppressive orders, the vocabulary of diversity, constructed as it must necessarily be out of the ethnocentric vocabulary it rejects, offers no strategy for motivating collective action to replace the ones it would abandon. It suggests no contemporary terms, nothing so powerful as the old appeals to "our common humanity," or proclamations that we are "all sinners alike," to explain why we should treat those who are "other," those who are different from ourselves, as we would treat those we accept as members of our community. What, in the absence of traditional religious and moral values, can preserve principles like egalitarianism after the demise of their eighteenth-century liberal rationales? What enforces the desire for trans-ethnic understanding after foundational justifications are discarded? What strategies do we have or can we construct for fulfilling the founding model, *e pluribus unum*, but in contemporary terms not of unity but of productive action in our diversity?

An emphasis on the rhetoricity of ethnocentrism refocuses attention on the role of literature[24] in cultural change by reminding us that changing the terms of culture, the forms of life, is a matter of the kind of rhetorical reweaving undertaken by *Native Son*. Though it may seem merely tautological, still it may be therapeutic to say that narratives of race, critical and fictive, are constituted in the language of race—the only language they have available to them. Thus, they are subject to and shaped by its features, its distinctions, the limits and possibilities of its established implications, the unspeakably complex web of verbal interrelations that comprise a vocabulary, and that vocabulary is itself enmeshed in the much larger linguistic web that articulates the forms of life. On this view, the rich are "rich" and the poor "poor." Blacks are "black," not by biology or conditions, but by virtue of all the familiar uses that word finds among speakers of the language. If they are not "negro" or "black" but "African American," then those new words self-consciously carry old freight. As Alger, Washington, and Wright collectively suggest, ethnic boundaries so construed cannot be crossed, since as *matters* of definition, they are, *by* definition, impermeable. That is their purpose. To actually cross them would mean, for example, to become "white," and although that is essentially what Washington has been accused of, we have seen that avoiding just such a "crossing" was the scrupulous preoccupation of his text. Revisionist accounts seeking inclusion, as Alger's and Washington's did, operate within the existing revisionist vocabulary of change and thereby end up reiterating and reinforcing familiar boundaries. The gestures of these narratives are, themselves, reiterated in critical and theoretical approaches to the subject because these approaches, in their turn, also are constituted out of the rhetorical features of ethnic discourse, the terms that have been employed to debate the subject, the very forms, that is, that debate seeks to change. This circularity is critical to mainstream/margin discourse.

Yet in all this talk of circularity and the immersion of revisionist impulses in the tradition, I don't mean to peddle pessimism about the possibility of change. In fact, I'm more inclined to see change as unavoidable than as impossible. And, despite the claims of Walter Michaels and others, there is no theoretical reason a narrative, and thus a society, cannot "escape" its existing conditions, alter its own forms, though, as Stanley Fish has so often said, it cannot do so just by wanting to. While works like Alger's offer the comfort of conventional reading, books like *Native Son* are important precisely as they give us an unfamiliar and therefore necessarily uncomfortable one, one that confuses and thus confronts our own usual terms. The exercise of that confronting is at once an implicit critique, a clearing of old understandings from the ground, and an early rhetorical move toward constructing new social forms. On the evidence of such texts, texts that treat writing as a matter of imaginatively recomposing the borders of language that are also the borders of ideologies, social change might be elided with acts of composing new vocabularies. If boundaries cannot be crossed, they can be redefined. This is, however, both a long-term and a freakish process.

Just what to do with texts, even if this is true, still looks like a tough question to many critics. The principal lesson pressed home by the dizzying complex of critical debates over this issue is that we have not, so far at least, developed particularly satisfactory accounts of the relationships scholars are trying to explain. The job of connecting literature with other discourses, of describing the larger cultural implications of individual texts, of connecting particular rhetorical acts into cultural rhetorics, of weaving multiple ethnic voices into a society, is bigger than the one recent historicist critics of American literature have undertaken.

In this connection, it is a particularly ironic commonplace that instruments of innovation tend, for the most part, to go unrecognized by those schooled in the old vocabulary, who have taken innovative vocabularies that revise traditional boundaries for everything from bad writing to shopworn wisdom. A test of the success of any developing criticism might be how effectively it deals with the "other," not just as a matter of learning to "respect differences," and certainly not by domesticating it in familiar narratives, whether oppressive or redemptive. Like Columbus in the "New World," the characters in *Native Son*, whether "racist" or "progressive," insistently see what is not there and prompt Bigger to do so as well. Bigger Thomas assumes he has an identity because he acted, just as America has been assumed to have an "identity"—a coherent national character—*because* it attained political nationhood. Each of these fantasies appeals to the same venerable and powerful interpretive habit (rather than merely to a particular cultural prejudice), an ethnocentric way of understanding that insists on inscribing the "other" into familiar accounts of the self and the known. That interpretive ethnocentrism is common both to critical interpretation of the textually new and to the ethnocentric treatment of "other groups." *Native Son* subjects such interpretation to ironic critique and lays bare its implications as a social model. Thus *Native Son* can be read as unmasking the interpretive assumptions that stand behind *both* the discourse of "America" and ethnic discourses. Readers committed to articulating a more socially engaged literary studies might take a cue from this detailed and rigorous refusal of traditional sides in ethnic debate and of the familiar, even comfortable, postures toward ethnicity they entail. In this light, alternative interpretive projects might be entertained less for their perceived consistency or inconsistency with particular ideological positions than for whether they promote new vocabularies and thus provoke us to understand not just something we did not know, but something we did not know we needed to know. By diverging from received forms, texts like *Native Son* penetrate the sometimes dark and tortuous paths of cultural change. In our current circumstances, readers cannot afford to disregard the transformative potentials of such excursions into unknown cultural forms or of the critical reconstructions they can inspire. Such works are, it seems to me, indispensable resources in the effort to articulate substantial cultural revision and thus to assist the future in its coming.

## Notes

1. Steven A. Holmes, *New York Times News Service*, in *The Oregonian*, February 2, 1994, p. A16.

2. If not a boy, then we have what might be called an "unauthorized account." The terms and implications change, as do the narrative strategies and generic conventions that amount to experiments in making sense of the conflicting terms involved.

3. Booker T. Washington, *Up from Slavery* (1901; rep. New York: Lancer Books, 1968), pp. 171–172.

4. Peter Carafiol, *The American Ideal: Literary History as a Worldly Activity* (New York: Oxford University Press, 1991).

5. William C. Spengemann most recently discusses the implications of "America" for developments in English language and literature in *A New World of Words: Redefining Early American Literature* (New Haven: Yale University Press, 1994). That work enforces the point that the narrative characteristics I am describing have, for a long time, been famously associated with romantic writing in general, a point which, as Spengemann shows, suggests that "American" narratives are not confined within the nation's boundaries or to the citizenry of the United States, but are a world-wide response to post-Medieval conditions, prominent among them the idea of a "New World." The other direction in which this cuts is to expand, as I try to do here, the horizon of texts to which the writing conventionally considered ethnic may be connected. Even the insistence of such writing on its own difference—especially that insistence—is not different.

6. See my earlier essays, "After American Literature," *American Literary History* 4 (Fall 1992): 539–549, and "Changing the World: The Rhetoric of Revisionism," *ADE Bulletin* (Spring 1992): 61–68.

7. Horatio Alger, *Ragged Dick* (1867; rep. New York: Collier, 1962).

8. Ibid., p. 2.

9. Ibid., p. 55.

10. For a discussion of the problems of imagining an identity around some affirmative model of poverty, see John Guillory, *Cultural Capital: The Problem of Literary Canon Formation* (Chicago: University of Chicago Press, 1993), p. 13.

11. Alger, *Ragged Dick*, p. 72.

12. Ibid., p. 58.

13. Ibid., p. 145.

14. Washington, *Up from Slavery*, p. 10.

15. Ibid., p. 120.

16. Richard Wright, *Native Son* (1940; rep. New York: Harper & Brothers, 1966).

17. Ibid.,p. 31.

18. Ibid., p. 44.

19. Ibid., p. 67–68.

20. Ibid., p. 123.

21. The murder of Bessie, which many readers would see as intentional and thus inconsistent with the portrait of Bigger I am sketching here, seems to me, on the contrary, the most inescapable example of Bigger's hopeless position, trapped between incompatible

and equally impossible options. While the killing lacks the reflex detachment of Mary's murder, the text takes great pains to inscribe it into the same dynamic of optionlessness, of the impossibility of purposeful action, that dominates the rest of the book and Bigger's life. The section in which Bigger is trying to figure out what he must do about the not particularly useful or trustworthy Bessie is repeatedly punctuated by variants of the line, "he can't take him with her and he can't leave her behind." This reiteration reminds Bigger and us, in an almost incantatory way, that he has no route of effective action. The result, throughout the book, is inaction or aborted action. Deprived of productive options, Bigger botches killing Bessie, just as he botches the rest of his life. He kills Mary without trying; he cannot kill Bessie (effectively) when he tries, and once again, this failure, built as it is into the dynamic of his life, contributes to his capture and death.

22. "How 'Bigger' was Born," *Native Son*, p. xiv.

23. Ibid., p. xxiv.

24. My use of this term is not meant to suggest any privileged status for belletristic texts. From a pragmatic perspective, "literature" is simply a word for texts, linguistic and otherwise, that are treated as literature—scrutinized, analyzed, and explained as rhetorical forms.

ASHRAF H. A. RUSHDY

# Reading Black, White, and Gray in 1968:
# The Origins of the Contemporary
# Narrativity of Slavery

The search for what David Bradley and Shelley Fisher Fishkin call an "integrated American Literature" promises to be an exciting project and a worthwhile one.[1] It is also going to prove an extremely difficult and long-term project, partly because the new focus on the positive and constitutive interplay of the black and white literary traditions poses some dangers as well promising many windfalls. One danger the project must confront will be that some critics will gloss over the substantial drama of conflict in intercultural literary engagements as they pursue a narrative of camaraderie between African-American and European-American authors and literary lineages. Another related danger is that some critics will use the occasion of this enterprise to develop arguments negating the different material and social conditions within which differently-situated American writers work. In other words, they will assiduously forget the power differential between black and white literary productions and deny the different levels of access black and white authors have to the cultural apparatus which forms the conditions by which literary works are produced, mediated, and received. In order to offset if not prevent these dangers, those of us who seek a more inclusive national literature must forego the desire for an easy resolution or a short-term *rapprochement*. Instead, we need to seek out the deeper meanings of conflicts in literary history and not forget that it is the social order of our nation, with its fundamental material inequities, that defines and determines the sites of contestation where those conflicts occur in our national literature.

Acting on such an imperative, we can then appreciate Cornel West's insight about what he defines as the pitfalls of canon-formation: that "ideologies of pluralism" which do not reconfigure the fields from which they arise are only strategies for concealing what could be "irresoluble conflict." Instead of hiding the incommensurability of certain clashing discourses and material interests, West advises us to focus on moments of "conflict, struggle and contestation." Focussing on those conflicts will not lead us away from whatever chances there are for an "integrated American literature," but rather allow us to explore one of the constitutive elements of that national literature. Eric Sundquist has recently defined as one of the essential paradoxes of American literature the fact that it is a literature which is "both a single tradition of many parts *and* a series of winding, sometimes parallel traditions that have perforce been built in good part from their inherent conflicts." The conflicts, in other words, are not moments of regression from an ideal but acts of positive struggle which have material effects on the terrain where they take place. Previously, that struggle has been figured as one in which so-called minority literatures contest racial stereotypes circulating in the dominant culture by revising those texts belonging to the so-called mainstream literature. One of the truly beneficial contributions that the new focus on the interplay of black and white literary traditions offers is that it rewrites the terms of that struggle. Instead of seeing only resistance, as important in itself as that is, we are also in a position to see the ramifications of that resistance, to see how conflicts effect transformations in given readerships, or what Tony Bennett calls "reading formations."[2] These conflicts, then, not only provide us with opportunities to define local acts of struggle in the field of cultural production, but they also allow us to examine the constitutive elements of a given readership in a specific historical moment. In other words, an exploration of the conflicts in American literary history will show us the *dynamic* interplay between an emergent, oppositional literature and an empowered, hegemonic literature—that is, it will show us both the site and the significance of the conflict as well as developing a narrative of the effects of that conflict.

The subject of this paper is the conflict that occurred in 1968 over William Styron's *Confessions of Nat Turner* and John Henrik Clarke's *William Styron's Nat Turner: Ten Black Writers Respond*. There are three reasons I wish to return to this debate and examine it anew within the terms I have discussed above. First, as we find ourselves in the midst of an enterprise that is largely about dialogue across racial lines, a dialogue in which we problematize "race" as the constituent and defining feature of the division itself, we would do well to discern how such dialogues were conducted in the past. The case of Styron, his critics, and his defenders is particularly instructive because it represents the most recent shift in cultural affairs in American modernity, taking place as it did in 1968, the most volatile year of the most volatile decade in this century. Since the contemporary impetus for the revision of the curriculum in American higher education and the drive towards multiculturalism in general are directly derived from those social movements of the sixties, we can learn a great deal about the origins of our present enterprise at the same time that we learn to avoid the mistakes attending those earlier attempts at multicultural dialogue.

Second, this debate also represents a foundational moment in the unstable relationship between race and readership. The debate I will be tracing occurs in two phases. In the first phase, African-American writers objected to the widespread praise granted Styron's novel by the white literary establishment and offered a thorough critique of the novel itself. White reviewers like C. Vann Woodward and Philip Rahv went so far as to suggest that "only a white Southern writer could have brought [the novel] off" since, as Rahv put it, "a Negro writer, because of a very complex anxiety not only personal but social and political, would have probably stacked the cards, producing in a mood of unnerving rage and indignation, a melodrama of saints and sinners." After June Jordan objected to Rahv's presumption, black critics objected to the novel itself in a variety of different forums, including Albert Murray's critique in the *New Leader*, Alice

Walker's in *American Scholar*, Darwin Turner's in the *Journal of Negro History*, and Poppy Cannon White's in the *Amsterdam News*. The most famous production, though, was that of the ten critics who contributed to the Clarke collection, whose publication initiated the second phase of the debate. In the second phase, European-American writers responded to the social and cultural politics of the critics in the Clarke collection by questioning the critics' reading strategies. (I will hereafter be referring to the black writers in the first phase as "critics" and the white writers in the second phase as "respondents"). Race, however, was not the only factor in this debate. Not only did some African-American writers and historians write positive reviews of Styron's book in highly influential journals, but both the critics and the respondents themselves were motivated less by racial obligations than by institutional ones.[3]

Most of the critics were careful to note that it was not simply Styron's biological "whiteness" that prevented him from producing a more satisfactory portrait of an African-American revolutionary. John A. Williams says explicitly that white writers can indeed write about blacks. When John Oliver Killens says that "Styron tells us *about* the story of Nat Turner, but he is not *of* the story," he is saying that Styron's alienation from the story is a result of his not having lived *culturally*, in black America. It is precisely like a person who "tries to sing the blues when he has not paid his dues." Likewise, Albert Murray notes that when members of the African-American literary community first heard that Styron was going to attempt a novel on Nat Turner's life, they felt it was a "cause for high hopes." African-American intellectuals "who keep check on such things were enthusiastic, and even the Black Nationalists, who place race above literature, were willing to wait and see." Indeed, so ardent a Black Nationalist as Loyle Hairston does not criticize Styron for his being a "white" writer, but for his inability to challenge the environmental conditions which created "whiteness" and an exclusively white literary tradition—that is, for his commitment to "reading human history in fundamentalist terms" that reflect "institutional white supremacy." Hairston notes that most white writers are "nurtured in the envenomed atmosphere of American racism," but he declares this fact just before he praises another white writer who wrote a novel about Nat Turner in 1967, Daniel Panger. The ten critics, then, do not object simply to Styron's race, but rather to the fact that his novel reflected the set of beliefs associated with an intellectual moment that was inimical to African-American subjectivity, a moment, in their opinion, that had been superceded in 1968 by developments both in the social order with the emergence of Black Power and in the academy with the fruition of the New Left social history. Therefore, the critics represented a position against what they believed to be an outdated but nonetheless hegemonic climate of opinion—one based on theories of African-American structural silence, historical victimage, and cultural absence. The respondents, on the other hand, notably Eugene Genovese, Martin Duberman, and Seymour Gross and Eileen Bender, defended not only Styron but the hegemonic climate of opinion which his novel reflected and the institutional arrangements over which that climate prevailed.[4]

Finally, it is important that we return to this debate, bringing with us the terms and goals of the present project, in order to explore the positive effects of this conflict in literary history. It is my argument that the full debate over Styron's and Clarke's texts formed part of a crucial transformation in the intellectual study of slavery—a transformation which has led to a renaissance of African-American literary representations of slavery in the three decades since the conflict. Before 1969, there were only two notable twentieth-century African-American novels about slavery in the United States. In 1936, Arna Bontemps published *Black Thunder*, a fictional treatment of Gabriel Prosser's 1800 Virginia revolt. In 1966, Margaret Walker published *Jubilee*, a fictional representation of the life of her maternal great-grandmother under the trials of slavery and during the travails of Reconstruction (which she began writing in 1934 as a senior at Northwestern).[5] These two novels constituted practically the only black fiction about slavery since Pauline Hopkins published *Contending Forces* in 1900. Since 1969, though, virtually dozens of African-American authors have written about slavery. In 1969, John Oliver Killens published *Slaves*; in 1971, Ernest J. Gaines published *The Autobiography of Miss Jane Pittman*. In 1976, Ishmael Reed's *Flight to Canada* appeared at the same time as Alex Haley's *Roots*. The late seventies saw Octavia Butler's *Kindred* (1979), Barbara Chase-Riboud's *Sally Hemings* (1979), the early eighties Charles Johnson's *Oxherding Tale* (1982), and the later eighties Sherley Anne Williams's *Dessa Rose* (1986), Toni Morrison's *Beloved* (1987), and Barbara Chase-Riboud's *Echo of Lions* (1989). In the early nineties, Charles Johnson published *Middle Passage* (1990), J. California Cooper *Family* (1991), and Caryl Phillips *Cambridge* (1991). The trend gained strength in 1994, when at least five more novels joined this partial list: Caryl Phillips's *Crossing the River*, J. California Cooper's *In Search of Satisfaction*, Louise Meriwether's *Fragments of the Ark*, Fred D'Aguiar's *The Longest Memory*, and Barbara Chase-Riboud's *The President's Daughter*.

These novels are not direct results of the conflict over Styron's novel, nor are they in any meaningful sense "responses" to his novel. Rather, these contemporary narratives of slavery emerged from a set of intellectual, institutional, and social conditions which the debate over Styron's novel and the Clarke collection crystallized and helped bring about. This contemporary renaissance of African-American writing, then, is a positive effect of a deep conflict which helped transform the cultural terrain of historical fiction about slavery. The specific conflict over Styron's novel was part of a social moment in which Black Power politics and New Left social history were attempting to claim institutional and intellectual space. The writers in the Clarke collection represented the cultural arm of the Black Power movement insofar as they were contesting the institutional arrangements that made possible Styron's novel; they also represented an aspect of New Left social history insofar as they challenged historical representations of slavery which systematically excluded slave testimony and folklore. These two elements of their critique of Styron were important because they helped change those institutional arrangements and helped transform the historical study of slavery.

Although they were published only about seven months apart, Styron's novel and Clarke's text are products of two distinct climates of opinion and represent two distinct readerships. The readerships are not distinct because of the race of specific readers but rather because of the ways acts of reading recreate prevailing schemes of racial difference. I would argue that this moment of extreme conflict between white and black intellectuals in 1968 helps us see how an intelligentsia with a racially defined subjectivity endorses a reading strategy which, in turn, consolidates and recreates that racially defined subject position. I would like, therefore, to explore how two distinct readerships take up a specific text and offer two distinct revisionary readings of that text. By examining material practices of reading, we are able to see how specific readerships are solicited and altered by a given conflict. In 1968, the text which both Styron and the critics take up is "Nat Turner." Their diverse readings of that text raise several key questions. What are the determinants of reading? How much do ideologies of the contemporary social order direct a reader's practices? How much do residually influential historical precedents of reading (what I call "first readings") govern a reader's actions? These are large issues that exceed the scope of the present paper, but I would like to initiate an exploration of these questions by examining specifically how Styron and the black critics read the text of Thomas R. Gray's *Confessions of Nat Turner* (1831). Although Gray's text is not the only contemporary account published in Turner's time—there were newspaper reports, and Samuel Warner published an account of the Southampton revolt before Turner had even been captured—it is the document which, as Henry Irving Tragle rightly notes, directly or indirectly has "provided the basis for most of what has been written, in both a fictional and a pseudo-historical sense, about the Southampton Revolt."[6] I will begin then by returning us to what are arguably the "first readers" of Nat Turner.

## Thomas Gray and Thomas Dew: The First Readings of Nat Turner

Thomas Gray's *Confessions of Nat Turner* is a text with an extremely curious dialectic; it is a collaborative effort in which the two collaborators are not only unequally situated, but are in fact quite distinctly opposed in their motives for producing the joint work. William Andrews has brilliantly shown that while Thomas Gray was intent on developing a portrait of an aberrant and contained revolt which was the "offspring of gloomy fanaticism," Nat Turner was intent on creating a self-portrait of a heroic and divinely-led prophet. While Gray wishes to know only the "history of the motives" for the revolt, Turner wishes to use the opportunity of the interview to construct a history of himself. This is a crucial event in the history of African-American self-representation, since Gray's *Confessions* contains the "first significant chronology of an African-American life in southern literature." What Andrews refers to as this "diametric collaboration" produces a "text in which the two men's myths of Nat Turner exist in a relationship of *différance* because of the traces of signification that link" each person's image of Nat Turner to the other's. Andrews concludes that given the conditions of the text as an act of "antagonistic collaboration," we should think of "Nat Turner" as a "product of the dynamics of the text itself." Eric Sundquist has recently added to this idea by suggesting that we can find a replaying of the entire phenomenology of slavery in Gray's *Confessions*. The *Confessions* contains a "slave revolt within the masquerade," writes Sundquist, for although "Gray's text serves to contain and suppress Turner's revolt by situating it within a description of fanaticism, it does not obliterate the meaning of the revolt as an event or as a textual reflection on religious and political principles of liberation." There are spaces in the interstices of the text where Nat Turner is able to assume a degree of subversive subjectivity precisely when Gray suffers "a momentary lapse in the countersubversive regulation of his own language."[7]

One of those key moments in Gray's text occurs when Gray collects himself to pronounce on the alleged dementia of his subject. "He is a complete fanatic," writes Gray, "or plays his part most admirably." Despite his stated goals of containing the revolt and preventing the spread of fear from future revolts amongst the citizens of Virginia and North Carolina, Gray cannot ultimately suppress his abiding suspicion that he has been an unwilling accomplice in the production of an image or idea that Turner controls. He cannot finally say that he understands or is able to define the essential madness of this man. Turner could well be a consummate actor, and Gray an unwilling director not fully in control of the production he is about to issue. Each time Gray attempts to offer a portrait of a singularly demented villain, he is forced to acknowledge the humanity and superhumanity of his subject. Wishing to impress his readers with the fact that Turner still bears "the stains of the blood of helpless innocence about him," Gray nonetheless cannot keep himself from also commenting on the fact that Turner is "clothed with rags and covered with chains." The body of Nat Turner, in other words, is not only a spectacle of guilt because it is stained with the blood of his victims, but it is also a commodified, ill-treated, and captive entity. Describing the "expression of his fiend-like face when excited by enthusiasm," Gray feels simultaneously impelled to note that Turner dares to "raise his manacled hands to heaven, with a spirit soaring above the attributes of man." In Gray's internally divided portrait, Turner's face may be demonic but his actions tend towards heaven. Although he had begun his narrative with the stated intent of laying to rest the "thousand idle, exaggerated and mischievous reports" which excite fear in the "public mind," Gray himself concludes his last look at Nat Turner with exactly that same fear he had set out to exorcise: "I looked on him and my blood curdled in my veins."[8] As a reader of Nat Turner, then, Thomas Gray is forced to attest to the ambiguity and the heroic nature of his subject. His madness might be a semblance, his religiosity might be sincere.

A year after Gray published his *Confessions*, Thomas Dew, the professor of political law at William and Mary (later to be named president of the college), wrote what most historians of the Old South consider the first book-length pro-slavery argument. Responding to the Virginia legislative debates of 1831–1832 concerning the future of slavery in the Old Dominion, Dew wrote a tract in which he showed the prohibitive cost of emancipation and colonization. He concluded a witty piece of writing with the belief that "the time for emancipation has not yet arrived, and perhaps it never will." Almost at the very outset, Dew situates his text in relation to the Southampton revolt. As much as Gray's *Confessions*, then, Dew's book employs a strategy of containment, noting the aberrant nature of that insurrection and showing the folly of pursuing a course of political action in any way conditioned by the aftermath of that revolt. He points out the foolishness of Virginia legislators' even choosing to debate the possibility of emancipation just six months after the Nat Turner revolt. "Any scheme of abolition proposed so soon after the Southampton tragedy," he writes, "would necessarily appear to be the result of that most inhuman massacre." Once slaves get the idea that their violent actions can lead to political changes, then in all probability, Dew notes, slaves will create more insurrections. Dew's major strategy is to show that the economics of emancipation make any political program for it impossible; his supplementary minor strategy, though, is to revise the popular understanding of the Southampton revolt and its leader. "Any man who will attend to the history of the Southampton massacre," he writes, will see at once that the revolt was the product of a "demented fanatic" and could have been prevented by one good solid white man. Had "Travis, the first attacked," woken up when Nat Turner had the ax over his head and "shot down Nat or Will, the rest would have fled, and the affair would have terminated *in limine.*" Dew was here repeating and exaggerating an idea the press had propagated as its containment measure. In the September 3, 1831, *Richmond Whig,* for instance, John Hampden Pleasants confidently asserted that "20 armed whites would put to the rout the whole negro population of Southampton." According to Dew, that would have been nineteen whites too many.

Mostly, though, Dew is concerned with containing the character of Nat Turner, which he does in two ways. First, he castigates the representation of discontented slaves and those who offer those representations—the abolitionists in the Virginia legislature, those political malcontents who are "subversive of the rights of property and the order and tranquillity of society." What they do, Dew argues, is "commit the enormous error of looking upon every slave in the whole slave-holding country as actuated by the most deadiy enmity to the whites, and possessing all that reckless, fiendish temper, which would lead him to murder and assassinate the moment the opportunity occurs." They are grievously in error, writes Dew. He insists that slaves are servile, dependent, abject, and cheerful beings. Repeating what some pro-slavery Virginia legislators had said in the debates and developing his own theories along the way, he argues that the typical Virginia slave in his or her "[c]heerfulness and contentment" is the "most harmless and happy creature that lives on earth." He remarks on the "quiet and contentment of the slave who is left unemancipated." He notes that the slave has the "intellect only of a child" and ought not to be set free in the "infancy of his uninstructed reason." The slaves of a good master, he writes, are "his warmest, most constant, most devoted friends." He concludes that a "merrier being does not exist on the face of the globe than the negro slave of the United States." Writing the first pro-slavery tract in America, Dew produces the "Sambo" stereotype in response to the fear aroused by Nat Turner's revolt. As intellectual historians of the 1830s have noted, the stereotype of the docile slave (the "Sambo" figure) emerged from a specific historical moment in response to the planter class' anxiety about Nat Turner.[9]

The second, interrelated strategy Dew employs is to reduce or eliminate the

ambiguity in Gray's own reading of Nat Turner. The Southampton revolt, writes
Dew, "originated with a fanatic negro preacher, (whose confessions prove beyond
a doubt mental aberration)."[10] Gone is the suspicion that Turner might be acting,
eliminated the speculation that Turner might have had cause for his revolt,
removed beyond a shadow of a doubt the idea that Nat Turner might actually
have had communication with that heaven he sought with his manacled hands.
In place of that ambiguity there is now a mentally aberrant preacher, nothing
more. To put it another way, Dew's reading strategy is to remove the "Gray"
from the text and make it a "black" and "white" issue. These two first readings
of Nat Turner, then, constitute the prehistory of the contemporary debate over
William Styron's novel. We can call the method of reading Nat Turner as an
ambiguous heroic revolutionary the "Thomas Gray reading strategy," and the
method of reading Nat Turner as an unambiguous religious fanatic the "Thomas
Dew reading strategy."

## White and Gray: William Styron's *Confessions of Nat Turner*

A year and a half before completing his novel, Styron told two of his interviewers
that he had discovered very little material when he began his research on Nat
Turner in 1949. There were a "few little newspaper clippings of the time, all of
them seemingly sort of halfway informed and hysterical and probably not very
reliable." In another interview conducted a month after the novel was published,
Styron noted that there was one text which provided him with most of his
information, as well as his title. He refers to Thomas Gray's *Confessions* as "the
single document that means anything."[11] Since Styron presents himself as a *reader*
of Gray's text, it is imperative for us to know what kind of readerly strategies
he employs. The first thing we need to do in order to determine Styron's readerly
options is to examine his interviews both before and after the publication of
*William Styron's Nat Turner: Ten Black Writers Respond*; this will give us a
sense of Styron as a reader in relation to the two first readings of Nat Turner
(that is, the Gray reading and the Dew reading). Once we have determined how
Styron represents himself publicly as a reader of Gray's text, we can examine
how Styron realizes his reading strategies in the production of his novel.

   In a 1963 interview with James Jones, Styron says that Turner was "an extraordinary man," a "man of *heroic* proportions." In an interview in September 1965,
Styron says that after he gave a reading at Wesleyan University, a student asked
him whether someone like Nat Turner would think in the literary language Styron
gave him. Styron responded sharply: "I had to tell him—I'm afraid it embarrassed
him—that I found that question very condescending to Negroes." Turner, he
informs his interviewers, "was a very complicated man. . . . He was educated—
not highly educated, but a man, I think, of some genius—and therefore one has
to allow him a mode of expression which will take in these complexities." He
added in an interview with George Plimpton that Turner's education "gave him
a sense of his own worth as a human being." Indeed, as he tells C. Vann
Woodward and R.W.B. Lewis, Turner was "one of the few slaves in history who

achieved an identity." Two things helped him imagine Turner. First, living with James Baldwin allowed him to conceive of "a black Negro, not a, you know, white Negro, but a black, black homely Negro" who possessed a sparkling intelligence. Second, he had to empathize with his hero to the degree of "turn[ing] myself into a unique slave." Once he has accomplished this act of supreme sympathy, Styron assumes a quixotic relationship with Nat Turner. Consider his comment to Robert Canzoneri and Page Stegner: "If you start finding out about Nat, discovering things about Nat, well, of course, every passage, every chapter, every section is kind of a revelation both for yourself and for Nat."[12] It is impossible to discern whether Styron is talking about his fictional Turner or the historical Nat Turner; moreover, it is intriguing to find him talking about his fictional creation as a living being.

Now there is nothing unusual about that. Most novelists who talk openly about their creative impetus say that they not only inhabit their fictional characters, but that they live with them. Few, however, so quickly turn on their characters and banish them from the house of fiction. In the interviews following the publication of the Clarke collection, Styron no longer talks about that heroic, intelligent, complex, educated man who was a "genius" of sorts. Instead, Styron tells Douglass Barzelay and Robert Sussman in 1968, "if you examine the testimony, the original *Confessions*, any intelligent person is going to be appalled" because the Nat Turner found there is "not very heroic looking at all." Moreover, as he tells Ben Forkner and Gilbert Schricke in an interview in 1974, the historical Nat Turner "was an almost insanely motivated religious fanatic" who possessed a "deranged mind." As a writer, Styron states, "I took the perfectly legitimate liberty of humanizing this man, or monster, by giving him a rational revolutionary plan, plus other talents." No longer quite so confused about the space between the historical and the fictional Nat Turners, Styron notes that "the real Nat Turner as opposed to the one I created were and are two different people." Indeed, it is safe to say that Styron is no longer Don Quixote; he has become Dr. Frankenstein. "I," he intones, "I gave this man a dimension of rational intelligence which he most likely did not really possess." As recently as 1992, he suggested that in his "countless" readings of Gray's *Confessions* he had "early on" discovered that Nat Turner was "a person of conspicuous ghastliness," a "madman" who was "singularly gifted and intelligent," but "mad nonetheless." In the end he had to conclude that "on the record Nat Turner was a dangerous religious lunatic."[13]

The image one gets here is of Styron as an unstable reader, a reader whose whimsy and whose present politics direct how he publicly represents his reading strategies, and whose quixotic attitude toward his characters sometimes leaves him slightly confused about the difference between historical figures and fictional characters. The important point, though, is that Styron's unstable reading strategy is not arbitrary. What he does, in fact, is enact each of the two first readings of Nat Turner. He reads as Gray before the controversy and as Dew after it. In neither case does he betray his novel, however, because there he exhibits both the sympathetic ambiguity of Gray and the rigid containment strategy of Dew. The difference, however, is that Styron did not use religious fanaticism as his

"Dew point," but rather sexual obsession—in particular, he argued for Turner's sexual obsession with a white teenage girl named Margaret Whitehead. To a large measure, the debate over Styron's novel is conducted around the figure of this young girl, whom Styron makes the object of Turner's most violent sexual fantasies and his most troubling religious epiphanies. At some points he fantasizes about raping her, and at the end of the novel he masturbates while dreaming of her and achieves what we are meant to assume is a semblance of salvific grace. More importantly, for my present interests, Margaret Whitehead is the figure around whom Styron organizes his reading of Gray's *Confessions*. She is a historical figure who is present in Gray's *Confessions*; and in both Styron's mind and those of his critics, she is linked to an absence in Gray's *Confessions*, namely Nat Turner's wife.

In 1992, Styron used the occasion of the twenty-fifth anniversary of his novel to elaborate on how he read the absence of Turner's wife in Gray's text. In the "process of using the *Confessions* as a rough guide," he writes, "I was struck by the fact" that Turner never refers to a "woman in a romantic or conjugal sense." This "absence was quite significant and I had to use my intuition to guess at its meaning." His intuition led him to read that absence in terms of the presence of the one woman Turner murdered during the insurrection—Margaret Whitehead. Although at first he had intended to make the relationship between Whitehead and Turner a relatively minor episode, he says he was "drawn irresistibly" to their relationship, which he then explored more fully in the novel. According to his critics, Styron's omission of Turner's wife was deliberate since he used that absence to produce a sexually-repressed black man constantly lusting after white women (for Margaret Whitehead turns out to be only one of a series of white women Styron's Turner spends his time fantasizing about sexually). Both the critics in 1968 and later scholars have shown that not only is there abundant contemporary evidence attesting to the existence of Nat Turner's wife, but that there are sound reasons for Turner's not wishing to reveal her existence to Thomas Gray. We also now know that Styron himself knew of the existence of Turner's wife, since he wrote in the margin of page 33 of his copy of William Drewry's *The Southampton Insurrection*—"Nat's wife: Fannie?"—while also speculating whether "Nat has seen his wife seduced by Travis" on the margin of the front blank sheet of that book.[14]

One can hardly fault Styron for failing to read an absence in a text; so, although he knew of the existence of Turner's wife, his desire to remain faithful to Gray's *Confessions* must have prohibited him from mentioning her. That leaves us with the question of Margaret Whitehead. She is mentioned in Gray's text; and she is apparently the only person Nat Turner did kill. Styron's greatest achievement, it seems to me, is to have worked into the very fabric of his novel a reading of Gray's text in which Nat Turner's murder of Margaret Whitehead signifies Turner's love or lust for her. Styron stated in 1992 that he based his reading of Turner's alleged lust or love for Margaret Whitehead on two crucial points: first, Nat Turner murdered only Margaret Whitehead, and, second, "after that murder his insurrection seems to quickly run out of speed." One of the discoveries he made in his reading of Gray's *Confessions*, as he told Canzoneri and Stegner, is that "Nat himself murders only one person, and the revolt sort of collapses internally once he has killed." In any case, he adds, "[t]hat's what my reading of the *Confessions* tells me." But not his alone, he concludes. "I think it's unavoidable in an honest reading of Nat Turner's confessions that he himself was almost unable to grapple with violence, to carry it out successfully." Finding himself fascinated by the fact that Turner murdered only one person, Styron argues that there "must have been—I say *must* have been because I have no proof, but I'm convinced—some kind of relationship between the two, and I think it was a very guarded sexual relationship." Once that theory is in place, Styron is left with no choice, no readerly options, but to draw the conclusion he has already arrived at. "I can't explain otherwise the fact" that Turner killed only "this one girl, an eighteen-year-old girl who's the only nubile girl, so far as I can find out, killed during the insurrection."[15]

Unfortunately, Styron is mistaken in each one of his premises here. Margaret Whitehead was not the only young woman killed during the Southampton insurrection. The slave rebels also murdered a seventeen year old woman who was engaged to be married the following day. Moreover, as Lerone Bennett pointed out in his reading of Gray's *Confessions*, there was a compelling reason Turner murdered only once. Nat Turner was "the *leader* of the Southampton insurrection," writes Bennett, and "generals seldom kill." Bennett quotes from Gray's *Confessions* to show how Nat Turner himself explained his role: "I took my station in the rear, and as it 'twas my object to carry terror and devastation wherever we went, I placed fifteen or twenty of the best armed and most to be relied on, in front, who generally approached the houses as fast as their horses could run; this was for two purposes, to prevent their escape and strike terror into the inhabitants—*on this account I never got to the houses, after leaving Mrs. Whitehead's, until the murders were committed*, except in one case. I sometimes got in sight in time to see the work of death completed, viewed the mangled bodies as they lay, in silent satisfaction, and immediately started in quest of other victims" (emphasis added). For the most part, as might be expected of "General Nat," Turner was directing rather than performing the sanguinary work of the revolt. Finally, there is hardly any warrant for suggesting that the revolt "runs out of speed" after Turner murders his one victim. After the rebels complete their work at the Whitehead household, they are prevented from murdering more families only because the families to whose houses they go are already fled. Nonetheless, after Nat Turner kills Margaret Whitehead, the rebels do go on to kill twenty-seven people. Since that constitutes practically half the total number killed during the Southampton revolt, it is absurd to say that the revolt "collapsed."[16]

Despite his mistaken premises, or perhaps because of them, Styron's reading of Gray is interesting precisely because we learn a great deal from what Styron chooses to omit or highlight in his rewriting of Gray's *Confessions*. Let us, for example, examine how Styron represents the acts of violence Turner inflicts on the three people he attempts to murder: Joseph Travis, Mrs. Newsome, and

Margaret Whitehead. In the first section of the novel, Styron quotes Gray's text on both of Turner's unsuccessful attempts. Styron has Gray read back to Turner the attempt on Travis: "it being dark I could not give the deathblow, the hatchet glanced from his head." Gray also reads back the incident regarding Mrs. Newsome: "I took Mrs. Newsome by the hand, and with the sword I had . . . I struck her several blows over the head." Yet in the third section, when Styron has Turner recall the events of the insurrection in his own mind, unmediated by Gray, these two events are vastly revised. On the initial attempt, Styron has Turner miss Travis "by half a foot, striking not Travis' skull but the headboard between him and his wife." Then he has Turner miss a second time, the "outside of the blade glanc[ing] lightly from [Travis'] shoulder." In the third section, also, Mrs. Newsome disappears entirely and is instead replaced by two anonymous victims whom Turner fails to kill. He recalls that, "two times when I had raised the glittering blade over some ashen white face, only to have it glance away with an impotent thud or miss by such an astonishing space that I felt that the blow had been deflected by a gigantic, aerial, unseen hand."[17] Styron's revision of Gray's version of the attempt on Travis' life is pretty easily explained; he wants to make Turner an irresolute and thoughtful individual for whom murder did not come easily. So he has him miss twice instead of once, and ensures that he never hits Travis on the head.

His decision to eliminate Mrs. Newsome is slightly more complex. Not only did it serve Styron's purpose to have Turner fail to murder twice more instead of once, but it also allowed him to eliminate the only other woman Nat Turner attempted to kill. It would indeed have proved difficult for Styron to include Mrs. Newsome, precisely because his confusion between violence and sexual desire would not permit it. Let me explain what I mean by returning to an interview in which Styron demonstrates his readerly strategies. In his interview with Woodward and Lewis, Styron adds that one needs to be a rigorous reader of Gray's text. Because the "original confessions of Nat are sketchy," he says, "one has to read between the lines constantly." He himself achieved that rigor by first establishing a state of absolute sympathy. "I had to plunge into some sort of psychological state in order to achieve the kind of insight I did. I hope it has some accuracy." That insight, he informs his interviewers, is that "since Nat killed no one else, and he killed this beautiful girl, considered one of the belles of the county, the psychological truth was that Nat did not hate her. He loved her, or at least had a passion for her." To buttress this logic, Styron adds: "I believe this must have been true. I cannot prove it. I think that if there is any psychological truth in these insights, it partially lies in the fact that one often wishes to destroy what one most earnestly desires."[18]

What Styron seems not to notice is that he has twisted the connection between sexual desire and the desire to destroy. There clearly is some "psychological truth" in Styron's insight; what one does desire one sometimes destroys. But that is not what Styron argues in his reading of Gray's *Confessions*. His argument is that since Nat Turner destroyed Margaret Whitehead, he must have desired her. Rather than arguing that one's desire sometimes results in violence to the desired object or person, he is arguing that Turner's violence signifies desire. In the one instance, violence is an aberrant effect of desire; in the other, desire is diagnosed through acts of violence. We know nothing about what Nat Turner may or may not have felt for Margaret Whitehead. We know that he killed her. From this information, which is that Nat Turner performed a violent act against her (because he happened to be in the right place at the right time, as Gray's *Confessions* show), Styron infers that he desired her. Violence is interpreted as desire.[19] By removing Mrs. Newsome from the novel, Styron is able to maintain that Turner acted on his violent desire only with Margaret Whitehead.

It is clear from Styron's statements in his interviews that Margaret Whitehead is the figure on whose presence he fundamentally bases his reading of Gray's *Confessions*. Indeed, one could say that Margaret Whitehead is nothing less than the figure Styron uses to inhabit and then appropriate Gray's *Confessions*. We saw that one of the ways Styron situates his novel in an intertextual relationship with Gray's is by quoting descriptions of Turner's acts from Gray's text in the first section of the novel and then rewriting those descriptions in an entirely different and more graphic way in the third section of the novel. This strategy of situating his novel intertextually in relation to Gray's *Confessions*, however, is only ancillary to Styron's most concerted strategy for appropriating Gray's text. Margaret Whitehead provides the means for Styron's appropriative reading, which in turn is based on his confusion between violence and sexual desire.

As Lerone Bennett pointed out, Styron's fundamental representational strategy in that attempt is to appropriate Gray's *Confessions* and to place himself in Gray's stead as "Nat Turner's Last White Man." He does this first by giving his book the same title as Gray's pamphlet. He then incorporates Gray's text into his novel. In the "Author's Note" introducing his *Confessions*, Styron calls Gray's text the "single significant contemporary document concerning this insurrection." He then prefaces his *Confessions* with Gray's own preface, entitled "To the Public." Finally, Styron exerts his energies in a concerted effort to situate his Thomas Gray (character) as the Thomas Gray (author), and his *Confessions* as a "dangerous supplement" to Gray's *Confessions*. He begins by having his narrator define the limits of the text of Gray's *Confessions*. When he is unable to respond to Gray, Styron's Turner thinks to himself: "I couldn't—not because there was no reply to the question, but because there were matters which had to be withheld even from a confession, and certainly from Gray." He goes on to inscribe his very silence into the text. "It was impossible to talk to an invention, therefore I remained all the more determinedly silent." Later, Turner will reinforce this skepticism: "I wondered just how much of the truth I was telling him might find its way into those confessions of mine that he would eventually publish."[20]

Moreover, Styron casts doubts on Gray's *Confessions* by suggesting that the text was a collaboration and not simply the autobiographical musings of Nat Turner. When Gray reads back part of Turner's statement, Turner is confused about the voice: "His words (mine? ours?)." At the same time, Styron insinuates that in his *Confessions* Turner is now telling the truth he was unable to tell Gray. He prefaces a description of his masturbatory fantasies with a Rousseau-like honesty: "I should tell it, even though it concerns a matter I would hesitate to dwell on had I not resolved to make this account as truthful as possible." He refers to the text which contains information not found in Gray's *Confessions* as "this account of my life" at the same time as he suggests that this is information he told Gray ("I told him," "as I told Gray"). Towards the end of the third section, Gray returns to the scene and brings with him the material text: "the folded paper notes to my confessions." Again, Styron's Gray pretends to have information which the historical Nat Turner never offered the historical Thomas Gray.[21]

Finally, Styron has the character of Gray validate the text we are about to read by reading into it precisely the point which Styron used to read Gray's *Confessions*. Styron's Gray prefaces his reading of Gray's *Confessions* by suggesting that he will pause over the interesting facets of the text: "while I recite the entire thing out, there are a few items that I haven't gotten entirely straight in my own mind and I want you to clarify them for me if you can." He pauses over two "items." The first concerns Turner's decision to murder a master he considered "kind." The second concerns the fact that Turner murdered only once. Gray addresses Turner on what he insistently calls this "main" point: "the main point is this, which you didn't tell me in so many words, but which I'm going to bring out now by deductive reasoning, as it were. The main point is that in this whole hellish ruction . . . you, Nat Turner, were personally responsible for *only one death*. . . . How come you only slew one? How come, of all them people, this here particular young girl?"[22] Gray will repeat this "main point" in the courtroom as a way of explaining the motivation for Turner's rebellion.

When Gray addresses the court, he asks generally pertinent questions regarding Turner's motives—"How did it happen? . . . From what dark wellspring did it flow? Will it ever happen again?"—before offering the sole source of the answers to these queries: "The answer lies here, the answer lies in the confessions of Nat Turner." The "confessions," of course, are the ones to follow, not the 1831 text. But that confusion between the two "confessions" is necessary for Styron to incorporate his major readerly interpretation into his novel through the mouth of Gray. Moreover, Styron's Thomas Gray has now become Thomas Dew. His purpose in addressing the court, he says, is "to demonstrate that the defendant's confessions, paradoxically, far from having to alarm us, from sending us into consternation and confusion, should instead give us considerable cause for relief." Unlike Dew, however, Styron's Gray does not relieve public consternation by arguing that Turner is a religious fanatic. The public has no reason to fear, he says, picking up a copy of the confessions, because "Nat Turner was personally responsible for only one murder. *One murder*—this being that of Miss Margaret Whitehead." The answer Styron's Gray offers for Turner's motivation centers entirely on the fact that Turner murdered only Margaret Whitehead, "a young girl in all her pure innocence." While the murder of Margaret Whitehead is itself "inexplicably motivated, likewise obscurely executed," Gray nonetheless intimates that it is clearly the linchpin for understanding Turner. Styron's Turner himself will attest as much. As Gray's voice drones on in the courtroom, Turner suddenly recollects several moments he shared with Margaret Whitehead, noting each detail about her appearance, her smell, her words. In other words, both Gray in court and Turner in his mind make Margaret Whitehead the central figure in the drama about to unfold.[23] While Gray refers to the second, third, and fourth sections of the novel as the "confessions of Nat Turner," which will answer his preliminary questions about motives, it is clear that the answer is the one given at the end of the first section. As Styron's Gray makes explicitly clear both to Turner himself in his reading of Gray's text and to the court which convicts Turner, the answer is Margaret Whitehead.

She is also the figure through whom Styron publicly revises and appropriates Gray's *Confessions*. Just as Styron assumed a quixotic attitude towards his hero when he spoke about Nat Turner in his interviews, so, too, when he talks about the figure of Margaret Whitehead he tends to assume a quixotic relationship to his book. His early comments to interviewers suggest that he was in the process of interpreting Gray's text. To Canzoneri and Stegner, he confided that there "must have been a relationship between Nat Turner and Margaret Whitehead, a very guarded sexual relationship." To Woodward and Lewis, he had suggested the same thing: "I believe this must have been true. I cannot prove it." When he was interviewed by George Plimpton, though, Styron was no longer reading Gray's *Confessions* with any kind of caution because he was no longer interpreting Gray's text; he felt that his text had become the reality of Nat Turner's life. "Nat's feelings for her [Margaret Whitehead]," he tells Plimpton, "were just as I described them in the book." Turner "was smitten by her, this paragon of the unobtainable, in some obscure and perilous way so that the killing of her was not only a matter of working out his frustration but possessing her soul and body as well."[24] In Styron's mind, then, Styron's *Confessions* have become Gray's *Confessions*. The historical Nat Turner felt for Margaret Whitehead just what Styron's *Confessions* tells us he felt. In his public representation of his book, Styron was arguing that his novel was no longer a reading but an enactment of historical fact.

The ten black critics were absolutely correct, then, when they contended that Styron was deliberately misrepresenting an African-American revolutionary hero and simultaneously appropriating the autobiographical document containing the written record of his life. Given the way Styron was representing his novel as being true to "the *known* facts," and given that historians were praising him for doing nothing less than producing an exact replication of Gray's text, it is no wonder that the critics felt compelled to return to and produce a corrective reading of Gray's *Confessions*, to insist on divorcing Styron's version of Nat Turner from Gray's version, and to demonstrate how Styron uses Margaret Whitehead as the figure through whom he appropriates Gray and transforms Turner. In doing so, the critics also raised a set of questions about the historiographical representation of slavery, about racial politics in the field of cultural production, and about the relationship between the social order and a literary text. They saw that Styron's *Confessions* was a novel which buttressed the failing but still dominant view historians took of American chattel slavery, while it also indirectly but ruthlessly criticized the Black Power movement. They also saw that it was being circulated and received as a master text in the white literary establishment. Their book was the first of a series of attempts by African-American intellectuals to counter the effect of Styron's text by showing the failings of the hegemonic climate of opinion about slavery, asserting the cultural principles of Black Power, and directly contesting Styron's reading of Thomas Gray's *Confessions*.

## Black and Gray: John Henrik Clarke's *Ten Black Writers Respond*

In many ways, *William Styron's Nat Turner: Ten Black Writers Respond* was not so much a reaction to Styron's novel as it was an exposition of the specific conditions which made that novel possible. However, the Clarke collection was also a testament to the fact that the conditions in American intellectual and social life were changing in 1968. Indeed, the publication of this remarkable volume was not merely a reflection of the changing social conditions of the late sixties; it was itself a part of the shifting power relations in cultural affairs in this period. As such, the Clarke collection was both a symptom of and an agent in the production of new conditions that would make possible different representations of slavery in the future. It is my argument here that the Clarke volume did in fact make possible the range of new representations of slavery that appeared between the seventies and the nineties. The Clarke collection managed to intervene in the academic study of slavery in a substantial way and helped set the agenda for the future historiographical representation of slavery. The writers in the Clarke collection not only defined the hegemonic forces directing Styron's reading of Gray's *Confessions*, but they also gave legitimacy to the resources and materials necessary to disrupt that intellectual hegemon. Those resources included slave testimony, folklore, and oral reminiscences. The Clarke collection not only used slave testimony strategically in its own volume, but it also had a noticeable effect on the study of slavery and the collection of materials for the future study of slavery. Here, I can best specify the effect the Clarke collection had on historical scholarship by examining the immediate change in the collection of material on the historical Nat Turner in the aftermath of the controversy over Styron's novel. In initiating a new project which respected slave testimony, the Clarke collection also set the agenda for the future fictional representation of slavery. This is so in the simplest sense because the Clarke collection helped change the historical debate over slavery, in turn creating a new historiographical portrait, which ultimately affected the later fictional representations of slavery.

   The first thing the writers in the Clarke collection had to do, though, was to show how the complex of ideas operative in the hegemonic climate of opinion governed Styron's reading of Gray. Lerone Bennett made the point that Styron's reading strategy was deliberate and followed a preordained pattern. According to Bennett, Styron "forces history to move within the narrow grooves of his preconceived ideas," and those "ideas" are formed by the climate of opinion about slavery coalescing around the dominant culture's belief that slaves were docile and that their families provided no meaningful countervailing support against the destructive aspects of enslavement. There is a "pattern in his distortion of the facts," writes Bennett, and "the pattern is meaningful." Styron's distortions of Nat Turner's psychic and domestic lives are replications of Stanley Elkins (who argued in 1959 that the system of slavery in the United States produced slaves who were peculiarly docile) and Daniel Patrick Moynihan (who employed Elkins's argument in his own thesis that the destructive effect of slavery on African-American families was still evident in lower-class black family life in 1965). Bennett rigorously demonstrated how Styron deliberately pursued a reading of Gray's *Confessions* premised on these two theses by showing precisely where Styron misquoted Gray.[25]

At the beginning of the novel, Styron's Gray tells Turner that he is "going to read the whole thing [the *Confessions*] out to you here." He starts quoting liberally from Gray's text. In one instance, he reads out a passage about Turner's early life: "And my mother strengthened me in this my first impression, saying in my presence that I was intended for some great purpose." In Gray's *Confessions*, though, the passage runs as follows: "And *my father and* mother strengthened me in this my first impression" (italics added). Whereas in Gray's text Nat Turner had referred to "my grand mother, who was very religious, and to whom I was much attached," Styron's Turner refers to "My mother, to whom I was much attached." Styron has the grandmother die before Turner is born and has her lose her religiosity altogether. Whereas Turner tells Gray that he grew up among the slaves in his community, who would often consult him when they pursued any "roguery," Styron has his Turner exhibit fairly thorough disgust with the field hands and nothing resembling respect or affection for other slaves (with the exception of Willis and Hark). Where Nat Turner tells Gray that he learned to read miraculously amidst his family—given a book one day to stifle his crying, he starts spelling out words to the "astonishment of the family"—Styron has the white Miss Nell teach Turner to read. In each instance, then, Styron rewrites Gray's text so that Turner's family plays a less significant role. By eliminating Turner's father, negating the extended family, and diminishing the importance of an extended communal network, Styron produces what Bennett rightly calls "a proper ADC slave family" and what Vincent Harding refers to as "a wretched precursor of the Moynihan report." It was this sensibility, this effort to read a text of slave testimony through the filter of the Moynihan Report, to which the critics objected. This is what they called the "deliberate" distortion of Nat Turner's own account of himself, and this is why they, unlike George Core, did not believe that "Styron's slight departures from the text of the original *Confessions* are beside the point."[26]

Moynihan, of course, was indebted to Elkins; and it is the Elkins thesis that the slaves in the Old South were docile "Sambos" which primarily governs Styron's reading of Gray's *Confessions*. Before, during, and after the controversy over *The Confessions of Nat Turner*, Styron consistently praised Elkins and maintained the importance of *Slavery* to his own fictional treatment of Nat Turner. In his 1963 review of Herbert Aptheker's *American Negro Slave Revolts*, Styron gave his most complete remarks about Elkins's book. Comparing Aptheker's argument about the ubiquity of slave revolts to Elkins's contention of their absence, Styron concluded that Elkins's book was a "brilliant analysis," which produced an accurate portrait of what "must have been the completely traumatizing effect upon the psyche of this uniquely brutal system, which so dehumanized the slave and divested him of honor, moral responsibility, and manhood. The character (not characterization) of 'Sambo,' shiftless, wallowing happily in the dust, was no cruel figment of the imagination, Southern or Northern, but did in truth exist." Nonetheless, despite his consistent admiration for Elkins, Styron did not produce a novel which is in any way a simple replication of the Elkins thesis. He portrays some slaves who were defiant, such as Nelson (who resisted his master's attempt to whip him), and others who were in the process of being transformed from "Sambos" into revolutionaries (such as Hark, whose response to spilling white blood is to feel himself no longer a "servant of servants" but rather a "killer of men").[27] Although Styron created a few slaves who were sometimes able to shed their servile and infantile personalities, most of the slaves Turner meets are in some way or other deeply-wrought variants of the "Sambo" character.

Bennett found Styron's use of the Elkins thesis also part of the "pattern" of reading the African-American past. According to Bennett, not only does Styron recreate the stereotype of "Big Black Sambo," but he actually has the effrontery to put the "Sambo thesis in Nat Turner's mouth." Indeed, like Elkins, Styron's Turner toys with the idea that a "Sambo" personality structure might be only an elaborate act before determining that it is truly a personality structure, and, indeed, the dominant personality structure of African-American slaves. According to Styron's Turner, in the presence of white people Hark became "the unspeakable bootlicking Sambo." The "very sight of white skin cowed him, humbled him, diminished him to the most fawning and servile abasement." Styron's Turner also insists that Hark is *acting* as a "Sambo" in order to play a role which protects him, both before and after his transformation into a "killer of men." Treating Hark as "a necessary and crucial experiment," Styron's Turner sets out to "destroy that repulsive outer guise" of "Sambo" and nurture "the murderous fury which lay beneath." At the end of his experiment, Styron's Turner recognizes that there might be slaves like Hark, slaves who possess an inner personality core which is not ultimately servile and infantile, at the same time as he is forced to acknowledge the "painful fact that *most* Negroes are hopelessly docile" (emphasis added). In the end, most of the slaves, including the ones who allegedly defended their masters against Nat Turner, are not like Hark or Nelson but more like Hubbard, who represents "some grotesque harbinger of all in black folk gone emasculate forever."[28]

What the critics objected to was that Styron utterly ignored the fact that his reading of slave personality-types was based on the strategy of containment employed by the pro-slavery polemicists in the aftermath of the Nat Turner revolt—that is, that Styron's representation of the docile slave was precisely the response of ideologues such as Thomas Dew to the spectre of Nat Turner. Ernest Kaiser found it sad that Styron should have chosen to employ "Elkins's false thesis," which he feels is based on a "southern racist fantasy." The critics pointed out to Styron that the "Sambo" stereotype was created amidst particular social conditions attesting to particular class anxieties. If "the majority of slaves were inert 'Sambos,' broken in mind and spirit, as Styron's Nat suggests," then why, Thelwell asks, did Southern state governments fill the "official record with so many requests for federal troops to guard against insurrection?" Bennett's major point is that Styron fails to acknowledge that the "Sambo" stereotype was created in the aftermath of the Nat Turner revolt as a means of containing the ramifications of that revolt. What Styron does not know or goes to great lengths to deny, writes Bennett, is that "antebellum southerners and their modern descendants had to believe that Sambo existed in order to deal with the contradictions of their own existence."[29] In other words, what Bennett, Thelwell, and Kaiser are suggesting is that Dew supplanted Gray in Styron's *Confessions*. Styron's text supported this subversion because Styron was reading Nat Turner through the filter of the complex of ideas associated with the Elkins thesis.

Having shown how Styron's reading strategy was governed by the dominant historical representation of American slavery and the political representation of contemporary African-American family life, the critics then proceeded to challenge what they considered Styron's act of cultural appropriation. They issued that challenge in two forms. On the one hand, they showed how Styron had misread African-American history and culture because he read those dynamic features of American cultural life through the filter of an eroding complex of beliefs about slavery; on the other, they criticized the methodologies of those historians who had produced that complex of beliefs and denied the value of slave narratives to their historical work by appending to their own volume a significant piece of slave testimony. They pointed out that Styron's *Nat Turner* was a response to a certain political imperative, and that it was founded on a reading strategy which was itself based on a certain set of historical statements which no longer possessed the validity they had assumed five years earlier. They insisted that the Nat Turner Styron represented in his novel was, like Thomas Dew's, based on the needs and demands of a white cultural imperative attempting to deny the meaning of slave resistance (in Dew's case) and the significance of contemporary Black Power politics (in Styron's).

They appended Gray's *Confessions* to their text as a way of returning the written historical record to public discourse so that people could see how Styron read and misread that remarkable piece of slave testimony; and also as a way of attesting to the emergence of new, literary Nat Turners whose own voices, unlike Turner's, needed no Gray intermediary. They claimed in their own text, preceding the one in which Nat Turner spoke for himself, that the Nat Turner who would be representative of African-American cultural life "still awaits a literary interpreter worthy of his sacrifice." "Black people today," wrote Charles Hamilton, "must not permit themselves to be divested of their historical revolutionary leaders." He concluded his essay by pointedly arguing that Styron's portrait was based on an act of cultural appropriation. The volume as a whole resonated with this point. John Henrik Clarke introduced the volume by maintaining that "our Nat is still waiting," and Mike Thelwell concluded it by stating that the history of Nat Turner "remains to be written." Immediately thereafter, as a guideline to what would be written, came the twenty-five pages of Gray's *Confessions*.[30] In this volume, Nat Turner was the eleventh black writer to respond. The writers in the Clarke collection, then, challenged Styron's local reading of Gray and, more generally, addressed themselves to the climate within which Styron and other historians read slave testimony. I would like now to turn from this conflict in American literary history and examine its ramifications. What immediate effect did the conflict have on the readership who entered and emerged from it? What deeper and more long-term effects did it have on later American cultural representations of slavery (both fictional and historical)?

## Black, White, and Gray: The Contemporary Narrativity of Slavery

The way to answer the first question is to examine the ways historians and critics read Nat Turner after Styron. On the one hand, Styron largely succeeded in appropriating Gray's text and making his novel the major intermediary for Nat Turner's life for the majority of readers who have published their responses to this novel. The evidence of his success exists in the virtually unanimous acclaim with which the novel was received by the white literary establishment and the validation it got from historians like C. Vann Woodward, Martin Duberman, and Eugene Genovese. As a sign of how completely Styron managed to appropriate Gray's *Confessions*, consider the fact that Genovese should presume to change the title of Gray's text. Since "Styron's novel has the same title as that Gray gave to the original," he writes, "I shall refer to the latter as Turner's *Testimony*." By giving Styron's book the title, Genovese indicates that the novel has supplanted the original, and that, one assumes, pretty well left Styron entitled to tell the story of Nat Turner. As another comment on how successfully Styron appropriated Nat Turner himself, we can cite the fact that in 1969 James Cone was compelled to add a caveat when he listed the heroes of black consciousness: "Nathaniel Paul, Daniel Payne, Nat Turner (not Styron's), Marcus Garvey, Elijah Muhammad, and Malcom X."[31] A final indication of Styron's successful appropriation of Gray's text is the fact that later historians of Turner's revolt would read Gray's *Confessions* through the filter of Styron's novel, attempting to answer the questions Styron posed to that text or to represent in an overdetermined fashion those features of Nat Turner's life which Styron eliminated.

Stephen Oates's essay on the Southampton revolt in the October 1973 issue of *American Heritage* is a case in point. On the one hand, Oates performs solid revisionist work in returning to the historical record what Styron removed from it or correcting what he distorted. For instance, Oates insistently restores Nat Turner's family—in one paragraph he notes that "[b]oth parents praised Nat," that "[h]is mother and father both told him that he was intended for some great purpose," and that "Nat was also influenced by his grandmother." He also asserts the existence of Nat Turner's wife, Cherry. On the other hand, though, Oates is not just responding to Styron's misrepresentations of historical events and negations of historical people; he also feels it necessary to respond to Styron's reading of Gray's *Confessions* by accepting the presuppositions Styron articulated through his fictional Thomas Gray. Oates probes into the reasons Turner did not kill more people, something which he describes as a mystery: "a fatal irresolution? the dread again?" When he reads the description of Turner's three unsuccessful attempts at murder, he spends an inordinate amount of energy explaining why Turner failed. His attempt at Travis's life is described as a "wild blow that glanced off Travis's head." Without any warrant at all, Oates casts Turner's attempt on Mrs. Newsome's life into intentionalist language—"evidently he could not bring himself to kill her"—instead of attempting to analyze any connection between Turner's lack of success and the inutile weapon he was using. Because his attention is so preoccupied with a desire to answer Styron's question about Turner's failure to murder more, Oates is compelled to pursue his own misreading of Gray's text.[32] While many historians believed Styron to be faithful to Gray's account, a historian like Oates, who contested Styron's fidelity to Gray, nonetheless believed himself bound to respond to those very questions Styron had posed to Gray's text.

The final sign of Styron's success is that he has been able to promote himself as the "origin" of the contemporary interest in Nat Turner and to convince others that he has the right to that title. Since 1967, Styron has rarely missed an opportunity to claim that he initiated the contemporary interest in Nat Turner. In the February 1974 issue of *American Heritage*, Styron published a letter in response to Oates's article in which he claimed, first, that Oates was not as "eminent" or as "sophisticated" a historian as Woodward, Duberman, and Genovese, historians who had "all publicly testified to the historical integrity of [his] vision of Nat Turner," and, second, that Styron himself was responsible for Oates's and other historians' interest in Nat Turner. He claimed that Oates was "happily engaged in the cottage industry I established up at the University of Massachusetts and elsewhere." In 1982, he again proclaimed that he had "never ceased being a little surprised at the bustling cottage industry which *The Confessions of Nat Turner* spawned during the subsequent years."[33] When he lists those works, he includes the two collections of materials relating to the rebellion, one edited by Eric Foner (1971) and the other by Henry Irving Tragle (1971), as well as the two casebooks devoted to the historical Nat Turner and Styron's novel—Melvin Friedman and Irving Malin's *William Styron's The Confessions Nat Turner: A Critical Handbook* (1970) and John Duff and Peter Mitchell's *The Nat Turner Rebellion: The Historical Event and the Modern Controversy* (1971)—and, finally, the two historical studies of the Southampton rebellion: F. Roy Johnson's *The Nat Turner Story* (1970) and Stephen Oates's *The Fires of Jubilee: Nat Turner's Fierce Rebellion* (1975). The fact that Styron's questions direct Oates's inquiry suggests that Styron is partially accurate in arguing that some of these books are indeed reactions to his novel, while others are at least informally affected by his novel. (It is also worth noting that when Styron lists those books which are products of his cottage industry, he fails to mention the book published the year before his, F. Roy Johnson's first book on the insurrection, *The Nat Turner Slave Insurrection* [1966], and the book published in the same year as his, Daniel Panger's novel *Ol' Prophet Nat* [1967]; the trouble with "origins," of course, is that one needs to deny so much to establish them.)

What Styron neglects to mention, though, is that these later books also do what he failed to do, and precisely what his critics accused him of failing to do,— namely, they consult the folk traditions of African-Americans. In his collection of material pertaining to the revolt, for instance, Eric Foner has sections on nineteenth-century African-American historians' representations of Nat Turner, on literary and journalistic representations of Nat Turner in the 1880s and on the centenary of his revolt in 1931, as well as a section on the contemporary "folk memory of Nat Turner." Henry Irving Tragle not only compiled all the relevant written historical material on the Southampton insurrection, but he also interviewed some sixty individuals regarding the folk tradition of the insurrection. After travelling to Southampton County in 1969 and interviewing both European Americans and African Americans living there, Tragle determined that it is "possible to say with certainty that Nat Turner did exist as a folk-hero to several generations of black men and women who have lived and died in Southampton County since 1831." F. Roy Johnson added some thirty-five pages of "new material provided by Black tradition and white tradition" to his second book on the Southampton revolt, *The Nat Turner Story*. He not only drew on William Drewry's account of his interviews with seventy-two residents of Southampton County, but he also interviewed an "even larger number of persons . . . for materials to make the present report the fullest yet." Moreover, he also listened to the "hundreds of folk tales" of the white and black folk traditions. In researching his book, Oates also traveled to Southampton County in the summer of 1973 in order to consult African Americans living there about the folk tradition of Nat Turner.[34]

These later writers and collectors, then, took up the important point raised by Albert Murray in his review of Styron's novel and Vincent Harding in his critique of it. When Harding had said that Styron did not use the "living traditions of Black America" (repeating Albert Murray's point that Styron did not employ the insights from "Negro folk heritage"), Genovese took issue with Harding's statement, arguing that "we have yet to be shown evidence that slaves and postslavery blacks kept alive a politically relevant legend of Nat Turner." Indeed, Genovese went so far as to call Harding's claim a "pretense" and argue that "if the existence of armed resistance to slavery is now generally appreciated, William Styron deserves as much credit as any other writer." In his response, Harding rightly took exception to Genovese's assumption of claiming to know "what is alive and well in the continuing traditions of Black America"; and he raised the crucial issue of what Genovese meant when he used "we" so freely. There is "another 'we'," writes Harding, "the black part of the pronoun, one might say," who live in the black tradition and who have a claim to be heard when stating a living knowledge about Nat Turner. Harding lists Frederick Douglass, Samuel Ringold Ward, Henry Highland Garnet, Harriet Tubman, and H. Ford Douglass as people who knew what it was to live with the "memory of Turner." He offers a succinct bibliography of black journals and materials which contain information about a tradition of slave resistance well before it occurred to Styron to inform African-American people of this tradition. And, finally, Harding mentions the folklore, particularly the folklore passed on by "great-grandparents and grandparents," the folklore generated within families between generations.[35]

In another forum, a panel discussion at the Southern Historical Association in New Orleans on November 6, 1968, held the day before Harding's rejoinder was published, Ralph Ellison informed William Styron himself that African-American familial oral lore contained historical figures from slavery, including figures associated with slave revolts. "This record exists in oral form," noted Ellison, "and it constitutes the internal history of values by which my people lived even as they were being forced to accommodate themselves to those forces and arrangements of society that were sanctioned by official history." Encapsulating what the black critics collectively maintained, Murray, Harding, and Ellison inform their white would-be informants that there is another historical, living tradition, what Ellison elsewhere called "our familial past," providing a supplementary and often subversive version of the past contained in the "official versions."[36] The work produced on Nat Turner after the controversy over Styron's novel took seriously what Ellison, Harding, and Murray were saying by researching the oral, the familial, and the cultural traditions in black America.

It is important to note how the critics' comments affected later work on Nat Turner—because it alerts us to the fact that Styron's success in appropriating Gray's *Confessions* was not complete. While his novel may have conditioned some future readers of Gray's *Confessions* to pursue answers to those questions Styron felt worth asking, the Clarke collection was able to initiate another project of collecting and making more public the folk heritage and the unwritten history of African-American cultural life under slavery. That project of collecting and publishing the oral testimony of ex-slaves and the descendents of ex-slaves, as we can see in retrospect, was going to change the reading patterns of those who would approach slave testimony in the next three decades. As Mike Thelwell noted in his contribution to the *New York Review of Books'* "Exchange on Nat Turner," the "evidence and materials concerning the slave culture and world view, although largely ignored, do exist." The "reality of slavery," he had written in his contribution to the Clarke collection, is to be found in the "testimony of the slaves themselves."[37] In a large measure, the Clarke collection opened up a new space and initiated a new interest in the resources available for those historians who wished to see slavery from the slave's point of view. More importantly, the writers in the Clarke collection also demonstrated that reading is itself an activity governed by institutional and social forces.

Because it did that, the Clarke collection also had an almost immediate effect on the readership which had so highly praised Styron's novel. Consider, for instance, the altered reading strategies of two writers, one a literary critic and the other a historian, each of whom reviewed both Styron's novel and the Clarke collection. In his *New York Times* review of Styron's *Confessions*, Eliot Fremont-Smith claimed that Styron's novel "resurrects" and "is based on" Gray's *Confessions*. Indeed, Fremont-Smith went so far as to argue that the novel "faithfully reflects . . . the voice of the real Nat Turner as it comes through in the actual confessions." So thoroughly does he believe in Styron's accuracy that when he himself reads Gray's *Confessions* he reads it through Styron's eyes. Fremont-Smith thinks that there are only two pertinent questions asked in Gray's *Confessions*—why did Nat Turner kill a kind master and why did Turner kill only once? Those, of course, are precisely the questions Styron put into his fictional Gray's mouth. In his *Village Voice* review of Styron's *Confessions*, Martin Duberman also argued that Styron was faithful to the historical record. Duberman argued that Styron's "determination to be true to the past," his "insistence on historical authenticity" in paying his "scrupulous debt to the past," led him "to put aside his subjective vision, his own truth, in order to serve those twenty-odd scraps of paper we call Nat Turner's 'confessions.' "[38] As we saw above, the critics demonstrated that Styron was not so scrupulous in his debt as Duberman suggested, nor so bound to Gray's text as Duberman and Fremont-Smith argue. What is more important here is the fact that historians and reviewers believed Styron to have produced the definitive reading of Gray's text. Once the Clarke collection entered public discourse, though, those historians and reviewers had to reassess Styron's reading of Gray.

In those reassessments, Fremont-Smith and Duberman both used the strategy of denying the validity of the very text which they had earlier praised Styron for reading and bringing to life. In his review of the Clarke collection, Fremont-Smith had to admit that Styron's reading of Gray was not definitive, and that it was, in fact, a "characteristically callous white-liberal appropriation of a Negro hero for the purpose of containing and destroying his mythological potency." What were once the "actual confessions" Styron rendered so faithfully have now become one myth among several. The subtitle of Fremont-Smith's review is "what myth will serve?" Likewise, in his review of *William Styron's Nat Turner: Ten Black Writers Respond*, Duberman had to admit that the "original confessions" were "filtered through the eyes and words of a white man and therefore automatically suspect." In a note he attached to the reprinting of this review in his 1969 collection of essays, Duberman added that he had been "wrong in saying that Styron had kept scrupulously . . . to all the details of Nat Turner's original 'confessions.' " He grudgingly confessed that the black critics had effectively showed how "Styron did change or omit a number of details in the confessions." At the end of his review, though, Duberman remained largely resistant to those very imperatives of New Left social history which the critics brought with them to the debate over Styron's novel. He claims to be still "leery of the 'oral tradition' which some of the writers [in the Clarke collection] are *reduced* to citing" (emphasis added). That "oral tradition," of course, would not only become a prominent feature of social history in the seventies and eighties, but it would also play a fundamental role in Duberman's own work after the debate. His magnificent biography of *Paul Robeson*, for instance, would have been unimaginable without the "oral tradition" on which he there draws with such expertise. More importantly, Duberman implicitly admitted that the Clarke collection's intervention had caused him to question his own local acts of reading. Although he had read "those confessions so many times in the past," and had quickly reread Gray's text once again when reviewing Styron's novel, it took the critics' reading to show him how his own (and Styron's) reading strategies were determined by the specific social conditions forming the hegemonic climate of opinion in America in the mid-sixties.[39]

The answer to the first question with which I concluded the previous section, then, is that the conflict over Styron's novel helped transform a readership in two specific ways. Some readers of Nat Turner began to gather materials from the folklore and oral traditions of African-American heritage, thus altering the field within which slavery and slave resistance would be studied in the future. Other readers of Styron's novel began to question their own strategic placement as readers who were institutionally and socially situated to read in a certain, determined way. Following 1968, historians of American chattel slavery pursued Thelwell's point about slave testimony in a more systematic and concerted fashion, while, concomitantly, readers of America's slave past learned to be vigilant about their own cultural situatedness by bringing folklore and other forms of the "oral tradition" to bear on the subject of slavery.

Taking up the second question, then, we can say that the long-term effects of this conflict are positive since the debate helped change the attitudes of historians who would write histories of slave culture and slave community life in the seventies. For instance, before 1968 Eugene Genovese had been extremely skeptical of the value of slave testimony for the study of the peculiar institution; after 1969, and after he himself participated in the debate over Styron's novel, Genovese had a radical change of heart, began heartily to endorse the use of slave testimony, and changed the project he had originally been working on to reflect his own changed attitude. The product of that change was, of course, the massive and ground-breaking *Roll, Jordan, Roll: The World the Slaves Made* in 1974.[40] Genovese's intellectual conversion is representative of a broader shift in historical representations of American chattel slavery, which, in turn, led to the emergence of a series of new African-American fictions about slavery. It is important to stress that the connection between the debate over Styron's novel and the contemporary narrativity of slavery is complex and not entirely direct. Under the old terms of an outdated model for exploring multiracial literary interactions, one might have insisted that African-American fiction about slavery emerging after 1969 was a response or reaction to Styron's representation. Under the new terms of a more rigorously historicist account of multicultural projects, we can see that there are several interrelated reasons for the outpouring of contemporary African-American fiction about slavery after 1969.

For one thing, there was an important generational shift in African-American life in the sixties. Toni Morrison pointed out that the African-American novelists of her generation—that is, novelists who began writing in the mid-to-late-sixties—were called on to provide a cultural forum for ancestral narratives which had hitherto existed in domestic spaces. The "novel is needed by African-Americans now in a way that it was not needed before," she wrote, because "[w]e don't live in places where we can hear those stories anymore." The generation of writers a century removed from the end of legal slavery in the United States took up the duty of supplementing if not enacting those familial tales. Moreover, this generational shift in the sixties had within it another generational shift equally important to the renaissance of contemporary African-American narratives of slavery: the shift from the Civil Rights movement to the Black Power movement. With the emergence of Black Power in 1966, African Americans developed a newly-empowered sense of black subjectivity and a renewed respect for black cultural practices and imperatives. This development positively affected writers of contemporary narratives of slavery. Most of the contemporary authors would agree with Sherley Anne Williams that while the Civil Rights movement was important because it "gave would-be writers of new African-American histories and fictions the opportunity to earn financial security and thus the time to write," it was essentially "the Black Power movement that provided the pride and perspective necessary to pierce the myths and lies that have grown up around the antebellum period as a result of Southern propaganda and filled us also with the authority to tell it as we felt it."[41]

There were also crucial institutional factors that made possible the renaissance of black writing about slavery. In the late sixties, publishers and other cultural institutions opened up some space for African-American writers. A *Newsweek* story in the summer of 1969, entitled "The Black Novelists: 'Our Turn,' " stated that there was a "black revolution" in literature which the publishing industry was quick to capitalize on. Whereas publishers had been uninterested in African-American authors earlier, they began "scrambling to add black writers to their lists" in the late sixties. And, of course, with the development of Black Studies programs in Northern, predominantly white universities between 1968 and 1969, there was a new demand for texts written by African Americans.[42] The late sixties, then, saw a social change with the emergence of Black Power, an intellectual change with the development of New Left social history, and an institutional change with the opening up of new opportunities in publishing and teaching black-authored texts. These changes together formed the conditions which led to the renaissance of African-American writing about slavery for the next three decades. Of course, it is not hard to see how the conflict over Styron's novel played a large role in both signifying the need for and promoting those changes. The writers in the Clarke collection constituted the vanguard of the Black Power intellectuals who initiated the challenge to the "Southern propaganda" about American slavery. They also represented the New Left social history in insisting on examining slavery "from the bottom up" by incorporating the testimony of slaves into the historical record. In some ways, the Clarke collection also attested to the existence of an emergent new readership which publishers would see as an opportune market. One of the things reviewers of the Clarke collection repeatedly noted is that *William Styron's Nat Turner: Ten Black Writers Respond* addressed a new kind of readership and presupposed a militant black audience.

These changes in American cultural life—social, intellectual, and institutional—made possible the novelistic treatment of slavery in African-American writing after 1969. Addressing a readership alert to new historiographical work on the strength of slave communities and the importance of slave culture, the authors of the seventies and eighties produced contemporary narratives of slavery which reflected and helped create a new climate of opinion about the American past. These contemporary narratives are heterogeneous, and I do not mean to suggest that they follow a paradigmatic pattern in their representations, but they also share several key strategies and concerns. The contemporary narratives of slavery insistently view slavery from the slave's point of view. Five of the novels adopt the form and conventions of antebellum slave narratives and literally assume the slave's point of view: Ernest Gaines's *Autobiography of Miss Jane Pittman*, Ishmael Reed's *Flight to Canada*, Charles Johnson's *Oxherding Tale* and *Middle Passage*, and Sherley Anne Williams's *Dessa Rose*. The other third-person historical novels are substantially based on a slave's perspective and often have lengthy sections in which the slaves speak for themselves or intimately remember their past (as is the case in both Barbara Chase-Riboud's *Sally Hemings* and Toni Morrison's *Beloved*).

It is to be remembered, of course, that Styron had also adopted the slave narrative form in his *Confessions*. The difference, however, is that while Styron was oscillating between the Dew and the Gray reading strategies, the novelists listed above employ oral productions which test the limits of and ultimately subvert the authenticity of any "official" history and challenge the presumed authority of those "first readers." The novelists who write contemporary narratives of slavery establish a dialectic between slave-masters' oppressive literary representations and the slaves' own liberating oral witnessing of slavery. In *The Autobiography of Miss Jane Pittman*, for example, the editor who is soliciting Miss Jane's story notes that what was "wrong with them books" of history was that "Miss Jane is not in them." In an interview, Gaines himself noted that his approach to research was driven by the desire to find out the information absent in those books. "Truth to Miss Jane is what she remembers. Truth to me is what people like Miss Jane remember. Of course, I go to the other sources, the newspapers, magazines, the books in the libraries—but I also go back and listen to what Miss Jane and folks like her have to say." Miss Jane's oral tale has enough integrity and authority so that the library research does not ultimately "authenticate" the story. Indeed, after reading the "books in the libraries," Gaines goes back to listen to "what Miss Jane and folks like her have to say" in order to test the truth of what the books are saying.[43] Later novels like *Flight to Canada, Beloved*, and *Dessa Rose* all represent that same struggle between a form of writing that would master and the practice of orality that would free the slave.

This changed attitude toward oral production—toward the collective folk heritage Albert Murray advised Styron to consult, the generational folklore Vincent Harding defined, and the familial narratives Ralph Ellison and Toni Morrison attested to—marks what might be the most important development in the contemporary narratives of slavery. With that development, the contemporary novelists signal their departure from the reading strategies of Styron's generation. They read absences in the historical record with more knowledge of how that record is compiled by acts of exclusion, with a greater sense of how the authority an official historical record claims is often a result of its ignoring or rendering mute the testimony of its exploited victims. They attend more carefully to what is present in that existent record and do not misread it through an over-zealous desire to find in it what Albert Murray calls the "folklore of white supremacy and the fakelore of black pathology."[44] Finally, they supplement that record by incorporating into it the testimony which was previously excluded. They therefore transform the record and simultaneously reconstruct its readership. Following the impetus of those brave critics of 1968, the contemporary novelists of slavery have incorporated into their novels a sensibility about oral productions of knowledge that causes their own readership to distrust the borders of anything in black and white, and, in this particular case, in Gray.

## Notes

1. David Bradley, "Foreword," to William Melvin Kelley, *A Different Drummer* (1962; New York: Doubleday, 1989), xi–xxxii, esp xviii. Shelley Fisher Fishkin, *Was Huck Black?: Mark Twain and African-American Voices* (New York: Oxford University Press, 1993), 128–144; Fishkin employs Bradley's term on p. 143.

2. Cornel West, "Black Critics and the Pitfalls of Canon Formation," in *Keeping Faith: Philosophy and Race in America* (New York: Routledge, 1993), 33–43, esp. 38, 34. Eric J. Sundquist, *To Wake the Nations: Race in the Making of American Literature* (Cambridge: Harvard University Press, 1993) 18. Tony Bennett, "Texts, Readers, and Reading Formations," *Bulletin of the Midwest Modern Language Association* (Spring 1983): 3–17.

3. Philip Rahv, "Through the Mists of Jerusalem," *The New York Review of Books* (October 26, 1967): 6–10, esp. 6. Cf. C. Vann Woodward, "Confessions of a Rebel: 1831," *The New Republic* (October 7, 1967): 25–28, esp. 28. June Meyers, "Spokesmen for the Blacks," *The Nation* (December 4, 1967): 597–599, esp. 597, 599; June Meyers is now June Jordan. Albert Murray, "A Troublesome Property," *The New Leader* 50 (December 4, 1967): 18–21. Alice Walker, in "The Revolving Bookstand: Recommended Summer Reading," *American Scholar* 37 (Summer 1968): 512–554, esp. 549–551. Darwin T. Turner, "[Review of Styron's *Confessions of Nat Turner*]," *Journal of Negro History* 53 (1968): 183–186. Poppy Cannon White, "Confessions of Nat Turner," *New York Amsterdam News* (November 25, 1967), 15. See also White, "'The African' vs. Nat Turner," *New York Amsterdam News* (December 9, 1967), 17. African Americans who wrote positive reviews of Styron's novel include James Baldwin, qtd. in Raymond A. Sokolov, "Into the Mind of Nat Turner," *Newsweek* (October 16, 1967), 65–69; John Hope Franklin, *Chicago Sun-Times Book Week* (October 8, 1967); Benjamin Quarles, *Social Studies* 59 (November 1968): 280; J. Saunders Redding, "A Fateful Lightning in the Southern Sky," *Providence Journal* (October 29, 1967), sec. W, p. 18; and Redding, in "The Revolving Bookstand: Recommended Summer Reading," *American Scholar* 37 (Summer 1968): 512–554, esp. 540–542. See Albert E. Stone, *The Return of Nat Turner: History, Literature, and Cultural Politics in Sixties America* (Athens: University of Georgia Press, 1992), 120, 104, 44, 120–126, 171, 393 (n. 25).

4. John A. Williams, "The Manipulation of History and of Fact: An Ex-Southerner's Apologist Tract for Slavery and the Life of Nat Turner; Or, William Styron's Faked Confessions," in *William Styron's Nat Turner: Ten Black Writers Respond*, ed. John Henrik Clarke (Boston: Beacon Press, 1968), 45–49, esp. 45. John Oliver Killens, "The Confessions of Willie Styron," in *William Styron's Nat Turner*, 34–44, esp. 36, 44. Killens, "The Confessions of Willie Styron," 44. Murray, "A Troublesome Property," 18, 20. Loyle Hairston, "William Styron's Dilemma: Nat Turner in the Rogues' Gallery: Some Thoughts on William Styron's

Novel *The Confessions of Nat Turner,*" *Freedomways* 8 (Winter 1968): 7–11, esp. 10. Hairston, "Rescuing Nat Turner from American History," *Freedomways* 8 (Summer 1968): 266–268, esp. 267. Daniel Panger's novel *Ol' Prophet Nat* is a much-ignored but important representation of Nat Turner which has suffered critical neglect mostly because it was distributed by a small press, John F. Blair Publishers, operating out of Winston-Salem. Eugene D. Genovese, "William Styron Before the People's Court," *New York Review of Books* (September 12, 1968): 34–38; reprinted in Genovese, *In Red and Black: Marxian Explorations in Southern and Afro-American History* (1971; Knoxville: University of Tennessee Press, 1984), pp. 200–217. Martin Duberman, "[Review of Clarke's *William Styron's Nat Turner: Ten Black Writers Respond*]," *New York Times Book Review* (August 11, 1968); reprinted in *The Uncompleted Past* (New York: Random House, 1969), pp. 216–222. Seymour L. Gross and Eileen Bender, "History, Politics and Literature: The Myth of Nat Turner," *American Quarterly* 23 (October 1971): 487–518. I discuss this debate in much more detail in a forthcoming study, *NeoSlave Narratives: Studies in the Social Logic of a Contemporary African American Literary Form,* chapters 3 and 4.

5. Margaret Walker, "How I Wrote *Jubilee,*" in *How I Wrote Jubilee and Other Essays on Life and Literature,* ed. Maryemma Graham (New York: The Feminist Press, 1990), 50–65.

6. Henry Irving Tragle, ed., *The Southampton Slave Revolt of 1831: A Compilation of Source Materials* (Amherst: University of Massachusetts Press, 1971), 301.

7. William L. Andrews, *To Tell a Free Story: The First Century of Afro-American Autobiography, 1760–1865* (Urbana: University of Illinois Press, 1986), 72. Thomas R. Gray, *The Confessions of Nat Turner* (Baltimore, 1831) repr. in Tragle, *The Southampton Slave Revolt of 1831,* 300–321, esp. 306. Andrews, "Inter(racial)textuality in Nineteenth-Century Southern Narrative," in *Influence and Intertextuality in Literary History,* ed. Jay Clayton and Eric Rothstein (Madison: University of Wisconsin Press, 1991), 298–317, esp. 305. Andrews, *To Tell a Free Story,* 76, 77. Sundquist, *To Wake the Nations,* 40–41, 43, 48.

8. Gray, *The Confessions of Nat Turner,* 305, 317, 303.

9. Thomas R. Dew, "Abolition of Negro Slavery," *American Quarterly Review* 12 (1832): 189–265; repr. in *The Ideology of Slavery: Proslavery Thought in the Antebellum South, 1830–1860,* ed. Drew Gilpin Faust (Baton Rouge: Louisiana State University Press, 1981), 23–77, esp. 77, 26, 68, 27, 67, 38, 57, 60, 65, 66. John Hamden Pleasants, *Richmond Whig* (September 3, 1831) repr. in *Nat Turner,* ed. Eric Foner (Englewood Cliffs, N.J. Prentice-Hall), 21. For a more thorough study of Thomas Dew's pro-slavery thought, see Dickson D. Bruce, Jr., *The Rhetoric of Conservatism: The Virginia Convention of 1829–1830 and the Conservative Tradition in the South* (San Marino, California: The Huntington Library, 1982), 179–188.

George Fredrickson notes that "open assertions of *permanent* inferiority [of Black people] were exceedingly rare" prior to the 1830s. After about 1830, though, following the rise of organized abolitionism in the North, the attempt by progressive Virginia legislators to propose the abolishing of slavery in the Old Dominion during the Virginia legislative debates in 1829–1830, and, especially, in the aftermath of the Nat Turner revolt, such open assertions flourish as did their inevitable counterpart—the "stereotype of the happy and contented bondsman." Winthrop Jordan also discovered that the "Sambo image of the slave simply was not reported . . . prior to the 1830's." George Fredrickson, *The Black Image in the White Mind: The Debate on Afro-American Character and Destiny, 1817–1914* (1971; Middletown, Conn.: Wesleyan University Press, 1987), 43, 52–53. Winthrop Jordan qtd. in Mina Davis Caulfield, "Slavery and the Origins of Black Culture: Elkins Revisited," in *Americans from Africa: Slavery and its Aftermath,* ed. Peter I. Rose (New York: Atherton Press, 1970), 171–193, esp. 186. Caulfield cites "personal

communication" for the Winthrop Jordan observation, and alludes to a paper he delivered
at the American Historical Association meetings in December 1964 (192, n. 45).

10. Dew, "Abolition of Negro Slavery," 25.

11. Robert Canzoneri and Page Stegner, "An Interview with William Styron," *Per/Se*
1 (Summer 1966): 37–44 repr. in *Conversations with William Styron*, ed. James L. W.
West III (Jackson: University Press of Mississippi, 1985), 66–79, esp. 67. C. Vann
Woodward and R.W.B. Lewis, "Slavery in the First Person: An Interview with William
Styron," *Yale Alumni Magazine* 31 (November 1967): 33–39, esp. 34.

12. James Jones and William Styron, "Two Writers Talk It Over," *Esquire* (July 1963):
57–59; repr. in *Conversations with William Styron*, 40–48, esp. 45. Canzoneri and Stegner,
"An Interview with William Styron," 70, 71. George Plimpton, "William Styron: A Shared
Ordeal," *The New York Times* (October 8, 1967): 2–3, 30–34, esp. 32. Woodward and
Lewis, "Slavery in the First Person," 36. Sokolov, "Into the Mind of Nat Turner," 67.
Woodward and Lewis, "Slavery in the First Person," 36. Canzoneri and Stegner, "An
Interview with William Styron," 70.

13. Douglas Barzelay and Robert Sussman, "William Styron on *The Confessions of
Nat Turner*: A *Yale Lit* Interview," *Yale Literary Magazine* 137 (Fall 1968): 24–35; repr.
in *Conversations with William Styron*, 93–108, esp. 100. Ben Forkner and Gilbert Schricke,
"An Interview with William Styron," *Southern Review* 10 (October 1974): 923–934 repr.
in *Conversations with William Styron*, 190–202, esp. 193, 192. Styron, "Afterword to the
Vintage Edition: Nat Turner Revisited," in Styron, *The Confessions of Nat Turner* (1967;
New York: Vintage International Edition, 1992), 341.

14. Styron, "Afterword to the Vintage Edition: Nat Turner Revisited," 443, 446. For
contemporary and near-contemporary reports of Nat Turner's wife, see *Richmond Constitutional Whig* (September 26, 1831); repr. in *The Southampton Slave Revolt of 1831*, 90–99,
esp. 92; Samuel Warner, *Authentic and Impartial Narrative of the Tragical Scene Which
Was Witnessed in Southampton County (Virginia) on Monday the 22nd of August Last*
(1831), repr. in *The Southampton Slave Revolt of 1831*, 281–300, esp. 296; Thomas
Wentworth Higginson, "Nat Turner's Insurrection," *The Atlantic Monthly* (August 1861):
173–187: repr. in Higginson, *Travellers and Outlaws: Episodes in American History*
(Boston, 1889), 276–326, esp. 280–281; and Henry Irving Tragle, "Styron and His
Sources," *Massachusetts Review 11* (Winter 1970): 135–153, esp. 145–146. For Turner's
reasons for hiding his wife's existence from Gray, see Anna Mary Wells, "An Exchange
on 'Nat Turner,' " *New York Review of Books* (November 7, 1968): 31. Cf. Daniel Panger,
*Ol' Prophet Nat* (Winston-Salem: John F. Blair Publishers, 1967), 58. For the information
on Styron's copy of Drewry's *The Southampton Insurrection*, see Arthur D. Casciato and
James L. W. West III, "William Styron and *The Southampton Insurrection*," *American
Literature* 52 (January 1981): 564–577, esp. 569 (n. 9).

15. Styron, "Afterword to the Vintage Edition: Nat Turner Revisited," 444. Canzoneri
and Stegner, "An Interview with William Styron," 68, 69, 75.

16. Warner, *Authentic and Impartial Narrative*, 287. Lerone Bennett, Jr., "Nat's Last
White Man," in *William Styron's Nat Turner*, 3–16, esp. 13–14. Gray, *Confessions of
Nat Turner*, 312, 313. Tragle, "An Approximate Chronology of the Southampton Slave
Revolt," in *The Southampton Slave Revolt of 1831*, xv-xviii.

17. Styron, *Confessions of Nat Turner*, 38, 39, 388, 389, 403–404.

18. Woodward and Lewis, "Slavery in the First Person," 37, 38.

19. Although the point I am making here about the confusion in Styron's reading
touches only peripherally on the subject, I would like to note that I am not denying that
in a society such as ours it is almost impossible to make firm distinctions between sexual

desire and violence. As Catherine MacKinnon has argued, it is necessary in a culture where sex is portrayed in violent imagery and violence is eroticized to make the point that "there is much violence in intercourse, as a usual matter." I also take Sharon Marcus's point about the "gendered grammar of violence" in the United States, and find extremely useful her distinction between "sexualized violence" and "subject-subject violence." See Catherine A. MacKinnon, "Sex and Violence: A Perspective," in *Feminism Unmodified: Discourses on Life and Law* (Cambridge: Harvard University Press, 1987), 85–92, esp. 88; and Sharon Marcus, "Fighting Bodies, Fighting Words: A Theory and Politics of Rape Prevention," in *Feminists Theorize the Political*, ed. Judith Butler and Joan W. Scott (New York: Routledge, 1992), 385–403, esp. 392, 396.

20. Styron, *Confessions of Nat Turner*, xi, xv, xviii, 34, 35, 393.

21. Ibid., 37, 172, 247, 252, 392, 394.

22. Ibid., 29, 33–34, 36–37.

23. Ibid., 83–84, 84, 85, 88.

24. Canzoneri and Stegner, "An Interview with William Styron," 69. Woodward and Lewis, "Slavery in the First Person," 38. Plimpton, "William Styron: A Shared Ordeal," 32.

25. Bennett, "Nat's Last White Man," 8. Stanley Elkins, *Slavery: A Problem in American Institutional and Intellectual Life* (1959; 3rd. ed. Chicago: University of Chicago Press, 1976) Daniel Patrick Moynihan, *The Negro Family: The Case for National Action* (Washington: Office of Policy Planning and Research, 1965).

26. Bennett, "Nat's Last White Man," 9, 11. Styron, *Confessions of Nat Turner*, 29, 31. Gray, *The Confessions of Nat Turner*, 306. Styron, *Confessions of Nat Turner*, 31. Harding, "You've Taken My Nat and Gone," in *William Styron's Nat Turner*, 21–33, esp. 26, 29. Cf. Mike Thelwell, "Back With the Wind: Mr. Styron and the Reverend Turner," in *William Styron's Nat Turner*, 79–91, esp. 82–83. George Core, *"The Confessions of Nat Turner* and the Burden of the Past," in *The Achievement of William Styron*, ed. Robert K. Morris and Irving Malin (1975; rev. ed. Athens: University of Georgia Press, 1981), 206–222, esp. 218.

27. Styron, "Overcome," *New York Review of Books* (September 26, 1963): 18–19. Styron, *Confessions of Nat Turner*, 100, 391.

28. Bennett, "Nat's Last White Man," 7. Styron, *Confessions of Nat Turner*, 55, 57, 58, 363.

29. Ernest Kaiser, "The Failure of William Styron," in *William Styron's Nat Turner*, 50–65, esp. 56, 57. Thelwell, "Back With the Wind," 87. Bennett, "Nat's Last White Man," 7.

30. Bennett, "Nat's Last White Man," 16. Charles V. Hamilton, "Our Nat Turner and William Styron's Creation," in *William Styron's Nat Turner*, 73–78, esp. 74, 78. John Henrik Clarke, "Introduction," in *William Styron's Nat Turner*, vii-x, esp. p. x. Thelwell, "Back With the Wind: Mr. Styron and the Reverend Turner," 91. Cf. Killens, "The Confessions of Willie Styron," 44. Gray, *The Confessions of Nat Turner*, in *William Styrons's Nat Turner*, 93–118.

31. Genovese, "William Styron Before the People's Court," 203. James H. Cone, *Black Theology and Black Power* (1969; San Francisco: HarperSanFrancisco, 1989), p. 131.

32. Stephen B. Oates, "Children of Darkness," *American Heritage* 24 (October 1973): 42–47, 89–91.

33. William Styron's letter in "Postscripts to History," *American Heritage* 25 (February 1974): 101. Styron, "Introduction," in *This Quiet Dust and Other Writings* (1982; New York: Vintage International, 1993), 6–7.

34. Foner, ed., *Nat Turner*, 141–151, 158–166, 172–174. Tragle, ed., *The Southampton Slave Revolt of 1831*, 12–13. F. Roy Johnson, *The Nat Turner Story: History of the South's Most Important Slave Revolt, With New Material Provided by Black Tradition and White Tradition* (Murfreesboro, N.C.: Johnson, 1970), 179–213, esp. 179–180. Oates, *The Fires of Jubilee: Nat Turner's Fierce Rebellion* (1975; New York: Harper & Row, 1990), 147–154.

35. Vincent Harding, "You've Taken My Nat and Gone," 29. Genovese, "William Styron Before the People's Court," 202. Harding, "An Exchange on Nat Turner," 35–37.

36. Ralph Ellison, William Styron, Robert Penn Warren, and C. Vann Woodward, "The Uses of History in Fiction," *Southern Literary Journal* 1 (Spring 1969): 57–90 repr. in *Conversations with William Styron*, 114–144, esp. 127. Ellison, "Hidden Name and Complex Fate: A Writer's Experience in the United States," in *Shadow and Act* (New York: Random House, 1964), 144–166, esp. 148.

37. Thelwell, in "An Exchange on Nat Turner," 34. Thelwell, "Back with the Wind: Mr. Styron and the Reverend Turner," 87, 87 (n. 2).

38. Eliot Fremont-Smith, " 'A Sword Is Sharpened,' " *New York Times* (October 3, 1967): 45. Fremont-Smith, " 'The Confessions of Nat Turner'—II," *New York Times* (October 4, 1967): 45. Duberman, "[Review of William Styron's *The Confessions of Nat Turner*]," *The Village Voice* (December 14, 1967); repr. in Duberman, *The Uncompleted Past*, 207–215, esp. 214–215.

39. Fremont-Smith, "Nat Turner I: The Controversy," *New York Times* (August 1, 1968): 29. Fremont-Smith, "Nat Turner II: What Myth Will Serve?," *New York Times* (August 2, 1968): 31. Duberman, "[Review of Clarke's *William Styron's Nat Turner: Ten Black Writers Respond*]," 220, 203, 221, 203.

40. I discuss Genovese's thinking about the use of slave testimony from 1966 to 1970 elsewhere; see *NeoSlave Narratives*, ch. 4. For his 1966 position, see Genovese, "The Legacy of Slavery and the Roots of Black Nationalism," *Studies on the Left* 6 (November-December 1966): 3–65, which contains the responses by Aptheker, Kofsky, and Woodward, and Genovese's rejoinder. For his 1970 position, see Genovese, "American Slaves and their History," *New York Review of Books* (December 3, 1970): 34–43; and Genovese, "The Influence of the Black Power Movement on Historical Scholarship," *Daeaalus* 1 (Spring 1970): 473–494. Cf. August Meier and Elliott Rudwick, *Black History and the Historical Profession, 1915–1980* (Urbana: University of Illinois Press, 1985), 260–262.

41. Toni Morrison, "Rootedness: The Ancestor as Foundation," in *Black Women Writers (1950–1980): A Critical Evaluation*, ed. Mari Evans (New York: Doubleday, 1984), 339–345, esp. 340. Sherley Anne Williams, "The Lion's History: The Ghetto Writes B[l]ack," *Soundings* 76 (Summer/Fall 1993): 245–259, esp. 248.

42. Robert A. Gross, "The Black Novelists: 'Our Turn,' " *Newsweek* (June 16, 1969): 94–98. Nathan Irvin Huggins, *Afro-American Studies: A Report to the Ford Foundation* (New York: Ford Foundation, 1985).

43. Ernest J. Gaines, *The Autobiography of Miss Jane Pittman* (1971; New York: Bantam Books, 1972), vi. Gaines, "Miss Jane and I," *Callaloo* (May 1978): 23–38, esp. 37–38.

44. Murray, *The Omni-Americans: Some Alternatives to the Folklore of White Supremacy* (New York: Da Capo, 1970), 7.

JEFFREY STEELE

# The Politics of Mourning:
# Cultural Grief-Work from
# Frederick Douglass to Fanny Fern

In the mid-nineteenth century, the figure of the mourner carried powerful cultural resonances. Familiar icons of mourning art channelled grief into recognizable and controllable patterns, defining it as one of the most "natural" human feelings. Representations of mourners draped over coffins or tombs appealed to people who needed reassuring postures in an age of high mortality rates. The domestication of mourning—in new "garden" cemeteries, ritualized patterns of dress, and popular narratives—gave a comfortable structure to encounters with death. This process is particularly evident in the imagery associated with the female mourner, who was transformed into a powerful cultural emblem.[1] In numerous finishing schools, girls were taught how to compose mourning pictures and samplers–training that imprinted on them the image of the female mourner as the natural signifier of grief. One widespread emblem was modeled upon an engraving by James Akin and William Farrison, Jr., entitled "America Lamenting Her Loss at the Tomb of General Washington." Beneath a weeping willow, a grieving woman leans against a pyramid emblazoned with the bust of Washington.[2] Both the drapery and posture of the female mourner suggest grief but also total submission to an absent (yet omnipresent) male authority. Such images remind us that mourning represented a major transition in most adult women's lives, since widows—who often lost their primary means of financial support—were ecomically vulnerable.

In many ways, the mourner is an ideal figure for a writer bent on expressing his or her sense of personal damage and loss. Mimicking a culturally sanctioned role, it can be used to blur the distinction between grief occasioned by specific deaths and a more general sense of pain motivated by the awareness of being oppressed. Through images of mourning, women writers could parody everyday postures of grief, seeming to promise a continuing subservience at the same time they indicated specific areas of oppression and discontent. According to Lauren Berlant, such a literary position, manifested in "modes of containment," was typical of nineteenth-century women's writing. Disguising social critique beneath a mask of "sentimentality," numerous women writers used apparently artless representations of "feminine" feeling to express "complaint" and "injury."[3]

One of the most familiar, and yet functional, images of female feeling was that of mourning. Traditionally, Juliana Schiesari argues, men have had greater access than women to the public representation of loss—most notably through the "*discourse* of melancholia." But while men have been provided with "the most privileged access to the display of loss," the representation of female suffering has been constrained to the extent that the idea of the *female* "melancholic" has been largely unthinkable.[4] At issue is the construction of a language enabling women to represent their sense of loss and disempowerment. Significantly, Schiesari finds such a language in the discourse of female mourning; "women," she argues, "have . . . characteristically represented their losses through a language that approximates a mourning for their . . . devalued status"; such a language, she continues, can easily expand into a consideration of "the structured denial of privilege for all women within patriarchal societies."[5] As we shall see, many nineteenth-century women writers used representations of mourning to express the awareness of loss within a culture that inhibited the full expression of their being.

Because of the racial politics of the time, the sentimentalized image of feeling had a somewhat different valence in African-American writing. In the nineteenth century, white readers found it difficult to connect with the full range of black experience. As Harriet Jacobs discovered, white women could not easily identify with "the figure of the sexually exploited female slave" (one of the stock images of abolitionist rhetoric). Such images of "sexual vulnerability" threatened their own privileged status as sexually pure "true women."[6] But if white readers could not connect with the image of the sexually violated black woman (or the brutalized black man, for that matter), they could read themselves into portraits of black mourning. In contrast to figures of sexual violence, sentimentalized images of mourning bridged racial and cultural differences, providing a direct link to the reader's heart. In the words of Shirley Samuels, sentimental constructs elicited patterns of "affect and identification" that made "connections across gender, race, and class boundaries."[7] As we shall see, both Frederick Douglass and Harriet Jacobs communicated most directly through sentimentalized portraits of themselves as mourners whose sense of loss appealed directly to their white readers' hearts.

Such communication becomes even more important when one considers the limitations placed upon female and black expression. In the nineteenth century, white men were granted a wide repertoire of expressive possibilities. But—in the case of women and African Americans—the expression of unauthorized depths of feeling threatened to violate conventional categories of being. As a result, only controlled representations of mourning by members of these groups were reassuring for white, middle-class men who prided themselves on their differentiation from such "excesses" of feeling. But such postures maintained their ideological value only so long as designated mourners adhered to familiar roles. Any open expression of unhappiness or discontent threatened to topple a cultural economy based upon the presence of subservient individuals, whose tears were contained within specific ideological frames that limited grief to "proper" occasions. Representations of unrestrained grief might blur such boundaries, washing into areas of subjectivity set aside as white male preserves.

Women writers, for example, worked within clearly delineated emotional boundaries that prohibited open complaint. We see this in Fanny Fern's 1852 newspaper article "The Tear of a Wife," which presents an ironic meditation on the dictum that "the tear of a loving girl is like a dew-drop on a rose; but on the cheek of a wife, is a drop of poison to her husband." "Matrimonial tears," Fern sardonically observes, " 'are poison.' "

> There is no knowing what you will do, girls, with that escape-valve shut off; but that is no more to the point, than—whether you have anything to smile at or not; one thing is settled—*you mustn't cry!* Never mind back aches, and side aches, and head aches, and dropsical complaints, and smoky chimneys, and old coats, and young babies! *Smile! It flatters your husband.* He wants to be *considered* the source of your happiness.[8]

While numerous nineteenth-century women did manage to express their grievances in their lives and texts, Fern's column is useful as an index of the emotional boundary that defined the permissible limit to female complaint. Tinging this boundary through dialogic intervention, Fern enables her readers to see the cultural limits constraining mournful female expression. At the same time, she politicizes women's mourning by suggesting that its causes are found in the inequitably gendered distribution of labor.

Just as female complaints disturbed the authority of husbands, black complaints were often perceived as threatening by white male readers. This emotional boundary is readily apparent in the two prefatory letters, written by the white male abolitionists William Lloyd Garrison and Wendell Phillips, that introduce the *Narrative of the Life of Frederick Douglass.* According to Phillips, a slave narrator such as Douglass was not expected (or, presumably, allowed) to make "wholesale complaints" that might detract from the "truth, candor, and sincerity" of his account. In a similar vein, Garrison defends the truth-value of Douglass's narrative by insisting that "nothing has been set down in malice, nothing exaggerated, nothing drawn from the imagination"—forms of emotional contamination that would hinder Garrison from considering Douglass's representation of his life as a "fair specimen" and a "case."[9] Expressions of uncontrolled subjectivity violated the narrative (and social) contract between slave narrator and white reader, by bringing into the text areas of unverifiable subjectivity. According to William Andrews, the white abolitionists believed that "the imagination was the wellspring of fabrications and exaggerations, and hence not to be acknowledged as part of the slave narrator's intellectual resources."[10] It is troubling to realize that a literary genre putatively devoted to the cause of emancipation depended in part upon culturally circumscribed standards of African-American literary expression. As Douglass later complained in *My Bondage and My Freedom,* his white sponsors wanted nothing but "the facts"—the "objective" description of the fugitive slave's history without any distortion.[11]

Given such restrictions, elegiac narrative modes ideally suited nineteenth-century women and African-American writers; for these literary forms are politicized from the beginning. Designed to convey a sense of loss, representations of mourning lend themselves to the expression of the anger, grievance, and dislocation that are part of each person's experience. The capacity to mourn is essential to the maturing of the self, since each person is faced with inevitable frustrations and must learn to accept absence and loss as part of the structure of his or her being.[12] From this perspective, it should not surprise us to find that many narratives of human development are tinged with elegiac (even tragic) tones, as they represent the various boundaries between infantile fantasies of omnipotence and existence in a world where all human agency is eventually limited. Such representations of limitation become even more powerful in the narratives produced by groups that have experienced a history of oppression. In a sense, members of oppressed groups find the work of mourning compounded by an original *ontological liability*: the definition of their persons as lacking the full range of agency or power available to other more privileged members of their culture. Socialized within preexisting structures of oppression, these persons must learn to grieve for the losses structured into their being, as they come to terms with the dominant culture's sense of outrage at their "very existence."[13]

Unless the victims of oppression can effectively mourn, they run the risk of remaining in positions of paralysis and silence. A paradigmatic expression of this danger is found in a twentieth-century text: Richard Wright's harrowing autobiography, *Black Boy*. After the murder of his Uncle Hoskins by whites jealous of his lucrative business, Wright and his family find their mourning blocked: "There was no period of mourning. There were no flowers. There were only *silence*, quiet weeping, whispers, and fear" (my italics). The calculated act of racial terrorism, designed to control the black populace, has its intended effect. In the face of "men who could violate my life at will," the young Wright (like the other members of his community) experiences an agonizing tension that paralyzes him, so that all he can feel is "blank and void within."[14] Later, when Wright's mother suffers a paralytic stroke, her infirmity becomes for him a profound symbol of the paralyzing silence that has been structured into his being by a racist society.

But at the moment when Wright sees the symbolism of his mother's paralysis, he is filled with the determination "to wring a meaning out of meaningless suffering."[15] In the words of Ralph Ellison, he creates a literary equivalent to the blues, displaying "the impulse to keep the painful details and episodes of a brutal experience alive in one's aching consciousness, to finger its jagged grain, and to transcend it."[16] Refusing to be terrorized into silence, Wright mourns the theft of his and his community's being. Around him, he sees African Americans who have succumbed to the terror of "the white death" that has induced in them a "paralysis of will and impulse." Not allowed to "act straight and human," they are "baffled" by a set of barriers that have altered the current of their lives.[17] Documenting the psychological and social effects of such oppression, Wright forces us to examine the human expense of such social structures. He compels the reader to share with him the liberating work of mourning the ontological loss structured into the lives of the oppressed.

We find similar patterns in the works of many nineteenth-century writers who encouraged the victims of oppression to recognize the political implications of their pain. An essential step in this process was the recognition of the damage of disabling subject-positions based upon the assumption of white male supremacy. Significantly, both Frederick Douglass and Margaret Fuller defined this posture of abjection as a form of "idolatry." One of the most insidious aspects of bondage, Douglass discovered, was the slaves' "reverence" for their distant "godlike" masters. Many of those around him were "trained from the cradle up, to think and feel that their masters are superior, and invested with a sort of sacredness." Even in the North, he confessed in *My Bondage and My Freedom*, he found it difficult to escape this internalized oppression, as he labored to free himself from the tendency to be a "hero worshipper," entranced by the spectacle of white male power.[18]

Margaret Fuller struggled against a similar pressure, as she measured the personal expense of idolatry. "I wish woman to live, *first* for God's sake," she observed near the end of *Woman in the Nineteenth Century*. "Then she will not make an imperfect man her god, and thus sink to idolatry."[19] Fuller's critique of female idolatry identified the culturally induced passivity of women as the occasion for a grief that must be mourned. For she saw that the incorporation of male idols within the female self created areas of damage. As a result, the goal of many of her texts was to define and begin to mourn the personal expense of such idolatry. Women, she laments in *Woman in the Nineteenth Century*, "are so overloaded with precepts by guardians . . . that their minds are impeded by doubts till they lose their chance of fair, free proportions." Later, she observes that the great women of the past "had much to mourn, and their great impulses did not find due scope."[20]

Luce Irigaray's critique of Freud's psychoanalytic theories helps to clarify the connection between such idolatry and mourning. Commenting upon Freud's theory of female "castration" (an analogue to what I have termed "ontological liability"), Irigaray suggests that masculinist constructions of the female self motivate a profound but unlocalized melancholy for women, who are taught that their bodies and psyches manifest a fundamental lack. As a result of such indoctrination, Irigaray argues, a woman's "ego suffers, helplessly, a defeat, a wound, whose effects are to be made out in the broad outlines of melancholia." Having been "castrated" by an ideology that misconstrues her being, she has structured within her psyche an undefinable loss.[21] Mutilated by the ideological context that gives her the very language of selfhood, the oppressed female subject is unable to mourn her status as a wounded woman.

As we know from writers such as Toni Morrison, a similar psychological dynamic operates for African Americans who have been taught to identify with white images of power and beauty. In *The Bluest Eye*, for example, a young African-American girl, Pecola, is alienated by the recognition that "all the world had agreed that a blue-eyed, yellow-haired, pink-skinned doll was what every girl child treasured."[22] In order to escape such alienation—to return to Fuller's and Douglass's terminology—nineteenth-century women and African Americans needed to recognize the frozen postures of idolatry that had encoded within them a vocabulary of lack. They had to bridge the gap between their sense of pain and their internalized images of an unapproachable power. As we shall see, the process of healing such a wound necessitates a "work of mourning" that reveals the extent to which the abject subject has incorporated within a phantom that is capable of controlling his or her life.[23]

Many early African-American texts focus the phantom of white racial oppression through pivotal acts of mourning. Early in Pauline Hopkins's serial novel *Hagar's Daughter* (1901-1902), there occurs a striking and familiar scene. Having gained control of the Enson estate after the disappearance of his brother Ellis, the novel's villain—St. Clair Enson—sells off most of his family's slaves. "On the morning of departure," we read,

> the small colony of black men and women sat and stood about the familiar grounds stunned and hopeless. Here most of them were born, and here they had hoped to die and be buried. The unknown future was a gulf of despair. Ellis was a good master, kind and considerate; *their sincere mourning for him was mingled with grief at their fate* [my italics].
> In the midst of a motley group Hagar stood with her child clasped in her arms,—hopeless, despairing.[24]

Reminiscent of similar scenes in nineteenth-century slave narratives, this moment conflates a specific act of mourning (at the supposed death of Ellis Enson) with a more generalized grief, which is motivated by the slaves' recognition of their own degraded and hopeless condition.

About to be sold, the slaves are unable to resolve their grief for either their missing master or their uncertain fate. But the observers of this scene (Hopkins's narrator and readers) understand the connection between the slaves' grief and their oppression; *they* can engage in a more general mourning that is unavailable to Hopkins's characters, whose lives seem trapped within an unending cycle of loss. As a result, this passage moves beyond the losses experienced by specific persons to a consideration of the unequal conditions of being that occasioned their original grief. Showing her readers the ways in which personal pain is grounded in external social conditions, Pauline Hopkins articulates the *politics* of mourning.

In the *Narrative of the Life of Frederick Douglass* (1845), we find a similar dynamic. Reconstructing his response to the sorrow songs of the slaves, Douglass recalls how he was struck with the "first glimmering conception of the dehumanizing character of slavery." After he learned to read, he became able to understand and interpret the lament found at the heart of slaves' lives. But at first, he did not understand the "deep meaning" of their mournful songs:

> I was myself within the circle; so that I neither saw nor heard as those without might see and hear. They told a tale of woe which was then altogether beyond my feeble comprehension; they were tones loud, long, and deep; they breathed the prayer and complaint of souls boiling over with the bitterest anguish.[25]

Within "the circle," Douglass had not yet learned how to transform lament into mourning. Each day, we can imagine, he heard the same bitter tones of "complaint" and "anguish," as he confronted the repetition of an interminable pain that found a partial outlet but no relief.

But, as Douglass recreated such moments in his autobiography, such pain was transfigured into a focused mourning. "Those songs still follow me," he asserts,

> to deepen my hatred of slavery, and quicken my sympathies for my brethren in bonds. If any one wishes to be impressed with the effects of slavery, let him go to Colonel Lloyd's plantation, and, on allowance day, place himself in the deep pine woods, and there let him, in silence, analyze the sounds that shall pass through the chambers of his soul,—and if he is not thus impressed, it will only be because "there is no flesh in his obdurate heart."[26]

In this passage, Douglass moves from a representation of the slaves' grief to a definition of his own mourning. Modeling the reader's response, he measures moral capacity in terms of the ability to feel and mourn the slaves' pain and suffering.

Evoking the deep tone of lament in the slaves' songs, Douglass articulates the *personal* expense of slavery. Through an act of identification with such anguish, his readers begin to *feel* the agony of bondage. The necessary resolution of this mourning process, this passage implies, must be the elimination of the oppressive conditions that occasioned the original grief. The antithesis of such a feeling response is the display of what Douglass calls a "heart . . . harder than stone," a detachment allowing one to view the sufferings of others while remaining "unmoved."[27] Throughout the *Narrative*, Douglass self-consciously characterizes his own position as mourner in opposition to such hard-hearted detachment. In moments such as the famous soliloquy on the banks of the Chesapeake ("O why was I born a man, of whom to make a brute!"), he shows his readers both "what the incident signified" and "how to *feel* about it"—an important step in the liberation of the African-American autobiographer.[28] As we identify with his sorrow, Douglass's lament for his degraded condition as a slave both mobilizes our sympathy and demands our political response.

A similar dynamic of mourning is found in scenes that express Douglass's grief for others. Perhaps the most vivid example is his extended lament for his grandmother, who was turned out to die because of her advanced age:

> She stands—she sits—she staggers—she falls—she groans—she dies—and there are none of her children or grandchildren present, to wipe from her wrinkled brow the cold sweat of death, or to place beneath the sod her fallen remains. Will not a righteous God visit for these things?[29]

Here, the expression of grief elides into an open indictment of the slave system that allowed such suffering. As the *vehicle* of insight, this scene of mourning engages readers' feelings at the same time that it redirects them to a larger source: we attend not only the death of a single woman but the suffering of countless slaves who have experienced similar brutality. Douglass's reference to God's judgment against such cruelty makes explicit the political link that is often expressed in his writing through scenes of mourning: it highlights the *politics of mourning*.

One of Douglass's most aggressive and outspoken assertions of such political engagement occurs in his famous oration, "What to the Slave is the Fourth of July?" Contrasting the patriotic celebrations of the northern white community with the despair of those still in bondage in 1852, Douglass contentiously asserts, "This Fourth of July is *yours*, not *mine*. *You* may rejoice, *I* must mourn." In this powerful address, he strives to wake his auditors to the unheard and unseen suffering of those still in captivity, by challenging them to share his mourning: "Fellow-citizens, above your national, tumultuous joy, I hear the *mournful wail* of millions, whose chains, heavy and grievous yesterday, are to-day rendered more intolerable by the jubilant shouts that reach them." As Douglass knows full well, his auditors will only realize the "scorching irony" of celebrating freedom in a slave-holding nation if they can respond to that "mournful wail" and learn to grieve for those still imprisoned within slavery.[30]

Other African-American writers, as well, understood that the representation of mourning could effectively wake their readers to a sense of unjust suffering. Two-thirds of the way through Harriet Jacobs's *Incidents in the Life of a Slave Girl* (1861), for example, there occurs a vivid chapter that focuses many of that work's central themes through the lens of mourning. As an apparent digression, Jacobs tells the story of "Aunt Nancy," a woman who was prevented by her arduous duty as servant and nurse for Mrs. Flint's children from bringing any of her own pregnancies successfully to term. Giving birth to six premature infants, her health "ruined by years of incessant, unrequited toil, and broken rest," Nancy has died. Ostensibly occasioned by the death of a mistreated relative, this chapter—an extended elegy—quickly becomes a lament for all the black women injured by the institution of slavery. In this regard, Nancy's failure to become a mother seems symbolic of one of the harshest aspects of slavery—its threat to maternity and the mother-child bond. Portraying herself as a suffering mother whose maternal instincts connect with those of her northern female readers, Jacobs demands that slavery's destruction of motherhood should be the occasion for a politicized grief. Standing at Aunt Nancy's grave, we need to see how she (following countless others) was destroyed by the "patriarchal institution" of slavery.[31]

In a brilliant maneuvering of the reader's attention, Jacobs—at the end of this chapter—positions herself, as well, as an object to be mourned. Over the previous seven chapters, she has detailed her sufferings while hiding from Dr. Flint in her grandmother's attic. Not the least of these sufferings was her anguish as a mother separated from her children, whose sufferings she could not directly relieve. One day, for example, her son Ben was bitten by a vicious dog and she could not care for him. "O, what torture to a mother's heart," Jacobs exclaims, "to listen to this and be unable to go to him"[32] Within this context, the following passage—at the end of the "Aunt Nancy" chapter—carries a powerful resonance: "We could also have told them of a poor, blighted young creature, shut up in a *living grave* for years, to avoid the tortures that would be inflicted on her, if she ventured to come out and look on the face of her departed friend" (my italics).[33] By portraying her seclusion for seven years in her grandmother's attic as a "living grave," Jacobs invites us to stand over the "tomb" of her life and mourn the losses she has experienced. Positioning herself as an object for our grief and sympathy, she compels her readers to identify with her suffering and to analyze its causes.

Jacobs's discussion of her anguish as a mother isolated from her children connects with the theme of maternity in the "Aunt Nancy" chapter. Throughout *Incidents*, one encounters other unforgettable portraits of slave women separated from their children. Jacobs recreates the anguish of a mother on auction day: "I saw a mother lead seven children to the auction block. She knew that *some* of them would be taken from her; but they took *all*." Elsewhere she depicts the outcry in church of a woman who had lost everything: "They've got all of my children. Last week they took the last one. God knows where they have sold her." She shows us a slave-mother of a light-skinned child, who passes by, muttering, "It's his own, and he can kill it if he will."[34] Each of these scenes demands that Jacobs's white, northern readers share her mourning for the losses experienced by slave mothers.

This pattern of shared mourning is especially important given the chasm that threatens to separate Jacobs from her white readers. As Hazel Carby has argued, perhaps the most difficult realization for northern female readers was a sense of their own cultural privilege as sheltered "true women" living in a world of clearly mapped moral values. This distance is perceivable in the famous tenth chapter of *Incidents*, where Jacobs laboriously justifies her decision to escape from the constant sexual harassment of Dr. Flint by sleeping with another white slave owner—an act that asserted her sexual agency. As Jacobs knows well, such sexual expression is unthinkable for a "true woman," who was valued for her subservience and chastity. Unable to share the comforts of "home" or the protection of male chivalry, Jacobs was forced "to reconstruct the meaning of her own life as woman and mother."[35] Part of this reconstruction was her attempt to convince her readers that "the slave woman ought not to be judged by the same standard as others," because "the condition of a slave confuses all principles of morality, and, in fact, renders the practice of them impossible."[36]

Adding to Jacobs's difficulties is the "implication" of her white readers in "the oppression of black women." "The barriers to the establishment of the bonding of sisterhood," Carby continues,

> were built in the space between the different economic, political, and social positions that black women and white women occupied in the social formation of slavery. . . . The ideology of true womanhood was as racialized a concept in relation to white women as it was in its exclusion of black womanhood. Ultimately, it was this racial factor that defined the source of power of white women over their slaves, for, in a position of dependence on the patriarchal system herself, the white mistress identified her interests with the maintenance of the status quo.[37]

This deep chasm could only be bridged if Jacobs's readers could be motivated to shift their identification from the white slave mistress, nominally a representative of "true womanhood," to the injured slave. As Carby points out, this process is partially facilitated by Jacobs's portrait of her caring grandmother, who is more of a "true woman" than any of the white characters in the South.

But in an equally important way, the reader's bond with Jacobs is motivated by the contrast she draws between white female characters placed at the beginning and at the end of her account. Her portrait of the stony-hearted Mrs. Flint (which occurs in the second chapter) stands in marked contrast to the image of the caring Mrs. Bruce found near the end. So mean that she would spit in the cooking pots so that the house servants could not eat from them, Mrs. Flint can see no further than her own sense of injury. She does not perceive the slave women in her household as objects of sympathy, or even pity, but rather as sexual threats. Infuriated by the knowledge that her husband has slept with numerous slave women on their plantation, Mrs. Flint is trapped within her own sense of sexual outrage. In a significant way, the portrait of Mrs. Flint undermines, in advance, the conservative set of sexual values that Jacobs challenges in chapter ten. Contained within the role of "injured wife," Mrs. Flint plays a narrow part in a moralistic narrative that is discredited from the beginning. Her failing is her incapacity to see beyond her own sense of hurt to the injury that the young Jacobs is experiencing as the object of Dr. Flint's unwanted sexual attentions. Mrs. Flint, we might say, can grieve for no one but herself.

As an antidote to such moral blindness, we encounter (near the end of Jacobs's narrative) the kindly Mrs. Bruce, a woman who is capable of attending to Jacobs's suffering. The response of Mrs. Bruce to Jacobs's sorrows seems paradigmatic of the role that Jacobs hopes her readers will play:

> But the *sadness of my face attracted her attention*, and, in answer to her kind inquiries, I poured out my full heart to her, before bed time. She listened with true womanly sympathy, and told me she would do all she could to protect me [my italics].[38]

In this scene, the representation of suffering (the "sadness" written on Linda's face) attracts "attention," soliciting a sympathetic response and a shared mourning. Recognizing the *difference* between her own sheltered experience and the horrors experienced by the black woman facing her, a white woman responds to her "sister's" grief.

Rather than exploiting the racial privilege of white, middle-class true womanhood, Mrs. Bruce moves beyond the sheltered circle of her home through an action—the harboring of a fugitive slave—that has the potential to revise the nineteenth-century ideology of separate spheres. Following the trajectory of those early female reformers who moved outside the home to care for the oppressed and injured members of society, Mrs. Bruce manifests a political sympathy that is grounded in her capacity to feel Jacobs's pain.[39] Mrs. Bruce's feeling response corresponds with what Jacobs, in her preface, calls a "realizing sense": "But I do earnestly desire to arouse the women of the North to a *realizing sense* of the condition of two millions of women at the South, still in bondage, suffering what I suffered, and most of them far worse."[40] The first step in making this connection, we have seen, is the depiction of herself and other slave women as suffering victims for whom her readers grieve. Without such mourning, Jacobs knows, their suffering will not be "realized"; it will remain an empty husk that lacks emotional content. Unless Jacobs's readers feel and share the pain of slave women, they will have nothing arousing them to action.

We find a similar model of sympathetic mourning in one of the earliest African-American novels—Harriet Wilson's *Our Nig* (1859). In a key passage, James Bellmont discusses with his aunt the vicious abuse of their black servant Frado by Belmont's mother and sister:

> I have seen Frado's grief, because she is black, amount to agony. It makes me sick to recall these scenes. Mother pretends to think she don't know enough to sorrow for anything; but if she could see her as I have, when she supposed herself entirely alone, except her little dog Fido, lamenting her loneliness and complexion, I think, if she is not past feeling, she would retract.[41]

Occurring in a novel that bears strong echoes of the slave narrative, this passage underscores an important dimension of the scenes of mourning also found in Douglass and Jacobs. The capacity to mourn is a *human* faculty, revealing a depth of subjectivity that contradicts any racist construction of African Americans as beings that lack feeling. Although Mrs. Flint views her as an unfeeling beast of burden, with no more "feeling for her children" than "a cow has for its calf," Harriet Jacobs shows her readers that her "mother's heart" bleeds.[42] Similarly, in *Our Nig*, Frado's lament refutes the position of James's mother (Mrs. Bellmont), who doesn't believe that Frado is capable of sorrow.

As an antidote to such views, the representation of Frado's lament has an important political function. "Oh, oh! . . . why was I made? why can't I die? Oh, what have I to live for?" Frado's lament recalls Frederick Douglass's famous cry of despair in his *Narrative*: "O God, save me! Oh God, deliver me! Let me be free! Is there any God! Why am I a slave?"[43] Both passages, we might say, construct "scenes of subjectivity" that provide their respective speakers with a humanizing representation of feeling. No white nineteenth-century reader could come away from either passage believing that black Americans lacked feeling. In the scene quoted above from *Our Nig*, James prefaces his depiction of Frado's grief with the exclamation: "But to think how prejudiced the world are towards her people!" Within this context, the representation of African-American grief has a pointed political function. Not only does it counteract one such prejudice by revealing a "human" feeling; it also suggests that such feeling has a tangible cause. To put it another way, it motivates black grief by showing its roots in an oppressive society.

Many similar issues are present in writing of white women writers at mid-century. Operating in nineteenth-century American culture was "a conventionalized iconography and stylized hagiography of dying women and children." In some quarters, the ideal of feminine beauty was "the tubercular look, which symbolized an appealing vulnerability, a superior sensitivity."[44] It comes as no surprise, then, that the pages of women's novels—during this era—were filled

with memorable deathbed scenes. Two of the most famous are the death of Little
Eva in Harriet Beecher Stowe's *Uncle Tom's Cabin* (1851) and the death of Beth
March in Louisa May Alcott's *Little Women* (1868).

In the narrative logic of *Uncle Tom's Cabin*, the moving death of Little
Eva motivates the ensuing death of her father, Augustine St. Clare. Apparently
distracted by his grief, St. Clare recklessly intervenes in a drunken brawl and
receives a fatal stab wound. While the ostensible result of St. Clare's death is
his deathbed conversion to Christianity, the most immediate effect is the breakup
of his plantation and the sale of the now vulnerable slaves. At this point, Stowe
efficiently displaces the process of mourning from Little Eva and her father to
the victims of slave-holding society. "We hear often," the narrator observes, "of
the distress of the negro servants, on the loss of a kind master; and with good
reason, for no creature on God's earth is left more utterly unprotected and desolate
than the slave in these circumstances." From this moment to the climactic death
of Uncle Tom as a result of the abusive treatment of Simon Legree, Stowe rarely
loses sight of the political benefits of mourning suffering slaves. "O there'll be
mourning, at the judgement-seat of Christ!" a voice sings out on the Legree
plantation. Such mourning (and judgment) is encountered again as Tom surveys
the degraded condition of the field-hands he is forced to labor with, and his
"whole soul overflowed with compassion and sympathy for the poor wretches
by whom he was surrounded." Most clearly of all, George Shelby's anguished
outcry at the deathbed of Uncle Tom stands as a model of response for Stowe's
readers: "O, don't die! It'll kill me!—*it'll break my heart to think what you've
suffered*,—and lying in this old shed, here!" (my italics).[45]

In her "Concluding Remarks," Stowe urges her readers to feel the "heartbreak,"
the "anguish," and "despair" of the slaves still suffering in bondage. She calls
for the "mothers of America" to arouse themselves to focused political action.
Significantly, the vehicle for Stowe's appeal is the most familiar and ritualized
mourning scene of all:

> By the sick hour of your child; by those dying eyes, which you can never forget;
> by those last cries, that wrung your heart when you could neither help nor save; by
> the desolation of that empty cradle, that silent nursery–I beseech you, pity those
> mothers that are constantly made childless by the American slave-trade! And say,
> mothers of America, is this a thing to be defended, sympathized with, passed over
> in silence?[46]

Redirecting her reader's grief at the loss of a child onto a politicized analogue
(the equivalent loss experienced by the slave mother), Stowe finally bases the
impact of her novel upon the capacity to mourn.

Related patterns of mourning are found in Louisa May Alcott's writing. Rather
than using scenes of mourning to focus directly upon the sufferings of the
oppressed, Alcott uses the death of Beth to deepen and redirect her characterization
of Jo March. Occupying a climactic position in *Little Women*, Beth's death
symbolizes the end of childhood for Jo, as it instills a new consciousness in her.
Taught "by love and sorrow," Jo returns to her stories, giving to them a new

and more sober realism. Eventually, Jo's sorrowful encounter with Beth's "prison-house of pain" chastens her egotism and occasions a new maturity.[47] In subtle, but important ways, Alcott suggests that sorrow plays a central role in the formation of female character. While the death of Beth is the ostensible cause of Jo's mourning, Alcott's readers (especially her female readers) are faced with more complicated patterns of grief. Marmee's suppressed anger, Jo's sacrifice of her tomboyish enthusiasm (when she marries Professor Bhaer), Amy's sly indirections–all reflect the restraints of women trapped in a world in which the only acceptable role is to be a "little woman," who performs appropriately in front of the father's admiring gaze.[48]

If Alcott hints in *Little Women* that the constrained circumstances of women's lives might justify the reader's mourning, an earlier novel—*Behind a Mask* (1866)—makes explicit the connection between female suffering and mourning. One of Alcott's most vivid characters, the scheming governess Jean Muir, is clearly a woman who has experienced enormous suffering. Significantly, Alcott (like Harriet Jacobs just a few years earlier) places her readers on a difficult moral terrain. On the one hand, Alcott's readers can condemn the actions of Jean Muir, an opportunistic fortune-hunter, as immoral—but only at the risk of maintaining their investment in a hierarchical code of values that privileges the secure life-style of comfortable English aristocrats over the claims of economi-cally vulnerable women. On the other hand, her readers can identify with Jean Muir. But in order to do so, they must replace their moralistic condemnation of her actions with a mournful recognition of her claims as a wounded woman.

Jean Muir, one of the characters remarks, "understands wounds better than anyone else in the house."[49] These wounds are both literal (knife wounds) and figurative. The divorced wife of an actor, Jean Muir knows full well that the only route to success—in her society—is to impersonate the role of "little woman" and to gain economic security through marriage to a wealthy man. Jean Muir's dilemma is shared by many of Alcott's readers, who also must present a "charming picture of all that is most womanly and winning" without appearing to manipulate their position on the marriage market. "Marriage," as Charlotte Perkins Gilman later commented, is what woman "is exhibited for. It is, moreover, her means of honorable livelihood and advancement. *But*–she must not even look as if she wanted it!"[50] Given her position in such a society, it comes as no surprise that Jean Muir disguises herself in order to appear more marriageable and that, beneath the mask of beauty, one finds a "gloomy woman . . . brooding over some wrong, or loss, or disappointment which had darkened all her life."[51] "Worn out with weariness and mental pain," Jean Muir reveals in privacy a suffering which many of Alcott's readers could identify with and mourn.

Fanny Fern's novel *Ruth Hall* (1855) depicts a similar dynamics of mourning. Ruth's movement from the position of "true woman" to independent journalist is motivated by the death of her husband Harry. Confronting a harsh world in which even her own relatives and in-laws refuse any form of economic assistance, Ruth finally discovers that writing for the New York papers will enable her to support her two children. She becomes an overnight sensation, as reader after reader is struck by the vivid realism of her articles. Fern makes explicit the link between Ruth Hall's literary success and her grief. For example, the most perceptive of her friends (Mr. Walter) realizes that "a bitter life experience" provides much of their strengths, while Ruth herself observes that "no happy woman ever writes. From Harry's grave sprang 'Floy' [Ruth's literary persona]." In a manner similar to the patterns of sympathy found in the narratives of Frederick Douglass and Harriet Jacobs, Mr. Walter's caring response provides a model for Fern's readers. Corresponding with him, Ruth realizes that his empathy for her writing grows out of his own acquaintance with suffering: since he knows pain, "his heart . . . readily vibrates to the chord of sorrow" in her writing.[52]

In a number of ways, Ruth Hall provides a profound analysis of the links between female creativity and mourning. Ruth Hall's strength (and by extension, Fern's) is grounded in a pain first apprehended through the Christianized language of nineteenth-century sentimentality, with its vivid iconography of female grief.[53] As Ruth expands the scope of her action and gains strength, she continues to maintain her position as a "true woman" who is a capable mother and a pious individual. At the same time, the novel's narrator uses the "sentimental" responses of love, sympathy, and religious faith as moral touchstones that enable the reader to evaluate the ruthless (literally, Ruth-less, since the Biblical pun seems intended) behavior of most of the novel's other characters. In this regard, it is no accident that the novel's final scene displays a moment of "*true* friendship" (and resolved mourning) as Mr. Walter, Ruth, and Ruth's children stand above Harry's tombstone. Ruth Hall has achieved fame and financial security, but she maintains her ties to the "sentimental" world in which the expression of heartfelt feeling (such as the act of mourning) is the most important moral touchstone.

In this regard, *Ruth Hall* is a superb example of what Jane Tompkins has called "sentimental power"—an attempt to expand domestic values from the home to American society at large. Since it enabled women writers to connect directly with (and modify) the values of their readers, the language of sentimentality became a powerful vehicle for such social change. At the heart of this sentimental vision, Tompkins finds a "sacred drama of redemption" focused, for example, through the heroic death of Little Eva in *Uncle Tom's Cabin*—an event that powerfully affects the lives of those around her. But the missing link in Tompkins's argument is the connection between the "ethic of sacrifice" displayed by a character like Little Eva and the transfigured lives of those influenced by her; she glosses over the dynamics underlying the "pervasive cultural myth which invests the suffering and death of an innocent victim with . . . the power to work in, and change, the world."[54] One of the keys to this dissemination of sentimental power lies in *the representation of mourning*. An essential element in the popular fiction of Stowe, Alcott, and Fern is their positioning of central characters as mourners, whose grief extends beyond specific losses to a consideration of the cultural conditions that make mourning a fit emblem of the female condition. Significantly, analogous scenes—demonstrating what we might term the "political power of sentimental mourning"—are found in the works of African-American writers such as Douglass, Jacobs, and Wilson.

In the middle of the nineteenth century, both African-American and white women writers were deeply influenced by the rhetoric of sentimentality. Members of both groups, in the words of Margaret Fuller, had "much to mourn." When she began writing an autobiography, the twentieth-century writer bell hooks recalls, she "considered the possibility that I had become attached to the wounds and sorrows of my childhood, that I held them in a manner that blocked my efforts to be self-realized, whole, to be healed."[55] In the nineteenth century, familiar narratives of feeling offered a way out of this impasse. Images of mourning pervaded every aspect of popular culture. Touching their readers at the most intimate level of emotional response, scenes of mourning mobilized their feelings at the same time that they provided obvious focal points for sympathy. Most Americans were already familiar with such appeals from the sentimentalized languages of nineteenth-century Christianity. In the hands of Frederick Douglass, Harriet Jacobs, Harriet Beecher Stowe, Fanny Fern, and many others, such images provided the perfect vehicle for reform.

## Notes

1. According to Barton Levi St. Armand, "The image of the mourning maiden had archetypal resonances for the popular culture" of mid-nineteenth-century America. *Emily Dickinson and Her Culture: The Soul's Society* (New York: Cambridge University Press, 1984), 42.

2. Betty Ring, *Let Virtue Be a Guide to Thee: Needlework in the Education of Rhode Island Women, 1730–1830* (Providence: Rhode Island Historical Society, 1983) 160, 171–189.

3. Lauren Berlant, "The Female Woman: Fanny Fern and the Form of Sentiment," in *The Culture of Sentiment: Race, Gender, and Sentimentality in Nineteenth-Century America*, ed. Shirley Samuels (New York: Oxford University Press, 1992), 268.

4. Juliana Schiesari, *The Gendering of Melancholia: Feminism, Psychoanalysis, and the Symbolics of Loss in Renaissance Literature* (Ithaca: Cornell University Press, 1992), 15, 31.

5. Ibid., 75, 77.

6. Karen Sanchez-Eppler, "Bodily Bonds: The Intersecting Rhetorics of Feminism and Abolition," in *The Culture of Sentiment*, 93, 96, 97. The conventional image of the "true woman," Barbara Welter explains, was of a woman who was domestic, submissive, pious, and sexually pure. The classic discussion of this role is her essay, "The Cult of True Womanhood, 1820–1860," in *Dimity Convictions: The American Woman in the Nineteenth Century* (Athens, Ohio: Ohio University Press, 1976), 21–41.

7. Shirley Samuels, "Introduction" to *The Culture of Sentiment*, 6.

8. Fanny Fern, "The Tear of a Wife," *Olive Branch*, August 28, 1852; rpt. *Ruth Hall and Other Writings*, ed. and introd. Joyce W. Warren (New Brunswick, N.J.: Rutgers University Press, 1986), 236.

9. *Narrative of the Life of Frederick Douglass*, in *The Classic Slave Narratives*, ed. Henry Louis Gates, Jr. (New York: New American Library, 1987), 253, 249.

10. William L. Andrews, *To Tell a Free Story: The First Century of Afro-American Autobiography, 1760—1865* (Urbana: University of Illinois Press, 1986), 135.

11. Frederick Douglass, *My Bondage and My Freedom*, ed. Philip S. Foner (New York: Dover, 1969), 361.

12. Eric Santner, *Stranded Objects: Mourning, Memory, and Film in Postwar Germany* (Ithaca: Cornell University Press, 1990), 11.

13. Nella Larsen, *Quicksand*, in *Quicksand and Passing*, ed. Deborah E. McDowell (New Brunswick, N.J.: Rutgers University Press, 1986), 29.

14. Richard Wright, *Black Boy (American Hunger)* (1944; restored ed. New York: Harper Perennial, 1993), 63–64, 86, 88.

15. Ibid., 117.

16. Ralph Ellison, "Richard Wright's Blues," in *Shadow and Act* (1953; rpt. New York: Vintage, 1972), 78.

17. *Black Boy*, 203, 218, 211.

18. Douglass, *My Bondage and My Freedom*, 39, 95, 251, 354.

19. Margaret Fuller, *Woman in the Nineteenth Century*, in *The Essential Margaret Fuller*, ed. Jeffrey Steele (New Brunswick, N.J.: Rutgers University Press, 1992), 346.

20. Ibid., 262, 267.

21. Luce Irigaray, *Speculum of the Other Woman*, trans. Gillian C. Gill (Ithaca: Cornell University Press, 1985), 69, 67.

22. Toni Morrison, *The Bluest Eye* (New York: Washington Square Press, 1970), 20.

23. According to Nicolas Abraham and Maria Torok, such incorporated images, "entombed" within the self, resist "all work of mourning." See "A Poetics of Psychoanalysis: 'The Lost Object—Me,' " *Substance* 43 (1984): 4.

24. Pauline Hopkins, *Hagar's Daughters* in *The Magazine Novels*, introd. Hazel V. Carby (New York: Oxford University Press, 1988), 72.

25. Douglass, *Narrative of the Life*, 263.

26. Ibid.

27. Ibid., 276.

28. Andrews, *To Tell a Free Story*, 103.

29. Douglass, *Narrative of the Life*, 284.

30. "What to the Slave is the Fourth of July?," appendix to *My Bondage and My Freedom*, 441, 442, 444.

31. Harriet Jacobs, *Incidents in the Life of a Slave Girl*, in *The Classic Slave Narratives*, ed. Henry Louis Gates, Jr. (New York: New American Library, 1987), 465, 466.

32. Ibid., 445.

33. Ibid., 466.

34. Ibid., 350, 339, 443.

35. Hazel V. Carby, *Reconstructing Womanhood: The Emergence of the Afro-American Woman Novelist* (New York: Oxford University Press, 1987), 50.

36. Jacobs, *Incidents in the Life*, 386, 385.

37. Carby, *Reconstructing Womanhood*, 51, 55.

38. Jacobs, *Incidents in the Life*, 494.

39. An excellent discussion of the growth of the nineteenth-century woman's movement out of early reform societies is found in Barbara J. Berg's *The Remembered Gate: Origins of American Feminism* (New York: Oxford University Press, 1978).

40. Jacobs, *Incidents in the Life*, 335.

41. Harriet Wilson, *Our Nig; or, Sketches from the Life of a Free Black*, ed. and introd. Henry Louis Gates, Jr. (New York: Vintage, 1983), 74.

42. Jacobs, *Incidents in the Life*, 427, 413.

43. Wilson, *Our Nig*, 74–75; Douglass, *Narrative of the Life*, 294.

44. Sandra Gilbert and Susan Gubar, *The Madwoman in the Attic: The Woman Writer and the Nineteenth-Century Literary Imagination* (New Haven: Yale University Press, 1979), 25; Susan Sontag, *Illness as Metaphor* (New York: Farrar, Strauss and Giroux, 1978), 30.

45. Harriet Beecher Stowe, *Uncle Tom's Cabin* (New York: Vintage/The Library of America, 1991), 371, 435, 459, 486.

46. Ibid., 514–515.

47. Louisa May Alcott, *Little Women* (New York: Collier Books, 1962), 482, 459.

48. Even though Mr. March is absent for most of the novel, the roles portrayed in this novel reflect the more generalized gaze of all the fathers in America, whose patriarchal values have shaped both Alcott's plot and the female roles she presents.

49. Louisa May Alcott, *Behind a Mask*, in *Alternative Alcott*, ed. Elaine Showalter (New Brunswick, N. J.: Rutgers University Press, 1988), 134.

50. Charlotte Perkins Gilman, *Women and Economics*, in *The Yellow Wallpaper and Other Writings* (New York: Bantam, 1989), 160.

51. Alcott, *Behind a Mask*, 106.

52. Fanny Fern, *Ruth Hall*, in *Ruth Hall & Other Writings*, 140, 175, 144.

53. In *19th-century American Women's Novels: Interpretative Strategies* (New York: Cambridge University Press, 1990), Susan K. Harris has argued that Fern alternates "sentimental" and "cynical" modes, ultimately "bringing the worldview implicit in the sentimental mode into doubt" (115, 112). I suggest that these two modes awareness often coexist.

54. Jane Tompkins, "Sentimental Power: *Uncle Tom's Cabin* and the Politics of Literary History," in *Sensational Designs: The Cultural Work of American Fiction, 1790–1860* (New York: Oxford University Press, 1985), 134, 128, 130.

55. bell hooks, "Writing Autobiography," in *Feminisms*, ed. Robyn R. Warhol and Diane Price Herndl (New Brunswick, N. J.: Rutgers University Press, 1991), 1036.

# Black and White Voices in an Early African-American Colonization Narrative: Problems of Genre and Emergence

One of the more remarkable documents from the early national period of American history was an 1826 "Memorial of the Free People of Colour to the Citizens of Baltimore," presenting the hope of a group of African Americans from that city to emigrate from the United States to Liberia, on the west coast of Africa. The memorial was not so remarkable because of the desire it expressed; it was one of many emigrationist documents dating as far back as 1773, when a group of Massachusetts slaves petitioned the colonial legislature for funds to resettle in Africa. Similar interests had received significant expression in New England during the 1780s and in the second decade of the nineteenth century, when African-American sea captain Paul Cuffe took a party of settlers to Sierra Leone, hoping to create trade relations involving African-American businessmen and African Americans on the African coast.[1]

What made the 1826 memorial remarkable was its peculiar provenance under the auspices of the "American Society for Colonizing the Free People of Colour of the United States," a group founded in 1816 and led by influential white Americans, rather than by African Americans themselves. Including heavy representation from the slaveholding states of the South, these white champions of African-American emigration acted primarily on the view that there was an essential incompatibility between white people and black and, thus, that the removal of black people—especially free black people—was imperative for the well-being of American society, and, in the view of more than a few, the security of slavery, as well.[2]

As a product of the American Colonization Society's efforts, the memorial occupied a complex place within the discussion of colonization. Among African Americans, the founding of the Society gave colonization new meaning. Prior to 1816, when colonizationist leadership was provided by African Americans themselves, the colonizationist enterprise, though showing meager results, evoked widespread interest and gained support from some of the most influential African-American leaders. Given the motivations behind the Colonization Society, however, many African Americans, including previous supporters, reacted with an opposition to colonization that continued to build through the decade of the 1820s. The memorial was intended to counter that opposition by providing a demonstration of African-American support. It was also intended to encourage increased white financial assistance, and to gain recruits for Liberia.

At the same time, because of its complex purposes, the "Memorial of the Free People of Colour" raised issues beyond that of colonization. Though not "literary" in any strict sense of the word, the document confronted questions of self-definition and national identity, for African Americans and Anglo-Americans alike, that were ultimately to play a profound role in the creation of American literary traditions. In particular, the memorial revealed complexities of "voice" and literary distinctiveness that continue to be important today.

Much of the "Memorial of the Free People of Colour" was addressed ostensibly to a white audience, and it began with a series of concessions to that audience justifying the colonizationist program. "We reside among you, and yet are strangers; natives, and yet not citizens," the memorialists began, attributing their position to "our difference of colour, the servitude of many and most of our brethren, and the prejudices which those circumstances have naturally occasioned." They expressed a profound pessimism about ever achieving "the benefits of citizenship" under the circumstances: "As long as we remain among you, we must (and shall) be content to be a distinct caste, exposed to the indignities and dangers, physical and moral, to which our situation makes us liable."[3]

They also conceded that the presence of free people of color caused real problems for the rest of American society: "It ill consists, in the first place, with your republican principles and with the health and moral sense of the body politic, that there should be in the midst of you an extraneous mass of men, united to you only by soil and climate, and irrevocably excluded from your institutions." They added, "Our places might, in your opinion, be better occupied by men of your own colour, who would increase the strength of your country." And they claimed to find good reason to seek a new home. Although not slaves, they said, "we are not free. We do not, and never shall participate in the enviable privileges which we continually witness." Having no opportunities, "our situation will and must inevitably have the effect of crushing, not developing the capacities that God has given us"(296).

The memorialists absolved the white audience from blame. Their presence in the United States was a legacy of slavery, they said, an institution that had been thrust upon America by the British during the colonial period. The people of the United States had shown their own objections through laws put into effect in 1808 to suppress the African slave trade. The memorialists hoped they could accelerate slavery's end by creating "a channel" which others, once freed, could follow, giving whites the possibility of freeing their slaves without swelling the ranks of free Negroes. This would further accelerate emancipation, since slaves would be replaced with white workers, and slavery could not compete with "the superior advantages of free labour" (296).

Liberia was one of several destinations emigrants might choose—"the world is wide." But the memorialists saw more than a few possibilities. Earlier settlers from America had prepared the way. Settlement had begun in 1821, and those who had gone before were already exercising the privileges of "freemen." Those "pioneers of African Restoration" had already begun to enjoy the necessities and comforts of "larger and older communities." Subsequent migrants had much to look forward to, and would soon prove themselves to be "republicans after the model of this republic. We shall carry your language, your customs, your opinions and Christianity to that now desolate shore, and thence they will gradually spread, with our growth, far into the continent." They added, "Africa, if destined to be ever civilized and converted, can be civilized and converted by that means only" (296–297).

The idea of mission defined the memorialists' hopes; it also justified the hardships black Americans would face leaving "a populous and polished society for a land where they must long continue to experience the solitude and ruggedness of an early settlement." Africa was "the only country to which they can go and enjoy those privileges for which they leave their firesides among you." As they said, "human happiness" is not the product of comforts. Those comforts "must be joined with equal rights and respectability," and with a hope for "the future prosperity and dignified existence" of future generations (297).

Colonization was a chance to build a nation, of which the colonists would be "the fathers." The hardships facing them would resemble those "your fathers suffered when they landed on this now happy shore," the memorialists reminded their white readers. There had been a "time when you were in a situation similar to ours, and when your forefathers were driven, by religious persecution, to a distant and inhospitable shore," they noted. "We are not so persecuted," readers were assured, "but we, too, leave our homes and seek a distant and inhospitable shore: an empire may be the result of our emigration, as of theirs." They concluded, "The protection, kindness and assistance which you would have desired for yourselves under such circumstances, now extend to us" (297, 298).

The complexities of voice in the memorial grew out of its efforts to represent African-American speakers interested in the white-led Colonization Society's venture. The interest in colonization it portrayed was genuine. The memorial was discussed at two large meetings. The first was held at the influential Bethel Church on December 7, 1826. There, the memorial was approved, signed by minister William Cornish, who chaired the meeting, and the meeting's secretary, Robert Cowley, a teacher. The other was held at the Sharp Street Church. The morning after the Bethel meeting, minister George McGill contacted Colonization Society officials to complain that notice of the Bethel meeting had been inadequate, urging the scheduling of another, several days later, at Sharp Street. Here, too, the memorial was adopted, signed by chairman James Deaver, a ropemaker, and freeborn boot and shoemaker Remus Harvey.[4]

The meetings were not the only evidence of interest. Even more telling, at least a few of those publicly associated with the document transformed their sentiments into action: George McGill moved to Liberia in 1827, where he achieved some prominence, serving a few years later as acting agent for the Society. Remus Harvey took his family there early in 1828; he became a teacher.[5]

But, if the document spoke for people genuinely interested in colonization, other questions of voice were more problematic. In particular, the document's authorship was far from clear. Though issued from meetings of free black Balti-moreans, it was also the product of a concerted attempt by two of the Colonization Society's white leaders in that city, Charles C. Harper and John H. B. Latrobe, working through the "African churches," to demonstrate black support for their efforts. They organized the initial meeting at Bethel to discuss both the general issue of colonization and the memorial itself; they were the officers McGill approached to set up the Sharp Street meeting. They were chiefly responsible for the memorial's publication as a handbill and in the Society's magazine, *The African Repository*.[6]

The role played by Harper and Latrobe raised problems which were widely recognized. The white Baltimore anti-slavery spokesman Benjamin Lundy, though not unsympathetic toward African colonization, reprinted the memorial in his *Genius of Universal Emancipation*, as "purporting to be from the people of color in Baltimore," and questioned "whether this memorial is, or is not, the voice of the *majority* of our colored people." In Philadelphia, long a center of opposition to the Colonization Society, three thousand members of the city's African-American community gathered on January 22, 1827, specifically to respond to the Baltimore memorial. Led by Jeremiah Gloucester and Richard Allen, the assembly produced a "Remonstrance" of its own, proclaiming the necessity that "the views of all should be known, and considered," and condemn-ing the memorial's presentation of "opinions and sentiments entirely erroneous; calculated by their circulation and adoption, materially to injure rather than benefit our brethren in these United States."[7]

Comments by Harper and Latrobe do not put the matter to rest. After the meetings, the memorial underwent some editing, chiefly having to do with "expressions" in which the memorialists "might seem to have speak [sic] too harshly of themselves." Such comments indicate the presence of a strong white hand in the memorial's composition: if Harper or Latrobe did not actually write it, they at least collaborated with those African-American leaders whose efforts they encouraged.[8]

Internal evidence argues for collaboration. The memorial used a variety of conventions that had already taken on a distinctive "black" or "white" character by 1826. There was a discernibly "white" hand in some of the memorial's concessions to its white audience: prejudice is described as "natural"; whites are absolved of the sin of slavery, blame for which is laid at the feet of the British. These ideas had been part of white colonizationists efforts since, at least, the Society's inception, and they had been just as conspicuously absent from African-American colonization rhetoric since the earliest days.[9]

Some of what was represented as an African-American view was no less tied to conventions of argument that were, by 1826, more identifiably "black" than "white." Most notably, the memorial put colonization squarely in the emancipa-tionist camp, ignoring contrary tendencies within the white colonizationist move-ment. The attachment of white colonizationists to antislavery was far from certain. Only a few months prior to publication of this memorial, Baltimore's *white* colonizationists had published a memorial of their own, renouncing any measures that might be "injurious or dangerous" toward the institution, and emphasizing the presence of slaveholders among their numbers. The "Memorial of the Free People of Colour" had none of this, asserting a link between colonization and emancipation that went back in African-American thought to 1773.[10]

There was also an African-American influence on the document's silences as much as on its words, on what it did not say as much as what it did. White colonizationists had frequently cited what they saw as the "degraded" state of free blacks as an argument for colonization. In a Baltimore address delivered the August preceding the memorial, Harper had himself argued in behalf of colonization on the ground that "emancipated blacks" left in the United States would "become a corrupt and degraded class, as burthensome to themselves as they are hurtful to the rest of society." He declared, "Free blacks are a greater nuisance than even slaves themselves" (although, in fairness, he added, "There are many free blacks who are honorable, honest, and enlightened, and for whom I entertain sincere respect").[11]

The memorial noted a lack of opportunities for free people of color, and, in stating that "beyond a mere subsistence, and the impulse of religion, there is nothing to arouse us to the exercise of our faculties, or excite us to the attainment of eminence" used words not far from Harper's. But it pointedly said nothing about free people of color as a "burthensome" class. Frustrated ambitions are lamented, not alleged corruption in African-American society. When Harper spoke of the excision of language in which the memorialists appeared to "speak too harshly of themselves," given the formulae of white colonizationists, the omitted "expressions" are easy to imagine.

Finally, and less obviously, even as the memorial cited a prejudice "naturally occasioned" by color, and even as it eschewed a demand for total equality, it trenchantly juxtaposed the condition of blacks with the values of the white audience. The memorialists described themselves as "surrounded by the freest people and most republican institutions in the world, and yet enjoying none of the immunities of freedom." In using such language, they showed themselves a people fully aware of American ideals and purposes, of the meaning of their own exclusion from the institutions of American life. That kind of juxtaposition had long roots in African-American rhetoric, the egalitarian tendencies of American rhetoric being set against a system of discrimination—against an actual enslavement of African Americans—too obvious to ignore.

Just as significant as these distinctive conventions and themes were those pointing toward an interplay of black and white rhetorical traditions in the memorial's composition. The theme of "African Restoration" had long figured in the rhetoric of white and black colonizationists alike, and both had seen a basis for that restoration in the influence African Americans could exert toward the conversion of Africans to Christianity, the education of Africans in "American" ways. Hopes for a colonizationist enterprise that would result in an independent black-led African republic had also been expressed, and with equal strength, by emigrationists from both groups.

Black and white "authors," then, made their presence equally apparent in the text of the "Memorial of the Free People of Colour." So strong was the presence of each that, given the complications of authorship, it would be easy to dismiss the memorial on grounds of its being neither adequately "black" nor adequately "white." But what the memorial shows is that the question of voice cannot be reduced to the ancestry of authors, its effort to create a credible African-American voice in support of colonization helping to indicate the complexities inherent in any concept of voice defined along "racial" lines.[12]

At the heart of the memorial's presentation of an African-American voice was a complex set of issues growing out of the positioning of that voice in relation to larger questions of speaking and silence. On the one hand, the memorial's mixture of concessions and hopes served to place its putative authors at the periphery of American society, in but not of America, proposing to take an action that would ratify that externality. On the other, as the memorial reveals, there were implications to combining peripherality and speaking that were volatile, difficult to control. These implications were rooted in a problem of authority, a problem of who can speak for whom.

Although the memorial was presented as speaking in a black voice, its white sponsors created a marginalized space for that voice by asserting an overtly white authority in the actual process of publication. They did this by virtue of publishing the memorial in the Society's *African Repository*, with the endorsement that implied. They also did so in a supporting introduction, apparently by Harper and Latrobe, underwriting the memorial's black voice with a more authoritative one that was openly "white." Such an introduction was not unusual in the early history of African-American letters. The use of introductory "authenticating" narratives, as Robert Stepto has called them, antedates the 1826 memorial: similar narratives appeared as early as the 1770s, with the publication of Phillis Wheatley's poetry, and continued through the Civil War.[13]

The purposes of these authenticating narratives were complex, as Stepto has shown. One was to "guarantee" the African-American voice behind the text, much as the white colonizationists did here. Although the sponsors never actually said the signatories were the memorial's writers, by presenting it as proof of the "daily effects produced by correct information concerning the Colonization Society, and the state of the Liberian Colony, on the minds of the free coloured population," they vouched for both its African-American origins and its authenticity as the product an African-American colonizationist voice. At the same time, here as elsewhere, by intruding on the text, by refusing to let the memorialists speak entirely for themselves, they located this putative African-American voice at the margins of the public discussion of colonization's merits.[14]

But authentication could work both ways. As the memorial's sponsors recognized, their program was not without moral ambiguity. They took pains, for example, to assure their readers of their good intentions, claiming in the introduction that, "to the hope and belief that we should contribute, essentially, to the improvement and happiness of the free people of colour, by establishing them in a community on the African coast, does the Colonization Society in a great

degree owe its existence." There was a sense in which the memorial endorsed
that claim, documenting the cooperation of African Americans in the venture,
authenticating the kind of self-definition the memorial's sponsors advanced in
their introductory remarks. The process of authentication found in the memorial's
publication was, thus, reciprocal, the memorialists validating the white colonizationists' claims as much as the white colonizationists validated those of the
memorial.[15]

However, such a reciprocal process of authentication also meant that these
white colonizationists were forced to assign a greater importance to the African-
American voice than they had, perhaps, intended. To provide authentication, the
memorial had to present a black voice that was itself politically and morally
authoritative, not nearly so marginalized as, on the surface, it might have appeared.
By locating authority on both sides of the racial divide, the memorial's "authors"
effectively undermined that marginal position the black voice was supposed to
occupy.

One result of this reciprocal authentication was, thus, an unsettling of the
relationship between black and white Americans upon which the enterprise of
colonization was usually based. The memorial, rather than fixing differences,
produced a tense contradiction involving issues of similarity and difference. The
contradiction is notable in the introduction. In some places, the sponsors sought
to stress distinctions—invidious distinctions—as primary: "We wish we could
add, that a disposition to secure, by their own efforts, the means of transportation,
were increasing equally with the desire for removal." The marginality such words
projected with respect to the virtues of self-reliance and independence was at
the heart of the case for colonization as a necessary removal.[16]

In other places characterizations of similarity predominated and help reveal
how challenging, and how uneasy, the combination of peripherality and authority
could be. The same "principles of human nature" that had led to the European
settlement of America would "excite a desire among the free people of colour"
to undertake the Liberian mission, the introduction assured its readers, giving
difference a contingency that was less obviously compatible with the marginalization African Americans were said to deserve.[17]

Within the memorial, the effect of its combining of marginality and authority
was to create an uneasy relation between the putative speakers and their audience.
When the memorial assumed a voice for "we" as opposed to "you," it spoke,
virtually without reflection, of the existence of two separate communities in
America, defined by color. Its concessions to marginality represented a codification of difference. The ironic framing of those concessions by juxtaposing the
condition of African Americans with the republican values of white Americans
added an edge of antagonism to the code, as did the apparently humble promise
to carry "your" institutions to African shores.

At the same time, the memorial contained much that subverted difference. For
one thing, there were notable efforts in the memorial to bridge rather than to
build on apparent gaps between African-American speakers and their ostensible
white audience. One such bridge was created by the imputation of antislavery

sentiments to that white audience, even as the memorial put colonization in the antislavery camp. Slavery had not been a matter of American choice, the memorial said. It was an inherited institution which all Americans viewed as a curse. However much the absolution echoed a familiar white argument, it also built a connection based on common ideals and common interests among speakers, sponsors, and audience.

Similarly, in the parallel drawn in the memorial between African colonization and the European settlement of North America—a motif appearing in the introduction as well—the document identified potential similarities between black and white Americans, basing both the imperatives and possibilities of colonization on those similarities. The memorial deepened that tie in its address to the audience, urging white readers to put themselves in the memorialists' place: "the assistance which you would have desired for yourselves under such circumstances, now extend to us." In the early nineteenth century, the language of empathy was widely understood to destroy barriers, an understanding that further complicated those notions of difference on which the memorial was supposed to be based.[18]

The subversion of difference was even more notable in the treatment of the one basis for difference that, unspoken, lay at the document's core, and at the foundation of the controversy surrounding it. This was the difference based on "race," as that word was understood in the latter 1820s. At the time this memorial was produced, there were growing debates among Americans over the issue of race, debates in keeping with efforts to place African Americans at the American periphery. For the most part, through the Revolutionary and early national periods, there was an "environmentalist" consensus among whites on racial differences: blacks were seen as inferior, but that inferiority was explained in terms of the pernicious effects of slavery and discrimination. Nevertheless, by the time of the memorial, an increasing number of whites had begun to think of race as a matter of innate differences, arguing that blacks were a permanently, innately inferior people. White colonizationists remained within the environmentalist camp, but innatist tendencies were far from absent in a colonizationist case built on convictions of permanent unassimilability.[19]

For a distinct African-American voice, this emerging debate posed special problems. Given connotations of inferiority attached to "racial" differences, there was a difficulty in trying to develop a distinct presence without playing into innatism and notions of hierarchy, undermining the authority which, in this case, the African-American voice required. For this reason, perhaps, the very concept of "race" was rendered problematic in the memorial. Thus, in conceding the place of black Americans as "an extraneous mass of men," the memorial appeared to concede not only a white desire for American homogeneity, but even that conviction of unassimilability at the core of the white colonizationist case. Nevertheless, in making that concession, the memorial stated, "our places might, *in your opinion*, be better occupied by men of your own colour" (emphasis added). The modifying phrase redefined the white drive for homogeneity, making clear that any "extraneous" position blacks had to occupy was the result of white opinion, and not inevitable. To adopt the language of the memorial, while prejudice might be "natural," the disabilities associated with "race" represented a white construct more than a matter of innate distinctions.

When the memorial got to the construct itself, the arbitrary character of "race" was still more fully maintained. Among the most significant ways in which this was done was one of the most subtle, and, at the same time, the most unmistakable. Speaking of African Americans as "an extraneous mass of men," the memorial described black and white Americans as being united "only by soil and climate," portraying blacks themselves as "natives, and yet not citizens." Both phrases, in the context of the 1820s, were filled with meaning.

The portrayal of black Americans as "natives" if not "citizens" took on meaning from the continuing African-American debate over colonization, and shows agreement between black proponents and opponents over a crucial term. Among white colonizationists, it was a commonplace to describe colonization as a repatriation of "the African" to "his native soil." In asserting an American nativity, and a tie to American "soil," the memorial denied this major motif in white colonizationist rhetoric, a denial reinforced by the refusal to acknowledge Africa as the only possible destination for African Americans—"the world," it said, "is wide." The memorial thus took a position closer to that of black opponents to colonization, who had consistently asserted an American nativity. An 1817 anti-colonization resolution had, for example, described the ancestors of black Americans as "the first successful cultivators of the wilds of America," asserting an entitlement "to participate in the blessings of her luxuriant soil, which their blood and sweat manured." The phrasing of the memorial was hardly likely to have been accidental, and undermined the essentially "racial" connections white colonizationists drew among color, an "African" nativity, and a permanent alienation from American life.[20]

Those connections were still further undermined by the reference to climate. Climate and race were closely connected in early American racial thinking. Differences in skin color were presumed to be related to climatic differences, and these were seen to have implications with regard to nativity, as well. Early colonizationism, white and black, asserted that "Africans" in America would, settling in Africa, thrive in a west African climate for which God, nature, or both had intended them. As early as 1787, a group of black colonizationists proposed to return to an Africa whose "warm climate is much more natural and agreable [sic] to us; and, for which the God of nature has formed us." Robert Finley, one of the founders of the Colonization Society, had argued for African colonization on the ground that Africa would be "a climate suited to their color, and one to which their constitution, but partially altered by their abode in this country, would soon adapt itself."[21]

When the memorial cited ties between black and white Americans based on climate as well as geography, it severed, however subtly, a "racial" tie intended to make black people more "African" than "American." The need to confront problems posed by innatism, compounding the difficulties of combining marginality with authority, made such climatic language untenable. Despite what white colonizationists might have felt, their purposes were such as to render problematic the racial implications of their efforts in ways they themselves may have only partially perceived: it was a subtle point, but one which helped to make the "difference of colour" cited near the memorial's beginning still more adventitious, still more contingent than the prevailing white orthodoxy, even at its most benevolent, would allow.

The 1826 "Memorial of the Free People of Colour" thus had much to say, not only about colonization, but about what it means to talk about "black" and "white" voices in a particular historical context. The memorial defined them, first, as distinct voices, the presence of distinction marked structurally by the white sponsors' introduction, setting an identifiably "white" text against one identified as "black," expressing an assumption that members of neither group could somehow speak for the other. The distinction was reinforced substantively by the assertion of a group identity—a "we" as opposed to "you" in the memorial, a "we" and "they" in the introduction—that implied an incompatibility of perceptions. It was further reinforced by the memorial's concessions to difference essential to the colonizationist cause.

At the same time, the distinctiveness of the African-American voice could not be divorced from issues of authority and authentication, for blacks and whites alike. As the memorial's approach to the issue of race indicates, it was an interplay of similarity and difference that gave the voice its credibility and significance, an interplay directly related to the complex position African Americans occupied in American society as a whole and in relation to the ideological formations of the new American nation.

The "Memorial of the Free People of Colour" thus reveals much about the imperatives for an African-American voice in the early nineteenth century. But it is also possible to move from these imperatives to a consideration of more general issues concerning "white" and "black" voices in American letters. One has to do with the nature of distinctiveness, as distinctiveness has been sought, or assumed, historically. Toni Morrison has noted the extent to which "American" and "white" have been synonymous in the history of the United States, influencing literature as much as anything else, and virtually demanding that any "black" voice be, somehow, distinctive. However, as the memorial makes plain, the specific character of that distinctiveness cannot be assumed; it must be expressed.[22]

There have been many methods for marking distinctiveness within a larger American context. Historically, linguistic markers have been important, creating a black voice through the evocation of a "black" English. Morrison discusses the use of such language among white writers going back to Edgar Allan Poe in the early 1840s; it was revitalized by the plantation-tradition writers of the latter nineteenth century, and has not wholly disappeared. Among black writers, a similar use of language entered the tradition forcefully with the "dialect poetry" of Paul Laurence Dunbar, James Edwin Campbell, and others in the 1890s, re-emerging at various points since that time.[23]

As the memorial helps emphasize, linguistic markers may be less important in themselves than in their ability to express differences that writers believe can be identified with a persona behind the words. However, as the memorial also helps emphasize, such efforts at distinction cannot be taken in isolation, because they are grounded in issues of power and authority, as well.

African-American writers have been sensitive to such issues, even as they have sought to confront the necessary distinctiveness which African-American literature has been taken to have. The use of "dialect," as it developed historically, provides strong evidence of this sensitivity. In the 1890s, black writers were careful not to let a linguistic distinctiveness equate with total marginalization, and mixed linguistically distinct writing with "standard English" in ways that created the kinds of juxtapositions found in the 1826 memorial, asserting both difference and equality of capability and purpose. Later writers employed a linguistic relativism intended to counter any hierarchical assumptions their use of language might evoke. The balancing of difference and similarity has been a major focus in African-American efforts to create an African-American voice.

But, as Morrison also stresses, the problems of similarity and difference have had as much impact on the "white" voice as on the "black," and the memorial suggests why. Morrison has called attention to what she terms an "African presence" in American letters, and, particularly, to the pervasiveness of that presence in Anglo-American tradition. Certainly, one of the more curious facts in American literary history has been the wholly gratuitous way in which white writers have evoked this presence, usually through African-American characters speaking in a putative black voice that is ludicrous and stereotypical. It is not surprising that figures like Poe or the plantation-tradition writers, with their white Southern obsessions, should have created an African-American voice that belittled African-American people, but more than a few writers not directly concerned with racial matters have kept the tradition alive. F. Scott Fitzgerald's insulting interjection of blacks in *The Great Gatsby* is jarring; Ernest Hemingway's similar treatment of blacks, tellingly discussed by Morrison, is no less unnecessary. More contemporary writers such as John Updike and Saul Bellow have maintained the tradition. It is difficult not to be struck by the ubiquity of the African presence; it is also difficult not to be taken by the gratuitously negative terms in which that presence has been given life.[24]

The problems revealed in the 1826 memorial indicate why this tradition has remained so vital. As its publication history shows, the evocation of a black persona was inseparable from the process of self-definition and self-justification in which its white sponsors were engaged. They were not the first to evoke a black persona to that end. As historian Carroll Smith-Rosenberg has said, during the earliest years of the republic, white writers engaged in the construction of images of Africans—and of Native Americans, as well—in whose very "negative characteristics," as assigned by whites, Anglo-Americans could create, by means of contrast, compelling versions of what "Americans" ought to be. In the era of the memorial, similar uses of a black persona were becoming increasingly common. In popular culture, for example, pioneering minstrel performers—white men in blackface—were helping white Americans define themselves, and the racial character of their society, by presenting a ludicrous black persona against which whites could measure their own superiority. Thus, the simple process of white self-definition had already made the "African presence" an essential element in Anglo-American society. It was but a short step from there to Poe, and beyond.[25]

At the same time, if the African presence has historically been an essential part of a white American self-definition, the moral ambiguities the memorial reveals have made that presence no less problematic, even unmanageable, from the white point of view. When white Americans felt compelled to take a black voice seriously, as colonizationists did in the "Memorial of the Free People of Colour," they unavoidably subverted the foundations of difference upon which their self-definition was based.[26]

Thus one can understand the more common approach, resting on stereotype and ridicule. Unable to escape the "African presence," white writers have had to find ways to make it manageable, to bring it under control by maintaining the sense of difference upon which the presence was supposed to be based. In the era of the memorial, this effort was embodied in minstrelsy or, during that same time, in ugly "Bobalition" broadsides, dialect parodies of black antislavery appeals designed to descredit both the cause and black contributions to it. In Anglo-American culture, and in Anglo-American letters, the creation of a black voice in more ridiculous, distancing forms has at least appeared to allow that voice to be used without the contradictions it could easily entail; hence, a perplexing tradition at least as old as the memorial itself.[27]

This analysis of what may seem an obscure document should, therefore, stress the contingencies which must be acknowledged in any discussion of "voice" in a nation where, as the memorial notes, race has been such a formidable element. Not only does the document help to illuminate the inseparability of "black" and "white" voices, but it also helps to indicate the conditions under which such terms as "black voice" and "white voice" even have the resonance so much taken for granted today.

The specific "voices" found in the 1826 memorial were tied, in part, to the issues that gave rise to it. But, as with colonization itself, those issues were endemic to the American understanding of race, and to the demands that understanding imposed upon black and white Americans alike. In those demands, rather than in any irreducible distinctions among Americans themselves, lie the deepest sources for the differing "voices" in American thought and letters.

## Notes

1. On early colonizationism, see Floyd Miller, *The Search for a Black Nationality: Black Emigration and Colonization, 1787–1863* (Urbana: University of Illinois Press, 1975), esp. Part 1; Philip J. Staudenraus, *The African Colonization Movement, 1816–1865* (New York: Columbia University Press, 1961), ch. 1–14; and, for whites, Winthrop Jordan, *White Over Black: American Attitudes Toward the Negro, 1550–1812* (1968; rpt. New York: Norton, 1977), esp. 546–69.

2. On the motives of the Society's founders, see Douglas R. Egerton, " 'Its Origin Is Not a Little Curious': A New Look at the American Colonization Society," *Journal of the Early Republic* 5 (1985): 463–480.

3. "Memorial of the Free People of Colour," *African Repository* 2 (1826): 295. Subsequent quotations are cited in parentheses, in the text.

4. Charles C. Harper to Ralph R. Gurley, December 13, 1826, in American Coloniza-
tion Society, Records, 1792–1864, vol. 1, Manuscript Division, Library of Congress,
Washington, D.C.; "Memorial of the Free People of Colour," 294, 298; *Freedom's Journal*,
May 18, 1827.

5. Harper to Gurley, December 28, 1826; Penelope Campbell, *Maryland in Africa:
The Maryland State Colonization Society, 1831–1857* (Urbana: University of Illinois
Press, 1971), 52, 64, 100; U.S. Congress, 28th Congress, 2nd Session, Senate Document
150, *Message of the President of the United States, communicating Information relative
to the operations of the United States squadron on the west coast of Africa, the condition of
the American colonies there, and the commerce of the United States therewith* [Washington,
1845], 172, 188. Within a year of the memorial's appearance, 70 free black emigrants,
along with about 50 freed slaves, were included among the 200 or so individuals who
left Baltimore for Liberia. Figures are taken from the *Message of the President*, just cited,
and from Archibald Alexander, *A History of Colonization on the Western Coast of Africa*
(Philadelphia: William S. Martin, 1846), 277–278. One of the few studies to examine
pro-colonizationist black thought under the auspices of the Colonization Society, is Marie
Tyler McGraw, "Richmond Free Blacks and African Colonization, 1816–1832," *Journal
of American Studies* 21 (1987): 207–224.

6. Harper to Gurley, December 13, 1826.

7. *Genius of Universal Emancipation* 2 (1826–1827): 94, 141.

8. Harper to Gurley, December 28, 1826.

9. The tradition of blaming the British for American slavery is noted in Duncan J.
MacLeod, *Slavery, Race and the American Revolution* (New York: Cambridge University
Press, 1974), 32–34.

10. "Memorial of the American Colonization Society, to the Several States," *African
Rrepository* 2 (1826): 54–61.

11. [Charles C. Harper], "Address of C. C. Harper," *African Repository* 2 (1826):
188–189.

12. See, on this, Eric J. Sundquist, *To Wake the Nations: Race in the Making of
American Literature* (Cambridge: Harvard University Press, 1993), 38, 43. See, also,
Shelley Fisher Fishkin, *Was Huck Black? Mark Twain and African-American Voices* (New
York: Oxford University Press, 1993).

13. Robert B. Stepto, *From Behind the Veil: A Study of Afro-American Narrative*, 2nd
ed. (Urbana: University of Illinois Press, 1991), 3–6; see, also, Sundquist, *To Wake the
Nations*, 45–46.

14. "Memorial of the Free People of Colour," 293, 294.

15. Ibid., 294.

16. Ibid.

17. Ibid., 293.

18. Jay Fliegelman, *Declaring Independence: Jefferson, Natural Language, and the
Culture of Performance* (Stanford: Stanford University Press, 1993), 40.

19. On the general acceptance of environmentalism, see George Fredrickson, *The
Black Image in the White Mind: The Debate on Afro-American Character and Destiny,
1817–1914* (1971; New York: Harper, 1972), 43–44; on emerging innatism, see Jordan,
*White Over Black*, 533–538, and Reginald Horsman, *Race and Manifest Destiny: The
Origins of American Racial Anglo-Saxonism* (Cambridge: Harvard University Press, 1981),
48–50; an early sense of the need to deny innatist ideas on the part of a white colonizationist
clearly motivated T. R., "Observations on the Early History of the Negro Race," *African
Repository* 1 (1825): 7.

20. *African Repository* 1 (1825): 90; *Poulson's American Daily Advertiser* (Philadelphia), August 12, 1817.

21. The early argument from climate is noted in Jordan, *White Over Black*, 554; the 1787 quotation is in Sidney Kaplan and Emma Nogrody Kaplan, *The Black Presence in the American Revolution*, rev. ed., (Amherst: University of Massachusetts Press, 1989), 208; Robert Finley, *Thoughts on the Colonization of Free Blacks* [Washington: N.p., 1816], 7.

22. Toni Morrison, *Playing in the Dark: Whiteness and the Literary Imagination* (Cambridge: Harvard University Press, 1992), 47.

23. Toni Morrison, "Unspeakable Things Unspoken: The Afro-American Presence in American Literature," *Michigan Quarterly Review* 28 (1989): 13–14. Reprinted, in part, in this volume.

24. For Morrison's discussion of Hemingway, see *Playing in the Dark*, 69–90.

25. Carroll Smith-Rosenberg, "Dis-Covering the Subject of the 'Great Constitutional Discussion,' 1786–1789," *Journal of American History* 79 (1992): 841–873; Eric Lott, *Love and Theft: Blackface Minstrelsy and the American Working Class* (New York: Oxford University Press, 1993).

26. See, also, Sundquist, *To Wake the Nations*, 52.

27. Lott, *Love and Theft*, 24–25; Shane White, " 'It Was a Proud Day': African Americans, Festivals, and Parades in the North, 1741–1834," *Journal of American History* 81 (1994): 35–36. See, also, Michael Rogin, "Making America Home: Racial Masquerade and Ethnic Assimilation in the Transition to Talking Pictures," *Journal of American History* 79 (1992): 1050–1077.

# Howells, Du Bois, and the
## Effect of "Common-Sense":
## Race, Realism, and Nervousness
## in *An Imperative Duty* and
## *The Souls of Black Folk*

In the composite picture which William Dean Howells, as his life work, has painted of America he has not hesitated to be truthful and to include the most significant thing in the land—the black man. With lies and twistings most Americans seek to ignore the mighty and portentous shadow of ten growing millions, or, if it insists on darkening the landscape, to label it as joke or as crime. But Howells, in his "Imperative Duty," faced our national foolishness and shuffling and evasion.

—W.E.B. Du Bois, 1912[1]


D u Bois's enthusiasm for "the composite picture which William Dean Howells ... has painted of America" requires some explanation. Except for an occasional busboy, waiter, or doorman, Howells's composite picture of American life in fact almost completely neglects what Du Bois calls "the most significant thing in the land—the black man."[2] Moreover, the novel Du Bois cites as an example of Howells's attempt to "face" our national evasion isn't about black life at all, but describes a beautiful young white girl's discovery, and subsequent concealment, of her remote black ancestry. In fact, Howells's only novel about race in America, *An Imperative Duty* (1891), has more often been considered an exercise in "foolishness and shuffling and evasion" than a progressive challenge to conventional representations of African-American life and character. Rhoda Aldgate's marriage at the end of the novel to Dr. Olney, a white nerve specialist who shares her secret, is itself a complicated act of evasion, carried out in the couple's mutual confidence that, as he puts it, "sooner or later our race must absorb the colored race; and I believe that it will obliterate not only its color but its qualities."[3] Instead of facing "the mighty and portentous shadow of ten growing millions," as Du Bois would have it, Howells more often practices an anxious neglect of African-American culture, preferring even here, in his only extended fictional meditation on American race and miscegenation, to bury black personalities in stereotype and caricature.

Du Bois's praise for *An Imperative Duty* is all the more puzzling when measured against contemporary opinion. The outspoken Anna Julia Cooper described the reaction of many black and white readers in 1892 when she objected to Howells's reliance on demeaning stereotypes of Irish and African Americans.[4] Instead of facing our national foolishness, Howells's realism, according to Cooper, reworks and perpetuates the tired old clichés of the plantation tradition by misrepresenting blacks as simple-minded, dutiful servants, "bootblacks and hotel waiters, grinning from ear to ear and bowing and curtseying for the extra tips."[5] A reviewer for the *Critic* struck a similar note, attributing the failure of *An Imperative Duty* to Howells's "ignorance of the subject," adding that the author "likes the race . . . as the Princess Napraxine likes the wolves in Russia—in theory and at a distance."[6] Frances Harper may have been inspired in part by a similar disappointment to write *Iola Leroy; or, Shadows Uplifted* (1892), whose heroine bears a striking resemblance to Rhoda Aldgate. After discovering the truth about her mixed-race identity, Iola rejects the chance to follow Rhoda into white society when she turns down the marriage proposal of another white doctor, instead fulfilling her obligation, or imperative duty, to comfort and uplift members of her race. Her story unfolds like a deliberate rewriting of Howells's novel from an African-American woman's point of view.[7]

After failing to impress contemporary readers and critics, *An Imperative Duty* has fared little better in the twentieth century. Houston Baker objects to the novel's "myopic" representation of Rhoda's decision to submerge her African-American identity, while Kenneth Warren has argued more subtly that Howells's critique of sentimental "duty," or what he sarcastically calls "dutiolatry" in the novel, betrays striking limits to the aesthetic range of his realism.[8] It would seem that for all Du Bois's remarkable insight as a cultural critic, he was nearly alone in his appreciation for Howells's racial novel, whereas a virtual chorus of opinion has for over a century echoed Anna Cooper's judgment that, on matters of race, "Mr. Howells does not know what he is talking about."[9]

Yet Du Bois had a number of important reasons for admiring a novel of such ill repute. To begin with, Howells's speculation on the psychology of racial difference set a crucial precedent for Du Bois by introducing the medical discourse of "double consciousness" into the context of racial and cultural identity. The term had wonderfully broad applications in scientific and literary discourses at the end of the nineteenth century, yet Du Bois followed Howells in making double consciousness the focal point of what Eric Sundquist has called Du Bois's "theory of diasporic consciousness."[10] The concept of African-American "two-ness" first took shape for Du Bois in an 1897 essay, published six years after the serial appearance of Howells's novel, and he later refined the idea in *The Souls of Black Folk* (1903), which includes the following, justly famous, lines:

> The Negro is a sort of seventh son, born with a veil, and gifted with second-sight in this American world—a world that yields him no true self consciousness, but only lets him see himself through the revelation of the other world. It is a peculiar sensation, this double-consciousness, this sense of always looking at oneself through the eyes of others, of measuring one's soul by the tape of a world that looks on in amused contempt and pity. One ever feels his two-ness—an American, a Negro; two souls, two thoughts, two unreconciled strivings; two warring ideals in one dark body, whose dogged strength alone keeps it from being torn asunder.[11]

Scholars have debated the intellectual lineage of Du Bois's famous concept exhaustively, noting its appearance in a variety of contexts.[12] Emerson employed the term "double-consciousness" in the essay "Fate," perhaps drawing on Goethe's similar idea, and related versions of the same romantic formulation have appeared in writers as diverse as John Greenleaf Whittier, George Eliot, and Henry James.[13] A more direct line of influence probably came from Du Bois's Harvard professor, William James, whose work on "alternating selves" and "primary and secondary consciousness" in *The Principles of Psychology* (1890) unquestionably stimulated Du Bois's thinking about race and identity during his Harvard years.[14] Du Bois was well versed in both romantic literature and the scientific discourse of experimental psychology, and it is likely that both traditions nurtured his concept of the crippling double-bind of African-American cultural identity. But it was from Howells—who was also supremely well-read in the relevant scientific and romantic literature—and from *An Imperative Duty* specifically, that Du Bois learned to envision double consciousness as a racial dynamic peculiar to African Americans. Writing in 1890, the same year that produced James's *Principles of Psychology*, Howells described Rhoda Aldgate's state of mind as she wanders alone through the streets of Boston, stunned by the revelation of her "servile and savage origin":

> All the while she seemed to be walking swiftly, flying forward; but the ground was uneven: it rose before her, and then suddenly fell. . . . Her head felt light, like the blowball of a dandelion. She wished to laugh. There seemed to be two selves of her, one that had lived before that awful knowledge, and one that had lived as long since, and again a third that knew and pitied them both. . . . In the double consciousness of trouble she was as fully aware of everything about her as she was of the world of misery within her. . . . (60)

The idea of double consciousness would of course become something entirely different in *The Souls of Black Folk*, where the term sets in motion a series of tense dualities between, for example, American materialism and African spiritualism, or, as Arnold Rampersad has explained, between "memory" and "amnesia" about the African past.[15] Neither William James's processual theory of human consciousness, nor Emerson's cosmic opposition between freedom and fate brought these dualities immediately into focus. Rhoda Aldgate's racial "two-ness," on the other hand, while clearly Jamesian in conception, translates the medical and romantic discourses of double consciousness into the murky language of racial identity, a gesture that is magnificently completed in *The Souls of Black Folk*. Du Bois was clearly struck by the image of Rhoda's attempt to negotiate a psychological crisis involving multiple selves, which he loosely referenced in his brief description of Howells's novel:

> Here was a white girl engaged to a white man who discovers herself to be "black." The problem looms before her as tremendous, awful. The world wavers. She peers beyond the Veil and shudders and then—tells her story frankly, marries her man, and goes her way as thousands of others have done and are doing.[16]

According to *The Souls of Black Folk*, the victim of double consciousness longs to attain the sure footing of "true self-consciousness," "to merge his double self into a better and truer self"—a tripartite model of identity that culminates ideally, one suspects, in a version of Rhoda Aldgate's "third" self, which "knew and pitied" the other two.[17]

Du Bois was shrewd to understand that Howells's image of racial anxiety placed the conceptual terminology of Jamesian experimental psychology at the disposal of the cultural critic; and while Howells was perhaps not the critic to take maximum advantage of the opportunity himself, we need not be overly puzzled at Du Bois's appreciative reading of *An Imperative Duty*. The novel gave him what he needed most: a psychological explanation of African-American identity in terms of nervous disorder, a "two-ness" that causes the world to "waver" and impedes "true self-consciousness." Howells, of course, had something entirely different in mind when he conceived of a love story between Olney, the nerve specialist, and a mulatta beauty. His story is about the therapeutic appropriation of blackness as a counter-force to white "over-civilization" and anxiety.[18] With an ingenious disregard for authorial intention, Du Bois inverts this gesture in *The Souls of Black Folk*, appropriating nervous disease as African-American cultural property, thus turning Howells's therapeutic argument on its head while making effective use of its conceptual machinery. Regarding matters of race, Howells may not have known what he was talking about, as Anna Cooper suspected, and in part for that reason his image of Rhoda Aldgate's psychological dilemma initiates a rich cultural exchange between writers on opposite sides of the color line, an exchange that takes place in and through the idea of double consciousness. To begin making sense of that concept in the context of Howells's larger career as a critic and novelist, it will be helpful look more closely at *An Imperative Duty* and to consider that novel's unique deployment of a longstanding relationship between race and neurasthenic discourse.

At the beginning of Howells's novel, Dr. Olney has returned from a long sojourn in Europe to open a practice among the "shrill-nerved women" of Boston (89). Having lost his comfortable income as a result of the panic of 1873, he is forced to abandon his dream of remaining in Italy with a quiet practice among the "nervous Americans who came increasingly abroad each year," and finds himself instead in the "bewilderingly strange" atmosphere of his native New England, "where nervous diseases most abounded" (10). Because he arrives in July, the neurasthenic sufferers are all out of town for the season, and Olney faces the depressing "social spectacle" of Irish and Negro street life, while "the handsome houses on the Back Bay, where nervous suffering . . . must mainly abide, . . . seemed to repel his intended ministrations with their barricaded doorways and their close-shuttered windows" (10). Shaken by this token of his tenuous relation to the fashionably sick, Olney becomes a nervous sufferer himself, beset by anxiety at the prospect of slipping below the level of social respectability. With four Irish waiters crowding so close that he can feel them breathing on his premature bald spot, the nerve specialist experiences "such a vertigo that he thought he must swoon into his soup," and the very idea of moving into a boarding-house to economize on expenses leaves him feeling "almost sick" (5, 10).

Olney's anxiety about his uncertain social position leads him to reflect at length about the encroaching lower classes. What bothers him most about the Irish is their tastelessly aggressive pursuit of an American dream of material success, the "awkward and rather stupid" vigor with which they seek to improve their condition by lining their pockets (5). Such vigor is threatening to Olney because it ignores precisely the intangible qualities of birth, manner, and education that constitute his tenuous claim to cultural authority. He observes, moreover, that the disconcerting flexibility of class distinctions has a damaging effect on the nerves of the upwardly mobile, as well as on himself. Whereas the first generation of Irish immigrants were "strong, sturdy, old-world peasants," the women of the next are "thin and crooked, with pale, pasty complexions, and an effect of physical delicacy" (4). Their "undeveloped gait," at once aggressive and uncertain, resembles Olney's faltering stride through the alien streets of Boston, though he takes care to deny the parallel. While he admits that, "as a general thing the Irish are quicker-witted than we are," they lack the essential Anglo-Saxon faculty of "mere common-sense." "At any rate," he concludes, "they seem more foreign to our intelligence, our way of thinking, than the Jews— or the Negroes even" (19).

If young, rising Irish Americans seem to encroach on Anglo-Saxon cultural authority by mimicking fashionable nervous disorders that were once the exclusive privilege of Back Bay Boston, then what appeals to Olney about the city's black population is its seeming acquiescence to an inferior social status. Surveying the American scene for the first time in many years, he finds African Americans to be "altogether agreeable" because, unlike the Irish, "the colored people keep to themselves" (6). As waiters, they exercise a welcome restraint, clothing their greed in a "smiling courtesy" and "childish simple-heartedness" that appear to Olney "graceful and winning" (5). He recognizes the pretense of this disguise but appreciates the good taste with which it is worn, noting the "innate feeling for style" possessed by even the most outlandish Negro "dandies." Moreover, their willingness to live separately in "their own neighborhoods, their own churches, . . . their own resorts," seems to guarantee African Americans a measure of emotional health amidst the chronically nervous white population (6). Unlike the "pale and crooked" second-generation Irish, black Bostonians strike Olney as "the only people left who have any heart for life here" (19). Neither time nor environment leaves its mark on their "hopeful and happy" faces, and Olney fancies "that Boston did not characterize their manner, as it does that of almost every other sort of aliens" (6).

With this elaborate preparation, the novel moves somewhat predictably toward a climax involving the central categories of race and nervousness. Olney is summoned late at night to care for an old acquaintance, Mrs. Meredith, who happens to be staying in the same hotel and is suffering from a mysterious anxiety, which Olney diagnoses as "suppressed seasickness" (16). He senses at once that her illness is of a moral, rather than physical, nature, and that if she could unburden herself of some secret, "she would probably need no medicine" (23). But with her niece Rhoda in the room, Mrs. Meredith remains tight-lipped about the source of her anxiety, and Olney has no desire to play the confessor to "one of those women, commoner among us than any other people," who has probably become "muddled as to her plain, every-day obligations by a morbid sympathy with the duty-ridden creatures of the novelist's brain" (23). Olney finds such women repulsive, though he is aware that his professional future depends upon their continued suffering.[19]

When Olney checks on Mrs. Meredith the following day, she is alone, and, after a great deal of hedging and many pregnant sighs, she reveals to him the cause of her shattered nerves. Rhoda, who has lived with the Merediths since infancy, is of "negro descent" (31). Mrs. Meredith has kept the secret of Rhoda's one-sixteenth black ancestry exclusively to herself since her husband's death, and might have carried it to the grave, except that Rhoda is on the verge of accepting a marriage proposal from a wealthy minister, whom Mrs. Meredith cannot bear to injure. Olney has difficulty focusing on the complicated question of Mrs. Meredith's duty, for he finds himself thrown into "a turmoil of emotion," which seems to override his earlier sympathetic observations about African Americans.

> His disgust was profound and pervasive, and it did not fail, first of all, to involve the poor child herself. He found himself personally disliking the notion of her having negro blood in her veins; before he felt pity he felt repulsion; his own race instinct expressed itself in a merciless rejection of her beauty, her innocence, her helplessness because of her race. The impulse had to have its course; and then he mastered it, with an abiding compassion, and a sort of tender indignation. (31)

This highly charged language makes Olney's "instantaneous mental processes" difficult to interpret, for he masters his race instinct with what seems like a more subtle version of the same thing, "tender indignation." His only clearly defined emotion is anger directed at Mrs. Meredith, who has allowed her "hypochondriacal anxieties" to threaten Rhoda's happiness.

When Mrs. Meredith finally works up the courage to tell Rhoda that her mother was an octoroon, the information produces an emotional chaos in which multiple selves vie for control of Rhoda's suddenly fractured identity. Walking alone through Boston's black neighborhoods in the dreamlike state of "double con-sciousness" cited above, she experiences a more profound version of her aunt's "suppressed seasickness," as the ground seems to heave and swell beneath her. Her competing selves are expressed in rapid emotional shifts, as Rhoda alternately identifies with "the blackness from which she had sprung" and recoils from "repulsive visages of a frog-like ugliness" (63–64). She attempts to regain control over consciousness by channelling her chaotic emotions into a sense of obligation ("What ought I to do? Yes, that is the key: Duty!" [60]), finally resolving to give up her suitor and go south to assist what may be left of her mother's family.

Meanwhile, the shock caused by Mrs. Meredith's revelation has begun to affect Olney in a similar fashion. As he leans over her dying body (she has taken an overdose of the sleeping narcotic he prescribed for her anxiety), Olney begins to lose "his fight with a sort of pluriscience in which it seemed to him that he

was multiplied into three selves" (69). Generally in Howells's fiction, the loss
of this fight signals a failure of the will and leads to immoral behavior.[20] Here,
on the other hand, Olney's loss of control over consciousness marks his recovery
of emotional health and a rebirth of sexual energy. He finds Rhoda increasingly
attractive, especially when she dons black mourning clothes, which "singularly
became her" (89). Howells clearly strains for language to describe Olney's
increasingly sexual obsession with the remote taint of Rhoda's "servile and savage
origin."

> [It] gave her a kind of fascination which refuses to let itself be put into words: it
> was like the grace of a limp, the occult, indefinable lovableness of a deformity, but
> transcending these in its allurements in infinite degree and going for the reason of
> its effect deep into the mysterious places of being where the spirit and the animal
> meet and part in us. . . . The mood was of his emotional nature alone; it sought and
> could have won no justification from his moral sense, which indeed it simply
> submerged and blotted out for the time. (90)

In order to win her surrender, Olney must convince Rhoda that her intention to
sacrifice their happiness because of an abstract sense of obligation to her African-
American relations in the South is the stuff of romantic fiction, and in no way
represents a common-sense response to circumstances. In answer to her histrionics
("Oughtn't I to go down there and help them; try to educate them, and elevate
them?" [96]), he replies with a therapeutic argument that has been implicit already
throughout the novel:

> The way to elevate them is to elevate *us*, to begin with. It will be an easy matter
> to deal with those simple-hearted folks after we've got into the right way ourselves.
> No, if you must give your life to the improvement any particular race, give it to
> mine. Begin with *me*. (96–97)

When Olney asks Rhoda to help his own race get "into the right way," he is
referring obliquely to the damaging effects of a pervasive "race instinct," which
Mrs. Meredith's revelation has forced him to confront even in himself, and which
he has ambiguously "mastered" with "tender indignation." But Olney's quest for
elevation and "improvement" through Rhoda is more directly a response to the
problem of nervous anxiety, a symptom of race instinct that besets virtually every
representative of the "Northern type" in the novel (89). Mrs. Meredith's sleeping
narcotic has already betrayed the ineffectiveness of scientific remedies, which
at best merely distract the sufferer. Here Olney proposes intermarriage as an
alternative therapy for neurasthenic disease, and offers himself as a test case.

The implication is that Olney's "hypochondria of the soul," his dubious New
England legacy, can be reversed, or at least treated, by a therapeutic infusion of
blackness, the "sunny-natured antetype" to American over-civilization (101). And
indeed Olney begins to look "young and strong" after his conquest; his vertigo
is replaced by a manly, forward-looking optimism ("I'm going to provide for
your future, and let you look after your past" [100]); and even his ever-present
bald spot begins to seem more like a mark of mature distinction than a sign of

congenital weakness. Their union is not quite the blissful resolution of comedy, for the lovers find no more than "the common share of happiness" in their life together, but then neither has Rhoda succumbed to the fate of the tragic mulatta of American romance.[21] Their marriage, as so often in Howells's fiction, signifies a compromise between untenable extremes, which in this novel are racially coded: "the tameness of the Northern type" merges with the savage "beauty of antiquity" (89).

Out of this almost allegorical compromise emerges a healthy perspective, beholden neither to the Puritan cult of "duty" nor to a purely carnal nature, a perspective Howells clearly associates with the literary mode of realism: "Their love performed the effect of common-sense for them, and in its purple light they saw the every-day duties of life plain before them" (99). The "effect of common-sense" is a realistic perspective, a mode of perception that embraces "simple honesty and instinctive truth," a "common sense" vision—as Howells explains in "Criticism and Fiction"—that works like a therapeutic corrective to "the self-distrust that ends in sophistication."[22] Sophistication, in this context, is a symptom of over-civilization and a source of anxiety; realism emerges as the "sunny-natured antetype" to romantic sophistry, which fosters the debilitating anxiety of "self-distrust." Realism, in other words, becomes a figure for health.

Howells was certainly not alone in diagnosing nervousness, or over-civilization, as an American epidemic toward the end of the nineteenth century, and he was by no means the first to draw a link between race and anxiety. George M. Beard's *American Nervousness* had announced an imminent crisis with millennial urgency in 1881, defining neurasthenia as a preliminary phase of insanity, to which only the highest civilizations are susceptible. The disease struck mainly "brain-workers" and women of the more "advanced" races, namely the Anglo-Saxon; and while members of "inferior" racial and social categories were at times diagnosed as "moderately nervous," such anomalies occurred only at "stopping-places between the strength of the barbarian and the sensitiveness of the highly civilized."[23]

This racially loaded medical discourse makes plain the remarkable paradox of neurasthenia and its therapies. Illness is a mark of social and intellectual distinction, a condition of suffering that is by definition inaccessible to African Americans, who can at best hope to be "moderately nervous." One of the functions of the disease, therefore, is to establish well-defined conceptual boundaries between "brain-workers" and laborers, whites and blacks, sufferers and non-sufferers. Yet as Olney's vertigo and Mrs. Meredith's "suppressed seasickness" imply, it is the very flexibility of these distinctions that generates nervousness in the first place. The fluttering hands and hot breath of the Irish waiters at his hotel leave Olney suffering classic neurasthenic symptoms, as he prepares to swoon with lady-like sensitivity into his soup at the beginning of the novel. Similarly, Mrs. Meredith's fatal anxiety is the result of her suppressed awareness that Rhoda embodies a major breach in the color line. For Howells, who attends to this paradox with subtle clarity, nervousness is both a sign of social distinction and a consequence of the instability of such distinctions.

African Americans perform a similarly paradoxical role in the discourse of neurasthenia. In one sense, the logic of nervous illness stems from the scientific racialism of nineteenth-century thought, in that it defines civilization as an absence of barbarism, white as an absence of black, suffering as an absence of health. Such a discourse obviously demonizes blackness as a threat to the stability of civilization and denies African Americans the status of nervous suffering. Yet when commentators coined the term "race suicide" during the second half of the nineteenth century, the danger they perceived to white civilization came not primarily from the lowest levels of society but from the highest, where an excess of nervous anxiety threatened to enervate white America, loosening its hold on power.[24] Sensitive to the this perceived danger, and to its sources in hypochondria, Howells was one of many neurasthenics to represent African Americans as both a threat and a therapy for the nation's cultural ills. Nervous Americans were advised to practice relaxation as a way to confront anxiety, and more than one manual encouraged whites to cultivate leisure by learning from "Oriental people, the inhabitants of the tropics, and the colored peoples generally."[25]

One of the most vociferous opponents of "race suicide," Theodore Roosevelt, preached a different therapy but also employed racially charged language to chastise "the timid and scholarly men in whom refinement and culture have been developed at the expense of the virile qualities."[26] Noting "grave signs of deterioration in the English speaking peoples," Roosevelt called for a restoration of masculine strength through the appropriation of barbarian energy. American expansionist foreign policy was thus a sort of therapeutic panacea for the flabby culture that ventured beyond its borders to assimilate the aggressive tendencies it so desperately needed, while spreading civilization to those who presumably needed it just as badly. Howells's image of a mixed-race marriage that produces "the effect of common sense" in Rhoda and Olney would have been outrageous to Roosevelt's sense of racial integrity, but Roosevelt has very much the same concept of health in mind when he writes that "fitness" comes only to "those races with an immense reserve fund of strength, common sense, and morality."[27] As in Howells, "common sense" is a politically ambiguous mediation of barbarism and civilization, perhaps epitomized in Roosevelt's image of the imperialist soldier who speaks softly and carries a big stick.

Howells's novel plays heavily on the same racially coded analysis of the American scene, but in imagining Olney's marriage to Rhoda as a common-sense "stopping-place" between barbarism and civilization, he attends more carefully than Roosevelt to the racial dynamics implicit in neurasthenic discourse. The black body in Howells's novel possesses, in effect, therapeutic value for the white mind. Moreover, Howells fabricates an image of blackness as a way to articulate a changing model of white subjectivity. Emotional complexity is by definition beyond the reach of the "inferior" races, according to the neurasthenic discourse in which Howells clearly participates, yet as Toni Morrison might explain, the "instantaneous mental processes" of the white subject in Howells's novel come into view only against a black background.[28] Olney's healthy manhood and "common-sense" perspective are achieved through an act of amorous cultural appropriation, an act that transgresses, without obscuring, the integrity of the color line.

As the parallel with Roosevelt's foreign policy implies, Olney's "conquest" of an African-American "antetype" is a traditional gesture, rooted in the twin legacies of American slavery and imperialism. If Olney's appropriation of black health has a familiar resonance, however, Du Bois accomplishes something almost revolutionary when he inverts the racial markers in Howells's neurasthenic discourse in order to appropriate white illness as African-American cultural property. Nervousness in Beard's classic study of the disease is a mark of social distinction, defined in opposition to the unsophisticated emotional well-being of the "inferior" races. Howells's narrator moves in step with this logic when he describes the "happy and hopeful" faces of African Americans, who are the only people left in Boston with any "heart for life" (19). Moreover, Rhoda's bout with double consciousness is anything *but* typical of black experience, according to Howells's representation of African-American life in the novel (101). Her mother's race is blessed with an abundant reservoir of "heaven-born cheerfulness," which it is Rhoda's misfortune partially to have lost through exposure to the Anglo-Saxon syndrome Howells calls "hypochondria of the soul." With remarkable audacity, Du Bois stands this logic on its head by describing nervous disorder as the ineluctable condition of African-American identity at the turn of the twentieth century. Blacks, not whites, suffer from "a painful self-consciousness, an almost morbid sense of personality and a moral hesitancy which is fatal to self-confidence."[29] Du Bois makes Rhoda's double consciousness, her wavering in the veil of blackness, a condition of African-American experience, thereby appropriating American nervousness as a status symbol that belongs properly to blacks. As Tom Lutz explains, "Du Bois is culturally enfranchising blacks by claiming that they are all, in effect, neurasthenic."[30]

Actually, Du Bois employs neurasthenic discourse as a selective marker in much in the same way as Beard and others. His critique of Booker T. Washington, for example, attributes Washington's personal success to a remarkable "singleness of vision," a "oneness with his age," that ironically disqualifies Washington as an effective spokesman for African-Americans—who, as nervous sufferers, are anything but at home in late-nineteenth-century America (43). In fact, temporal discontinuity is at the heart of African-American anxiety, according to Du Bois:

> The worlds within and without the Veil of Color are changing, and changing rapidly, but not at the same rate, not in the same way; and this must produce a peculiar wrenching of the soul, a peculiar sense of doubt and bewilderment. Such a double life, with double thoughts, double duties, and double social classes, must give rise to double words and double ideals, and tempt the mind to pretence or to revolt, to hypocrisy or to radicalism. (202)

As with Rhoda, the "peculiar wrenching of the soul" makes its way directly to the mind, to consciousness, where nervous disease expresses itself as a culturally empowering disorder, a form of vertigo or seasickness available not to Washington's "unquestioning followers," but to the supersensitive black sufferers who make up Du Bois's constituency.

Other black writers also relied on the discourse of neurasthenia to overturn longstanding stereotypes of African-American character. Charles Chesnutt, for example, begins *The Marrow of Tradition* (1901) by contrasting Aunt Jane's abundant maternal warmth and nurturing black energy with the physical and spiritual frailty of her neurasthenic Southern white mistress, Mrs. Carteret. These stock characterizations tend to break down in the next generation, however, where African Americans find themselves occupying a "borderline between two irreconcilable states of life," where they possess neither "the picturesqueness of the slave" nor the "unconscious dignity of those [for] whom freedom has been the immemorial birthright."[31] As in Du Bois, this border line is a site of "doubt and bewilderment," which tends to usurp Mrs. Carteret's privileged neurasthenic suffering. Young African Americans, according to Chesnutt's narrator, have entered

> the chip-on-the-shoulder stage, through which races as well as individuals must pass in climbing the ladder of life,—not an interesting, at least not an agreeable stage, but an inevitable one, and for that reason entitled to a paragraph in a story of Southern life, which, with its as yet imperfect blending of old with new, of race with race, of slavery with freedom, is like no other life under the sun.[32]

As Howells made clear, the pervasive nervousness of "the Northern type" is both a symptom of the "imperfect blending of . . . race with race," class with class, and an attempt to reaffirm inflexible social distinctions capable of resistance to change and mobility—hence the wonderfully double-edged sword of neurasthenic discourse. Chesnutt removes some of the circularity of this logic by figuring the "chip-on-the-shoulder stage" as a mere way station on the evolutionary road to perfect emotional health.

Du Bois's concept of double consciousness is part of a more radical deployment of Howells's neurasthenic discourse, one in which Africa, and not just "the picturesqueness of the slave," looms in the anxiety-stricken consciousness of the "black folk." Where Howells appropriates black health as an antidote to nervous suffering among representatives of the "Northern type," Du Bois assumes white illness as a complex metaphor for African-American identity. Moreover, while they move in very different directions, both authors hint at the relation between double consciousness and literary realism. Rhoda, according to Du Bois, "peers beyond the Veil and shudders and then—tells her story frankly."[33] To tell her story any other way than "frankly," Du Bois implies—with "simple honesty and instinctive truth," as Howells might put it—would be to distort the two-sided, common-sense vision that is unique to her experience.

In fact, recalling the novel more than twenty years after its publication, Du Bois was mistaken when he described Rhoda's narrative sincerity in *An Imperative Duty*, for Rhoda does not tell her own story. Howells originally intended to make Olney the first person narrator when he jotted notes for an epistolary novel entitled "The Letters of Olney" in 1883, and only later did he settle on the use of an omniscient narrator. There is a wonderfully appropriate—if coincidental— symmetry, however, in Du Bois's memory of *An Imperative Duty* as a first-person confession by a black neurasthenic and Howells's original intention to write a first-person confession by a white neurasthenic. The confusion over point of view, fanciful though it may be, emphasizes the image of Howells's novel as a site of dynamic cultural exchange, with Howells and Du Bois positioned beside one another on the richly contested psychological terrain of double consciousness.

## Notes

1. William Edward Burghardt Du Bois, "As a Friend of the Colored Man," *Boston Evening Transcript*, February 24, 1912: 12. Du Bois's column, originally published as part of a seventy-fifth birthday tribute to Howells, is reprinted in *Critical Essays on W. D. Howells, 1866–1920*, ed. Edwin H. Cady and Norma W. Cady (Boston: G. K. Hall, 1983), 215.

2. African-American characters perform important roles in some of Howells's early writings, including a sketch entitled "Mrs. Johnson," *Atlantic Monthly* (Jan. 1868), reprinted in *Suburban Sketches* (New York: Hurd & Houghton, 1871). More often they perform cameo roles, as in *A Hazard of New Fortunes*, ed. David J. Nordloh et al. (1890; rpt. Bloomington: Indiana University Press, 1976) and *An Open-Eyed Conspiracy* (New York: Harper, 1897).

3. William Dean Howells, *An Imperative Duty*, ed. David J. Nordloh et al. (1891; rpt. Bloomington: Indiana University Press, 1969), 27. Subsequent references to this edition are provided in the text.

4. The serial version of the novel was severely criticized for its degrading representation of Boston's Irish population, which Howells modified for book publication. For an account of the novel's reception, see Martha Banta's "Introduction" to the Indiana edition, ix–xi.

5. Anna Julia Cooper, *A Voice from the South* (1892; rpt. New York: Oxford University Press, 1988), 206.

6. *The Critic* (Jan. 16, 1892): 34. Quoted in Banta, ix.

7. No evidence of a direct relationship has been uncovered, but several critics have discussed the striking parallel between Howells's *An Imperative Duty* and Harper's *Iola Leroy*, usually in order to highlight the inferiority of Howells's novel. See, for example, Kenneth Warren, *Black and White Strangers: Race and American Literary Realism* (Chicago: University of Chicago Press, 1993), 66–67.

8. Houston A. Baker, Jr., *Workings of the Spirit: The Poetics of Afro-American Women's Writing* (Chicago: University of Chicago Press, 1991), 34; Warren, *Strangers*, 65–66.

9. Cooper, *Voice*, 201.

10. Eric J. Sundquist, *To Wake the Nations: Race in the Making of American Literature* (Cambridge: Harvard University Press, 1993), 571. There is no definitive evidence that Du Bois read Howells's novel prior to 1897, though it is extremely likely that he did. As a graduate student at Harvard in 1891, when the serial version appeared, Du Bois would almost certainly have felt a personal stake in Howells's representation of the city's African-American community, and it might reasonably be supposed that he discussed the novel with his professor, William James, who read *An Imperative Duty* that year and spoke very highly of it in correspondence with Howells. Moreover, when Du Bois did mention the novel in his 1912 telegram to the *Boston Evening Transcript*, he incorrectly identified Rhoda as the first-person narrator, implying that his comments were based on a relatively distant memory.

11. W. E. B. Du Bois, *The Souls of Black Folk: Essays and Sketches* (Chicago: McClurg, 1903), 3.

12. Among those scholars is Kenneth Warren, whose discussion of Henry James's use

of the phrase "double consciousness" in *The Ambassadors* is qualified by an excellent reminder that the "teasing repetition" of this key term ought not to dominate understanding of Du Bois's thought (12). Following Warren's example, I have attempted, wherever possible, to ground my own analysis in what Warren calls literary historical "concretions," and to treat double consciousness less as a "teasing" leitmotif than as a contested early-modern intellectual terrain, where Howells, Du Bois, and other writers from various disciplines momentarily converge upon one another.

13. The connection with Emerson has been most thoroughly explored by Brian A. Bremen in "Du Bois, Emerson, and the 'Fate' of Black Folk," *American Literary Realism* 24 (Spring 1992): 80–88, while Dickson D. Bruce, Jr., provides a more panoramic discussion of possible influences in "W.E.B. Du Bois and the Idea of Double Consciousness," *American Literature* 64 (June 1992): 299–310. Other important discussions of the evolution of Du Bois's concept include Arnold Rampersad, *The Art and Imagination of W.E.B. Du Bois* (New York: Schocken, 1990) and David Levering Lewis, *W.E.B. Du Bois: Biography of a Race* (New York: Henry Holt, 1993).

14. Du Bois surely read William James's *Principles of Psychology* some time after its release in 1890, and he was probably also aware of James's essay "The Hidden Self," published for a popular audience in *Scribner's Magazine* during the same year. The essay introduced American readers to new models of multiple consciousness advanced in the work of the French psychologist Alfred Binet, whose *On Double Consciousness* must be considered yet another source for Du Bois's concept of African-American identity. Eric Sundquist discusses the work of Binet and James, remarking that the latter "provided the key to a theory of diasporic consciousness that was capable of yoking together the conception of a split-off, perhaps hidden but in any case culturally oppositional 'personality' and the conceptions of race nationalism comprised by the ideological watchword 'African Personality' " (571).

15. Arnold Rampersad, "Slavery and the Literary Imagination: Du Bois's *The Souls of Black Folk*," in *Slavery and the Literary Imagination*, ed. Arnold Rampersad and Deborah McDowell (Baltimore: Johns Hopkins University Press, 1989), 118.

16. Du Bois, "Friend of the Colored Man," 217–218.

17. Du Bois, *Souls*, 4.

18. Jackson Lears discusses the notion of "over-civilization" in *No Place of Grace: Antimodernism and the Transformation of American Culture, 1880–1920* (New York: Pantheon, 1981).

19. Howells's authorial voice seems to resonate clearly in Olney's expression of disdain for Mrs. Meredith's "morbid sympathy with the duty-ridden creatures of the novelist's brain," yet it would be wrong to suggest that the author consistently shares Olney's perspective. Howells is noticeably critical of Olney's class and race consciousness, even as he mocks Rhoda's and Mrs. Meredith's hyper-sensitivity to the stigma of race. A "common-sense" vision, he implies throughout the novel, would mediate between the two.

20. Like Rhoda and Olney, Angus Beaton in *A Hazard of New Fortunes* is "in possession of one of those other selves, of which we each have several about us" (126). In his case, however, the unpredictable movements of consciousness are a sign that "his will was somehow sick" (394).

21. George N. Bennett explains that Howells negotiated a difficult compromise between comedy and melodrama in *An Imperative Duty* by composing an "abstract comedy." See *The Realism of William Dean Howells: 1889–1920* (Nashville: Vanderbilt University Press, 1973), 94–105.

22. Howells, *Criticism and Fiction and Other Essays*, ed. Clara and Rudolph Kirk (New York: New York University Press, 1959), 12.

23. George M. Beard, *American Nervousness: Its Causes and Consequences* (New York, 1881), 186, 16. The cultural logic of neurasthenia in early-modern America is explored masterfully by Tom Lutz in *American Nervousness, 1903: An Anecdotal History* (Ithaca: Cornell University Press, 1991).

24. Lutz explains that the term "race suicide" was popularized by Edward A. Ross, a University of Wisconsin sociologist, who advocated strict immigration laws and incentives for reproduction among whites as measures to forestall dilution of the more "advanced" races in America (82).

25. See William Dean Howells, "Editor's Study," *Harper's Monthly* 89 (Oct. 1894): 799–801; William James, "The Gospel of Relaxation," *Scribner's* 25 (April 1899): 499–507; William A. Hammond, "How to Rest," *North American Review* 153 (August 1891): 215–219.

26. *The Letters of Theodore Roosevelt*, ed. Elting E. Morison (Cambridge: Harvard University Press, 1951), 1:508.

27. *The Works of Theodore Roosevelt*, 20 vols. (New York: Scribner's, 1926), 13:358–359, quoted in Lutz, *Nervousness*, 81.

28. Toni Morrison, *Playing in the Dark: Whiteness and the Literary Imagination* (Cambridge: Harvard University Press, 1992).

29. Du Bois, *Souls*, 202. Subsequent references to this edition are provided in the text.

30. Lutz, *Nervousness*, 264.

31. Charles W. Chesnutt, *The Marrow of Tradition*, ed. William L. Andrews (New York: Penguin, 1992), 245.

32. Chesnutt, *Marrow*, 245.

33. Du Bois, "Friend of the Colored Man," 217–218.

CARLA L. PETERSON

# The Remaking of Americans:
# Gertrude Stein's "Melanctha" and
# African-American Musical Traditions

Shortly after completing *Three Lives* in 1906, Gertrude Stein wrote a letter of lament from Paris to her friend Mabel Weeks: "I am afraid that I can never write the great American novel. I don't know how to sell on a margin or do anything with shorts or longs, so I have to content myself with niggers and servant girls and the foreign population generally." To explain her aesthetic choices and to underscore her affinity with such "foreign" peoples, Stein appropriated the language of the uneducated and in particular of black dialect: "Leo he said there wasn't no art in Lovett's book and then he was bad and wouldn't tell me that there was in mine so I went to bed very missable but I don't care there ain't any Tschaikowsky Pathetique or Omar Kayam or Wagner or Whistler or White Man's Burden or green burlap in mine at least not in the present ones. Dey is very simple and very vulgar and I don't think they will interest the great American public. I am very sad Mamie."[1]

What Stein's lament first addresses is her early ambition to write a *great* novel that would be *American*, and to do so from a position abroad in France. Stein would later attribute her inspiration for *Three Lives* to two great European modernists—Flaubert, author of the composite *Trois contes* and obsessed pursuer of *le mot juste*, and Cézanne, innovator of a new technique of heavy block brush strokes. In *The Autobiography of Alice B. Toklas*, Stein recalled: "She had begun not long before as an exercise in literature to translate Flaubert's Trois Contes and then she had this Cézanne [portrait of a woman] and she looked at it and under its stimulus she wrote Three Lives."[2] Still later she asserted that it was the aesthetic sensibility of these two Frenchmen that had enabled her to put into practice a new "realism of composition": distinctions between central and subordinate ideas disappear, "one thing [becomes] as important as another thing [and] each part is as important as the whole." In the literary text, such realism of composition is characterized by "a constant recurring . . . a marked direction in the direction of being in the present" that results in the creation of a "prolonged present."[3]

Critics have argued that Stein's development of such modernist literary techniques converged with modernist painters' new interest in African art, in particular the mask that flattens out surfaces and abstracts individual features.[4] I would argue, however, that in *Three Lives* Stein's aesthetic inspiration is equally American, as Grant Richards, a British publisher who rejected her manuscript, was all too well aware: "Moreover, there is the question of scene and atmosphere, both in this case so very American that the ordinary English reader would be a little at a loss."[5] I would further argue that this inspiration derives quite specifically from Baltimore and, in the case of "Melanctha," from African-American Baltimore. Indeed, Stein in her *Autobiography* acknowledged African-American culture as an important source of her own modernist beginnings: "Gertrude Stein had written the story of Melanctha the negress, . . . which was the first definite step away from the nineteenth century and into the twentieth century in literature" (54).

Adopting the critical paradigm elaborated by Raymond Williams in *The Politics of Modernism*, I suggest that Stein in Paris occupied the modernist situation of the emigré. For Williams, modernism can be explained only in terms of its specific historical moment. This moment is characterized by the end of organic community and the development of global socioeconomic transformations that encourage massive international migrations of peoples, whether forced or voluntary, to ever expanding imperial and capitalist metropoli. As a consequence the city attains increasing importance, first as a geographic borderland where disparate groups of peoples live together in strange propinquity and where the dislocation of individuals often results in isolation and loneliness, and second as a site in which immigration leads to an estrangement and denaturalization of language, which is no longer perceived as customary but as arbitrary and conventional. Thus the imperial metropolis extends "over a new range of disparate, often wholly alien and exotic, cultures and languages."[6]

Such an analysis of modernism's historical moment aptly describes the migratory pattern of Daniel Stein's family from Allegheny, Pennsylvania, where Gertrude was born in 1874, to Austria, France, and then to Baltimore and Oakland, as well as Stein's self-imposed exile to Paris in 1903; and it may well explain the perception by others of Stein's "foreign" use of the English language.[7] But I would also contend that it accurately portrays the city of Baltimore at the turn of the century and hence of Bridgepoint, the fictionalized Baltimore of *Three Lives* inhabited by "niggers and servant girls and the foreign population generally." Indeed, from the 1880s on Baltimore was a fast-growing city, workers drawn to it because of its rapid expansion of manufacturing and industry. By the mid-1880s its population included a large number of factory workers in the coal and oyster industries, in canning, glass blowing, brickwork, carpentry, electrification, and in clothing sweatshops; in addition, women labored as domestics, laundresses, and needle workers. Given the sharp increase in transatlantic migration in the last decades of the nineteenth century, many of these workers were ethnically Irish, German, Italian, and Eastern European immigrants, as well as African Americans who constituted approximately 15 percent of Baltimore's population in 1890; religiously, they were Catholic, Protestant, and Jewish.[8] According to a 1907 study of housing conditions in Baltimore, this working population lived not only in segregated tenement and alley districts, but also in mixed ones: "In the [Albermarle street] tenement district the large majority of the inhabitants were Russian Jews, with a smaller number of Italians, and a sprinkling of other nationalities. . . . The [Biddle] alley district . . . is occupied largely by negroes with a sprinkling of native white families, and a remnant of the colony of clean, hard-working, thrifty Germans, who seem to have constituted the original inhabitants."[9]

Stein herself lived in Baltimore, first with her aunt and uncle, the Bachrachs, from 1892 to 1893, then with her brother, Leo, and later with a friend, Emma Lootz, from the fall of 1897 to early 1902, when she was a student at the Johns Hopkins medical school. As her biographers have noted, Stein had direct contact with the city's immigrant and African-American population. According to a cousin, "everybody was attracted to Gertrude—men, women and children, our German maids, the negro laundresses." More specifically, Gertrude and Leo's housekeeper was a German immigrant named Lena Lebender who in *Three Lives* is fictionalized as "the good Anna" and gives her name to "the gentle Lena." Finally, Stein's choice of residence during her medical school years suggests a necessary acquaintance with this minority population. Rather than confine herself to the solidly middle-class German Jewish enclave around Eutaw Place in the northwestern part of the city where the Bachrachs and the Cone sisters lived, Stein established herself to the east in a more heterogeneous neighborhood, first at 215 East Biddle Street, then at 220 East Eager Street, a street Lootz remembered as "nice enough . . . except for the hens floating down the gutter." These residences were not far from the black middle-class neighborhood of West Biddle Street beyond which lay the Biddle alley district; and the Hopkins medical school was located in the middle of another poor black area through which Stein was obliged to pass in order to reach the hospital and in which she delivered babies to fulfill the requirements for her course in obstetrics.[10]

In *Q.E.D.*, Stein's first sustained fictional effort written in 1903 after she had abandoned medical school and moved to Paris, she appears to have deliberately turned her back on Baltimore; thus her protagonist and fictional self, Adele, remarks: " 'We are all agreed that Baltimore isn't much of a town to live in.' "[11] The novella appears to be exclusively preoccupied with Stein's dilemma over her own psychosexual situation; as critics have noted, the triangular lesbian relationship of Adele, Helen Thomas, and Mabel Neathe is a reenactment of Stein's own tormented relationship with May Bookstaver and Mabel Haynes that took place between 1901 and 1903.

*Q.E.D.*, however, also hints at larger modernist concerns that are later fore-grounded in *Three Lives*. The text's point of departure is geographic displacement, here the transatlantic voyage, which becomes the enabling condition of modernist psychological experience but also reaffirms the vital "need of the country to which one belongs, . . . for the particular air that is native" (99). More specifically, the native place for the working out of such experience is the American city, Baltimore, but especially New York and Boston; and it is Stein's fictional self, Adele, who comes to typify the modernist individual lost in the urban crowd and reveling in it as a space of potential liberation. Finally, the novella enacts the search to define native character, in this case American womanhood: the female protagonists are "distinctly American but each one at the same time bore definitely the stamp of one of the older civilisations, incomplete and frustrated in this American version but still always insistent" (54). If Helen is "the American version of the English handsome girl" (54) and Mabel "sufficiently betray[s] her New England origin" (55), Adele is denied any form of relationship to an older civilization but suggests "a land of laziness and sunshine" (55–56), a description that will reappear in "Melanctha" in association with "the negro."

By the time she started writing *Three Lives*, Stein's imagination had drifted back to Baltimore, which, fictionalized as Bridgepoint, becomes the central site of experience in all three stories. The good Anna and the gentle Lena of the first and last stories respectively represent Stein's "servant girls and the foreign population generally," and through them the narrative explores issues of geographic displacement and European immigration. Both Anna and Lena come from Germany to America and enter into service; Anna and her mother "came second-class, but it was for them a long and dreary journey"; Lena is "patient, gentle, sweet and german. She had been a servant for four years and had liked it very well."[12] As immigrants, Anna's and Lena's relationship to their older native language is suddenly ruptured and their use of the new dominant language remains strange and unnatural. As menial workers in an urban environment, both women suffer acutely from their dependent situation and its ensuing loneliness; they can survive neither the harshness of working-class conditions in a rapidly developing capitalist metropolis nor the compulsory heterosexuality that patriarchy enforces on them.

Both "The Good Anna" and "The Gentle Lena" thus explicitly point to the ways in which nationality, class, and gender shape the lives of their protagonists. Yet, issues of race lurk just below the surface as Stein's fictional narratives echo the contemporary racial discourse that had become increasingly virulent as a consequence of the widespread immigration of the European poor in the 1880s and 1890s. Emerging Anglo-Saxon nativist ideologies affirmed the separation of Europeans into different biological types and ultimately races, asserting the inherent inferiority and progressive degeneration of Eastern and Southern European immigrants and the consequent need to maintain Anglo-Saxon racial purity in the interest of national survival.[13] In "The Gentle Lena," Lena's American cousins resort to racial analogy to mock their immigrant cousin's social inferiority: "They hated to have a cousin, who was to them, little better than a nigger" (246). But it is only in "Melanctha," the last of the stories written, that Stein chose to represent "niggers" fully.

I suggest that to write "Melanctha" Stein turned to black popular cultural forms with which she had come into contact during her Baltimore years. In analyzing these appropriations, I am following Toni Morrison's injunction that we need to investigate what she has called "Africanism" in American literary texts.[14] Such critical activity forms part of a larger cultural project committed to the deconstruction of racial categories. According to this project, race can no longer be viewed as a biological construct, since human genetic variability between "races" is no greater than that within a given "race," and since the term "race" is often used to describe what are in fact ethnic experiences—historically acquired—of blacks in the United States. Rather, race must be seen as an ideological construct conditioned by social, cultural, and historical factors. As Aldon Nielsen has argued, race is "a consummately empty signifier, that is constituted out of a people's desire ... to name themselves as not-other"; an "empty signifier," race acquires meaning only when invested with particular social and cultural constructions by given groups or individuals.[15]

In studies of African-American culture, critics such as myself have worked to assess the ways in which African Americans have negotiated "blackness" throughout our history, creating social institutions, economic networks, and cultural forms that have enabled the emergence of black subjectivity and historical agency. In turning to white writers, however, we need to look at how blackness has served as a strategy for their definition and redefinition of themselves as white Americans. To quote Aldon Nielsen once again: "In writing themselves into history *as* white writers ... white authors of our past ... were founding their essential subjectivity upon, depended for their very being upon, the existence of black people."[16] White identity is revealed to be dependent on blackness in some fundamental way, and hence blackness becomes an inescapable condition of Americanness. This blackness is most often not historically contextualized, however, but exists as something other, that which Michael Rogin has called "the surplus symbolic value of blacks," whether born of fear, desire, or aspiration to power and control.[17] Yet paradoxically, what this symbolic value points to is the existence in the United States of a complex racial borderland where blood lines are often blurred and cultural traditions merged. African-American critics need, then, to analyze the ways in which this borderland gestures toward a shared culture but also reaffirms existing hierarchies and power relations.

I want to argue that in "Melanctha" Stein appropriated African-American musical traditions to assert her Americanness in opposition to the European high culture of Flaubert and Cézanne, while at the same time marking her distance and alienation from the dominant American culture—that which forced her admission: "I don't know how to sell on a margin or do anything with shorts or longs." A newly-arrived emigré in Paris, Stein occupied the position of outsider, the immigrant stranger who is both unassimilated and unassimilable. Linguistically, she found herself, to paraphrase Williams, liberated from the dominance of the "old, settled language" and in the presence of a "new, dynamic language." Yet Williams himself warns against any rigid opposition between these two languages, noting that the "uses of a language of connection and of forms of intended communication remained an emphasis and an intention of [those] social groups ... whose specific existence had been blurred or contained within the imposed 'national' forms," while the new language could be "deliberately manipulative and exploiting."[18]

Indeed, in "Melanctha" Stein invented a modernist discourse that was rooted more in the geographic and linguistic borderland culture of the American metropolis than in the "dynamic" languages of Europe. To create this new language,

Stein worked toward, in Williams's words, "a deliberate running-together, cross-fertilization, even integration of what had been hitherto seen as different arts, aspir[ing] to develop language towards the condition of music, or towards the immediacy and presence of visual imagery or performance."[19] And she was able to achieve her purposes by turning to contemporary musical traditions—coon songs, early folk-blues, and ragtime music—of African Americans, one of those "social groups" whose "specific existence" the dominant culture had hoped to "blur or contain within the imposed 'national' language." As we shall see, however, not all of these musical traditions can be said to be purely African-American either in origin or in practice. They are, in fact, inextricably linked to other American ethnicities, underscoring the incredible complexity of race and race relations at the turn of the century.

Stein appropriated these African-American musical forms because their images were useful to her as she sought to work out her sense of both her Jewishness, which, she increasingly felt, differentiated and isolated her from her larger social community, and her lesbianism, which, as *Q.E.D.* attests, she was slowly coming to acknowledge. As many critics have noted, Stein projected herself most explicitly into "Melanctha" as the light-skinned doctor, Jeff Campbell, the "whitest" of all the characters in terms of his values and behavior and the most critical of black working-class mores. Yet, Stein also made use of her black lower-class characters—Rose Johnson, James Herbert, and Melanctha herself—to explore personal, sexual, and familial conflicts; in the text, blackness functions as a means of both self-expression and denial.[20] Stein's exploitation of these images is thus double-edged, encompassing a repulsion against blacks as foreign and primitive, on the one hand, and an attraction to them as emblematic of free sexuality and vibrant womanhood on the other. In short, if we need to question Stein's total adherence to Flaubert's and Cézanne's "realism of composition" and modernist criticism's exclusive focus on the experimental quality of her writings, we also need to avoid the caricaturing of Stein as a "white supremacist" guilty of offensive racial stereotyping.[21]

Musical history indicates that Baltimore was a central site for the development of African-American musical culture at the turn of the century. Although Stein nowhere makes specific reference to this music, both the external evidence provided by her proximity to black neighborhoods and the internal evidence of her prose suggest her acute awareness of it. Furthermore, we know that Stein was intensely attuned to the sound of voices, commenting in the *Autobiography* that "I don't hear a language, I hear tones of voice and rhythms" (70). More particularly, in a Radcliffe theme of 1895 Stein recorded the strong impression made on her by the "negro" sounds of Baltimore: "Baltimore, sunny Baltimore, where no one is in a hurry and the voices of the negroes singing as their carts go lazily by, lull you into (the) drowsy (wakin) reveries. . . . To hear the negro voices in the distance and to let your mind wander idly as it listeth, that is happiness. The lotus-eaters knew not the joys of calm more completely than a Baltimorean."[22] It was Stein's rendering of these sounds that Richard Wright was responding to when he wrote that "while turning the pages of 'Melanctha,' I suddenly began to *hear* the English *language* for the first time in my life. . . . English as Negroes spoke it: simple, melodious, tolling, rolling, rough, infectious."[23]

Perhaps the earliest negro sound that Stein would have heard in Baltimore in the 1890s was the coon song, sung by whites and blacks alike, that had developed out of earlier minstrel and road show traditions. Its lyrics relied on caricature and racist stereotyping in order to ridicule and lampoon blacks as uncivilized and primitive people. In such songs as "All Coons Look Alike to Me," "My Coal Black Lady," "May Irwin's 'Bully' Song," or "Mister Johnson Turn Me Loose," black men, in Edward Berlin's words, "are portrayed as ignorant, gluttonous, thieving (stealing chickens, watermelons, and pork pies), gambling, cowardly, shiftless, and violent (most often wielding a razor); the women are sexually promiscuous and mercenary, often leaving one 'honey' (which rhymes with 'money') for another." The racism of the language and imagery is overt and undeniable. In "May Irwin's 'Bully' Song," for example, the male protagonist boasts about his successful confrontation with the "bully" in the following terms: "I riz up like a black cloud and took a look aroun'/ There was dat new bully standin' on the ground/ I've been lookin' for you nigger and I've got you found/ Razors 'gun a flyin', niggers 'gun to squawk."[24]

Tremendously popular at the turn of the century, coon song shows were a readily available form of entertainment as individual performers and companies toured widely, stopping in all major cities, including of course Baltimore. It is to this tradition, I suggest, that Stein turned in order to portray Melanctha's father, James Herbert, her last lover, Jem Richards, and her friend, Rose Johnson, characters who appear at the beginning and the end of the story, thereby providing its frame. Jem is the typical "young buck" of coon songs (216); the description of the fight between Herbert, "fierce, suspicious, . . . look[ing] very black and evil," and the coachman John is strongly reminiscent of the tradition's representations of black men: "Suddenly between them there came a moment filled full with strong black curses, and then sharp razors flashed in the black hands that held them flung backward in the negro fashion, and then for some minutes there was fierce slashing" (94); finally, Rose Johnson, "a real black, tall, well built, sullen, stupid, childlike, good looking negress . . . [who] had the simple, promiscuous unmorality of the black people" (85–86) may well bring to mind the burlesque heroine of "My Coal Black Lady": "This coal black lady, She is my baby, . . . Her color's shady, But she's a lady."[25]

It is important to remember, however, that despite its racist content, the coon song tradition was not a purely white form, but was born of mixed blood lines. Its origins lay in an earlier minstrel tradition that itself combined Euro-American art forms—dances such as the Irish jig and clog, Scottish and Irish folk songs, musical instruments like the tambourine and fiddle, songs and stories of the American frontier—with African-American elements such as dance-steps, folk expressions, and instruments like the banjo and the jawbone.[26] Similarly, coon songs were written and performed not only by whites but by blacks as well; one of the earliest songs, "All Coons Look Alike to Me," was written and first sung by the famous black entertainer, Ernest Hogan. Yet black performers such as Hogan, Billy Kersands, Bob Cole, Billy Johnson, and J. Rosamund Johnson did not simply adapt themselves unthinkingly to the coon song tradition but subverted it, seeking, following Houston Baker's formulation, *"the mastery of form"* in order then to engage in *"the deformation of mastery,"* so that the minstrel mask ultimately became "a governing object in a ritual of *non-sense"* composed of mere sounds. This deformation of mastery is perhaps nowhere more evident than in black performers' subversive questioning of the authenticity of both the tradition and its practitioners; Bert Williams and George Walker underscored the fraudulent identity of white performers when they advertised themselves as "Two *real* Coons," while Ernest Hogan's claim to being "the unbleached American" implicitly hinted at the alien status of all those other bleached Americans.[27]

It is quite possible that Stein patterned the characters of Rose and Sam Johnson after the protagonists of the antebellum minstrel song "Coal Black Rose," whose lines echo faintly in "My Coal Black Lady." According to music historians, the plot of "Coal Black Rose" was developed into an Ethiopian opera entitled *Oh Hush! or the Virginny Cupids* that was first performed in 1833 and subsequently became "one of the most frequently revived pieces in the entire repertoire of American minstrelsy."[28] This piece portrays the rivalry between the bootblack, Sambo Johnson, and his boss, Cuff, in their courtship of "coal black Rose," and the ultimate success of Sambo, although Cuff does get his revenge at the end in his physical assault on Sambo. Sambo and Rose are held up to ridicule as black characters who are foolish enough to try to ape middle-class conventions of courtship; it is easy to see how they might function as prototypes of Stein's Sam and Rose Johnson. Significantly, although the lyrics of "Coal Black Rose" were American, the music derived from British folk tradition.[29] Such a mixed genealogy underscores the inextricable entanglement of white and black cultural forms in the nineteenth century and invites us to reinterpret with renewed seriousness Stein's narrator's insistence that the "real black" Rose Johnson "had been brought up quite like their own child by white folks" (86).

I would argue that Stein's creation of these frame characters, born of mixed racial heritage, allowed her to articulate highly charged childhood family conflicts that continued to haunt her, enabling her both to discharge anger against, and reconstitute understanding of, past events and individuals by means of projection, disguise, and displacement. For example, as Richard Bridgman has noted, many of Stein's fictional fathers, including James Herbert, are "domineering, suspicious, impatient and brutal" and may be seen as projections of Daniel Stein.[30] Further, Rose Johnson may be viewed as Stein's imaginative response to the figure of the ineffectual, victimized wife/mother (both Stein's and Melanctha's own); deliberately rejecting both housewifery and motherhood to ensure her own survival, Rose transfers her domestic obligations onto Melanctha and neglects her own child until it dies: "Rose Johnson was careless and negligent and selfish, and when Melanctha had to leave for a few days, the baby died. . . . Rose and Sam her husband were very sorry but . . . neither of them thought about it very long" (85).

In the late 1890s composers began to put coon songs to syncopated rhythms, giving rise to a new musical form, ragtime, which, from its beginnings, was intimately associated with Baltimore, birthplace of the great rag pianist Eubie Blake. Although originally merely an instrumental accompaniment to the coon song, ragtime rhythms gradually came to dominate the lyrics, which became less explicitly racial in content, and then disappeared altogether. Syncopation has been considered a distinctly African-American form that improvisationally disrupts the regularity of the stressed beats of a musical composition by emphasizing a normally unstressed beat or by delaying, pushing, or interpolating a beat; counterpoint is created when the right hand imposes such rhythmic irregularities upon the left. If ragtime began as the instrumental accompaniment of coon songs, it soon gained wider currency as composers started applying syncopated rhythms to classical music. In such situations, rag became dependent on European musical expression, whose regularity it worked to disrupt; once again the blood lines between black and white cultural forms became blurred. Given its African-American rhythmic and improvisational nature, however, rag remained an expression of freedom and subversion.[31]

Blake, who has left us a fascinating first-hand account of the development of ragtime, started his musical career in 1898 at the age of fifteen playing the piano in such Baltimore "bawdy houses" as Aggie Shelton's and Annie Gilly's, as well as at Alfred Greenfeld's saloon. In his reminiscences he recounts how ragtime music was one of those negro sounds that permeated the atmosphere of Baltimore, and we may speculate that it eventually reached Stein herself. Annie Gilly's, for example, was located on East Street, some blocks to the west of the Johns Hopkins hospital; furthermore, according to Blake, African-American street bands accompanying funerals often passed the corner of Jefferson and Ann streets directly in front of the hospital: "Well, the people would sing and the band would play, you know, funeral music, dirges. Now on the way back, see, they play the very same melodies—he's buried now, see—in ragtime. Oh, how they'd swing!"[32] Finally, we may wonder whether Eubie Blake's real name, James Hubert, does not find itself echoed in the name of Melanctha's father, James Herbert.

Eubie Blake's reminiscences are especially significant for their perception of how race, ethnicity, and sexuality shaped the practice and performance of ragtime and how boundaries between different racial and ethnic groups at times weakened and became blurred, illustrating once again the borderland nature of the modernist metropolis. Aggie Shelton's, for example, was located in a black neighborhood, but Aggie herself was of German background and spoke in a "thick Teutonic accent"; if Eubie, the entertainer, was black, "the girls were all *white*, and of course so were the customers." Finally, different rags were seen to appeal to different social groups; Jesse Pickett, composer of "The Dream Rag," a piece that Blake himself learned to play, "often called it 'The Bull Dyke's Dream' because of its strong impact on the lesbians who worked in sporting houses, who crowded around the piano wherever he went, crying 'Hey, Mr. Pickett!! Play The Dream.' "[33]

Heightened awareness of the syncopated rhythms of ragtime music invites us to rethink and rephrase the many incisive analyses made by Stein scholars concerning the modernist experimental style of "Melanctha." Thus, Marianne DeKoven's and Lisa Ruddick's references to the story's narrator as "obtuse" may in fact intimate the presence of syncopation. According to these critics, the narrator is "obtuse" because she is unable to tell her story properly and give her narrative direction, because she fails to provide an internal logic to her narration of events, so that linear causality is noticeably absent. More specifically, the narrator shows signs of a "collapse of emphasis"; consequently, "the dramatic outlines are flattened." Finally, she reveals herself incapable of subordination, of placing in the background those events that are less important than others.[34] I would suggest that rather than being "obtuse," the narrator of "Melanctha" may in fact be ragging on conventional notions of narrative logic, causality, emphasis, and subordination that are the hallmark of the dominant literary tradition. The peculiarity of the narrative style of "Melanctha" is confirmed by DeKoven's comment on the degree to which it differs from that of both "The Good Anna" and "The Gentle Lena"; the "compact, evenly stressed rhythms" of the two earlier composed stories "are transformed by repetition in 'Melanctha' into a wavelike cadence with phrases or measures emphasized by rhymes." To support her argument DeKoven quotes a narrative passage in which the prose "rushes forward freely and then halts at each '-er' rhyme," creating a strange push-and-stop effect:

> Now when her father began fiercely to assail her, she did not really know what it was that he was so furious to force from her. In every way that he could think of in his anger, he tried to make her say a thing she did not really know. She held out and never answered anything he asked her, for Melanctha had a breakneck courage and she just then badly hated her black father.
>
> When the excitement was all over, Melanctha began to know her power, the power she had so often felt stirring within her and which she now knew she could use to make her stronger. (95)

Such a combination of abrupt shift in rhythm, repetition of "-er" syllables, and accumulation of staccato rhymes contradicts traditional Western notions of prose regularity and hints at the presence of syncopation.[35]

As Ruddick has pointed out, Melanctha and the narrator share many stylistic traits, given their similar tendency toward a form of mind-wandering marked by repetition, offbeat stresses, and lack of subordination.[36] Melanctha is prone to syncopated rhythms as well, and her use of syncopation is particularly effective in her conversations with Jeff Campbell, contributing in important ways to the evolution of Jeff's character. As noted earlier, Stein's foremost identification is with the logical, bookish, scientific Jeff, who stands outside black popular culture, offering the reader a distanced perspective on it as he decries the tendency of "colored people" toward "excitements" and "this running around business" (117). Yet if Jeff insists on his disgust with such irregular living, Melanctha quite rightly points out the degree to which he is also attracted to "queer folks": " 'I can't say as I see just what you mean when you say you want to be good and real pious, because I am very certain Dr. Campbell that you ain't that kind of a man at all, and you ain't never ashamed to be with queer folks Dr. Campbell' " (120).

Jeff's dissociation from this urban culture of excitements leads him ironically to participate in another world of the senses, that of the pastoral: "Jeff always loved to watch everything as it was growing, and he loved all the colors in the trees and on the ground, and the little, new, bright colored bugs he found in the moist ground and in the grass he loved to lie on" (149). Much as in the case of the sensuous Adele in *Q.E.D.*, Jeff's affinity to nature suggests his openness to a world that is neither rational nor scientific, but rather appeals directly to senses that are capable of being excited.

It falls to the sexually adventurous Melanctha, whose experiences include both the heterosexual and the homoerotic, to open Jeff up to this world of sensual excitement, and she does so in their many lengthy conversations which play themselves out in a counterpoint of voices as Melanctha responds to the regularity of Jeff's discourse by means of syncopation. When Jeff comments that religion is "a good way for many people to be good and regular" (118–119), she questions his use of these terms and reminds him of his willingness to associate with "queer folks." Jeff initially resists shifting rhythm, complaining that she goes too "fast" for his "slow way of doing" (163). But he eventually gives up his regular rhythm to syncopate, hesitating, repeating words, interpolating additional phrases—"you see," "really," "it's like this way with me"—in his search for greater emotional knowledge:

> "You see, Melanctha, really, it's just like this way always with me. You see, Melanctha, its like this way now all the time with me. You remember, Melanctha, what I was once telling to you, when I didn't know you very long together, about how I certainly never did know more than just two kinds of ways of loving, one way the way it is good to be in families and the other kind of way, like animals are all the time just with each other, and how I didn't ever like that last kind of way much for any of the colored people. You see Melanctha, it's like this way with me. I got a new feeling now, you been teaching to me."(158)

If Melanctha may be loosely associated with the syncopated rhythms of ragtime, she can be linked even more closely with the early folk-blues. In contrast to the coon songs, blues music and lyrics are more purely African-American and exhibit strikingly different perspectives on, and attitudes toward, the African-American folk. Although the blues as a formal musical structure (a twelve-bar, three-line, AAB form) was not known until around 1910, folk-blues originated much earlier out of the vernacular music of Southern blacks—hollers, work songs, love songs, and spirituals; these were simple one-verse oral compositions consisting of a single line repeated three times that expressed the singer's intense feelings of sadness, lonesomeness, and abandonment, as for example in the line "Got no mo' home dan a dog, Lawd." Many early singers and composers have insisted that it is impossible to locate a specific time and place for the origin of the blues— " 'The blues? Ain't no first blues! The blues always been' "—especially since early blues singers were wanderers who carried their music from place to place via the railroad, the river, and the road. Ma Rainey recalled that she heard the blues for the first time quite by accident in a small town in Missouri in 1902, while Eubie Blake is said to have exclaimed: " 'Blues in Baltimore? Why, Baltimore is the blues!' "[37]

As critics have noted, the protagonists of the blues—both male and female—are individuals who are down on their luck, perhaps because they have lost their money or job, or more often because they have been betrayed by a wife/girlfriend or husband/boyfriend; sexual desire, fulfillment, and betrayal are central to the blues. Friendless and alone in the world, these individuals may turn to drink to numb their pain or leave home to wander about aimlessly and sing the blues; railways, dockyards, and roads become important settings of their experience. In the lyrics the representation of black womanhood is complex and sometimes contradictory. Women are sexually experienced, highly adept at "rolling" their "jelly"; and they are hard-drinking, connoisseurs of whiskey, gin, and rum. But if women singers tend to lament their victimization at the hands of two-timing men, male singers regard women as manipulative and duplicitous. Internalizing the racist aesthetics of the dominant culture, these men often prefer brown or yellow women to black as objects of sexual desire; yet they sometimes also acknowledge that these lighter-skinned women are not as trustworthy, and ultimately turn back to black women. Finally, particular suspicion is directed toward women who choose to spend time together and "don't think about no man": "Ketch two women runnin' togedder long, / You can bet yo' life dere's somethin' gwine wrong."[38]

A blues sensibility permeates "Melanctha," determining the story's geographic setting and shaping the destinies of both Melanctha and Jane Harden, who, as critics have noted, are fictional projections and reconfigurations of May Bookstaver / Helen Thomas and Mabel Haynes / Mable Neathe, respectively. As Melanctha gradually detaches herself from her family shortly after her father's razor fight with John, she starts to wander, much like her own creator Stein. Blues fashion, she strays "sometimes by railroad yards, sometimes on the docks or around new buildings" (96). In these places she meets black workers who are not hesistant to name female sexuality in the language of the blues: " 'Hullo sis, do you want to sit on my engine,' and, 'Hullo, that's a pretty lookin' yaller girl, do you want to come and see him cookin' " (98); or " 'Do you think you would make a nice jelly?' " (102). As blues women, Melanctha and Jane Harden are headstrong, passionate, and deliberately flout social convention to insist on their geographic mobility and freedom to express their sexuality as they please. If both of them are "yaller," it is because in the world of the blues it is the light-skinned women who are the most self-sufficient and unpredictable. Moreover, in blues lyrics the name Jane is often attached to women who make sure they get their own way: "My Jane's a gal gits all she can, / If you ain't got it, she hunts another man."[39] Jane Harden's independence is evident in the narrator's description of her vast worldly experience, her hard drinking ("Jane Harden had many bad habits. She drank a great deal, and she wandered widely" [104]), and of course in her suggested lesbianism, expressed through her strong attachment to Melanctha: "Jane grew always fonder of Melanctha. Soon they began to wander, more to be together than to see men and learn their various ways of working" (105).

It is Melanctha, however, whose very name suggests the blues, who is the primary blues figure of the story. She rambles in such blues sites as the railroad

yard and the docks, hoping to gain "real experience" by getting to know the
"natures" and "various ways of working" of the men who labor there (97, 95);
and for a time she challenges traditional sexual mores as she and Jane choose
to "run together." But Melanctha's blues nature is embodied above all in her
"complex, desiring" personality that draws her first to Jane, then to Jeff Campbell,
and finally to Jem Richards, in search of "real, strong, hot love" (87, 122); and
it is her consequent disappointment in this search that leads her to name herself
as a blues woman in a conversation with Rose that occurs at the beginning of
the story and is then recalled twice at the end:

> Sometimes the thought of how all her world was made, filled the complex, desiring
> Melanctha with despair. She wondered, often, how she could go on living when she
> was so blue.
>
> Melanctha told Rose one day how a woman whom she knew had killed herself
> because she was so blue. Melanctha said, sometimes, she thought this was the best
> thing for her herself to do.
>
> Rose Johnson did not see it the least bit that way.
>
> "I don't see Melanctha why you should talk like you would kill yourself just
> because you're blue. I'd never kill myself Melanctha just 'cause I was blue." (87)

Stein's text here indeed sings the blues.

As critics have noted, Stein was aware from a very early period in her life of
the sensual side of her nature; one of her Radcliffe themes portrays a "dark-
skinned girl" who is filled with "passionate yearnings" and "wild moods," and
a notebook entry comments on "the Rabelaisian, nigger abandonment . . . bitter
taste fond of it" to which she was clearly attracted.[40] Thus, even though Stein
projects herself in "Melanctha" into the more sober character of Jeff Campbell,
she nonetheless betrays a strong identification with those "complex, desiring"
aspects of her female protagonist, an identification kept carefully veiled within
the culture of the blues. Indeed, sexual ideologies of this period viewed the
homosexual, in particular the lesbian, as a hybrid (neither woman nor man) and
thus as degenerate; furthermore, according to these ideologies, it is the black
woman who, through the supposed malformation of her genitalia, comes to
embody the lesbian most fully: "the overdevelopment of the clitoris . . . lead[s]
to those 'excesses' which are called 'lesbian love.' The concupiscence of the
black is thus associated also with the sexuality of the lesbian."[41] Seen from the
perspective of the dominant culture, the vital image of black womanhood in the
blues lyrics from which Stein constructed her portrayal of Melanctha is transformed into one of degeneracy.

The foregoing analysis is meant to suggest the possibility of Stein's deep
familiarity with both coon songs, descended from mixed blood lines, and ragtime
music, performed in ethnically mixed settings and appealing to diverse sexualities,
as well as her attraction to the representation of blues women as independent and
sexually experimental. In imaginatively appropriating these African-American
musical traditions with which she had become familiar while living in Baltimore,

Stein turned to a culture that offered her representations of masculinity, femininity, and sexuality through which she could explore personal, familial, and social issues that had followed her on her transatlantic migration.[42] Yet from the point of view of the dominant culture, these musical traditions were perceived as degenerate because of their association with blackness and also with deviant lesbian sexuality, itself linked, as we have seen, to blackness. Thus, if "Melanctha" suggests Stein's fascination with African-American popular music, it also reflects her need to distance herself from it, out of fear of being assimilated to blackness, of actually being identified as a "nigger." The story embodies modernism's ambivalence over the loss of organic community and the flowering of borderland cultures in which the liberating fluidity of personal identity also becomes a source of anxiety.

Such fears were not entirely implausible to a Jewish woman who had inhabited an American metropolis at the turn of the century. Sander Gilman has argued that European anti-Semitic traditions had for centuries identified Jews as blacks, first through religious iconography that portrayed Jews as the Antichrist, and then through interpretations that asserted the physical similarity between Jews and blacks. Gilman has further shown how the physical reality of "plica polonica," a disease that plagued Eastern European Jews living in conditions of filth and poverty and blackened their skin, became a marker of their unhygienic nature, hypersexuality, and ugliness, linking them to blacks. In the United States, the massive immigration of foreign populations in the 1890s transformed American cities into geographic borderlands, and recently arrived Eastern European Jews came to be regarded by the dominant culture as little different from blacks. In this moment of social change, according to Michael Dobkowski, the Jew was readily perceived as the racial Other, the unwholesome and filthy slumdweller, the uncivilized and morally degraded foreigner who is ultimately incapable of being assimilated into Anglo-Saxon society.[43]

Even more radical were those views that asserted Jews to be of non-European origin; most typically, Jews were believed to be descended from an Asiatic race, specifically the Mongoloid Khazars.[44] At the extreme, a few race theorists even speculated on the historical admixture of Negro blood with the Jewish race. In a 1910 monograph, Arthur T. Abernethy asserted that "the Jew of to-day is essentially Negro in habits, physical peculiarities and tendencies." Such theories would eventually culminate in the better-known writings of Lothrop Stoddard, who argued that "it was also probably during their Egyptian sojourn that the Jews picked up their first traces of Negro blood. A Negroid strain undoubtedly exists in Jewry; to it the frizzy or woolly hair, thick lips, and prognathous jaws appearing in many Jewish individuals are probably due." Jews and blacks are further linked through the visible signs of physical degeneracy, marked by "deformed skulls, protruding jaws, and low brain weights," proving them to be races out of their proper place, and promising their eventual extinction.[45] Degeneracy has occurred because by the end of the nineteenth century neither of these displaced races is pure but rather hybridized. Jews continue to carry the stain of their early infusion of Negro blood while more recent racial miscegenation has given rise to the mongrelized mulatto. As these theories continued to assimilate Jews to blacks, many racial characteristics originally ascribed to blacks became attributed to Jews, in particular that of unrestrained and deviant sexuality. Here, finally, theories of racial degeneracy converged with those of sexual degeneracy.

It was from these images of degeneration that Stein ultimately sought to distance herself. Indeed, such standard conflations of racial and sexual deviancy may well explain her curious endorsement of Otto Weininger's treatise *Sex and Character*, published in 1906, in which the intersections of race and sexuality are very differently configured. Weininger condemns the Jewish race, which bears the mark of the Negro particularly in its "readily curling hair," since, according to him, this race is "saturated with femininity" and lacking in individuality, dignity, ethical sensibility, self-control, and genius. In contrast, Weininger praises the homosexual, rejecting sexual inversion as psycho-pathological and symptomatic of degeneration, and asserting that such inversion is "merely the sexual condition of these intermediate sexual forms that stretch from one ideally sexual condition to the other sexual condition." The "ideally sexual condition" is of course that of the male, and thus the homosexual woman who contains a large proportion of maleness in her becomes the subject of Weininger's intense admiration.[46]

One of the strategies through which some turn-of-the-century Jewish performers such as Al Jolson, Eddie Cantor, and Sophie Tucker sought to deal with the dominant culture's assimilation of Jewishness to blackness was by means of blackface, a representational strategy that emphasized the instability and volatility of the two groups' relationship to one another. When such Jewish performers assumed blackface, they were assimilating themselves to blacks; blackface then also became a means through which they could hide their real identities as Jews.[47] Yet, female blackface entertainers like Sophie Tucker also betrayed a real fear of identification with blacks and a need for racial reassurance when they insisted on revealing their true identity at the end of the performance. Forced to adopt blackface when a booking agent found her "so big and ugly," Tucker came to value the make-up; it functioned as a protective mask, freeing and enabling her to become the "World-renowned Coon Shouter." Yet her deliberate distance from blackness is all too obviously asserted in her compulsion at the end of the act "to peel off a glove and wave to the crowd to show I was a white girl," and in her obsessive investment in her own whiteness: "My own hair under the wig was a mass of burnished gold curls. Nature and my Crimean ancestors had done that for me. They had given me, too, my smooth, fine skin, that was pleasingly white now, since I had learned how to care for it."[48] Finally, as Michael Rogin has pointed out, such a revelation of what lies beneath blackface also functioned as part of a process of Americanization whereby Jewish performers hoped to assert their racial distance from blacks and embark on a path of upward mobility.[49]

Much like these Jewish entertainers, Stein may be said to adopt a form of blackface performance in writing "Melanctha." To the extent that she projected herself into the characters of Jeff and Melanctha, Stein was both identifying with blacks and using blackface as a protective mask behind which to explore personal sexual issues. But such a form of identification was also fraught with psychic dangers; blackface came then to function as a distancing mask behind which Stein flaunted her own whiteness. If racial distancing is unequivocal in Stein's stereotyping of certain of the frame characters, a more complex ambivalence is at work in the triumphant survival of Rose Johnson at the end. And if the story concludes with the demise of the two blues women—the disappearance of Jane Harden from the narrative and the death of Melanctha—the lessons of the blues live on in Jeff Campbell: "Jeff always had strong in him the meaning of all the new kind of beauty Melanctha Herbert once had shown him, and always more and more it helped him with his working for himself and for all the colored people" (207); and finally, the syncopated rhythms of ragtime endure beyond the narrated events in the style of the narrator herself.

In writing "Melanctha" Stein found herself caught in a complex web of racial contradictions. She was both powerfully drawn to African-American popular musical culture at the turn of the century, which offered her representations of strong, vibrant women unavailable to her in other artistic traditions, and she was repulsed by these images out of fear of being assimilated to them through her double identity as a Jew and a lesbian. These dual tendencies are fully inscribed in the racial discourse of "Melanctha."

## Notes

1. Quoted in James R. Mellow, *Charmed Circle: Gertrude Stein & Company* (New York: Praeger, 1974), 77.

2. Gertrude Stein, *The Autobiography of Alice B. Toklas* (New York: Vintage Books, 1960), 34. All further references are to this edition and will be placed parenthetically within the text.

3. Gertrude Stein, "A Transatlantic Interview 1946," in *Gertrude Stein: A Primer for the Gradual Understanding of Gertrude Stein*, ed. Robert Bartlett Haas (Los Angeles: Black Sparrow Press, 1971), 15–16; "Composition as Explanation," in *A Stein Reader*, *Gertrude Stein*, ed. Ulla F. Dydo (Evanston, Ill.: Northwestern University Press, 1993), 498.

4. See, for example, Michael North, *The Dialect of Modernism: Race, Language, and Twentieth-Century Literature* (New York: Oxford University Press, 1994), 59–65.

5. Quoted in *The Flowers of Friendship: Letters Written to Gertrude Stein*, ed. Donald Gallup (New York: Octagon Books, 1979), 54.

6. Raymond Williams, *The Politics of Modernism: Against the New Conformists* (London: Verso, 1989), 77–78; for a similar application of Williams's theories to Pound and Eliot, see North, *The Dialect of Modernism*, ch. 4.

7. Richard Bridgman, *Gertrude Stein in Pieces* (New York: Oxford University Press, 1970), 6.

8. Sherry H. Olson, *Baltimore: The Building of an American City* (Baltimore: Johns Hopkins University Press, 1980), 200–229.

9. Association for the Improvement of the Condition of the Poor, *Housing Conditions in Baltimore* (Baltimore: Charity Organization Society, 1907), 12, 16.

10. Quoted in Elizabeth Sprigge, *Gertrude Stein: Her Life and Work* (New York: Harper and Brothers, 1957), 23, 39; Robert Crunden, *American Salons: Encounters with European Modernism* (New York: Oxford University Press, 1993), 165, 177.

11. Gertrude Stein, *Q.E.D.* in *Fernhurst, Q.E.D., and Other Early Writing* (New York:

Liveright, 1971), 72. All further references are to this edition and will be placed parenthetically within the text.

12. Gertrude Stein, *Three Lives* (New York: Vintage Books, 1936), 24, 239. All further references are to this edition and will be placed parenthetically within the text.

13. For a full discussion of Anglo-Saxon nativist ideologies at the turn of the century, see John Higham, *Strangers in the Land* (New York: Atheneum, 1975), ch. 6.

14. Toni Morrison, *Playing in the Dark: Whiteness and the Literary Imagination* (Cambridge: Harvard University Press, 1993), 6.

15. Aldon L. Nielsen, *Writing Between the Lines: Race and Intertextuality* (Athens: University of Georgia Press, 1994), 16.

16. Ibid., 11.

17. Michael Rogin, "Blackface, White Noise: The Jewish Jazz Singer Finds His Voice," *Critical Inquiry* 18 (Spring 1992): 417.

18. Williams, *Politics of Modernism*, 79.

19. Ibid., 70.

20. See also Lisa Ruddick, *Reading Gertrude Stein: Body, Text, Gnosis* (Ithaca: Cornell University Press, 1990), 33.

21. On Stein's racism, see Sonia Saldivar-Hull, "Wrestling Your Ally: Stein, Racism, and Feminist Critical Practice," in *Women's Writing in Exile*, ed. Mary Lynn Broe and Angela Ingram (Chapel Hill: University of North Carolina Press, 1989), 185; on Stein as an experimental writer, see Marianne DeKoven, *A Different Language: Gertrude Stein's Experimental Writing* (Madison: University of Wisconsin Press, 1983). In a later study, DeKoven seeks to correct her earlier "oversight" of Stein's racial stereotyping by analyzing Stein's reference to "Melanctha" as the first step into twentieth-century literature, *Rich and Strange: Gender, History, Modernism* (Princeton: Princeton University Press, 1991), 229, 68.

22. Quoted in Rosalind S. Miller, *Gertrude Stein: Form and Intelligibility* (New York: The Exposition Press, 1949), 139.

23. Quoted in *Richard Wright: Books and Writers*, ed. Michel Fabre (Jackson: University Press of Mississippi, 1990), 151.

24. Edward A. Berlin, "Ragtime Songs," in *Ragtime: Its History, Composers, and Music*, ed. John Edward Hasse (New York: Schirmer Books, 1985), 72; Edward A. Berlin, *Ragtime: A Musical and Cultural History* (Berkeley: University of California Press, 1980), 33.

25. W. T. Jefferson, "My Coal Black Lady" (M. Witmark & Sons, 1896).

26. Robert C. Toll, *Blacking Up: The Minstrel Show in Nineteenth-Century America* (New York: Oxford University Press, 1974), 27–51; Eric Lott, *Love and Theft: Blackface Minstrelsy and the American Working Class* (New York: Oxford University Press, 1993), 92–96.

27. Houston A. Baker, Jr., *Modernism and the Harlem Renaissance* (Chicago: University of Chicago Press, 1987), 15, 21, 20; *The Afro-American*, April 11, 1903.

28. Gary Engle, ed., *This Grotesque Essence: Plays from the American Minstrel Stage* (Baton Rouge: Louisiana State University Press, 1978), 1.

29. Hans Nathan, *Dan Emmett and the Rise of Early Negro Minstrelsy* (Norman: University of Oklahoma Press, 1977), 159–160.

30. Bridgman, *Gertrude Stein in Pieces*, 10.

31. Terry Waldo, *This Is Ragtime* (New York: Hawthorn Books, 1976), 34–35.

32. Quoted in Al Rose, *Eubie Blake* (New York: Schirmer Books, 1979), 12–13.

33. Ibid., 21, 22; Robert Kimball and William Bolcom, *Reminiscing with Sissle and Blake* (New York: Viking Press, 1973), 42.

34. DeKoven, *A Different Language*, 28, 37; Ruddick, *Reading Gertrude Stein*, 33–37.

35. DeKoven, *A Different Language*, 42–43.

36. Ruddick, *Reading Gertrude Stein*, 33–35.

37. Abbe Niles, *Blues: An Anthology*, ed. W. C. Handy, rev. Jerry Silverman (New York: Da Capo Paperback, 1990), 12, 20, 61; quoted in Eileen Southern, *The Music of Black Americans*, 2nd ed. (New York: W. W. Norton, 1983), 330.

38. *The Blues Line*, ed. Eric Sackheim (Hopewell, N.J.: Ecco Press, 1993), 288; Niles, *Blues*, 13.

39. Howard W. Odum and Guy B. Johnson, *Negro Workaday Songs* (New York: Negro Universities Press, 1969), 144.

40. Miller, *Gertrude Stein*, 141–142; Linda Wagner-Martin, *"Favored Strangers": Gertrude Stein and her Family* (New Brunswick: Rutgers University Press, 1995), 80.

41. Sander L. Gilman, "Black Bodies, White Bodies: Toward an Iconography of Female Sexuality in Late Nineteenth-Century Art, Medicine, and Literature," *Critical Inquiry* 12 (Autumn 1985): 218.

42. Stein's awareness of her acts of cultural appropriation, as well as her anxiety over their legitimacy, are fully intimated in a passage in her later *Autobiography* in which she suggested that Negro culture does not necessarily belong to the Negro, but should be presumed to be universal, while at the same time accusing this culture of "nothingness": "Gertrude Stein did not like hearing him [Paul Robeson] sing spirituals. They do not belong to you any more than anything else, so why claim them, she said. He did not answer. . . . Gertrude Stein concluded that negroes were not suffering from persecution, they were suffering from nothingness" (238). I thank Sterling Stuckey for pointing this passage out to me.

43. Sander L. Gilman, *Difference and Pathology: Stereotypes of Sexuality, Race, and Madness* (Ithaca: Cornell University Press, 1985), 31–32, and *The Jew's Body* (New York and London: Routledge, 1991), 172–173; Michael N. Dobkowski, *The Tarnished Dream: The Basis of American Anti-Semitism* (Westport, Ct.: Greenwood Press, 1979), 146–147.

44. Robert Singerman, "The Jew as Racial Alien: The Genetic Component of American Anti-Semitism," in *Anti-Semitism in American History*, ed. David A. Gerber (Urbana: University of Illinois Press, 1986), 116.

45. Arthur T. Abernethy, *The Jew a Negro, Being a Study of the Jewish Ancestry from an Impartial Standpoint* (Moravian Falls, N.C., 1910), 105; Lothrop Stoddard, "The Pedigree of Judah," *The Forum* 75 (March 1926): 326; Nancy Stepan, "Biological Degeneration: Races and Proper Places," in *Degeneration: The Dark Side of Progress*, ed. J. Edward Chamberlain and Sander L. Gilman (New York: Columbia University Press, 1985), 98–99.

46. Otto Weininger, *Sex and Character* (1906; rpt. London: William Heinemann, 1975), 303, 306, 48.

47. Rogin, "Blackface, White Noise," 420, 439.

48. Sophie Tucker, *Some of These Days* (Garden City, N.Y.: Doubleday, 1945), 33, 35, 60.

49. Rogin, "Blackface, White Noise," 440, 447.

# The Master's Tools Revisited:
# Foundation Work in Anna Julia Cooper

B lack women at the World's Columbian Exposition in 1893 neatly divided themselves into two categories—marginalized insiders standing within the Fairgrounds and clear-cut outsiders. Inside, speaking in the building that housed the Haitian exhibition, was a small group of women, including the Washington, D.C., teacher and writer, Anna Julia Cooper. Hers was a quick five-minute delivery, calling on women to "take our stand on the solidarity of humanity, the oneness of life." Standing outside the gate, distributing pamphlets about women's marginalization at the Fair, stood the anti-lynching crusader Ida B. Wells. Wells delivered a protest much more direct than Cooper's. She called her pamphlet "a clear, plain statement of facts concerning the oppression put upon the colored people in this land of the free and home of the brave."[1] Her fiery work began with a history of slavery and included graphic descriptions of lynching in the United States. Common sense might suggest that Wells and those standing with her *outside* the Fair's walls were the radicals, those fighting for the most dramatic changes for women.

Likewise, the scholars who have recovered Cooper's work from obscurity often group her in the camp demanding less radical change. Hazel V. Carby and Mary Helen Washington help us understand Cooper's analysis of "patriarchy" and "imperialism" in her 1892 book of essays *A Voice From the South*.[2] But Washington finds Cooper too much the insider. "I must confess to a certain uneasiness about Cooper's tone in these essays, a feeling that while she speaks for ordinary black women, she rarely, if ever, speaks *to* them," says Washington.[3] Cooper adopts a high tone and instead of addressing black women's hand-to-mouth existence, she writes about education and Women's Clubs. Washington adds: "Her voice is not radical."[4]

Surely, bread and butter issues seized the minds of black women then. But asking whether Cooper speaks *to* or *for* black women, or speaks from *inside* or *outside*, doesn't lead us to Cooper's most important contribution. By design, Cooper did not unleash a fusillade of facts as Wells did, for she believed the facts would fall on deaf ears. Instead, Cooper worked on a different level. She rooted out beliefs that moved people to treat black women as chattel—beliefs that guided racist and sexist thinking about black women—and she recast them. Cooper stepped inside the minds of her audience and quietly laid a foundation to change their convictions. Readers walked away with new radical definitions of African Americans' and women's places in America that at first might not have been apparent to them. Only if readers stopped to piece together what they had taken in from *A Voice from the South* would they realize that Cooper audaciously sought to recast how society thinks. With refined rhetorical skills, then, Cooper overcame her marginalized status. She implicitly *created* the audience she wanted to speak to and *remade* the black woman in society's eyes. "The struggle with nature is over," she says in one essay, "The Status of Women in America," "the struggle with ideas begins."[5] Cooper had taken her battle to a higher level.

Just as Frederick Douglass's dialogic use of the open letter granted him a sudden promotion in society—from voiceless ex-slave to writer employing a 300-year-old-form—Cooper appropriated the methods—and the rights—of classical rhetoric to take power.[6] Cooper delineated her propositions quietly to rework definitions at the heart of the debate. Whether or not readers agreed with Cooper's explicit demands for reform, they put down her book with new implicit definitions of education, of women's role in society, and of race. In hijacking her audience's values, perhaps Cooper reflected the advice of Alexander Crummell, a man she considered as wise as "Moses and the Prophets." "Words are vital things," said the rector of St. Luke's Church in Washington, D.C. "They cannot enter the soul as passive and inoperative things."[7] Only with new definitions of training, race and gender could black women begin to work free of white oppression and a hand-to-mouth existence, if they ever could.

Cooper's method did not go unnoticed by the era's readers, who were more familiar with classical rhetoric than we are today. Albion Winegar Tourgée noted that "Rarely has the unsparing pencil passed so lightly over the pages of a book of essays as it did over the pages of this 'Voice from the South.' " "Cogently and forcibly written," said the Detroit *Plaindealer*, and the *Chicago Inter-Ocean* added, "The argument is keen . . . so pointed and honest as to be convincing for its justice."[8]

Yet Audre Lourde has said that the master's tools will never bring down the master's house. "Most Western literary genres are, after all, essentially male," argue feminist critics Sandra Gilbert and Susan Gubar, "devised by male authors to tell male stories about the world."[9] At the same time, Gilbert and Gubar show how successful women writers of the nineteenth century often implanted a second meaning in the text: "Parodic, duplicitous, extraordinarily sophisticated, all this female writing is both revisionary and revolutionary, even when it is produced by writers we usually think of as models of angelic resignation."[10] Indeed, Cooper may have adopted a male world's literary form, and she may have based her claims on assumptions inherent in the domestic sphere. But this does not make her an insider. Cooper used these methods to gather rhetorical force, to induce the audience to nod 'yes' while she slipped in a new, sometimes revolutionary, concept. Cooper might have been inside the master's house instead of seeking its destruction from outside, but she was quietly placing a new dictionary into the master's library, one that could change forever how the master read his own books.

Our digging then should begin with Cooper's education in rhetoric at St. Augustine's Normal and Collegiate Institute in North Carolina, at Oberlin and in her faculty position as a teacher of Latin in Washington, D.C. At these schools she learned the tools that would set her apart from other activists like Ida B. Wells and Mary Church Terrell. In her writing, Cooper argued differently than either Wells or Terrell. Instead of firing facts machine-gun style until she overwhelmed her audience with evidence, as Wells did, and instead of winding inductively from homey examples to broader missions for women, as Terrell did, Cooper built tight deductive arguments using the skills of classical rhetoric she learned in her youth. She quickly convinced her audience to agree with her on some point of general moral standards, and while their heads were nodding "yes," she rewrote their assumptions governing women's rights, women's right to education, and even the definition of race.

Gaining the education to wage these battles did not come easily to Cooper. When she attended St. Augustine's in 1873, the school organized its first Greek class but excluded women by designating it only for ministry students. "A boy, however meager his equipment and shallow his pretensions, had only to declare a floating intention to study theology and he could get all the support, encouragement and stimulus he needed," she later complained in *A Voice* (77). But Cooper would not be kept down by a lack of support. She got into the Greek class, and by the time she requested admission to Oberlin College as a twenty-three-year-old widow, she had read in Greek about three-hundred pages of text, including Xenophon, Plato, Herodotus and Thucydides, and in Latin, Caesar's seven books of commentaries, Cicero, and six books of Virgil's *Aeneid*.[11] Once at Oberlin in 1881, Cooper drank in the standard classical education of the era, which included a steady diet of rhetoric courses. She took the course offered her sophomore year, plus a logic course—then considered one of the ancillary fields of rhetoric— and three more courses in her junior year. And in her senior year, Cooper took courses in Plato and two more terms of rhetoric.[12] After graduating from Oberlin, she then taught Latin at the M Street School in Washington, D.C., for nearly the next forty years.[13]

Cooper's interest and training in rhetoric gives us a springboard to ask what it means to be a woman who used these skills to speak out. During the late nineteenth century, schools considered rhetoric one of the basic skills imparted to students. Oberlin so prized students' speaking ability that juniors met four days a week to focus on the physical preparation for speech, including, "Position, Breathing, Flexibility and Looseness of Throat, Depth of Vibration or Chest Resonance, 'Touch' and Articulation," according to the Oberlin College Catalogue for 1883–1884. "A complete system of Vocal Exercises will be given," the catalogue said, "designed to secure strength, ease, and durability of Voice."[14]

Rhetorical training at the time did not consist simply of chest and breathing exercises. Rhetoric's strength lies in its ability to mold concepts. In the nineteenth century, rhetoric theorists believed they rooted their practices in natural laws, laws that gave writers and orators powerful ammunition. "Of one who assumes to instruct and direct a body of men in a matter connected with their common interests," Cooper read in her sophomore class rhetoric text, "we expect that he will realize the importance of that which he advocates and the seriousness of the occasion."[15] These skills allowed orators and writers in a democracy to shape minds and change society. Mastering the rhetorical form thus allowed the skilled rhetorician—always defined as a man—to participate in the world's great issues, argued John Bascom, author of a leading rhetorical treatise of the time.[16] "When as a writer and speaker he puts himself in a communion with men, in giving law to their thought," says Bascom, "he gives law, also, to the nation's language."[17] And, in a democracy, he can give law to the land.

This white rhetorical strategy implicitly excluded black women like Cooper. As Claudia Tate points out in *Domestic Allegories of Political Desire: The Black Heroine's Text at the Turn of the Century*, white women held "exalted cultural value" and moved in "patriarchal society for producing heirs and regulating moral, spiritual, and emotional values." Society cast black women far below white women on the social hierarchy, stereotyped them as sluttish, and clung to an image of them as almost non-human. "Black women had expendable value," Tate says, "as base items of consumption."[18] Many black women in the 1890s struggled to exercise their right to speak, including Cooper's Oberlin classmate, Mary Church Terrell.[19] For years, Terrell had been eager to lecture on race in the United States. "When, however, my husband consented," she said, "some of his friends were so shocked and horrified that words simply failed them as they attempted to express their disapprobation."[20] Even among African Americans, gender tripped her up.

Cooper faced hardships similar to Terrell's. She says in her introduction to *A Voice* that "the 'other side' has not been represented by one who 'lives there.' And not many can more sensibly realize and more accurately tell the weight and the fret of the 'long dull pain' than the open-eyed but hitherto voiceless Black Woman of America."[21] Yet Cooper escaped the traps that sought to silence her. By embracing the rhetorical practice, Cooper moved away from race- and gender-based assumptions about who can write. By implicitly making herself a member of the government—a lawgiver—she upset the accepted order. Her "Woman vs. The Indian," for example, closes with a peroration intended to direct readers' moral development. She urges them to a higher level, a level that she already has laid before them, and she calls on her readers to align their thinking with "the supremacy of the moral forces of reason and justice and love in the government of the nation" (126).

The shape of Cooper's argument made another statement: she would accept no compromise. Rhetoric uses two opposing sides to investigate issues.[22] In her introduction to *A Voice*, she explains her task in terms of setting facts before a jury, and she casts her entire book as evidence in a trial. In "Woman vs. The Indian" for example, she establishes an opposition—Cooper versus white women who want to exclude blacks from their clubs. She sets out the agreed-upon-facts, defines the terms, refutes the racist women's arguments, and calls for a new moral and philosophical order on this topic. One cannot chose a middle ground.

Cooper's technique for building her arguments also sets her apart from other women of the period and illustrates how she manipulated male-dominated rhetorical styles for her own means. Bascom put much distance between feminine forms of expression and the necessary skills of a rhetorician. Strong rhetoricians considered memory the weakest way to marshal facts and only reluctantly used memory in a proof. Bascom identified memory with the feminine, slipping into the feminine pronoun when discussing it.[23] Bascom also warned male readers away from forms that dwelt on the emotions or that led the reader inductively from the specific to a broader point. Anecdote limited inductive reasoning's general applicability, he said, and its power.

Early feminists intentionally fashioned an inductive rhetorical style to avoid challenging the male order too forcefully. Aware that their power to speak was suspect, these women struck a more personal tone and relied on personal experience, in effect asking the audience to participate. "As a less authoritative and aggressive style," says Karlyn Kohrs Campbell, "it was a less confrontational violation of taboos against public speaking by women."[24]

Mary Church Terrell illustrates this feminine inductive approach in 1906. In "What It Means to Be Colored in the Capital of the United States," Terrell leads the reader through example after example of the indignities that she faced in Washington. "As a colored woman I might enter Washington any night, a stranger in a strange land, and walk miles without finding a place to lay my head," she writes.[25] Terrell struggles to find a restaurant that will serve her and a seat on mass transit to the Washington Monument. Only after Terrell leads us through these personal trials, and other ordeals by individuals she knows in Washington, D.C., does she make the overarching statement of her essay, which comes in its last sentence: "[T]he chasm between the principles upon which this Government was founded, in which it still professes to believe, and those which are daily practiced under the protection of the flag, yawns so wide and deep."[26] While Terrell effectively makes her point, she has not assumed the power of someone who can lay down principles or laws and then drag the audience by the collar through them.

Frances Willard, the head of the Woman's Christian Temperance Union, who wrote during Cooper's time, slightly modified this rhetorical pattern. Unlike earlier feminists, Willard uses deductive reasoning but conceals the premises of her arguments by embowering them in flowery statements.[27] In 1890, for example, Willard wrote "A White Life for Two," in which she argues for a new role for women. Then she adds: "To meet this new creation, how grandly men themselves are growing; how considerate and brotherly, how pure in word and deed!"[28] She clothes her assertion for women's power in flattery for men.

Contrast this with "The Higher Education of Women," Cooper's discussion of the new woman who gains the right to education:

> The question is not now with the woman "How shall I so cramp, stunt, simplify and nullify myself as to make me eligible to the honor of being swallowed up into some little man?" but the problem, I trow, now rests with the man as to how he can so develop his God-given powers as to reach the ideal of a generation of women who demand the noblest, grandest and best achievements of which he is capable; and this surely is the only fair and natural adjustment of the chances. (70–71)

None of Willard's "grandly growing men" here. Cooper drops "the problem" at men's door. Moreover, instead of starting the essay with personal experience, as

Terrell did, Cooper begins it with an image of traditional white male power: a book produced in Paris. "The author declares that woman can use the alphabet only as Molière predicted they would," she razzes, "in spelling out the verb *amo*" (48). Cooper takes the audience head on, and invokes icons of high culture only to make fun of their provinciality. Before our eyes have traveled halfway down the page, Cooper shows us that she can enter the Western tradition's dialogue *and* signify on it. By the time we reach the bottom of the page, Cooper's ironic voice has trotted Ovid, Penelope, Andromache, Lucretia, and Petrarch's Laura by the reader, and there can be no more questions about her right to speak. The essay then proceeds from a premise—that the "civilized world" needs women to keep it civilized—and develops Cooper's point: those civilizing women need to hone their skills with education. The "little man" in Cooper's prose will just have to live with the new, more educated, woman, she says, and Cooper doesn't hesitate to point a finger at the group that needs to make a change. Thus, Cooper moves in the deductive fashion, from the general to the concrete, and she does it without flinching. She leads her readers to the source of their backward attitudes and demands that they change.

Cooper uses deductive reasoning again in "Women vs. The Indian" to trounce Southern white women's reasoning abilities. "Now the Southern woman," she taunts, "was never renowned for her reasoning powers, and it is not surprising that just a little picking will make her logic fall to pieces" (108–109). These women believe that "because her grandfather had slaves who were black, all the blacks in the world of every shade and tint were once in the position of her slaves" (109). First Cooper uses analogy to show how the argument fails in its entirety. "The black race constitutes one-seventh the known population of the globe," she says. "That [the white lady's] slaves were black and she despises her slaves, should no more argue antipathy to all dark people and peoples, than that Guiteau, an assassin, was white, and I hate assassins, should make me hate all persons more or less white" (109). Do not blithely reason from the particular to the general, Cooper warns here. Because President James Garfield's assassin was white doesn't mean all white people are assassins.

Then Cooper represents their argument as a syllogism to pinpoint the fallacy of thought: "Civility to the Negro implies social equality. I am opposed to *associating* with dark persons on terms of social equality. Therefore, I abrogate civility to the Negro" (109–110). She displays an analogous syllogism—spaced on the page as if it were appearing in a logic text:

> Light is opposed to darkness.
> Feathers are light.
> Ergo,
> Feathers are opposed to darkness.

> The 'social equality' implied by civility to the Negro is a very different thing from forced association with him socially. (110)

In four short sentences, Cooper lays waste the Southern women's argument.

Despite her use of deductive logic, Cooper appeared less threatening to readers by anchoring her reasoning in safe and familiar waters: women's claim to the domestic sphere. Once she had pulled readers into that sphere and assured them of the ground rules, she could play with the audience's assumptions about women's role in society. Readers continued their journey, believing that the timeworn truisms of domesticity—which denied women their rights—guided the argument. By the time readers finished the essay, they found that Cooper had inserted new definitions, ones that assumed a new woman, with much more radical rights.

While the notion of the domestic sphere appears limiting to many readers today, Claudia Tate shows us that we have to place ourselves in the historical context to understand its significance for contemporary readers. At the time, the domestic ideal had a much different meaning to black women like Cooper than it did to whites like Willard. In the post-reconstruction world, black women could not be expected to reject a notion that the woman's world was the domestic one. Because slavery had never allowed them to have a home and family, they first had to secure that right. "After all, such heroines could hardly reject what had not been broadly within their domain to embrace," argues Tate about the women in African-American novels of the period. By holding on to the domestic, the black woman becomes a symbol of racial advancement.[29]

Consider first the tactics of Frances Willard, who stands on the more conservative side of Cooper, because Willard wraps her demands in domestic values but softens them until they recede into much less radical aims. To change women's roles changes little in society, she says. "Woman is becoming what God meant her to be and Christ's Gospel necessitates her being," Willard says in "A White Life for Two," "the companion and counselor[,] not the incumbrance and toy of man."[30] She wants women to have a different position in society, but this position isn't going to make us see our most closely held beliefs—something so basic as racism—anew.

Ida B. Wells's style stands on the other end of the spectrum from Willard and still shows us what Cooper does *not* do. As Hazel Carby explains, Wells zeros in on a specific moral wrong: the ways white males manipulated black men's and women's bodies for political ends.[31] She dwells less on redefining roles and race than she does on pinpointing morally reprehensible conduct and calling for its end. Unlike Cooper, Wells relies on an onslaught of facts drawn from white newspapers. "Out of their own mouths shall the murderers be condemned," she says in *A Red Record*.[32] Wells further establishes an aura of fact by quoting herself in *A Red Record*, making herself the authority, the source to which any writer, including Ida B. Wells in this case, would turn for the answer. And on this accretion of detail, deliberately and relentlessly, Wells founds her case for change.

Cooper argues, however, that facts don't work. "It is absurd to quote statistics showing the Negro's bank account and rent rolls," she says in "Womanhood: A Vital Element in the Regeneration and Progress of a Race," "to point to the hundreds of newspapers edited by colored men and lists of lawyers and doctors," while society makes black women chattel (25). Cooper understood that hard figures poured into a biased mind will go nowhere.[33] For deeper change, one needs to examine readers'— and society's—basic assumptions about women and race. Cooper must change readers' preconceptions so they can *see* the facts. Attack the problem at its root— at the basic cognitive level that whites use to understand African Americans—and redefine the notion of black women in the era.

Thus, if Cooper stands between both Wells and Willard in style, she surpasses them both in the radical changes she asks of the audience. Clothed in her learned rhetorical forms, Cooper remakes what it means to be a woman and what it means to be black in America. As her audience agrees with her on the flag-waving issues of God and country, she hijacks notions of domesticity, of women's role in education, and of race.

Accordingly, Cooper uses the domestic sphere to do something more than establish the black woman's right to have a family and home. Her writing uses the domestic sphere for leverage in building a more powerful and radical deductive argument. In "Woman vs. The Indian," for example, she leads readers into the peroration, rousing them to higher thoughts and exalted feelings, culminating in one stunning periodic sentence that illustrates reasoning central to her entire essay:

> Let her try to teach her country that every interest in this world is entitled at least to a respectful hearing, that every sentiency is worthy of its own gratification, that a helpless cause should not be trampled down, nor a bruised reed broken; and when the right of the individual is made sacred, when the image of God in human form, whether in marble or in clay, whether in alabaster or in ebony, is consecrated and inviolable, when men have been taught to look beneath the rags and grime, the pomp and pageantry of mere circumstance and have regard unto the celestial kernel uncontaminated at the core,—when race, color, sex, condition, are realized to be the accidents, not the substance of life, and consequently as not obscuring or modifying the inalienable title to life, liberty, and pursuit of happiness,—then is mastered the science of politeness, the art of courteous contact, which is naught but the practical application of the principal of benevolence, the back bone and marrow of all religion; then women's lesson is taught and woman's cause is won—not the white woman nor the black woman nor the red woman, but the cause of every man or woman who has writhed silently under a mighty wrong. (124–125)

Here, Cooper immediately frames the discussion as a trial—every interest has a right to a hearing—and thus we know that there can be no compromise, one side will have to win. She uses two basic building blocks—the position as society's shaper that her rhetorical role grants her, and the notion of domesticity—and she uses them to mold how readers approach race, class, and gender. She calls on readers to reassess their own values and not to let surface characteristics interfere with people's "life, liberty, and pursuit of happiness." She thus writes women and blacks back into the Declaration of Independence. Her deft handling of the male rhetorical form has helped her insert African Americans into the most basic document of the Union, making them part of her unstoppable sweep of history.

Cooper further redefines the domestic sphere. First, she delivers the traditional take on women's roles to the audience—succor the trampled. She begins a sentence that appears to describe traditional jobs for women by forecasting a time "when the right of the individual is made sacred, when the image of God in human form ... is consecrated and inviolable." But Cooper suspends the sentence between the first introductory clause and the subject and verb that we expect will follow. She inserts a series of modifiers to these truisms about women's labor, and she then reroutes the real point. She broadens our definition of who should receive help, and thus broadens our definition of women's work.

She first establishes what that women's sphere should include. By modifying "God in human form" with the phrases "whether in marble or in clay, whether in alabaster or in ebony," she pairs two substances that have the same constitution— marble and clay, for both come from the God's earth, yet stand apart because one is shiny and one is dull. Then by association, she presents two other sub- stances, alabaster and ebony, in the same light, carrying over the sense of kinship from the first pair to this new pairing. Although the new pair consists of different colors—white and black—we group them with the first pair because they're both natural substances. Cooper implicitly pulls white and black under the same Godly banner, grouping them in our minds with marble and clay. Cooper, who slew the Southern woman's logic with a swift syllogism, here defies a simple logical progression—what does clay have to do with wood?—and instead opts for creating a new unit in our minds. Cooper's audience believed that blacks and whites arose from very different stocks. Her task was to unite them under the notion of "human being." With her new groupings, these substances can be different—one white and the other black—yet the same—all part of God's dominion. From here, she need only show us that society denies a part of the whole, a portion of the "celestial kernel uncontaminated at the core," its proper rights to demand our action. Put this way, the task becomes clear. God's dominion is women's dominion, and their labor is redefined. Only when America bridges this gulf will women's work be done. For her part, the writer Cooper has finished her work before we even have reached the sentence's subject and verb.

After Cooper recasts what women's work means, she finishes the thought begun so long ago: "Then is mastered the science of politeness, the art of courteous contact." She has already won her point. Only then—when women stand up to claim proper rights for all of the whole—she says, can the coveted domestic power be claimed for one's own. Cooper here uses her rhetorical tools to find a niche within the dominant myth of domesticity. She then carves out a new function for herself, for women and for blacks. With such a large task before them, the women's movement needs all the soldiers it can muster—white and black.[34]

Cooper also applies her redefining magic in another essay, "The Higher Educa- tion of Women." When she speaks about educating women, she argues, as does Willard, that an educated woman can wisely chose a mate rather than run pell- mell into the arms of the first available man.[35] Once Cooper uses the domestic argument to demand education for women, she sets out to redefine what women are to do with it; in fact, once again, to redefine the domestic sphere. In one long sentence in "The Higher Education of Women," she pushes the narrative along, making the audience *think* that their definition of woman has been reaf- firmed, and then subverts it by redefining the notion of womanhood and redirecting what women can do with their education:

> [T]o-day there are one hundred and ninety-eight colleges for women, and two hundred
> and seven coeducational colleges and universities in the United States alone offering
> the degree of B.A. to women, and sending out yearly into the arteries of this nation
> a warm, rich flood of strong, brave, active, energetic, well-equipped, thoughtful
> women—women quick to see and eager to help the needs of this needy world—
> women who can think as well as feel, and who feel none the less because they

think—women who are none the less tender and true for the parchment scroll they bear in their hands—women who have given a deeper, richer, nobler and grander meaning to the word "womanly" than any one-sided masculine definition could ever have suggested or inspired—women whom the world has long waited for in pain and anguish till there should be at last added to its forces and allowed to permeate its thought the complement of that masculine influence which has dominated it for fourteen centuries. (50–51)

Cooper starts out with well-established facts—the story told so far about the growth of colleges. She tells us that colleges are sending out women with traits that everyone can approve of—strong, brave, energetic, well-equipped. In mid-sentence—"a warm, rich flood of strong, brave, active . . . women"—she uses parallel phrases that at first fit snugly with everyone's understanding of woman-hood, namely women who are "quick to see and eager to help the needs of this needy world." Who can deny Cooper here? Having built on these easy-to-swallow premises, Cooper's sentence has momentum. Then she hammers out the edges of what the audience considers feminine: "women who can *think* as well as feel." This is the contested territory. Cooper quickly buttresses her argument with a chaismus which argues that this "thinking" strengthens the very traits that the audience is most comfortable accepting in women: "who feel none the less because they think." Cooper consolidates her ground with another defining clause, one that buttresses traditional beliefs—"none the less tender and true." So far, Cooper sounds almost like Frances Willard, only she hasn't pushed the flowery phrasing so far.

But then Cooper works her cultural insurrection, suggesting that these educated women are all the more women—in a "deeper, richer" sense—than "any one-sided masculine definition could ever have suggested or inspired." Cooper argues for a new definition of womanliness, one that men could never have thought of. She takes this new definition and gives it weight in her audience's eyes by arguing that the world *needs* the strength of these better-equipped women to do the work. She calls women a "complement of that masculine influence," thus not calling for an overthrow but suggesting that the world's intellectual, cultural, and political forces are not complete until women's ideas are added to them. Then she pushes her point further. In mid-phrase, Cooper tucks in her most revolutionary concepts by demanding that women's ideas be "allowed to perme-ate" the world's thought. With "permeate" she seeks to overturn the male concep-tion of women *and* the male way of viewing the world to make women's thought part of the undivided whole. Cooper shows us what this permeation means: "Religion, science, art, economics, have all needed the feminine flavor" (57). Men can close nothing off to women.

Cooper makes similar moves with the notion of race. Like other writers of the era, she often speaks of mulatta women and their plight. Claudia Tate persuasively argues that novelists in Cooper's time, like Pauline Hopkins, were creating a new racial stock from mulattos. This was a "transitional racial and class status," argues Tate, that after emancipation created a new niche for African Americans in society. The slave was transformed from the chattel of the master to a new position "grounded in virtue, education, and hard work." In other words, writers like Hopkins used a fuzzy race background to move society's judgmental lens from skin color to individual accomplishment.[36]

Cooper also used light-skin heroines in her work, such as the "cream-colored applicant" in "Woman vs. The Indian," who was denied a place in Wimodaughsis (82). Like the novelists Tate writes about, Cooper isn't lifting the mulatto above those with darker skins. In extolling women's abilities to reform in "The Status of Women in America," she talks about their fierce loyalty: "You do not find the colored woman selling her birthright for a mess of pottage" (139). But the mulatta becomes a weapon to show that skin color is an "accident, not the substance of life" (125). Cooper mocks the whole notion of blood lines in "Woman vs. The Indian." "If your own father was a pirate, a robber, a murderer, his hands are dyed in red blood, and you don't say very much about it. But if your great great great grandfather's grandfather stole and pillaged and slew, and you can prove it, your blood has become blue and you are at great pains to establish the relationship" (103). Blood stands for little in the work that Cooper imagines for humankind, but she also questions whether it means anything by itself. The slave owner, for example, has created false divisions based on blood. "He sowed his blood broadcast among them, then pitted mulatto against black, bond against free, house slave against plantation slave, even the slave of one clan against like slave of another clan" (102). Cooper makes race a social distinction rather than a biological one. "Purity" rests in the mind.

It was a quality of mind that Cooper sought to create in her audience. Artists "have wrought into their products, lovingly and impartially and reverently, every type, every tint, every tone that they felt or saw or heard" (176), she says in one *Voice* essay, and they integrate these colors into their work. The artist controls the ultimate meaning of the piece. "For each of us truth means merely the representation of the sensations and experiences of our personal environment, colored and vivified, fused into consistency and crystallized into individuality in the crucible of our own feelings and imaginations" (176–177).

And this is what Anna Julia Cooper has done in *A Voice from the South*. She has used the rhetorical skills of the educated white man to package her own social criticism, a critique that fused the types, the tints and the tones of the world into a consistent whole. And in a close reading of how she crafts these new definitions, we see that she may be standing on the inside, as she did at the World's Columbian Exposition, but, from the insider's place, Anna Cooper has crafted a new world order.

*Notes*

I owe thanks to Karen Hust and Shelley Fisher Fishkin for their helpful comments and gracious support.

1. Anna Julia Cooper, speech at the World's Columbian Exposition, quoted in Jeanne Madeline Weimann, *The Fair Women* (Chicago: Academy Chicago, 1981), 123, and Ida B. Wells, *Crusade for Justice: The Autobiography of Ida B. Wells*, Alfreda M. Duster, ed. (Chicago: University of Chicago Press, 1970), 117.

2. Hazel V. Carby, *Reconstructing Womanhood: The Emergence of the Afro-American Woman Novelist* (New York: Oxford University Press, 1987), 96–97, and Mary Helen Washington, "Introduction," in Anna Julia Cooper, *A Voice from the South* (1892; rpt., New York: Oxford University Press, 1988), xxvii–liv.

3. Washington, "Introduction," xxix–xxx.

4. Ibid., xxxi. More recently, Elizabeth Alexander in " 'We Must Be about Our Father's Business': Anna Julia Cooper and the In-Corporation of the Nineteenth-Century African-American Woman Intellectual," *Signs: Journal of Women in Culture and Society* 20 (Winter 1995): 336–357, looks at other sides of Cooper's work. Alexander argues that Cooper writes her body into the text of *A Voice*, thus creating a space for the African-American woman intellectual. While Alexander notes Cooper's rhetorical sophistication, she is more concerned with Cooper's right to speak as an intellectual than she is with tracing how Cooper remaps the public debate.

5. Anna Julia Cooper, *A Voice*, 132. Future references will appear parenthetically in the text.

6. Shelley Fisher Fishkin and Carla L. Peterson, "We Hold These Truths to Be Self-Evident," in Eric J. Sundquist, ed., *Frederick Douglass: New Literary and Historical Essays* (New York: Cambridge University Press, 1990), 189–204; see especially pages 196–198.

7. Alexander Crummell, "The Need of New Ideas and New Aims," in *Africa and America: Addresses and Discourses* (Springfield, Mass: Willey & Co., 1891), 19. Cooper's comment about Crummell's wisdom is found in *A Voice*, 24.

8. Quoted in M. A. Majors, *Noted Negro Women: Their Triumphs and Activities* (Chicago: Donohue & Henneberry, 1893), 285–289.

9. Sandra M. Gilbert and Susan Gubar, *Madwoman in the Attic* (New Haven: Yale University Press, 1979), 67.

10. Ibid., 80.

11. Handwritten letter of John E. C. Smedes, reproduced in Louise Daniel Hutchinson, *Anna Julia Cooper: A Voice From the South* (Washington, D.C.: Smithsonian Institution Press, 1981), 35.

12. Course listing, Anna Julia Cooper file, Oberlin College Archives, 392.

13. Hutchinson, *Anna Julia Cooper: A Voice*, 148.

14. Oberlin College Catalogue, 1883–1884, 60.

15. Ibid., 65, lists "Hepburn's Manual" as the text for the second term, second semester Rhetoric course. I believe this refers to A. D. Hepburn, *Manual of English Rhetoric* (Cincinnati: Wilson, Kinkle & Co., 1875). Quote appears on 255.

16. Nan Johnson, *Nineteenth-Century Rhetoric in North America* (Carbondale: Southern Illinois University Press, 1991), 246. Johnson also drew my attention to Bascom's *Philosophy* as a leading rhetoric text of the era.

17. John Bascom, *Philosophy of Rhetoric* (New York: Woolworth, Ainsworth & Co., 1872), 135.

18. Claudia Tate, *Domestic Allegories of Political Desire: The Black Heroine's Text at the Turn of the Century* (New York: Oxford University Press, 1992), 25.

19. Karlyn Kohrs Campbell, *Man Cannot Speak For Her, Volume I: A Critical Study of Early Feminist Rhetoric*, Contributions in Women's Studies, No. 101 (New York: Greenwood Press, 1989), 151.

20. Mary Church Terrell, *A Colored Woman in a White World* (Washington D.C.: Ransdell, 1940), 158. Quoted in Campbell, *Critical Study*, 151.

21. Cooper may exaggerate somewhat. Condit and Lucaites argue that National Negro Conventions beginning in 1830 started a debate about equality that sometimes sought to extend the definition of freedom beyond gender. See Celeste Michelle Condit and John

Louis Lucaites, *Crafting Equality: America's Anglo-African Word* (Chicago: University of Chicago Press, 1993), 77–80. In short, other black women had spoken. But this doesn't cancel Cooper's general point that black women rarely were included in public debate.

22. See Richard A. Lanham's discussion of "Dissoi logoi," 57–59, and of "Arrangement: The Parts of an Oration," 171–174, in *A Handlist of Rhetorical Terms, Second Edition* (Berkeley: University of California Press, 1991).

23. Bascom, *Philosophy of Rhetoric*, 66.

24. Campbell, *Critical Study*, 12–15, quote appears on 14.

25. Mary Church Terrell, "What It Means to Be Colored in the Capital of the United States" (1906). Reprinted in *Man Cannot Speak For Her, Volume II: Key Texts of the Early Feminists*, compiled by Karlyn Kohrs Campbell, Contributions in Women's Studies, No. 102 (New York: Greenwood Press, 1989), 422.

26. Ibid., 432.

27. Campbell, *Critical Study*, 129.

28. Frances E. Willard, "A White Life for Two" (1890), reprinted in Campbell, *Key Texts*, 325.

29. Tate, *Domestic Allegories*, 138. Ann du Cille makes a similar point in *The Coupling Convention: Sex, Text, and Tradition in Black Women's Fiction* (New York: Oxford University Press, 1993), 50. Nina Baym also has argued that critics must begin to see the domestic story as part of an allegory of black people taking a role on the national stage. See Nina Baym, "A Refusal to Be Other," *American Quarterly* 46 (September 1994): 434–440, especially page 439.

30. Willard, "A White Life," 325.

31. Carby, *Reconstructing Womanhood*, 111–115.

32. Ida B. Wells, *A Red Record* (Chicago: Donohue & Henneberry, 1894). Rpt. in Ida B. Wells-Barnett, *On Lynchings: Southern Horrors, A Red Record, Mob Rule in New Orleans* (Salem, New Hampshire: Ayer, 1991), 15.

33. For a stunning example of a writer missing the point of Wells's cold, hard facts, see Thomas Nelson Page, "The Lynching of Negroes—Its Cause and Its Prevention," *North American Review* (January 1904): 33–48. Page uses the same figures as Wells does in *The Red Record*, and, incredibly, he still draws the conclusion that lynchings result from black men raping white women. After a Southern mob lynched Sam Hose, W.E.B. Du Bois decided that hard facts would not sway the country. He then turned his efforts from data-intensive sociology to persuasive journalism. See W.E.B. Du Bois, *Dusk of Dawn: An Essay Toward an Autobiography of a Race Concept* (1940). Reprinted in Du Bois, *Writings* (New York: Library of America, 1986), 602–603.

34. Cooper's facility with definitions in this sentence mimics what she does in the essay as a whole. She draws on her audience's universal disdain for bullies, shows that bullies treat African-American women badly, and reminds readers that women are responsible for taming these bullies. By placing bullies in the same group with racists, Cooper makes both the target for women's civilizing influence. See especially 85–90.

35. Compare with Willard, "A White Life," 334–335.

36. Tate, *Domestic Allegories*, 147.

ROBERT S. LEVINE

# The African-American Presence
# in Stowe's *Dred*

In "Unspeakable Things Unspoken," Toni Morrison maintains that "the presence of Afro-American literature and the awareness of its culture" should inform our readings of white-authored texts, for "the presence of Afro-Americans has shaped the choices, the language, the structure—the meaning of so much American literature." As an example, Morrison remarks on how newly resonant "meanings" become available in the works of Melville when his writings are "scoured for this presence and the writerly strategies taken to address or deny it." Morrison's essay has given rise to a methodology of "scouring"—critical efforts to disclose in white-authored texts deeply embedded African-American influences that have about them (presumably for white authors) the scandalous taint of "miscegenation."[1] In the case of Harriet Beecher Stowe, however, no such "scouring" is required, and no such scandal need be reported, for Stowe regularly acknowledged African-American influences on her writings, most notably in her 1853 *A Key to Uncle Tom's Cabin*. In addition to discussing the influences of Frederick Douglass, Josiah Henson, J.W.C. Pennington, Lewis Clarke, Solomon Northup, and Lewis Hayden, among others, on *Uncle Tom's Cabin*, Stowe reveals in *Key* that she sees herself as engaged in an ongoing dialogue with these important black writers of the period, writers whose influence, implicitly and explicitly, can also be discerned in her "other" antislavery novel, *Dred: A Tale of the Great Dismal Swamp* (1856).[2]

Published four years after *Uncle Tom's Cabin*, *Dred* has become a missing text in Stowe's canon. Judged by many critics to be racist and a botch, an embarrassment to Stowe and her admirers, the overwhelming response to *Dred* has been simply to ignore it. This decision to ignore is the true embarrassment, for it exposes contemporary critical practices as unwilling to deal with Stowe's complex and contradictory racial politics in *evolution*; as unable to attend to black influences on Stowe's texts, except when those influences "expose" her mendacity and blindness; and as reluctant to challenge essentialist notions of Stowe's inability to imagine slavery from a black perspective. This essay attempts to challenge current critical orthodoxies by resituating *Dred* in relation to contemporaneous African-American discourses on slavery and racism. Stowe's encounters with African Americans during the years 1852–1856 in particular had a major impact on her conception of black culture in *Dred*, a novel which, with its heroic portrayal of a militant black conspirator modelled on Nat Turner, can be regarded as an African–American inspired revision of *Uncle Tom's Cabin*. As we shall see, Stowe's exchanges with African-American writings and personalities

after the publication of *Uncle Tom's Cabin* had a dramatic effect on her racial
politics. Attending to the African-American presence in her 1856 novel helps us
to see that *Dred* is a fundamentally different book from *Uncle Tom's Cabin*, a
book that is far more engaged with African Americans' perspectives on their
situation in antebellum culture. Insofar as it explodes critical myths about her
purported blindness to African-American realities, *Dred* is critical to an understanding of Stowe's career.

As an example of Stowe's post-*Uncle Tom's Cabin* readiness to attend to
African-American perspectives, we might best begin with a brief consideration
of her views on Liberian colonization. In a well known contemporary attack on
*Uncle Tom's Cabin* in *Frederick Douglass' Paper*, to which Stowe subscribed,
the black emigrationist Martin R. Delany criticized Stowe for her apparent advocacy of colonization as a solution to America's racial problems, facetiously
hoping that in *Key* she has "renounced Colonization as she had made a public
avowal of it [in *Uncle Tom's Cabin*]." In response to Delany's criticisms, Douglass
asserted that Stowe may have become "more of an abolitionist now than when
she wrote that chapter." The evidence suggests that Stowe in fact did change her
mind on colonization, perhaps in response to this very letter exchange. Not only
did she send a letter to the May 1853 meeting of the American and Foreign Anti-
Slavery Society declaring that she was "not a Colonizationist," but in *Key* itself
she implicitly renounced colonizationism. The final chapter of *Key*—"What Is
To Be Done?"—says nothing about colonization, arguing instead for antiracist
strategies to bring about black elevation. She proclaims to her white readers:
"As far as in you lies, endeavor to secure for them [free and enslaved blacks],
in every walk of life, the ordinary privileges of American citizens."[3]
Following the publication of *Uncle Tom's Cabin*, Stowe, as America's best
known white antislavery writer, attempted to do just that. In the process, she
considerably enlarged her range of experiences with African Americans. As
recounted in *Key*, in 1852 she helped the slave Milly Edmondson to purchase
her children from slavery, raising the funds to send two of her daughters to
Oberlin. That same year she corresponded with Harriet Jacobs about the possibility
of helping her to write up her life history, and she entertained Sojourner Truth
for several days at her home. One year later she entertained Douglass at her
home. While in England in 1853, Stowe had numerous first-hand encounters
with black abolitionists, including William Wells Brown, William G. Allen,
William and Ellen Craft, and Samuel Ward. She writes about Ward in her 1854
*Sunny Memories of Foreign Lands*: "All who converse with him are satisfied
that there is no native difference between the African and other men." In the
spirit of such egalitarianism, Stowe championed the careers of two black female
performers, the singer Elizabeth Greenfield and the actress Mary Webb, for
whom she wrote *The Christian Slave* (1855), a dramatic version of *Uncle Tom's
Cabin*. She also wrote the introductions to three major African-American texts
of the 1850s: William C. Nell's *The Colored Patriots of the American Revolution*
(1855), Frank J. Webb's *The Garies and Their Friends* (1857), and Josiah Hen-

son's *Truth Stranger Than Fiction* (1858). In a review essay of 1856, "Anti-Slavery Literature," she again spoke to the impact of black writers on her thinking, praising the autobiographies of Henson, Bibb, Clarke, Douglass, and William Wells Brown for the ways in which they allowed readers "to know how a human heart like our own felt and thought and struggled, coming up in so strange and unnatural a state as that of slavery."[4]

But did Stowe's encounters with African-American writings and people during the 1850s serve the ends of knowledge or appropriation? It must be said that most critics regard these encounters as guided by Stowe's paternalistic racialism.[5] But her racialism, I would suggest, which can be acknowledged as a cultural donné, makes all the more remarkable the range of her interactions with African Americans and her ability to learn from these interactions. More importantly, perhaps, it should be stressed that figures such as Douglass, Jacobs, Ward, and Nell were hardly passive in their interactions with Stowe. Douglass, for example, sought to enlist Stowe in his project of establishing a black mechanics institute. Sojourner Truth sought to instruct Stowe on black religiosity. It would be useful to consider the ways in which Truth, an African American whose "presence" (like Douglass's) can be discerned in Stowe's *Dred*, attempted to do this.

Stowe described her 1852 encounter with Truth in a sketch entitled "Sojourner Truth, the Libyan Sibyl," which appeared in the April 1863 *Atlantic* and was reprinted in the 1878 *Narrative of Sojourner Truth*. Jean Yellin writes of Stowe's portrayal of Truth: "Stowe's Libyan Sibyl is passive. She possesses knowledge but she cannot act on it; further, because her language cannot readily be understood, no one else can use her knowledge as the basis for effective action."[6] Such a reading, however, is confuted by even a cursory glance at Stowe's text, which begins with an account of an actively engaged Truth arriving at Stowe's house in request of an interview with the famous author of *Uncle Tom's Cabin*. Stowe describes her initial encounter with Truth:

> She seemed perfectly self-possessed and at her ease,—in fact, there was almost an unconscious superiority, not unmixed with a solemn twinkle of humor, in the odd, composed manner in which she looked down on me. Her whole air had at times a gloomy sort of drollery which impressed one strangely.
> "So this is *you*?" she said.
> "Yes," I answered.
> "Well, honey, de Lord bless ye! I jes' thought I'd like to come an' have a look at ye. You's heerd o' me, I reckon?" she added.

It is Truth who initiates and shapes the dialogue; it is Truth who "looks down" on Stowe with "an unconscious superiority"; it is Truth who seems "perfectly self-possessed." Rather than deferring to Stowe, she aggressively seeks to ascertain whether Stowe knows who *she* is; and rather than deferring to Stowe's husband and the other ministers at the Stowes' home, she asserts her own qualifications to be a preacher: "When I preaches, I has jest one text to preach from, an' I always preaches from this one. *My* text is 'WHEN I FOUND JESUS!' "[7]

Truth's apprehension of Godhead and her ability to love her enemies are presented by Stowe as absolute forms of knowledge, knowledge that resonates, I would argue, precisely because of, rather than in spite of, Stowe's use of dialect to render Truth's speech. As Truth herself realized, whites took greater notice of her preachings when she theatricalized herself as an "African" illiterate whose perspective was radically different from white middle-class perspectives. As a recent biographer remarks, Truth, though capable of speaking more conventional English, "seemed to keep her speech considerably homely, ungrammatical, and in dialect because she found her audiences liked it that way. . . . In a sense she molded her public image around her illiteracy." Similarly, it could be argued that Truth during her visit "molded" herself for Stowe, not only deliberately speaking in dialect, but also, in ways calculated to keep her off balance, moving in and out of what Stowe terms "a sort of reverie." Truth thus must take some responsibility for encouraging Stowe to describe her "religious element" in terms of racialist stereotypes of the "barbaric," "wild, savage" African.[8]

In a brilliant speculative account of the characterization of Nat Turner in Thomas Gray's 1831 "Confessions of Nat Turner," Eric Sundquist likewise raises the possibility "that Turner himself had staged a performance for Gray and his audience, adopting the guise of religious madness in order to protect other slaves or potential plots, or simply to exercise his intelligence and imagination."[9] In doing so, Turner would have cunningly asserted an "authorship" role in Gray's text. (Given the influence of the "Confessions" on *Dred*, as attested by Stowe's reprinting of large portions of the text in the novel's Appendix, we might also grant him a posthumous "authorship" role in *Dred*.) Though Stowe's relation to Truth and other African Americans is quite different from Gray's relationship to Turner, Sundquist suggestively points to the ways in which an African-American presence in white-authored texts can, at times, be an actively created presence. We need to resist the paternalistic tendency of regarding blacks as always the "victims" of racialist representations.

Robert Stepto has discussed, with respect to *Uncle Tom's Cabin*, "the complex relationship between Stowe's novel and the many Afro-American antislavery texts published in the late 1840s and 1850s," noting that Stowe took pains to seek "the forms of black testimony that could both counter and corroborate the white testimony she already had in hand." In composing *Dred*, however, Stowe involved herself in something more complex and risky than simply countering and corroborating, for she was engaging African-American writers who, in many instances, had actively responded to her novel. Stepto argues, for example, that Stowe turned to Nat Turner as a subject for her second novel in response to Douglass's "The Heroic Slave" (1853), his revisionary celebration, in response to Stowe's Uncle Tom, of black revolutionary violence.[10] *Dred* thus must be viewed, in part, as the result of Stowe's creative exchanges with Frederick Douglass. In my reading of *Dred* I will be discussing several other such moments where Stowe responds to black voices and perspectives that have themselves responded to her writings. In this respect, one of the large aims of the reading of *Dred* that follows is to resituate Stowe's second novel in the midst of the black rhetoric that, I am suggesting, helped to bring it into being.

*    *    *

Despite its antislavery agenda, *Dred* seems oddly indebted to the plantation novel tradition inaugurated by John Pendleton Kennedy, beginning rather conventionally by focusing on the eighteen-year-old plantation belle, Nina Gordon, and her "crisis" of the moment: that she has accepted three marriage proposals from suitors. Because her parents are dead and her younger brother, Tom Gordon, has adopted "every low form of vice," Nina is expected to play a central role in watching over the slaves of her North Carolina plantation.[11] In view of such paternalism, it is not surprising that we are presented early on with a number of stock black characters, such as the "mammy" Aunt Katy and the scheming stablehand Old Hundred. But, unlike Kennedy, Stowe introduces us to rather substantial and complex black characters. Supervising the plantation, for example, is a slave named Harry, described by one character as "a very clever quadroon servant" (1: 24). Loyal and enormously intelligent, Harry, unbeknownst to Nina, also happens to be her older half-brother. As in Douglass's *Narrative* and *Bondage*, Brown's *Clotel*, Jacobs's *Incidents*, and many other works by black writers, Stowe's account of the genealogical backgrounds of the Gordon family exposes the licentiousness of the patriarchal master.[12] Caught between his love for his wife Lisette, the slave of a French Creole woman, and his love for Nina, Harry declares his envy (in the manner of Douglass in his autobiographical narratives) of those slaves who (supposedly) have never thought about their condition: "How often I've wished that I was a good, honest, black nigger, like Uncle Pomp! Then I should know what I was" (1: 76).[13]

But how thoughtless and content are "good, honest" blacks? Appearing to fit Harry's description is Old Tiff, the slave of an impoverished woman, Sue Cripps, with distant connections, Tiff pridefully insists on believing, to the "aristocratic" Peytons of Virginia. Introduced as he cares for Sue in a shabby room wherein are "medicinal-looking packages, a turkey's wing, . . . some bundles of dry herbs" (1: 97), Tiff in effect is presented as doctoring Sue through the art of conjure.[14] Indeed, as Tiff speaks of God in this Africanized spiritual space, Sue experiences a vision of heaven just before she dies; unlike the more conventional white preachers introduced later in the novel, Tiff thus has brought forth a convert from his syncretic Afro-Christian vision. His subsequent decision to become the guardian of Sue's children could be taken as a form of lackeyism, but it is more to the point, I think, to view his guardianship as a genuine act of love in which he transcends the bounds of race to care for the vulnerable children. Tiff also transcends the bounds of gender, as throughout the novel Stowe emphasizes the ways in which he resembles "an old woman" (1: 98). At times the "womanly" Tiff seems similar to, and partly modelled on, Sojourner Truth. For example, in the course of teaching the children how to speak "proper" English, Tiff insists that his own use of dialect is a matter of free choice: "Old Tiff knows what good talk is. Ain't he heard de greatest ladies and gen'lemen in de land talk? But he don't want de trouble to talk dat ar way, 'cause he's a nigger! Tiff likes his own talk—it's good enough for Tiff" (1: 278) . As a self-theatricalized "nigger," Tiff, like Sojourner Truth, can retain a modicum of power in a racist culture by appearing knowable and unthreatening to whites.

When Tiff first arrives at Nina's to announce the death of Sue, Aunt Milly, the slave of Nina's aunt, admiringly refers to him as a "faithful old creature" (1: 123). Milly, who emerges as one of the central characters of the novel, herself initially appears to be the "good, honest" slave of the plantation novel. When younger, Milly had married a "mulatto man, on a plantation adjoining" (1:60), and had a number of children who, one by one, were sold to distant plantations. Without sentimentalizing afflictions as somehow necessary for conversion, Stowe exalts Milly, as she exalted Milly Edmondson, Sojourner Truth, and Josiah Henson, for a Christlike capacity for suffering, remarking on how most "souls" would be broken by such experiences: "where one soul is thus raised to higher piety, thousands are crushed in hopeless imbecility" (1:61).[15]

By moralizing on Milly's experiences, Stowe, in these initial descriptions, exerts her command over the character. But when Milly makes her next major appearance in the novel, she tells her own story to Nina and draws out her own moral. In this sense Milly's narration speaks to, and reveals key aspects of, Stowe's interactions with Sojourner Truth; for what emerges of interest here are not simply the details of Milly's story that correspond to Truth's story, but the reordering of power relations that such storytelling can bring about. Describing her angry response to her mistress's betrayal of her promise not to sell her youngest son Alfred into slavery, Milly tells of how she shook her mistress by the shoulders and cursed her (as Truth similarly cursed her mistress for selling her youngest child). Unlike Truth, however, who resourcefully reclaimed her son, Milly relates a sadder story of how the self-educated Alfred was killed by the overseer he boldly sought to resist. This leads her, in a moment similar to that described by Truth, to demand that God take vengeance on her mistress. According to Milly, she walked into her mistress's room with Alfred's bullet-riddled jacket, and forcefully declared: "You killed him; his blood be on you and your chil'en! O, Lord God in heaven, hear me, and *render unto her double!*" (1: 219). The narrator describes the rhetorical scene: "Nina drew in her breath hard, with an instinctive shudder. Milly had drawn herself up, in the vehemence of her narration, and sat leaning forward, her black eyes dilated, her strong arms clenched before her, and her powerful frame expanding and working with the violence of her emotion . . . like the figure of a black marble Nemesis in a trance of wrath. She sat so for a few minutes, and then her muscles relaxed, her eyes gradually softened; and she looked tenderly, but solemnly, down on Nina" (1: 219).

In telling her life history to a white auditor, Milly both represents and affects power reversals, with the large implication being that proslavery idealizations of hierarchical relations on the plantation fail to speak to the reality of black rage. This point is worth underscoring, for up to this point in the novel black perspectives have remained subordinate to the focus on Nina's growing love for Edward Clayton, an antislavery reformer who owns a slave plantation where he is "training" (1: 42) blacks for their eventual freedom. But shortly after Milly narrates her life history, a new black perspective is introduced into the novel that even more boldly challenges racial hierarchies and ideologies. That perspective is in effect summoned forth by another manifestation of black rage. Furious at his half-brother Tom's sadistic efforts to purchase Lisette as his (sexual) slave, Harry declares to Nina, in the spirit of George Harris, "I hate your country! I hate your laws" (1: 175). Though Nina (with Clayton's help) purchases Lisette, thereby providing her with some protection, Tom continues to assert his mastery over Harry, striking him in the face with a whip when he encounters him by the Dismal Swamp. At which point there emerges from the swamps a Herculean black man who, like Milly, wears a marker of his Africanity, a turban, but unlike the Christic Milly, also carries a knife, hatchet, and rifle. Harry's offhand response to his unnerving appearance is this: "O, it is you, then, Dred!" (1: 241).

Harry's immediate recognition of "Dred," who, prior to this relatively late moment, nearly 250 pages into an approximately 700 page novel, has not even been mentioned in the text, enacts a point of rupture, as readers will initially find themselves disoriented by their own lack of knowledge of the existence and motives of this swamp-dwelling black. Alice C. Crozier has influentially argued that changes in "the style and direction of the novel occur quite abruptly halfway through with the sudden introduction of the wild pariah of the Great Dismal Swamp, Dred"; and she asserts that these changes were the direct result of Stowe's anguished response, in the midst of writing *Dred*, to Preston Brooks's caning of Charles Sumner. Yet the caning occurred in May of 1856, only several months before the publication of the novel. I want to suggest that what truly brings about the novel's transformation is the emergence of the repressed—the "naturalized" black presence that supports both the plantation and the plantation novel. In this sense, what we experience with the introduction of Dred is less a transformation than a revelation: that to this point our reading of the plantation (novel) has been thoroughly inadequate.[16]

When Dred steps forth from the swamps to address Harry, Stowe describes him, to the point of obsession, in terms of his body: He is a "tall black man, of magnificent stature and proportions," whose bulging muscles suggest "herculean strength" (1: 240).[17] But Dred, we quickly learn, is more than just a body. He is the leader of the maroons of the Dismal Swamp, fugitive slaves who constitute a revolutionary community plotting against Southern slave culture. An immediate African-American source for Stowe's revisionary thinking on black revolutionary violence would have been W. C. Nell's 1855 *The Colored Patriots*. As Stowe wrote in her introduction to that volume, Nell's "collection of interesting incidents" promises to "redeem the character of the race from [the] misconception" that they are "deficient in energy and courage." By 1855 that "misconception" ironically had much to do with Stowe's valorization of Uncle Tom. Given that Nell in 1851 had already extolled the heroism of black militance in a pamphlet version of *Colored Patriots*, Nell's book may be read as an effort to revise *Uncle Tom's Cabin* under the legitimating authority of Stowe herself. In addition to describing the participation of blacks in the Revolutionary War and the War of 1812, Nell also celebrates black insurrectionism, placing the conspirators Denmark Vesey and Nat Turner in an American patriotic tradition. Nell's longest section is on "The Virginia Maroons," whom he describes in this way: "The Great Dismal Swamp, which lies near the Eastern shore of Virginia, and, commencing near Norfolk, stretches quite into North Carolina, contains a large colony of negroes, who originally obtained their freedom by the grace of God and their own determined energy, instead of the consent of their owners, or by the help of the Colonization Society." A consecrated group of revolutionaries, the colony has "endured from generation to generation," Nell proclaims, "and is likely to continue until slavery is abolished throughout the land."[18]

Inspired by Nell, Stowe similarly represents Dred and his accomplices as revolutionaries in the tradition of the American patriots who "purchased for our fathers a national existence" (1: 257). Like Nell, she also portrays the maroons as the heirs of Vesey and Turner, presenting Dred literally as the son of Vesey and metaphorically as a stand-in for another "son" of Vesey—Nat Turner. Known by overseers throughout the region for "his desperate, unsubduable disposition" (1: 254), Dred as a young man had resisted a bullying overseer: "In the scuffle that ensued Dred struck him to the earth, a dead man, made his escape to the swamps, and was never afterwards heard of in civilized life" (1:255). As Stowe remarks, whites' terror at the knowledge of the existence of this militant black and his ever-expanding swamp community acted as "a considerable check on the otherwise absolute power of the overseer" (1:255). In this respect, she presents Dred and his community of conspirators as Sundquist suggests we should regard Turner and his community of conspirators—as successfully trading in the "power of retributive terror."[19]

Believing that he may well be God's chosen prophet to avenge the "oppression and injustice" (1: 256) of the enslavers, Dred (in the manner of Nat Turner) "would fast and pray for days; and then voices would seem to speak to him, and strange hieroglyphics would be written upon the leaves" (1: 257). In an apparent racialist account of blacks' special capacities to achieve such a spiritualistic state—to become, in effect, God's mediums—Stowe writes of how they "are said by mesmerists to possess, in the fullest degree, that peculiar temperament which fits them for the evolution of mesmeric phenomena; and hence the existence among them, to this day, of men and women who are supposed to have peculiar magical powers" (2: 6–7). Stowe's notions of blacks' "peculiar" access to the spiritual may well speak to her encounter with Truth, as well as to her reading of the black abolitionist John Langston's "The Intellectual, Moral, and Spiritual Condition of the Slave," which appeared in Douglass's 1854 fundraising volume *Autographs for Freedom*, to which she also contributed an essay. Langston makes special claims for the African American's "spiritual faculty which, when cultivated, enables him [sic] to recognize God in his spiritual manifestations, to discern and appreciate spiritual truths, and to feel and relish the gentle distillations of the spirit of divine love as they fall upon his heart like dew upon the grateful earth."[20] Stowe's interest in black spiritualism would also have had more general sources in her culture's interest, indeed implication, in African religions.[21] According to historians of antebellum slave religion, spiritualistic practices suggest exchanges between West African religions and Christianity. The syncretic linking of traditional African religions' beliefs in "spirit possession and mediumship" to Christian notions of the Holy Spirit contributed to what can be called the "Africanization" of American Christianity—one of *Dred's* large subjects.[22]

Viewing Dred in this larger cultural context, particularly given that Stowe emphasizes the roles of his African grandfather and the sorcerer Gullah Jack in forming his religious and political sensibility, helps us to see that Stowe means to represent Dred's Afro-Christianity as a legitimately revolutionary antislavery perspective. Nowhere is this more apparent than in the climactic camp meeting at the midpoint of the novel. Presenting the meeting, with its occasionally wild outbursts of enthusiastic energies and spiritual visions, as a signifier of the Africanization of Christianity,[23] Stowe makes Dred into the true minister of the camp meeting, one who preaches to the group a lesson very similar to what Stowe preaches at the end of *Uncle Tom's Cabin*: that for sinners the true God is not the Christ of love but the Christ of vengeance, figured in the voice of the prophets and Jehovah in the Old Testament. Journeying to the camp meeting after witnessing the death in the swamps of a fugitive slave, and after apprehending, as if "in a somnambulic dream" (1:294), God's command to " 'be a sign unto this evil nation!' " (1: 295), Dred from out of the darkness interrupts the corrupt slaveholder Father Bonnie's sermon on Revelation and Last Judgment to speak himself on judgment, wrath, and vengeance. As he preaches with the sort of devotional energy that Clayton links to the African's "tropical lineage and blood" (1: 299), and that Stowe herself links to Dred's "savage familiarity with nature" (1: 321), Stowe keeps the point of view fixed on the whites, who can barely make sense of what Dred is saying, and cannot even see him. Yet the auditors are stirred by his passionate declarations, fearing that they may well have come under the judgment of a genuine prophet: "there crept through the different groups wild legends of prophets strangely commissioned to announce coming misfortunes" (1: 321).[24]

Soon after delivering his "sermon" on God's eventual righting of wrongs, Dred "plunged into the thickets, and was gone" (1: 329). He is simultaneously "gone" and ubiquitous, for it is difficult not to read all subsequent events of the novel in relation to our knowledge of his lurking presence. From this perspective, Clayton's and Nina's efforts to obtain legal redress for Milly, shot in the arm by a drunken employer to whom she had hired herself out, seem naive, particularly as they imagine themselves as coming to the aid of a helpless child-like woman. Much more aware of the power-dynamic central to slavery is Clayton's father, the chief justice of the North Carolina Supreme Court, who overturns a jury decision in Milly's favor with a clear statement of the legal principles upholding slavery: "THE POWER OF THE MASTER MUST BE ABSOLUTE, TO RENDER THE SUBMISSION OF THE SLAVE PERFECT" (2: 103).[25] In response to his father's ruling, the idealistic lawyer Clayton decides to resign from the profession, even as he paternalistically chooses to retain over his slaves the "legal relation of owner simply as a means of protecting my servants from the cruelties of the law" (2: 108). But Clayton is not the only key character in attendance at the court; the mulatto slave Harry Gordon also witnesses the ruling. As observed by the uncomprehending younger Clayton, Harry responds with a visceral and politicized anger that seems of a piece with Dred's: "his face became pale, his brow clouded, and . . . a fierce and peculiar expression flashed from his dark-blue eye" (2: 105).

With the depiction of Harry's rage, "The Cloud Bursts"(2: 111), as Stowe titles the subsequent chapter. A cholera epidemic strikes the region, and Stowe, through her Biblical references, makes connections between the fatal disease and the Biblical judgment of vengeance—" 'The pestilence that walketh in darkness' " (2: 111)—that such a plague could be taken to represent. In William Wells Brown's *Clotel* (1853), a novel that may well be "present" in *Dred* (Stowe met Brown in England the year he published his novel), a similar connection between fever and vengeance is developed through the presentation of the militant black leader Picquilo. Described as "a bold, turbulent spirit . . . (who) from revenge imbrued his hands in the blood of all the whites he could meet," Picquilo, like Dred, lurks in the Dismal Swamp and is introduced into the novel at the time of the cholera epidemic of the early 1830s—the time of Nat Turner's rebellion. Stowe too insists on the link between cholera and Turner's brand of revolutionism, having Dred remark when he learns about the coming of the cholera epidemic: "Nat Turner—they killed him; but the fear of him almost drove them to set free their slaves! . . . A little more fear, and they would have done it" (2: 89).[26]

And yet despite Dred's hopes, Nina, who succumbs to cholera several hundred pages before the end of the novel, fails to free her slaves, thereby leaving "her people" vulnerable to the "uncontrolled power of a man like Tom Gordon" (2:138). But given the presence of Dred and his compatriots in the swamps, and given the Dred-like rage of "her people" at white oppressors, how vulnerable are they? Apparently not as vulnerable as Nina and Clayton feared; for when Tom, in attempting to take possession of Harry, strikes the resistant slave with a "gutta-percha cane" (2:145) of the sort Preston Brooks used to strike Charles Sumner, Stowe's black surrogate Sumner violently returns Tom's blow, and then escapes to the swamps with his wife Lisette. Within the maroon community, Harry initiates a letter exchange with Clayton that marks the growth of his "black" political consciousness. Informing Clayton that he has been reading widely in American Revolutionary history, Harry poses the large question raised earlier in the novel by Dred's "father" Denmark Vesey (and in Douglass's famous 1852 "What to the Slave is the Fourth of July?"): "If it were proper for your fathers to fight and shed blood for the oppression that came upon them, why isn't it right for us?" (2: 201). Clayton's advice to the swamp-dwelling Harry is to continue to be patient, as militancy "would only embitter the white race against them [blacks], and destroy that sympathy which many are beginning to feel for their oppressed condition" (2:210).

That patience (and sympathy) has its limits, however, is revealed in Stowe's subsequent representation of the breakdown of the white southern community as presided over by the intemperate, power-driven Tom Gordon. After leading a mob attack on an antislavery minister (and his wife), Tom uses his gutta-percha cane to strike Clayton, as he struck Harry, "in the vicinity of the swamp" (2: 270). In doing so, Stowe sardonically notes, Tom "proved his eligibility for Congress" (2: 271) . At the same time, Clayton, in attempting to resist Tom, proves his eligibility for the swamps. Rescued by Harry and Dred, who breaks Tom's arm in the exchange, the unconscious Clayton is carried off to be nursed within the maroon community. His arrival serves as Clayton's baptismal moment, as it were, into a black revolutionary perspective. Over the course of several interviews with Dred, whom he self-protectively regards "as a psychological study" (2: 291), Clayton begins to approach an understanding, however limited, of African-American revolutionism, eventually concluding "that nothing but the removal of some of these minds from the oppressions which were goading them could prevent a development of bloody insurrection" (2:302).

Stowe, through Clayton, therefore suggests near the end of the novel her own sense that there are "goads" to black insurrection. As for the morality of acting on those goads, Stowe addresses the issue through an ongoing "debate" between Milly and Dred, a debate which is informed by her sense of an exchange that took place between Sojourner Truth and Douglass in 1852. Stowe writes of the exchange in her 1863 article on Truth: "Douglass had been describing the wrongs of the black race, and as he proceeded, he grew more and more excited, and finally ended up saying that they had no hope of justice from the whites, no possible hope except in their own right arms. It must come to blood; they must fight for themselves and redeem themselves, or it would never be done." Truth's withering, silencing response, according to Stowe, is this: "Frederick, *is God Dead?*"[27] In the wake of the Emancipation Proclamation, Stowe means to emphasize that, contrary to Douglass's expectations, whites did come to the aid of blacks in what she (and Truth) increasingly came to view as a holy war of millennial redemption. But in *Dred*, written before the war began, Stowe writes out of a cultural moment of greater uncertainty about the uses of, or need for, black violence. Though she positions her Truth character in the camp of Christian patience and forgiveness, Stowe's alliance with Milly (Truth) is not all that firm, and she allows Dred (an "excited" Douglass) equal place and stature in articulating the rationale for slave insurrectionism.

The debate between Milly and Dred is initiated in the novel's first volume when Harry meets Dred in the swamps after being struck by Tom Gordon. Though he resists Dred's call for militant action, he feels Dred's pull, and remarks: "I will not be a slave" (1:243). Milly then arrives on the scene to articulate an alternative position based on the virtue of Christian forgiveness, seemingly triumphing when Harry returns to the plantation and Dred returns alone to the swamps. The debate is resumed in the novel's second volume precisely at that moment when Harry seems most a part of Dred's community. Awaiting the return of their compatriot Hark (named after one of Nat Turner's co-conspirators), the fugitives seem on the verge of taking some sort of violent action against slaveowners. Around a campfire, the men "clasp their hands in a circle, and join in a solemn oath never to betray each other" (2: 224). Each member then steps forward to tell his life history; within the circle, all of their voices are honored. The meeting resembles the African ring ceremonies that, as historian Sterling Stuckey observes, honored ancestors at burials and thereby ritually linked successive generations.[28] Stowe points to the linkages among generations by remarking on how Dred is reading from "the Bible of Denmark Vesey" (2: 214). And it soon becomes clear that the ceremony has been functioning as a burial ceremony of sorts as well, for news arrives that Hark has been tortured and killed by Tom. Dred's response is to call for a "day of vengeance" (2: 233) in which blacks simply kill as many whites as possible. Whereupon Milly enters the scene, singing of Christ as a peaceful, loving Lamb.

Milly's entrance at this particular moment thus brings to focus the ongoing debate between Dred and Milly on the proper course of black action to combat slavery. The critical consensus is that Milly, in articulating a pacifist religiosity similar to that informing *Uncle Tom's Cabin*, wins the debate, both in terms of theology and action, as Dred ultimately fails to launch a successful rebellion. As one critic asserts, Milly "persuades him [Dred] to at least postpone his plans."[29] But how persuasive is she? And to what extent does Stowe privilege her position? Milly, because of her own victimization at the hands of enslavers, can claim that she has "been whar you be" (2: 233). She urges Dred and his associates, in terms that even Clayton comes to regard as limited, that they should strive to be like Christ in their patient suffering; they should await "de new covenant" (2: 233). Dred's response can seem to suggest capitulation to her vision: "Woman, thy prayers have prevailed for this time! . . . The hour is not yet come!" (2: 234). But the fact is that just *prior* to Milly's arrival Dred had already decided to wait, announcing to the group from within his trance-like state that, though he now perceives only "silence in heaven . . . , [w]hen the Lord saith unto us, Smite, then will we smite!" (2: 232). We should also note that Stowe herself challenges Milly's appropriation of Christic Lamb imagery as a signifier of nonviolence, for shortly after Dred declares his intention of postponing vengeful action, the narrator declares that "the wrath of the LAMB" (2: 276) can be "a strong attribute of the highest natures; for he who is destitute of the element of moral indignation is effeminate and tame" (2: 275).

Dred's desire to "smite," therefore, retains a privileged place in the novel, not even to be annulled by Milly's Christlike insistence on patience. What prevents Dred from putting his desires into action, in addition to his apprehension of God's silence at this particular moment, is what prevented other slaves from leading successful rebellions: the hegemony of slavery. Additionally, Stowe makes Dred's honesty and heroism a cause of his "fall," for it is precisely his heroic decision to venture out on his own to spy on Tom's drunken crew that leads to his death. Returning to the group bleeding from a wound in his breast, Dred is himself described in Christlike spiritual terms, with the large implication being that his imminent death has every promise of being as redemptive and sacred as Eva's (and Tom's) in *Uncle Tom's Cabin*. Even with respect to Nina's death, I would argue that the two chapters on Dred's death constitute the sacred space of the novel.[30] As Stowe describes *Dred*'s "majestic and mournful" death (2: 299): "It was evident to the little circle that He who is mightier than the kings of earth was there" (2: 295). Stowe has not simply "killed off" Dred or otherwise aligned herself with Milly. She has instead figured a glorious, redemptive, fraternal death in the "hush harbor" of the swamps that, as we shall see, has an impact even on Milly. A historian of slave religion remarks on how in "the secrecy of the quarters or the seclusion of the brush arbors ('hush harbors') the slaves made Christianity truly their own."[31] At the Afro-Christian burial of Dred, Stowe insinuates herself into this sacred community by echoing in her narrative commentary an earlier appeal that Dred had made to his fellow conspirators to serve as God's covenanted "witnesses" (2: 298). What needs to be addressed here, in light of this sacred witnessing, is the large question that Stowe raised in *Key*: "What Is To Be Done?"[32]

Clayton's answer to this question is, as I have said, to insist upon the importance of educating and eventually emancipating the "four hundred odd" (1: 27) slaves of his plantation. His reformism, Crozier asserts, "assumes an extremely patronizing attitude toward the slaves."[33] But Douglass and other free blacks concerned with the elevation of the slaves could also be patronizing in their insistence on the slaves' need for the sort of education that would help them to prosper in bourgeois society.[34] In assuming that he knows what is best for the former slaves, however, Clayton can seem somewhat smug, in large part because this white reformer, until his arrival in the swamps, possesses such a limited knowledge of black perspectives. Not surprisingly, then, his reformist vision can seem naive and limited. And yet, Stowe does appear to be sympathetic to his reform project, especially as put into practice by his sister Anne Clayton, whose program of black elevation through education, industry, and hygiene (similar to Douglass's own temperance emphases in the New Bedford sections of *Narrative* and *My Bondage and My Freedom*) is presented unironically as a sensible way of preparing former slaves for freedom.[35] Nevertheless, as Anne herself confides to Nina, the education project is hopeless as long as Southern whites refuse to offer their support. It is only near the end of the novel, when Edward returns from the swamps to confront the social anarchy unleashed by Tom Gordon, that he reaches a similar conclusion. His friend Russel assesses the situation after a mob burns down their plantation's black school house, concluding that Anne and Edward have one of two options with their slaves: "You must either send them to Liberia, or to the Northern States" (2:323). They choose to do neither.

It is simply mistaken, then, to say that "Stowe again wrote favorably of colonization in her novel *Dred*."[36] Rather than arguing for colonization, Stowe, like Delany, Henson, and Mary Shadd Cary, though in somewhat different terms, argues (in part) for black emigration to Canada. Using funds secured from selling their plantation to purchase a "valuable tract of land" (2: 330) in western Canada, Clayton and his sister help to establish a black township that, with its integrated schools and thriving farms, quickly emerges as "one of the richest and finest [towns] in the region" (2: 330). In a footnote Stowe informs her readers that the community's success mirrors the success of the Elgin settlement. Founded in 1849 by William King, a Presbyterian minister, the Elgin Community, just south of Chatham, Ontario, where Martin Delany emigrated the year of Dred's publication, emerged during the 1850s as one of the most successful black communities in Canada. Though paternalism was undoubtedly central to King's modus operandi, his large goal was to empower the black participants by allowing them voting and property rights.[37] In her portrayal of the Claytons' Canadian commu-

nity, Stowe takes care to underscore the central place of the black members:
Harry emerges as one of the principal leaders; Dred's former associate Hannibal,
"instead of slaying men, is great in felling trees" (2: 331); and Jim, Tom Gordon's
former slave, has become an industrious farmer. That said, Clayton never seems
to renounce his "superintending" role (2: 57).

Given the persistence of white paternalism in this reform community, then, it
is crucial to note that Stowe presents the Claytons' emigration project as but one
of several possibilities for the novel's black characters. While Russel asserts that
Clayton must either "send" the blacks of his plantation to the North or to Liberia,
Stowe describes blacks who are not "sent" but rather make their escape, on their
own terms, to New York. They do so in such a way as to suggest that Stowe
may have been revising Douglass's 1853 "The Heroic Slave," his revision of
*Uncle Tom's Cabin*, in order to make it "blacker." She does so by depicting the
slaves' flight as a shared effort dependent upon black fraternity and community.
In "The Heroic Slave," the black rebel Madison Washington recounts to the
white abolitionists Mr. and Mrs. Listwell how he escaped to "the dismal swamps,"
where he lived a solitary existence for five years until, after being displaced by
a fire, he was apparently betrayed by a black lumberer to whom he had given a
dollar to purchase food.[38] In *Dred*, following the death of Dred, Stowe portrays
black lumberers who enable the escape of slaves, for all along, she writes, the
lumberers had linked themselves to Dred's subversive group, providing them
with "secret supplies" and even "attend[ing] some of Dred's midnight meetings"
(2: 303). These sympathetic lumberers, rather than betraying the maroons, hide
them on a ship to Norfolk, the first of several stopping points on their way North.

Significantly, Dred's compatriots are not the only slaves who make their way
North. Milly too decides to escape; she proves to be not so acquiescent and
patient after all. Her pretext for escaping is that such an action would benefit
her grandchild; without the child, Stowe writes, Milly would have remained
"patiently in the condition wherein she was called, and bearing injustice and
oppression as a means of spiritual improvement" (2: 304). Arguably, by linking
her to a grandchild, Stowe rescues Milly from what the novel increasingly suggests
would have been a pointless martyrdom at the hands of Southern enslavers. In
the novel's final chapter, Stowe, through her depiction of Milly, conveys her
belief that blacks can and should have a role to play in the United States. After
the passage of several years, Clayton arrives in New York to find that Milly
lives "in a neat little tenement in one of the outer streets of New York, surrounded
by about a dozen children, among whom were blacks, whites, and foreigners.
These she had rescued from utter destitution in the streets, and was giving to
them all the attention and affection of a mother" (2: 333).[39] Surprised by the
inclusive nature of Milly's reformism, Clayton remarks: "I see you have black
and white here" (2: 333). In response Milly affirms the integrationist ideals so
central to the antislavery and social reform programs of W. C. Nell and Douglass:
"I don't make no distinctions of color,—I don't believe in them. White chil'en,
when they 'haves themselves, is jest as good as black, and I loves 'em jest as
well" (2: 334). The humor here, and the concomitant biting social point, is

conveyed through Milly's "black"-centered rhetoric that has her affirming the equality of the races, not by arguing that blacks are, or can be, as good as whites, but rather by insisting that whites one day can be as good as blacks.[40]

Milly's Sojourner Truth-like ability to love whites, despite what we have seen of Tom Gordon and his drunken minions, is to the very end of the novel shared by Tiff. Like Milly, he has decided to escape to the North with the beloved white children under his charge. At first he and the children live with Milly and her grandson in their "humble tenement" (2: 329); eventually a distant aunt bequeaths to the children the Peyton fortune, and they move on to better things. In the novel's concluding chapter Tiff attends the wedding of the eldest child, Fanny, to the son of Clayton's friend Russel, and in effect renounces the absurd notions of Peyton superiority that have seemingly played such a large role in guiding his actions: "when all's said and done, it's de man dat's de thing, after all; 'cause a gal can't marry all de generations back" (2: 336). Yet in the novel's final paragraph, the motherly Tiff pridefully remarks that Fanny's baby is "de very sperit of de Peytons" (2: 337). Tiff here is nothing less than ridiculous, as even he has come to realize, but his love for Fanny and pride in her family can be regarded as a sign of his strength (he acts upon, rather than is embarrassed by, the "inappropriateness" of his love). With her images of Milly's and Tiff's nurturing transracial love, Stowe concludes the novel with a more hopeful picture than critics have generally recognized of blacks successfully finding a place in, and having an impact upon, Northeast culture.

But the novel doesn't end with the final paragraph; it offers at least one more answer to the question of "What Is To Be Done?" For immediately following the depiction of Tiff comes a three-part Appendix, the first section of which reprints "a few extracts" (2: 338) from Thomas Gray's "Nat Turner's Confessions" (the other two sections discuss slavery in legal and ecclesiastical contexts). Actually, Stowe reprints virtually all of the "Confessions," with a couple of key exceptions. She cuts most of Thomas Gray's negative comments on Turner; she cuts Gray's political moralizing; and, most crucially, she cuts Gray's reassurances to his Southern readers that "fortunate for society, the hand of retributive justice has overtaken them [Turner and his accomplices]; and not one that was known to be concerned has escaped."[41] By implicitly suggesting that some of Nat Turner's retributive accomplices may still be at large, Stowe means to participate in the political terror inspired by Turner. Further, by noting in her prefatory comments on the "Confessions" that one of Turner's "principal conspirators in this affair was named Dred" (2: 338), Stowe presents rebellion as a logical, perhaps even sacred, response to slavery that will be passed along by blacks from generation to generation until slavery is abolished. As she remarks in "The New Year" (1865), published in the *Atlantic* several months before Lee's surrender: "The prophetic visions of Nat Turner, who saw the leaves drop blood and the land darkened, have been fulfilled. The work of justice which he predicted is being executed to the uttermost."[42] Responsive to and aligned with the prophetic Nat Turner, the ultimate African-American presence in her novel, Stowe in *Dred*, as much as Melville in his equally prophetic "Benito Cereno" (1855), anticipated, promoted, and helped to supply the terms for understanding the bloodshed of the Civil War.

Because of the centrality of *Uncle Tom's Cabin* to Stowe's canon (and American culture), the belief has persisted that Stowe valorized but one black response to slavery: the pacifist religiosity of Uncle Tom. From the late nineteenth century on, black novelists in particular have sought to contest and revise that dominant, and troubling, image of black heroism.[43] In this essay I have been arguing that blacks' contestation of Stowe's racial politics began with the publication of her great best-selling novel, and that specific black responses, along with a range of other antebellum black discourses, ultimately impelled Stowe to rethink and revise her view of black heroism. Whether or not we view Dred as an alternative to or extension of Uncle Tom, it is important that we recognize not only his important place in Stowe's imagination and politics, but also the African-American interventions that helped to bring forth such a compelling figure.[44] Stowe, more than most white writers of the time, was responsive to African-American texts and people, and she is deserving of greater recognition for her unusually brave engagements. But given the fact of her racialism, she should perhaps be viewed less as a transcendent than a representative white writer whose texts inevitably were shaped by what Morrison terms "the presence of Afro-Americans." In this larger sense, then, it is my hope that my reading of Stowe's *Dred* will contribute to the ongoing project of both recovering and reconceptualizing the interplay between black and white voices and perspectives in antebellum culture.

## Notes

1. Toni Morrison, "Unspeakable Things Unspoken: The Afro-American Presence in American Literature," *Michigan Quarterly Review* 28 (1989): 3, 11, 18, 6. Reprinted, in part, in this volume.

2. Not for nothing has Judie Newman suggested that *A Key to Uncle Tom's Cabin* "might more properly be described as the key to *Dred* " ("Introduction" to Harriet Beecher Stowe, *Dred: A Tale of the Great Dismal Swamp* [Halifax, England: Ryburn Publishing, 1992], 14). For a suggestive reading of *Dred* in relation to antebellum black culture, see also Ellen Moers, "Mrs. Stowe's Vengeance," *New York Review of Books*, 3 September 1970, 25–32.

3. *Frederick Douglass' Paper*, 29 April 1853, 3; *Frederick Douglass' Paper*, 6 May 1853, 2–3; Thomas F. Gossett, *Uncle Tom's Cabin and American Culture* (Dallas: Southern Methodist University Press, 1985), 294; Harriet Beecher Stowe, *A Key to Uncle Tom's Cabin; Presenting the Original Facts and Documents Upon Which the Story is Founded. Together With Corroborative Statements Verifying the Truth of the Work* (1853; rpt. Port Washington, New York:, Kennikat Press, 1968), 252. On Douglass and Stowe, see Robert S. Levine, *"Uncle Tom's Cabin* in *Frederick Douglass' Paper*: An Analysis of Reception," *American Literature* 64 (1992): 71–93.

4. Harriet Beecher Stowe, *Sunny Memories of Foreign Lands*, 2 vols. (Boston: Phillips, Sampson, and Company, 1854), 2:105; Stowe, "Anti-Slavery Literature," *New York Independent*, 21 February 1856, 1.

5. See, for example, the critical accounts of Stowe's interactions with Jacobs in Jean Fagin Yellin, Introduction to Harriet A. Jacobs, *Incidents in the Life of a Slave Girl* (Cambridge: Harvard University Press, 1987), xviii–xix; Karen Sánchez-Eppler, *Touching*

*Liberty: Abolition. Feminism, and the Politics of the Body* (Berkeley: University of California Press, 1993), 85–86; and Joan D. Hedrick, *Harriet Beecher Stowe: A Life* (New York: Oxford University Press, 1994), 249. Among other things, these critics attack Stowe for her "insensitive" efforts to authenticate Jacobs's story, while failing to note the irony that Jacobs's autobiography was not taken seriously by critics until Yellin managed to authenticate her story.

6. Jean Fagin Yellin, *Women and Sisters: The Antislavery Feminists in American Culture* (New Haven: Yale University Press, 1989), 82, 81.

7. Harriet Beecher Stowe, "Sojourner Truth, the Libyan Sibyl," in *Narrative of Sojourner Truth; A Bondswoman of Olden Time, With a History of Her Labors and Correspondence Drawn from Her 'Book of Life'*, intro. Jeffrey C. Stewart (1878; rpt. New York: Oxford University Press, 1991), 152, 153, 154.

8. Carleton Mabee, with Susan Mabee Newhouse, *Sojourner Truth: Slave, Prophet, Legend* (New York: New York University Press, 1993), 65; Stowe, "Sojourner Truth," 152, 159, 161, 169.

9. Eric J. Sundquist, *To Wake the Nations: Race in the Making of American Literature* (Cambridge: Harvard University Press, 1993), 49.

10. See Robert Stepto, "Sharing the Thunder: The Literary Exchanges of Harriet Beecher Stowe, Henry Bibb, and Frederick Douglass," in *New Essays on Uncle Tom's Cabin*, ed. Eric J. Sundquist (New York: Cambridge University Press, 1986), 137, 151–152.

11. Harriet Beecher Stowe, *Dred; A Tale of the Great Dismal Swamp*, 2 vols. (Boston: Phillips, Sampson and Company, 1856), 2:47. Future page references to *Dred* will be supplied parenthetically in the text.

12. Stowe also makes the racialist suggestion that genealogy helps to explain the slave's character. Harry, we are told, "inherited much of the temper and constitution of his [Scottish] father, tempered by the soft and genial temperament of the beautiful Eboe mulattress who was his mother" (1:45). Yet whatever role Stowe initially suggests "genetics" may have played in the formation of Harry's character, she comes to place a much greater emphasis on the ways in which condition contributes to the growth of Harry's "black" political consciousness.

Unsurprisingly, the novel has a number of other equally troubling racialist moments, most of which I will not be adducing in what I concede is a somewhat polemical essay that simply takes for granted that Stowe failed to transcend the racialism of her times. For a provocative discussion of the progressive, antislavery uses of racial stereotyping, see Arthur Riss, "Racial Essentialism and Family Values in *Uncle Tom's Cabin*," *American Quarterly* 46 (1994): 513–544.

13. After reading antislavery texts in *The Columbian Orator*, Douglass famously remarks on the slaves, "I envied my fellow-slaves for their stupidity" (*Narrative of the Life of Frederick Douglass, An American Slave*, ed. Houston A. Baker, Jr. [New York: Penguin Books, 1982], 84).

14. On Tiff and conjure, see Gossett, *Uncle Tom's Cabin and American Culture*, 299–300.

15. Stowe praised Henson for renouncing desires for vengeance on whites and thus exemplifying "the great Christian doctrine of forgiveness." See her Preface to Josiah Henson, *Truth Stranger Than Fiction: Father Henson's Story of His Own Life* (1858), rpt. in *An Autobiography of the Reverent Josiah Henson*, ed. Robin W. Winks (Reading, Mass.: Addison-Wesley Publishing Company, 1969), 3.

16. Alice C. Crozier, *The Novels of Harriet Beecher Stowe* (New York: Oxford University Press, 1969), 39. See also Edmund Wilson, *Patriotic Gore: Studies in the Literature of the Civil War* (New York: Oxford University Press, 1962), 36–37.

17. Critics have responded negatively to these initial descriptions. Sánchez-Eppler remarks, for example, that "Stowe has not so much described Dred as built his body" (*Touching Liberty*, 29). Sundquist maintains that the large implication of Stowe's phreno-logical descriptions is to suggest that revolutionism is "a species of insanity" (*To Wake the Nations*, 79).

18. William C. Nell, *The Colored Patriots of the American Revolution*, intro. Harriet Beecher Stowe (1855; rpt. New York: Arno Press, 1968), 5, 227–228, 229. On Nell, see Robert P. Smith, "William Cooper Nell: Crusading Abolitionist," *Journal of Negro History* (1970): 182–199.

19. Sundquist, *To Wake the Nations*, 71. On maroon communities, see also Herbert Aptheker, "Maroons Within the Present Limits of the United States" (1939), rpt. in *Maroon Societies: Rebel Slave Communities in the Americas*, ed. Richard Price (Baltimore: Johns Hopkins University Press, 1979), 151–167. On swamp imagery in *Dred*, see David C. Miller, *Dark Eden: The Swamp in Nineteenth-Century American Culture* (New York: Cambridge University Press, 1989), 55–102. In "Violence and Sacrificial Displacement in Harriet Beecher Stowe's *Dred*" (*Arizona Quarterly*, 50 [1994]), Richard Boyd accuses Stowe of pursuing a "racist agenda" (57) in depicting Dred as an imitative version of Tom Gordon, his "white model/rival" (57). Boyd's ahistorical René Girardean reading fails to take account of Stowe's implication in black culture, and, more crucially, fails to distinguish between the master's and slave's uses of power.

20. J. Langston, "The Intellectual, Moral, and Spiritual Condition of the Slave," in *Autographs for Freedom*, ed. Julia Griffiths (Rochester: Wanzer, 1854), 148–149. Stowe contributed "A Day Spent at Playford Hall" to this volume.

21. As Lynn Wardley brilliantly argues, the reformist spiritualism of the 1840s and 1850s, so central to *Uncle Tom's Cabin*, "resonated with West African religious beliefs" ("Relic, Fetish, Femmage: The Aesthetics of Sentiment in the Work of Stowe," *Yale Journal of Criticism* 5 [1992]: 171) . On slave religion in *Uncle Tom's Cabin*, see Hedrick, *Harriet Beecher Stowe*, 214–216. On Stowe's personal interest in spiritualism, see Marie Caskey, *Chariot of Fire: Religion and the Beecher Family* (New Haven: Yale University Press, 1978), 287–331.

22. Alfloyd Butler, *The Africanization of American Christianity* (New York: Carlton Press, 1980), 137, passim. See also Lawrence W. Levine, *Black Culture and Black Consciousness: Afro-American Folk Thought from Slavery to Freedom* (New York: Oxford University Press, 1977), 3–189; Albert J. Raboteau, *Slave Religion: The "Invisible Institu-tion" in the Antebellum South* (New York: Oxford University Press, 1978); and John W. Blassingame, *The Slave Community: Plantation Life in the Antebellum South* (New York: Oxford University Press, 1979), 3–148.

23. In her important study of the backgrounds of such syncretism, Michel Sobel remarks that whites, through their sharing with blacks of religious camp meeting experiences in the late eighteenth and early nineteenth century, became "more 'open' to ecstasy and spiritual life, ready and willing to have 'experience,' and to share their experience with others" (*The World They Made Together: Black and White Values in Eighteenth-Century Virginia* [Princeton: Princeton University Press, 1987], 203).

24. James M. Cox maintains that Dred's "linguistic identity as an Old Testament prophet promising an apocalypse is directly at odds with Mrs. Stowe's New Testament commitment to abject humility as the Christian virtue" ("Harriet Beecher Stowe: From Sectionalism to Regionalism," *Nineteenth-Century Fiction* 38 [1984]: 463). But for an interesting reading of *Dred* that explores the ways in which Stowe sought to link the Old and New Testaments through a dualistic conception of the novel's characters and settings, see Theodore R. Hovet, *The Master Narrative: Harriet Beecher Stowe's Subversive Story*

*of Master and Slave in Uncle Tom's Cabin and Dred* (Lanham: University Press of America, 1989).

25. Judge Clayton's decision echoes a famous 1829 decision of North Carolina Judge Thomas Ruffin; Stowe discusses Ruffin in *Key*, 70–71. On legal issues in *Dred*, see Lisa Whitney, "In the Shadow of *Uncle Tom's Cabin*: Stowe's Vision of Slavery from the Great Dismal Swamp," *New England Quarterly* 66 (1993): 552–569.

26. William Wells Brown, *Clotel; or, The President's Daughter* (New York: Collier Books, 1970), 172. In linking plague to Dred's militant perspective, Stowe taps into conventional fears of the period that linked cholera to political subversion. See Charles E. Rosenberg, *The Cholera Years: The United States in 1832, 1849, and 1866* (Chicago: University of Chicago Press, 1962). On swamps and popular notions of infection, see also Miller, *Dark Eden*, 13.

27. Stowe, "Sojourner Truth," 168. The exchange probably took place in Salem, Ohio, though Wendell Phillips, Stowe's source, heard that it took place in Boston. Stowe also wrote about the exchange in an 1860 issue of the New York *Independent*. See Mabee, with Newhouse, *Sojourner Truth*, 85. Also useful is Patricia R. Hill, "Writing Out the War: Harriet Beecher Stowe's Averted Gaze," in *Divided Houses: Gender and the Civil War*, eds. Catherine Clinton and Nina Silber (New York: Oxford University Press, 1992), 260–278.

28. Stuckey, *Slave Culture*, 16, passim.

29. Mabee, *Sojourner Truth*, 89. Hedrick likewise claims that Dred's "Old Testament militancy is stilled by the words of Milly" (*Harriet Beecher Stowe*, 259); and Charles H. Foster goes so far as to argue that the novel displays "Milly's conversion of Dred to Christian pacifism" (*Rungless Ladder: Harriet Beecher Stowe and New England Puritanism* [Durham: Duke University Press, 1954], 85).

30. Hedrick remarks that it "is a measure of Stowe's failure to make him [Dred] come alive for the reader that we do not care when he dies" (*Harriet Beecher Stowe*, 260). Whether Hedrick, and like-minded readers, care or not, there is every indication that the maroon community cares, that Stowe cares, and that Stowe wants her readers to care. I find the scene affecting and unique to antebellum literature.

31. Raboteau, *Slave Religion*, 212.

32. Stowe, *Key*, 250.

33. Crozier, *The Novels of Harriet Beecher Stowe*, 37.

34. On middle-class aspects of black self-help, see Frederick Cooper, "Elevating the Race: The Social Thought of Black Leaders, 1827–1850," *American Quarterly* 24 (1972): 604–625.

35. At the center of the Claytons' project are efforts to teach the slaves "to be consistently orderly and cleanly" (2: 49–50). On the importance of hygiene to Stowe's social and political thought, see Lora Romero, "Bio-Political Resistance in Domestic Ideology and *Uncle Tom's Cabin*," *American Literary History* 1 (1989): 715–734. It is worth noting that Stowe, following the Civil War, established a school for free blacks in Mandarin, Florida. See Alex L. Murray, "Harriet Beecher Stowe on Racial Segregation in the Schools," *American Quarterly* 12 (1960): 518–519. For a useful discussion of Stowe's racial politics following the Civil War, see Gossett, *Uncle Tom's Cabin and American Culture*, 321–336.

36. Marva Banks, "*Uncle Tom's Cabin* and Antebellum Black Response," in *Readers in History: Nineteenth-Century American Literature and the Contexts of Response*, ed. James L. Machor (Baltimore: Johns Hopkins University Press, 1993), 219. Banks's source for her assertion would seem to be not Stowe's novel, but Thomas Graham, who in 1973 wrote that "in her next antislavery novel *Dred*, [Stowe] again wrote favorably of

colonization" ("Harriet Beecher Stowe and the Question of Race" [1973], in *Critical Essays on Harriet Beecher Stowe*, 133); and, in what seems to be an echoing of her reading of Graham and Banks, Susan Marie Nuerberg writes that "in her next antislavery novel, *Dred* (1856), Stowe once again embraces colonization" ("The Rhetoric of Race," in *The Stowe Debate: Rhetorical Strategies in Uncle Tom's Cabin*, eds. Mason I. Lowance, Jr., Ellen E. Westbrook, and R. C. De Prospo [Amherst: University of Massachusetts Press, 1994], 262).

37. As historians of the settlement remark, "More than any other, the principle of self-help reflected the character of Elgin" (William H. Pease and Jane H. Pease, *Black Utopia: Negro Communal Experiments in America* [Madison: State Historical Society of Wisconsin, 1963], 92). By underscoring the importance of black participation to the success of the Claytons' community, Stowe similarly extols the value of black self-help. Richard Boyd thus overstates when he argues that Clayton's Canadian project allows him to maintain "his coercive power" over the slaves ("Models of Power in Harriet Beecher Stowe's *Dred*," *Studies in American Fiction* 19 [1991]: 27). On Martin Delany's close ties to William King and the Elgin community, see Floyd J. Miller, *The Search for a Black Nationality: Black Emigration and Colonization, 1787–1863* (Urbana: University of Illinois Press, 1975), esp. 252–257.

38. Douglass, "The Heroic Slave," in *Frederick Douglass: The Narrative and Selected Writings,* ed. Michael Meyer (New York: Modern Library, 1984), 313. In his narration to the Listwells, Washington suggests that the lumberer's possession of a dollar raised the suspicions of whites, who may have tortured him into betraying Washington.

39. Stowe supplies a footnote informing the reader that her depiction of Milly here is informed by yet another African-American "presence," one Aunt Katy, "an old colored woman" and former slave, who "established among these destitute children the first Sunday-school in the city of New York" (2: 334).

40. The image of Milly at the novel's ending argues against Gossett's reading that Stowe has lost confidence that "blacks have sufficient intelligence and will to enable them to live as equal citizens in a free society" (*Uncle Tom's Cabin and American Culture*, 303). As Stowe portrays the situation, it is the whites who lack the intelligence and will to live up to the nation's egalitarian ideals.

41. See Thomas Gray, "The Confessions of Nat Turner," in *The Nat Turner Rebellion: The Historical and the Modern Controversy*, ed. John B. Duff and Peter M. Mitchell (New York: Harper & Row, 1971), 14. Stowe cuts, for example, Gray's statements that Turner was motivated by "hellish purposes" (13) and acted with "fiend-like barbarity" (27).

42. Harriet Beecher Stowe, "The New Year," rpt. in *Household Pacers and Stories* (1868; rpt. Boston and New York: Houghton, Mifflin and Company, 1896), 437. In "Writing Out the War," Hill argues that Stowe, in the context of the Civil War, saw Turner's militant beliefs as "too dangerous a concept for a freed slave to espouse" (274).

43. See Richard Yarborough, "Strategies of Black Characterization in *Uncle Tom's Cabin* and the Early Afro-American Novel," in Sundquist, ed., *New Essays on Uncle Tom's Cabin*, 45–84.

44. For a provocative discussion of similarities between Nat Turner and Uncle Tom, see Wilson Jeremiah Moses, *Black Messiahs and Uncle Toms: Social and Literary Manipulations of a Religious Myth* (University Park: Pennsylvania State University Press, 1982), 63–64.

# Sentimental Abolition in Douglass's Decade: Revision, Erotic Conversion, and the Politics of Witnessing in "The Heroic Slave" and *My Bondage and My Freedom*

If the volume now presented to the public were a mere work of art, the history of its misfortune might be written in two very simple words—TOO LATE. The nature and character of slavery have been subjects of an almost endless variety of artistic representation; and after the brilliant achievements in that field, and while those achievements are yet fresh in the memory of the million, he who would add another to the legion, must possess the charm of transcendent excellence, or apologize for something worse than rashness.

—Editor's preface, *My Bondage and My Freedom*, 1855[1]

Frederick Douglass stands as the only African American of the nineteenth century to receive sustained and serious critical attention. Amidst the celebration and republications of previously underaddressed works by African Americans, Douglass's work continues to be central; in the 1990s two volumes of critical essays and an additional award-winning biography have taken their places amongst Douglass scholarship. Criticism that addresses Douglass's artful narrative representations is now plentiful enough that another essay might easily be dismissed with the two words quoted in the epigraph—"TOO LATE."[2] Yet, in the opening sentences of his preface, the editor of Douglass's *My Bondage and My Freedom* refers to the very dynamics that justify another article that takes Douglass as its subject. The subtle, though not oblique, reference to *Uncle Tom's Cabin*[3]—the brilliant achievement fresh in the memory of millions—alerts contemporary readers of Douglass's post-Stowe writings not only to the politics of authority and revision at work in his novella "The Heroic Slave" (1853) and his second autobiography (1855), but also to his complicated negotiation of sentiment.

Douglass distances himself from Garrisonian moral suasion at the very same time that he adopts a heightened sentimentality as a rhetorical strategy in his own fictional and autobiographical writings. While the Douglass of the *Narrative* (1845), his first autobiography, does not engage in consistent sentimental renderings of domesticity, the 1855 narrator does. Recent critics acknowledge Douglass's use of sentiment and of Stowe, while some emphasize his simultaneous search for, relation to, and reconstruction of (white) paternal power and the rhetoric of the U.S. revolution.[4] While I touch upon Douglass's articulation of reconstituted manhood, my focus on Douglass's rhetorical use of sentimentality is slightly to the (Adamic) side of theirs.

Deborah McDowell notes that *"My Bondage and My Freedom* reveals more clearly than the first narrative that Douglass's rewriting of his own origins does more than satisfy the dictates of abolitionism. It also makes intelligible Douglass's and the movement's problematical relation to the feminine."[5] To McDowell's analysis I would add that Douglass's genealogical revisions also illuminate his, and abolitionism's, complicated relation both to the feminized, and to the erotically fraternal. In paradoxical ways, Douglass's post-Stowe writings bring to the fore questions of how domestic ideology informs abolitionist strategies. Douglass's auto-biographical projects call for the consideration of racial aspects of sentimentality that take into account domesticity's influence beyond a woman's sphere.

What I call "sentimental abolition"[6] renames, and, I hope, allows us to retheorize, the heightened connection between abolition and what is too often considered the separate sphere of sentimentality.[7] Sentimental abolition coincides with, and borrows from, the power of extended domestic spheres popularized in reformist communities and culture in the 1830s and 40s; it stresses the affectional over the authoritative, or, in other words, emphasizes that the heart is the only true site of change and redemption. Sentimental abolition's emphasis on the affectional also distances it from political reform.[8] These terms, however, are not dichotomous; Douglass's sentimental abolition allows him to explore emotive arenas in order to energize political protest. In claiming sentimental abolition as a category, I'd like to further assert that its emphasis on transforming the public through the affectional realm facilitates a particularly eroticized means of conversion to the antislavery cause. Not only do Georgianna in William Wells Brown's *Clotel* and Mrs. Bird in *Uncle Tom's Cabin* bring their partners to espouse abolition, for example, but fictional slave *heroes* convert white male characters by first touching their hearts.

Douglass revises Stowe by both deemphasizing women's centrality in "The Heroic Slave" and *My Bondage and My Freedom* and by striving to convert his characters and readers by linking emotive sympathy to judicial standing. As Douglass moves away from Garrisonian abolition and embraces political action and the promise of the constitution, he is aware that although his gendered strategies and his political positioning have changed, his political position as a legally disfranchised man who is African American has not. In the years that lead to the Dred Scott decision (1857) Douglass is increasingly concerned with questions of Black social and political agency. Although he is exasperated with being a moral witness, an objectified icon on the Garrisonian abolitionist platform, he is acutely aware that white men are the only reader-citizens imbued with standing as witnesses; they are his only politically embodied readers, the only ones, that is, with a "vote."

White men become, then, the primary object of Douglass's political desire, and he turns them into the objects of *desiring* in "The Heroic Slave." Douglass makes a representational choice to recognize that only the white male gaze and ear have the actual power to confirm his slave protagonist Madison Washington's subjectivity.[9] Douglass pairs the patriarchal and political power of the gaze with what is cast as the feminized vulnerability and penetrability of the ear in both contemporary critical and slave narrative discourse. Through the white male response to Madison's invasive sensorial presence, Douglass attempts to seduce white male readers to antislavery activism as a means of achieving future Black rights and subjectivity.

In this chapter I will address Douglass's quest for status as an independent agent in the sphere of political rights, where witnessing, converting witnesses, and gaining standing as witness in one's own right, are increasingly problematic. Examining Douglass's rewriting of Stowe's famous *Uncle Tom's Cabin* chapter "The Senator is but a Man" in "The Heroic Slave," his own autobiographical revision of his Aunt [H]Ester's beating,[10] and "The Heroic Slave" 's white Northerner Listwell's conversion to abolitionism, will reveal how Douglass weds sympathy to standing. Ultimately, in his revision of himself and of Stowe, I contend that as he (again) writes women's voices out of his texts, he locates his political intervention within the language of domestic affection and sentimental abolition. Further, instead of simply mimicking the cultural norms of heroic manhood,[11] his recognition of available representational strategies and Black racial and sexualized positioning combines to produce an eroticized bond between men.

A glance at the historical record gives context to Douglass's move away from Garrisonian moral suasion and his continuous use of the rhetoric of sentimental abolition. After two years of forced, if pleasant, post-*Narrative* exile, Douglass came back from London in 1847 with his freedom papers and enough money to begin his own newspaper—both gifts, so to speak, from English abolitionists. He was disappointed with Garrisonian responses to his initiative, for they were "opposed to the idea of [his] starting a paper, and for several reasons. First, the paper was not needed; secondly, it would interfere with [his] usefulness as a lecturer; thirdly, [he] was better fitted to speak than to write; fourthly, the paper could not succeed" (*MB*, 393). As a result, Douglass moved to Rochester, New York, and founded *The North Star*, which he soon merged with political abolition-ist Gerrit Smith's paper and renamed *Frederick Douglass' Paper* to reflect his continued editorial control.[12] Douglass began to reconsider his positions on voting; he endorsed political candidates and, in 1852, became actively involved in Gerrit Smith's successful bid for Congress. He also rethought his previously Garrisonian ideas about the antislavery nature of the constitution, and crystallized his former uneasiness about nonviolence as an abolitionist strategy.[13]

Although Douglass's descriptions in *Bondage* gloss over the explosiveness of the split and the bitter melee that ensued, during his break with the Garrisonians Douglass was maligned as an apostate in one of the most public personal divisions of the abolitionist movement. In the December 9, 1853, edition of *Frederick Douglass' Paper*, he described the break as an attack charged "with a bitterness ever increasing and a steadiness and violence only characteristic of malice, deep, broad, lasting in its worst form."[14] Douglass devoted almost a whole issue of his paper to responding to and reprinting the attacks on his personal life and political stances.

By 1853, Garrison was not the only major antislavery figure with whom Douglass had to reckon. The historical record also elucidates the overlappings and convergences between Douglass's "The Heroic Slave" (1853) and Stowe's *Uncle Tom's Cabin* (1852). Douglass himself had written a glowing review of *Uncle Tom's Cabin* in 1852. The next year Stowe's *A Key to Uncle Tom's Cabin* was greeted with panegyric praise in Douglass's paper. That year, when Douglass accepted Stowe's invitation to visit at her home, the two authors had much to discuss. While other Black leaders had condemned the colonizationist stance in *Uncle Tom's Cabin* and, in strong language, had raised questions about Stowe's free use of slaves' stories as her own, Douglass had been relatively gentle and had tried to forge alliances. Together with James McCune, a doctor who held advanced degrees from the University of Glasgow and the most prominent Black reformer in New York City, and James Pennington, another renowned fugitive narrator, Douglass petitioned Stowe to help them raise funds for a Black industrial college. In 1853, it looked as if their alliance would be successful.[15] In that year the National Negro Convention also reconvened, and acknowledged the prominence of the two writers. In their call for reconvention the organizers listed as reasons: the Fugitive Slave Act, segregated schools, colonization, social, economic and political barriers and "withal the propitious awakening to the fact of our condition at home and abroad, which has followed the publication of *Uncle Tom's Cabin*." They went on to cite Stowe's influence in their opening address, and to elect *Frederick Douglass' Paper*, where "The Heroic Slave" was first published, as their official organ.[16]

"The Heroic Slave"'s protagonist, an actual and successful slave mutineer named Madison Washington, and Douglass's life also converge in ways that might make Madison appealing to Douglass. Both make their initial escapes in 1835 and both come to the fore as public figures in 1841. Douglass uses Stowe's hero as a point of departure for Madison Washington. When, in Madison's opening soliloquy, he refers to a disembodied character, Tom, as if his readers have a context, of course they do: "If Tom can do it," meaning survive/escape, "so can I," Madison muses. As he breaks away from Garrisonian abolition, Douglass consciously circulates the image of Madison Washington to rewrite Stowe's pacifist vision and to counter the ex-slave autobiographer Josiah Henson's figure, whose popularity surged after he became known as the authentic model for Stowe's religious martyr, Uncle Tom.

This historical aside helps to situate the cultural context in which Douglass was maneuvering. Despite his shift to political abolition, in 1853 both he and Stowe were more rhetorically invested in conversion than in coercion. As a literary strategy, this situates them within a model of internal change rather than external regulation aligned with what Richard Brodhead calls "disciplinary intimacy." Brodhead explains that

> a first feature of this *collectively* composed disciplinary model is that it requires authority to put on a human face. A second feature is a purposeful sentimentalization of the disciplinary relation: a strategic relocation of authority relations in the realm of emotion and a conscious intensification of the emotional bond between the authority figure and its charge.[17]

Disciplinary intimacy leads to a move from the authoritative to the affectional. Garrison's pronouncement, "Let us aim to abolitionize the consciences and hearts of the people and we may trust them at the ballot box or anywhere,"[18] is a direct application of the theories of affectional rule that Douglass never rejects. What Douglass does invert is the relationship between "the authority figure and its charge." He insists that Garrison's "us" and "them" should be concepts free of the white paternalism and prejudice characteristic of both the movement and the broader culture.

What I would like to suggest is that the affectional is a slippery terrain, particularly in an era where homosexuality has not yet been defined.[19] Abolitionist Lyman Cobb suggests that "the parent or teacher should, first of all, secure the LOVE and AFFECTION of his children or pupils. He will then have an unlimited control over their minds and conduct."[20] Madison and Douglass are, of course, nothing if not teachers in an affectional realm which leaves the field of eroticized pedagogy wide open. "The Heroic Slave" also serves as a post-script to Douglass's 1852 letter to Charles Sumner, in which he had written that, in relation to Garrison, "I stand something like a child to a parent."[21] Douglass publicly realigns his relation to Garrison in prose by becoming Listwell's abolitionist teacher and "father." He reclaims slave authority and upsets abolitionist paternalism. In doing so, the categories of fraternal and erotic love blend into each other in "The Heroic Slave" as they do in *Uncle Tom's Cabin*.[22]

In 1853 Douglass consciously replicates and revises Stowe's stratagies, carefully shifting the meanings Stowe assigns to Tom's body, its circulation, and Tom's "escape," in an effort to attract rather than alienate both Stowe and her/their readers. His "Section II," a scene at the home of the Listwells, is a case in point; it is an explicit refiguration of the oft-quoted Senator Bird chapter in *Uncle Tom's Cabin*. One might characterize Listwell as the co-protagonist of "The Heroic Slave." He is a Northerner who is so overwhelmed by Madison's speech and presence when, on a trip South he happens upon the slave, that he becomes an abolitionist. In both Douglass's "Section II" and Stowe's "It appears that a Senator is but a Man," a fugitive interrupts a white Ohio familial scene replete with the familiar signs of domesticity. Douglass echoes Stowe's opening, which reads: "The light of the cheerful fire shone on the rug and carpet of a cosey parlor, and glittered on the sides of the teacups and well-brightened teapot, as Senator Bird was drawing off his boots" (*UTC*, 132). In his own first lines Douglass writes, "Five years after [Listwell's trip South], Mr. and Mrs. Listwell sat together by the fireside of their own happy home. . . . The children were all gone to bed. A single lamp burnt brightly within" (*HS*, 31). Douglass's virtual replication of the fugitive Eliza's appearance at the Birds's door will soon overturn the maternal ethic Stowe advances. Mrs. Bird is the moral force that both Eliza and Stowe's readers recognize; it is Eliza's appeal to Mrs. Bird that convinces the senator to follow his heart, and, faced with a fugitive slave, to act differently than he votes. In contrast, Madison relates his story at the sympathetic request of Mr. Listwell, who, of course, listens well. Even when he interrupts Madison, he facilitates and affirms Madison's story; as Robert Stepto puts it, Listwell authenticates rather than questions.[23]

Mrs. Listwell's interruptions, unlike her husband's, distract from rather than advance Madison's story and cause. When she breaks in on Madison's description of a hair-breath escape and exclaims, "Oh! The old wretch! He had betrayed you," Madison calmly responds, "I think not" (42). Mrs. Listwell, pointedly, does not listen well, and Douglass brings this home when she interrupts Madison a second time, the only other instance in which she speaks during the text. As Madison for the second time recalls stealing chickens in order to feed himself, an activity that Mr. Listwell earlier defended, she instead exclaims "But you didn't eat food raw? How did you cook it?" (44). "It seemed quite a relief to Mrs. Listwell to know that Madison had, at least, lived upon cooked food" the narrator quips; "women have a perfect horror of eating raw food" (44). While in Stowe good women understand slavery's evil better than their male counterparts, in Douglass's novella, as in his narratives, actual women (as opposed to woman-as-mother-as-trope) are ridiculed or erased.

In "The Heroic Slave," home and family—other familiar tropes of domestic rhetoric in antislavery writing—are displaced by the primary ties between Madison and Listwell. When Madison ventures back to the South to rescue his wife Susan, she, like Douglass's own wife Anna Murray, and like the memory of his mother, is mute.[24] Susan's one direct vocalization, a shriek, leads to their discovery, her death, and Madison's recapture. Moreover, neither Listwell's nor Washington's children—the loss of whom provides the bond between the Birds and Eliza—are any more than props. Washington mentions them as an afterthought; he never tries to see or rescue them, and after Susan's death Douglass doesn't even bother to account for what happens to them.

Douglass's revision of Stowe's Bird passage could be interpreted as an example of male revolutionary politics displacing a domestic ethic. Even though Douglass does incorporate domestic rhetoric and insists that slavery contradicts the morality of a Christian nation, one could argue, as Eric Sundquist does, that for Douglass "the primary tropes of family and home became archetypes of the nation-state not by virtue of a visionary feminism, a new rule of domesticity, but by their identification with the 'manly' principles of revolutionary politics."[25] Sundquist hints at the difference between the affectional models of visionary feminism and moral suasion as I would configure them, and bourgeois individual rights. Yet his opposition between a "visionary feminism" and the " 'manly' principles of revolutionary politics" resists taking fully into account the feminized rhetorical grounding of Douglass's move to the political and "paternal." Douglass incorporates "womanly" models more fully than Sundquist's argument admits. In attempts at conversion—religious in Stowe, or secular in Douglass—sentiment and sympathy are affectionately bound; that is, they fall within the realm of visionary feminism and sentimental abolition. Additionally, both slide into a masculinized discursive economy which escapes sanitized boundaries for "proper" viewing and hearing relations.

Douglass revises himself rather than Stowe as he translates into writing what he overhears and oversees in the beating of his Aunt [H]Ester; it is, for him, "the blood stained gate," his "entrance to the hell of slavery" (N, 51). The two passages work quite differently; in the Narrative, his framing emphasizes sentiment, while in *Bondage* he moves from language's inability to convey sentiment to language's inadequacy without attendant rights. In the *Narrative* he writes, "I have often been awakened at the dawn of day by the most heart-rending shrieks of an own aunt of mine. . . . No words, no tears, no prayers, from [the master's] gory victim seemed to move his iron heart from its bloody purpose" (51). Douglass affirms his emphasis on the heart, on the connection of language, of words, to tears and prayers, when he goes on, "I wish I could commit to paper the *feelings* with which I beheld it." Deborah McDowell and Francis Smith Foster, among others, have elucidated the voyeuristic reproductions Douglass both is complicit in and creates in this rendition.[26] That he testifies to witnessing such an "exhibition," and it being a most terrible "spectacle," actualizes his lamentation of being doomed to be "a witness and *participant*" in such "outrages" (my italics).

Without mitigating the force of these fine arguments, I would add that in the *Narrative* Douglass's language positions the author's character, the young Douglass, as a witness against slavery through the medium of inexpressible but shared sentiment and feeling with the reader, whom he hopes to convert into being a similar witness. Douglass may move the reader to excitement, to borrow his description of Listwell's feelings upon overhearing Madison's laments. The question is then what to do with the aligned feelings of fear and paralyzation that he himself experiences as, "so terrified and horror-stricken at the sight [of Ester's beating he] hid [him] self in a closet, and dared not venture out till long after the bloody transaction" (*N*, 52). Douglass cannot allow his readers to become overwhelmed into similar passivity. By creating a sympathetic link between the young Douglass and the reader—both experience the inexpressibility of language—he provides an interpretative path of sentiment: even if the reader can't process the feelings that his description evokes, Douglass counsels that s/he should use them as a catalyst to protest slavery.

Douglass's rendition in the second narrative shifts his focus from sympathetic bonds established through the inexpressible feelings that Ester's beating elicits to the language of judicial redress. After describing the beating in detail he writes, "Language has no power to convey a *just* sense of its awful criminality" (*MB*, 88, emphasis mine). Douglass implies in the first passage, and makes explicit in the second, that language is not adequately expansive; it has "no power to convey." Yet language in both instances is simply a medium. What does not remain constant is Douglass's focus on its purpose; he moves the reader from language's inadequacy in relation to the feelings of the heart as he writes in 1845, to an emphasis on criminality and justice ten years later. One reason language has "no power" in 1855 is that the African-American witness still has no standing in the judicial sense. Douglass's position as outsider looking through the slats of Master Anthony's kitchen closet, in which he sleeps, simulates his position as outsider in the court—as witness he, like his language, has no power. By making white readers witnesses—and by implicitly offering judicial means as a more effective medium for their language—he attempts to grant antislavery witnessing standing and to imbue language with political power.

Douglass attempts to generate wider white antislavery support in part because he recognizes the increasing encroachment upon and instability of Black rights. He thus anticipates Justice Taney's pronouncement in Dred Scott: that slaves and free blacks "are so inferior, that they had no rights which the white man was bound to respect."[27] Douglass's changing description of [H]Ester's beating reflects his translating the "subjective" language of sentiment to the "objective" codification of official discourse. When, for example, in *Bondage* Douglass reports how many lashes Ester receives, the numbers, unlike her cries, seem to leave little room for pro-slavery imbued meaning. By 1853 Douglass simultaneously accepts and resists what contemporary legal critic Patricia Williams forwards: that "white statements of black needs suddenly acquire the sort of stark statistical authority that lawmakers can listen to and politicians hear. But from Blacks, stark statistical statements of need are heard as strident, discordant, and unharmonious."[28] Douglass does not appeal to the court itself, but provides the data to those who can; he encourages white witnessing as a temporary measure in the fight for collective Black standing, standing that would promote more than individual Black self-expression.[29]

In both descriptions of [H]Ester's beating Douglass works to form a sympathetic link with his readers;[30] how he directs the energy that connection creates differs in each account. Robert Levine argues that for Douglass "the ability to sympathize was a key indication of one's humanity, and those whom he believed possessed capacities for sympathy—such as Stowe—were viewed as nearly transcending the limits of race." Levine goes on that "between Douglass and Stowe, as Douglass in 'The Heroic Slave' presents it between Washington and Listwell, power is shared and mutually constitutive."[31] Douglass, I would counter, is considerably less idealistic, for he realizes that the reader/listener/Listwell does not transcend race, and that power is not shared. This is precisely why Douglass needs white readers as witnesses, and why, again, he weds sympathy, tears, or language's emotive power to standing in his rewriting of [H]Ester and in his discription of Listwell's and Madison's relationship.

Because the racial and gendered identities of Douglass's characters are compound, we never find ourselves simply in the company of equally endowed men who have, through sympathy, transcended race. Douglass does not use "the male couple as a figure of an inherently democratic union of equals which could serve as the basis for a new social organization," as Robert Martin argues Melville does in the same decade.[32] One might expect that the definitively male discourse of rights, as Douglass employs it in his move toward adopting the founding fathers and individual liberalism, might provide fertile ground for the kind of homoerotic play that Martin outlines. Yet liberalism's emphasis on private rights, self-sufficiency and individualism excludes the collective, inwardly binding, affectional ways of knowing and exchanging that issues of witnessing bring to the fore. Douglass does make fraternity at once erotic and social. But the politics of his narrative conversions in "The Heroic Slave" presuppose the fact that his transracial couplings are not democratic unions of equals.

Douglass elicits sympathy by connecting it to horror and titillation through the sexualized (and tortured) bodies of [H]Ester and Madison, and by positioning their bodies as objects of the readers's voyeuristic gaze. The sexualization of representation is a crucial marker in the shift from the affectional to the erotic in antislavery literature. In countless narratives sexual exploitation—not issues of desire, self, and liberty framed by relations of capital and property, for example—is presented (at least ostensibly) as the ultimate reason to speak against slavery. Slavery often "begins" for its narrators at the moment they understand the sexual threat it presents. Narrators often inscribe the difficult politics of witnessing in these passages. Witnessing is almost always bound up with sex in slavery.

Representations of abolitionist conversion are also often sexually encoded. Within the affectional model of disciplinary intimacy, where Douglass and Stowe make their protagonists their teachers, Black men, as often as white women, instigate white male transformation. In the textual economies of these two authors at least, one result of "successful" male interracial interaction is the shift from elicited abolitionist love to (illicit) homoeroticized prose.

Heterosexualized attraction, so often a part of the hero's stature, is not an option in Douglass's portrait of Madison Washington. To give voice to what Karen Sánchez-Eppler characterizes as the "always suppressed possibility of the white women's desire for the Black man"[33] would almost certainly alienate his readers of either race. Black female affirmation, on the other hand, would be ineffective as a medium of conversion, because her desire was continually ignored, denied, or denigrated. White male desire, then, logically affirms Madison's status as hero. Happening upon the unaware Madison in the woods, Listwell observes that he was

> of manly form. Tall, symmetrical, round, and strong. In this movements he seemed to combine, with the strength of the lion, a lion's elasticity. His torn sleeves disclosed arms like polished iron. His face was "black, but comely." . . . His whole appearance betokened Herculean strength; yet there was nothing savage or forbidding in his aspect. (*HS*, 28)

After taking note and stock of Madison's overwhelming physicality, the narrator registers Listwell's explicit desire:

> As our traveler gazed upon him, he almost trembled at the thought of his dangerous intrusion. Still he could not quit the place. He had long desired to sound the mysterious depths of the thoughts and feelings of a slave. . . . He listened again for those mellow and mournful accents, which, he says, made such an impression upon him as can never be erased. He did not have to wait long. There came another gush from the same full fountain; now bitter, and now sweet. (28)

The erotic nature of Douglass's language is fairly self-evident. Listwell has little reason to "tremble" for his personal safety. He himself notes that despite Madison's Herculean strength, "there is nothing savage or forbidden in his aspect. A child might play in his arms, or dance on his shoulders" (28). Douglass's language both explicitly refers to the "behemoth" Uncle Tom, on whose shoulders Little

Eva plays, and simultaneously imbues Madison with a manly, rather than maternal, aspect. Listwell's voyeuristic (and appreciative) gaze catches Madison in a state of mental and physical undress. The switch from the visual, to the aural, to the gustatory confirms the suggestive scopophilic frame. Listwell has long desired to "sound" "depths" and is rewarded with an ejaculatory "gush," "now bitter, now sweet." It is the heightened invasiveness of his senses that assures Listwell's conversion-seduction. Far away from the rights rhetoric of the founding fathers, Douglass's language transfers the affectional model of sentimental sympathy into a highly eroticized exchange.

In the erotically fraternal version of sentimental abolition that Douglass presents here, his discourse of conversion insists upon the sexual charge of listening, and so anticipates Harriet Jacobs's use of the ear as a metaphor for sexual violation. Douglass creates "a narrative situation that he must have desired in his journalistic career . . . an interdependent relationship between the white abolitionist . . . guided by an authoritative black leader," as Shelley Fisher Fishkin and Carla Peterson aptly point out.[34] Yet in the passage describing Listwell's first encounter with Madison, testifying and witnessing become not only interdependent acts, they become interpenetrative ones. In case the reader has missed this point, Douglass writes that after Madison has left, Listwell "stood half hoping, half fearing the return of the sable preacher to his solitary temple. The speech of Madison rung through the chambers of his soul, and vibrated through his entire frame" (29). Listwell's titillated state is followed by a *petite morte* of sorts. The Northerner has been taken; he has been possessed, and through this, reborn. Later in this passage Listwell, who has listened well, declares "from this hour I am an abolitionist." Douglass marshalls the penetrative power of speech and the dangerous power of sexual titillation in order to gain a convert to the antislavery cause.

Ultimately the bonding that takes place between Madison and Listwell leads back to a rhetoric of conversion that readers can recognize as both fraternal and feminized, where the two terms are not oppositional but mutually constitutive. Later, when Listwell happens upon the recaptured Madison, whom he imagines he is linked to by a "supernatural power, a wakeful providence or an inexorable fate" (*HS*, 58), sentiment rather than revolutionary rights rhetoric is the site of their link. Douglass describes Listwell's thoughts in affectional language: "His feelings were . . . bitter and excited and his heart was full with the fate of poor Madison (whom he loved as well as admired)" (57). Despite this masculinized arena, Douglass's homoeroticism, like Stowe's, is expressed in the affectional language of sentiment and suasion rather than through rights discourse.

Douglass extends his use of sentimental tropes and language regularly used to express an expansive and empowering sentimental ideology as he simultaneously embraces individual and formal rights. While Douglass replaces Stowe's maternal ethic with a fraternal one, he does not dispense with affectional rhetoric, a central ideological linchpin of domesticity and sentimental abolition. Although by the early fifties Douglass has actually supported Free-Soil candidates and embraced the constitution, Madison Washington's narrative role parallels Douglass's authorial one: both depend on persuasive speech's emancipating power. Madison's liberatory strategy reflects Douglass's rendition of the slave who counters his master's arguments about the peculiar institution and persuades his master to grant him his freedom in Douglass's first formal primer, "The Columbian Orator." Each of the narratives and the novella he writes during what I call "Douglass's decade" seeks to convert whites through language that touches their core and compels them to work for abolition. Douglass offers affectional means of relation, voice, and sentiment as the medium for change.

Sentimental abolition is an important critical category because it names the models and mechanisms of domesticity that inform, but are not limited to, moral suasion. Domestic ideology's influence—which is not simply contained in the bodies and presences of women—provides the weft between sentiment and standing, between the fraternal and the feminized. Moreover, in antislavery writings that deal with the erotically charged representations of Black bodies engaged in transracial relations, affectional discourse acts as a catalyst for further sexualization, whether the object of desire be a man or a woman, whether the subject of desiring be a woman or a man.

## Notes

At the University of Michigan, Ann Arbor, I would like to thank the Center for African-American and African Studies (CAAS) for the fellowship that allowed me to research and write this paper. The University of Chicago's CAAS invited me to present an earlier draft, and I appreciate the helpful feedback I received. I would also like to thank Arthur Aubin Saint-Flannigan, Tyler Steben and especially Jacqueline Goldsby and Eric C. Williams for their useful suggestions at the final stages of this piece.

1. Frederick Douglass, *My Bondage and My Freedom* (New York: Dover, 1969). All subsequent Douglass quotations are cited as follows: *MB*: *My Bondage and My Freedom*; *N: The Narrative Life of Frederick Douglass*, ed. Houston Baker (New York: Penguin Books, 1982); *HS*: "The Heroic Slave" in *Three Classic African-American Novels*, ed. William L. Andrews (New York: Mentor, 1990).

2. See William Andrews, "*My Bondage and My Freedom* and the American Literary Renaissance of the 1850s," in *Critical Essays on Frederick Douglass*, ed. William Andrews (Boston: G.K. Hall & Co., 1991), 133–147; Eric J. Sundquist, ed., *Frederick Douglass: New Literary and Historical Essays* (New York: Cambridge University Press, 1990); William S. McFeely, *Frederick Douglass* (New York: W. W. Norton and Co., 1991).

3. Harriet Beecher Stowe, *Uncle Tom's Cabin* (1852; rpt. New York: Macmillan, 1962). Subsequent references are cited *UTC* within the text. Slave narrators in the fifties often make explicit reference to Uncle Tom or to Stowe. Solomon Northup's 1853 narrative is dedicated to Stowe. "The Heroic Slave" and *A Key to Uncle Tom's Cabin* also appear in the same year. Harriet Beecher Stowe, *A Key to Uncle Tom's Cabin* (rpt. New York: Arno Press, 1969); J. Solomon Northup, *Twelve Years a Slave* (Baton Rouge: Louisiana State University Press, 1968).

4. I refer most recently to Richard Yarborough, Eric Sundquist, and William Andrews. The latter two lament that Douglass's second narrative has been largely overlooked, and

argue for its centrality by addressing the paternal issues the text raises. Sundquist pays particular attention to Douglass's revisionary use of Stowe. See William Andrews, *To Tell a Free Story* (Chicago: University of Chicago Press, 1988); Eric J. Sundquist, *To Wake The Nations: Race in the Making of American Culture* (Cambridge: Harvard University Press, 1993); Sundquist, "Frederick Douglass: Literacy and Paternalism," 120–132; Andrews, "*My Bondage and My Freedom*," 133–147, both in Andrews, *Critical Essays*. For the most thorough treatment of "Heroic Slave," see Yarborough, "Race, Violence, and Manhood," in Sundquist, *New Essays*, 166–188. For work on Douglass's objectification of the black female, see especially Deborah E. McDowell, "In the First Place: Making Frederick Douglass and the Afro-American Narrative Tradition," in Andrews, *Critical Essays*, 192–214; and Valerie Smith, "Three Slave Narratives," in Smith's *Self-Discovery and Authority in Afro-American Narrative* (Cambridge: Harvard University Press, 1987).

5. McDowell, "In the First Place," 199.

6. The term "sentimental abolition" was used in the early 1860s to connote a hyper-diluted abolitionism. I mean to situate the term within the very different register set by recent work on the interconnections between abolition, domesticity, and feminism.

7. For important work that illustrates "the degree to which domestic and sentimental antislavery writings are implicated in the very oppressions they seek to reform," see Karen Sánchez-Eppler, "Bodily Bonds: The Intersecting Rhetorics of Feminism and Abolition," especially 93; and Laura Wexler, "Literary Eavesdropping, Domestic Fiction, and Educational Reform," 9-38, both in *The Culture of Sentiment*, Shirley Samuels, ed. (New York: Oxford University Press, 1992). For a reading of Harriet Wilson's *Our Nig* as a critique of bourgeois domesticity, see Gabrielle Foreman, *Sentimental Subversions: Reading, Race and Sexuality in the Nineteenth Century* (Berkeley: UMI Dissertation Service, 1992), 124-138.

8. Current "needs" and "rights" debates in contemporary critical legal studies (CLS) both echo and help to illuminate the practice and politics of abolitionist fractures. Moral suasion loosely corresponds to what CLS calls "needs discourse": CLS's skepticism about the law as a place of resort for the disfranchised corresponds to moral suasionists' distrust of the law and constitution. CLS's utopian strain, its emphasis on contractual alienation and its wish for a more communal world, echoes the secular extensions of Garrisonian, radical, nonsectarian, and anti-sabbatarianism activism and belief in morality as the highest authority.

9. The various ramifications of Douglass's choice are precisely what in Yarborough's estimation mar his novella. See "Race, Violence, and Manhood," 179–183. For a different reading, see Robert Stepto, "Storytelling in Early Afro-American Fiction: Frederick Douglass's *The Heroic Slave*," in *Black Literature and Literary Theory*, ed. Henry Louis Gates, Jr. (New York: Metheun, 1984), 175–186.

10. In the first narrative she is called Hester, in the second Ester; he explains the shift saying he is writing from sound.

11. Smith and McDowell argue that ultimately Douglass revises and reinscribes male patriarchal norms. Yarborough argues that in "Heroic Slave" Douglass "was ultimately unable or unwilling to call into question the white bourgeois paradigm of manhood itself," *New Essays*, 183.

12. Acutely aware of the racial dynamics of readership, Douglass was again disappointed when only twenty percent of his subscribers were African-American.

13. Douglass and Gerrit Smith were both later involved in John Brown's raid on Harper's Ferry. After Brown was apprehended, Douglass was forced to flee the country to avoid arrest. Brown became a martyr and Douglass's warrant was dropped; he eventually came home unmolested.

14. *Frederick Douglass' Paper*, 9 December 1853.

15. After promising that she would raise monies for the school, Stowe changed her mind; she never fully explained why. See McFeely's biography and Waldo Martin, *The Mind of Frederick Douglass* (Chapel Hill: University of North Carolina Press, 1984). Also see Robert Levine, "*Uncle Tom's Cabin* in *Frederick Douglass's Paper*: An Analysis of Reception," *American Literature* 64 (March 1992): 81.

16. See Eric Foner, *The Life and Writings of Frederick Douglass*, 2 vols. (New York: International Publishers, 1950), 2:29.

17. Richard Brodhead, "Sparing the Rod: Discipline and Fiction in Antebellum America," in *The New American Studies,* ed. Philip Fisher (Berkeley: University of California Press, 1991), 145.

18. *The Liberator*, March 13, 1840.

19. Homosexuality as a category, and thus as an *identity*, didn't form until the late 1800s. For work on earlier models of emergent homosexual relations and representation, see Michael Lynch, " 'Here is Adhesiveness': From Friendship to Homosexuality," *Victorian Studies* 29 (Autumn 1985): 68; Robert Martin, "A Note on the Use of the Term 'Homosexual,' " in Martin, *Hero, Captain, and Stranger* (Chapel Hill: University of North Carolina Press, 1986); James Creech, *Closet Reading/Gay Writing: The Case of Melville's Pierre* (Chicago: University of Chicago Press, 1993). In contrast, see Donald Yacavone, "Male Friendship in Abolitionist Circles," in *Meanings for Manhood: Constructions of Masculinity in Victorian America*, ed. Mark C. Carnes and Clyde Griffen (Chicago: University of Chicago Press, 1990), especially 89–93. Also see Nancy Cott, "Passionlessness: An Interpretation of Victorian Sexual Ideology, 1790–1850" *Signs* 4 (Winter 1978): 233.

20. Broadhead, "Sparing the Rod," 161

21. Andrews, *Critcal Essays*, 143.

22. See Gabrielle Foreman, " 'This Promiscuous Housekeeping:' Death, Transgression, and Homoeroticism in *Uncle Tom's Cabin*," *Representations* 43 (Summer 1993): 51–72, for a reading of homosocial desire between St. Clare, Tom, and St. Clare's manservant Adolph.

23. Stepto, "Storytelling," 183.

24. In *My Bondage and My Freedom* Douglass writes, "It has been a life-long standing grief to me, that I knew so little of my mother; and that I was so early separated from her. The counsels of her love must have been very beneficial to me. . . . I take few steps in life, without feeling her presence; but the image is mute, and I have no striking words of her's treasured up," 57.

25. Sundquist, *To Wake the Nations*, 109

26. McDowell crystallizes, develops, and examines the broader ramifications in her essay, perhaps the best work on Douglass's narrative objectifications of women. See "In the First Place," especially 201–204. Also see Frances Foster, " 'In Respect to Females. . . .': Differences in the Portrayals of Women by Male and Female Narrators," *Black American Literature Forum* 15 (Summer 1981).

27. *Dred Scott v. Sanford. Reports of Cases Argued and Adjudged in The Supreme Court of The United States*, December Term, 1856, Vol. 19 (Washington D.C: William Morrison, 1857), 407.

28. Patricia Williams, *The Alchemy of Race and Rights* (Cambridge: Harvard University Press, 1991), 152.

29. Even after he left the Garrisonian antislavery circuit and assumed the editorship of *The North Star*, Douglass continued to speak widely. He was also the underground railway agent in Rochester, was involved with abolitionist Gerrit Smith's run for Congress, and with several of John Brown's activities.

30. Building on the work of feminist scholars and historians, Robert Levine notes that "Sympathy is a key concept here . . . Douglass, as the *Narrative* and his remarks on *UTC* reveal, thought that the ability of the writer to create in the (white) reader a sympathetic identification with the plight of the slave was central to a text's potential to bring about social change," "An Analysis of Reception," 74.

31. Ibid., 85.

32. Martin, *Hero*, 11.

33. Sánchez-Eppler, "Bodily Bonds," 103.

34. For work on Douglass's journalism, see Shelley Fisher Fishkin and Carla Peterson, " 'We Hold These Truths to be Self-Evident': The Rhetoric of Frederick Douglass's Journalism," in *New Essays*, 200.

# The Blind Leading the Blind:
# The Racial Gaze as Plot Dilemma
# in "Benito Cereno" and "The Heroic Slave"

B y virtue of "The Heroic Slave" and "Benito Cereno," Frederick Douglass and Herman Melville share an affinity that has often been alluded to but never explored in depth. It is undeniable that the two texts demonstrate numerous points of contact: their historical proximity, their mutual acts of transforming factual events into fiction, their use of slave rebellions as source material, and, finally, their depictions of democracy in a state of contradiction, straining against itself. Having acknowledged these aspects I want to move swiftly past them to a more compelling feature these texts share in common. Both novellas dramatize the "racial gaze," a mode of voyeurism that takes on aoristic significance in the context of nineteenth-century American racial relations. Under the auspices of the racial gaze, difference and hierarchy come together within a procedural nexus.[1] This is not to suggest that Douglass's and Melville's purposes were the same. Nor is it to suggest their sources led them to identical points of emphasis. However, we need to pay close attention to the manner in which "The Heroic Slave" and "Benito Cereno" utilize the racial gaze as a way of organizing the plots of their fictions. By pairing Douglass and Melville we can come to understand how these fictions have the complementary aim of positing arguments which subvert the visual sphere as the zenith of representational modes.

To understand the significance of the racial gaze, one needs to understand the emergence of an irrefutable correlation between visualization and persuasion during the nineteenth century. As Peter Brooks suggests, the dominant nineteenth-century tradition of realism

> insistently makes the visual the master relation of the world, for the very premise of realism is that one cannot understand human beings outside the context of the things that surround them, and knowing those things is a matter of viewing them, detailing them, and describing the concrete milieu in which men and women enact their destinies. To know, in realism, is to see, and to represent is to describe.[2]

One finds further evidence for Brooks's claim by noting that by the middle of the nineteenth century the visual sphere had come to play an important role in foregrounding difference, and racial difference in particular. As Elizabeth Johns has demonstrated so ably in her excellent study of American genre painting, the "politics of everyday life" were such that African Americans were an ambiguous presence, on the margins to be sure, but necessary to concretize the visual

representation of social status, providing even poor whites with a group of
nonsovereigns who were unarguably beneath them." More importantly, it was
New York, and not the antebellum South, which served as the "prime location
... of the cultural construction and perpetuation of African-American character
across the United States."[3] The visual sphere provided Northern whites during
the antebellum period with a set of procedures by which to reinforce the African-
American presence as "one of relationship"[4] and difference, where

> autonomy, and thus authority and power, was reserved for white figures. Moreover,
> white painters avoided any reference to activities that actually defined the place of
> blacks. There were no scenes of labor, a scant few ... of blacks in white homes as
> servants, and virtually none of black females. ... White artists did not depict black
> males as heads of, or even as members of, families; they did not show blacks in
> what Emerson called an "original relation to the universe"—that is, in a world even
> circumscribed, the terms of which they defined themselves.[5]

In short, Johns concludes, "African-American men had to be perceived as power-
less and foolish for current social and political arrangements to prevail." Johns's
assessment of American genre painting during the antebellum period is useful
because it articulates the manner in which the visual sphere constructed the
African American's presence as a wholly public manifestation. Indeed, to construct images of an African-American private life would be to depict danger, a
threat to the status quo.

Douglass and Melville take advantage of this circumstance and utilize it as
the conceptual pivot for their respective narratives. In each novella, one finds
visual details playing an important role in the plot, as if both texts were especially
aware of how visual information serves to construct racial identity. Each of these
fictions asserts Douglass's and Melville's shared recognition that the problem
of transforming democracy was likely to involve the shedding of a great deal of
blood along with a hopelessly outmoded sign system that invested heavily in the
visual sphere. Thus, by looking at their management of the visual sphere, I will
argue that both Melville and Douglass subvert the social power of the gaze by
undermining the relationship between interpretation and visualization.

I want to corroborate the validity of the Douglass/Melville diad by first working
out how each writer implements the racial gaze as a symbolic gesture. "Benito
Cereno" is a narrative which represents the "black look" as a source of pleasure.
"The Heroic Slave" is driven by a different narrative procedure, that of first
destabilizing the racial gaze and then positing aurality, acts of listening, as viable
forms of representation. Further, both texts call attention to the act of scanning
visual "remains" and placing them into a narrative context. Turning to Melville
first, we find that the novella concludes with the death of Babo, leader of the
insurrection aboard the *San Dominick*. The description of Babo's demise is worth
quoting:

> Some months after, dragged to the gibbet at the tail of a mule, the black met his
> voiceless end. The body was burned to ashes; but for many days, the head, that hive
> of subtlety, fixed on a pole in the Plaza, met, unabashed, the gaze of the whites.[6]

Melville's language proposes that the affair reaches its conclusion because Babo's head is separated from his body. However, as the narrator takes care to inform us, Babo has, from the moment of his capture, refused to speak, choosing silence over speech of any form. The narrator, bearing more than a trace of Captain Delano's sense of racial superiority perhaps, attributes this silence to Babo's realization that "all was over," moving from conjecture to ventriloquism to argue that the slave's reticence plainly states, "Since I cannot do deeds, I will not speak words." But this interpretation of Babo's decision needs to be questioned. Should we accept the narrator's characterization of Babo's silence as an act of resignation or submission? For Babo's silence is just as easily read as an act of resistance, a recognition of "the use his words would be put to by the Spanish court"[7] and his unwillingness to cooperate. The "order" we find restored at the close of the court proceedings culminates not only in Babo's death, but the installation of his head on a pike in the Plaza, where his lifeless countenance can gaze at— and be gazed upon by—the whites who require reassurance that the matter has come to a successful end and that the threat has passed.[8]

Certainly, the strategy of severing the heads of rebellious slaves from their bodies has a dual purpose. Not only is it meant to signify the restoration of order, but also to remind the surviving slaves what fate will befall them should they choose a similar course. In short, Babo serves as both visual trope of power and palliative gesture, for if he is a tangible symbol of the power of the slave-owner (and the State's endorsement of that power), he would seem to be, just as well, a symbol of the powerlessness of the slave, reinforcing the notion that whites not only have more power than blacks but also that the state will respond in like manner to any rebellious threat they may choose to mount in the future. What insures this reading is that Babo's head functions, not as cipher, where meaning is randomized, given over to the free play that results from its detachment from an interpretive matrix, but as sign, where a system exists to insure the production of meaning. The spectators on the plaza, then, are secure not only because the matter has been closed, but also because the head is installed within a system foregrounded by the racial gaze. And yet, this interpretive matrix is threatened by entropy because it is Babo's head, as a "hive of subtlety," that asserts a refusal to fit comfortably into the category of either cautionary tool or visual artifact. The result, as Melville would have it, is that the relationship between the visual sphere and white supremacy is rendered unstable. This is substantiated further in the proceedings of the inquest, during which "the official Spanish documents" remind us that Babo is the engine of the entire plot on board the *San Dominick*, and that he thus directly refutes the myth that blacks are the examples of docility, meekness, or infantilism that Delano would have them be. Rather, as Babo demonstrates, his actions are the result of an intellect capable of grasping the nuances of the slaveholder's cultural conventions so completely that he orchestrates a mimetic performance whose reproduction of the status quo is nearly beyond rupture.

Thus Melville's language resists attributing a sense of finality to Babo's death. Indeed, we find that Babo's gaze meets "unabashed, the gaze of the whites" and further that it is directed "towards St. Bartholomew's church, in whose vaults slept then, as now, the recovered bones of Aranda." If we are to believe Melville's description, Babo acquires an even greater level of daring in death, where his contempt for his captors need not be masked. He becomes a figure who does not shrink from his role in the insurrection, nor does he drop his eyes in submission as would be expected of a living slave. Rather, he looks without shame at his handiwork; if anything, death has fortified Babo's gaze.[9] What this also suggests is that Babo's head does not sit as comfortably within the established system of signs as the tribunal would imagine.

Rather than leaving Babo's gaze outside the realm of intentionality, Melville invests the dead man's look with power. When directed across the Plaza, Babo's gaze exists on two planes: the physical plane, whereby one can follow the gaze from a point of origin to a destination, and a critical plane on which Babo's gaze articulates the instability of the cultural codes sustaining white supremacy. Indeed, the head announces with great certainty that the codes have been broken and that the violence necessary to settle the question of slavery will need to be enacted on an even grander scale (via a civil war perhaps). Melville fixes this idea into place by extending Babo's gaze across the plaza, where it settles upon the monastery, "where, three months after being dismissed by the court, Benito Cereno . . . did, indeed, follow his leader." The death of Cereno, some three months after the conclusion of the proceedings, where he testified to the criminal acts of the Africans on the *San Dominick*, is of a piece with Babo's unrelenting gaze. Though we have little textual evidence to substantiate the claim, I want to assert that Melville attributes Cereno's death, by way of the same irony to be found in much of the narrative, to Babo's presence. This is underscored by the novella's last sentence—its use of semi-colons that connect Babo, Aranda, and Cereno as a conceptual whole—which reads:

> The body was burned to ashes; but for many days, the head, that hive of subtlety, fixed on a pole in the Plaza, met, unabashed, the gaze of the whites; and across the Plaza looked toward St. Bartholomew's church, in whose vaults slept then, as now, the recovered bones of Aranda; and across the Rimac bridge looked toward the monastery, on Mount Agonia without; where, three months after being dismissed by the court, Benito Cereno, borne on the bier, did, indeed, follow his leader. (Melville, 2554)

Though their deaths occur at different intervals, Melville's grammatical construction asserts, nonetheless, that each has met his respective end because of his connection to the institution of slavery. Moreover, that Cereno is said to have "follow[ed] his leader," recalls the ironic joke Babo uses to remind his captives of his ability to link symbolism and violent force and insists that Babo is a man of his word; as Cereno's "leader" during the rebellion aboard the *San Dominick*, he has preceded the Spaniard into death. And while the ordeal aboard the *San Dominick* was a trying one, Melville suggests that Cereno has met his demise because Babo has kept his promise.

This is foreshadowed during Cereno's final, and famous, encounter with Captain Delano when the latter asserts, "You are saved. . . . you are saved: what has cast such a shadow upon you?" Cereno concludes the dialogue when he states, simply, "The negro." While there has been a great deal of interest in this exchange, its significance is underscored in the next sentence, where Cereno gathers "his mantle about him, as if it were a pall." Melville refers, of course, to the loose cloak Cereno wears draped over his shoulders. With an eye toward a more modern usage, mantle is also "something which envelopes, covers, or conceals." Here, the mantle that Cereno attempts to draw about him is that of racial superiority. While Cereno's statement could be dismissed as paranoia, I would offer that Melville had a more chilling intention and his use of language. His conflation of "mantle" and "pall" argues for a reading of white supremacy as a form of living death which takes on visual form. For this reading to be in any way a stable one, we need to recognize Delano's presence within the configuration. Melville's use of irony indicates it is Delano's obtuseness, his failure to be moved by the rebellion to a new way of seeing, that demonstrates the nature of the affliction to the fullest. Thus, in addition to the literal remains, the bodies of the three men directly involved in the affair on the *San Dominick*, there is yet a fourth body, Captain Delano's, whose inability to grasp the humanity of black slaves makes his gaze as ineffectual as that of Aranda, Babo, and Cereno. Indeed, in Melville's subversive tale Delano's gaze emblematizes darkness, for despite all the visual details at his disposal, he remains unmoved; he is incapable of recognizing slavery as an equally oppressive and corrosive event.

But "Benito Cereno" also speaks to the inadequate supply of "light" democracy focuses upon the dilemma of slavery. Though the slaves aboard the San Dominick might have instructed him on the lengths to which slaves yearning to be free would go to achieve their liberation, Delano does not make the necessary conceptual jump to view a slave rebellion as an assertion of democratic principles. This also makes us reconsider his exchange with Cereno. When he asks what "has cast such a shadow. . . ." upon Cereno, the reply forces us to examine Delano's role in this construction. The exchange between the two men is characterized by Delano's fixation on visual evidence and Cereno's shift to a metaphoric mode. Delano's belief that Cereno has been "saved" arises from his sense that democratic procedure has redeemed the Spanish captain and that good has vanquished evil. The American captain believes democracy, as a white man's domain, is restored to potency because the rebellion has been crushed. But Cereno's awareness that he is irreversibly implicated by the black bodies figuratively casting a shadow over him makes him aware that his role in the parody aboard the *San Dominick* has the lasting effect of discrediting democracy as well.

Babo's presence on the plaza signifies the instability of visual signs. The rebellion he stages on the *San Dominick* unmasks white supremacy as a discourse that can not only be learned by blacks but reduced to a performance, much to the detriment of those who enact blind adherence. Moreover, that Cereno is forced by circumstance to narrate the tale for its inclusion in the written proceedings of the hearings means that that instability is reinscribed into the very system used to lock black inferiority into place. We must read Cereno's silence as his realization that the rebellion has dislocated him from the assumption (which Delano still holds) that language functions as the site of power. As Jon Hauss has argued, Cereno "does not know, or will not find, words for his shattering experience."[10] The encounter on board the *San Dominick* has upset the master/slave hierarchy; here it is Babo who plays the role of ventriloquist, coercing Cereno's speech throughout. When at last he and Delano can exchange a word as fellow ship captains and, thus, as "equals," Babo's lingering presence, like his gaze, has a debilitating effect upon the Spaniard, as if the two are inseparably linked.

Frederick Douglass makes a similarly compelling effort to subvert the racial gaze. Like Melville, he is concerned with representing the remains of a slave rebellion at sea. But instead of the physical remains that close "Benito Cereno," Douglass proffers a historical record, which contains textual "remains." Hence he writes:

> The State of Virginia is famous in American annals for the multitudinous array of her statesmen and heroes. She has been defined by some as the mother of statesmen. History has not been sparing in recording their names, or in blazoning their deeds. Her high position in this respect, has given her an enviable distinction among her sister States. With Virginia for his birthplace, even a man of ordinary parts, on accounts of the general partiality for her sons, easily rises to eminent stations.[11]

Douglass offers Virginia as the birthplace of men who dominate the public sphere. The racial gaze is embedded in the act of reading, which is implied by the "annals" which describe the deeds of Virginians. Here again we find not only an instance of visual evidence, but the fact that that evidence is reified in textual form. The "multitudinous array" which is American history is not, in Douglass's view, merely a question of regional origins, rather it is an intentional arrangement that requires literacy to decipher. It is both a record of past achievement and, as Douglass intimates, a blueprint for success in the future. What "remains" is a historical record, a visual representation of excellence that seems to allude to natural circumstance. But the use of a tone of detachment calls attention to the act of omission, which Douglass's narrator makes clear by shifting to a more engaged rhetorical posture, indicating the record is incomplete:

> Yet not all the great ones of the Old Dominion have, by the fact of their birthplace, escaped undeserved obscurity. By some strange neglect, one of the truest, manliest, and bravest of her children, one who, in after years, will, I think, command the pen of genius to set his merits forth, holds now no higher place in the records of that grand old Commonwealth than is held by a horse or an ox. (Douglass, 25)

Douglass's narrator takes great pains to construct Virginia as symbolic territory where its "native sons" are invested with the power to govern and lead. And yet he does not give utterance to the fact that the terms of inclusion among Virginia's pantheon of heroes are racially inflected. What is given voice, albeit of a muted sort, is the need for a revisionary act of composition, carried out by one whose "genius" (on the order of Douglass's, of course) can liberate a figure worthy of enshrinement who, by an act of miscategorization, is placed among the lower orders.

Further, the narrator displaces the task of reconciling this discrepancy in Virginia's history onto those who formulated the faulty system of classification. Thus, he asserts:

> Let those account for it who can, but there stands the fact, that a man who loved liberty as well as did Patrick Henry—who deserved it as much as Thomas Jefferson—and who fought for it with a valor as high, an arm as strong, and against odds as great, as he who led all the armies of the American colonies through the great war for freedom and independence, *lives now only in the chattel records* of his native State. (Douglass, 25; my emphasis)

Again, the issue is one of remains—and what remains, of course, is a textual paradox of epic proportions. How, the narrator asks, can a figure on the order of men so conspicuously associated with American ideals be excluded from a place within a "legitimate" text? Moreover, Douglass employs a rhetorical posture that implies that the figure currently categorized as "chattel" made an important contribution to the American Revolution.

The reader is forced to contend with a failed act of historical preservation: the man in question, though a historical figure of great importance to American freedom, "lives now only in the chattel records of his native State." The history of Virginia involves an act of misplacement, a failure of the visual system foregrounding the relationship between textuality and historical veracity. Douglass leaves the obvious connection between the racial identity of his subject and his inclusion in historical discourse as a connotative gesture, the significance of which the reader must discern. Though such a gesture runs the risk of creating disinterest in the reader, Douglass's narrator nonetheless suggests that there may yet exist ways to augment the story and thus persuade the skeptic of his subject's merit. The inadequacy of the historical record notwithstanding, the task remains one of reconstructing this individual's actions and placing him correctly in the historical record. But to accomplish this, the reader must be loosed from a reliance on the racial gaze. The narrator begins this turn toward the main body of his narrative by articulating the conditions which accompany the act of locating the individual in question:

> *Glimpses* of this great character are all that can be presented. He is brought to *view* only by a few *transient incidents,* and these afford but *partial satisfaction.* Like a guiding star on a stormy night, he is seen through the parted clouds and the howling tempests; or, like the gray peak of a menacing rock on a perilous coast, and he is seen by the *quivering flash* of angry lightning, and he again *disappears* covered with mystery. (Douglass, 25–26; my emphasis)

What must be emphasized here is Douglass's use of language that refers to the act of looking, but here words like "glimpses," "transient," "partial satisfaction," and "quivering flash," all suggest the impossibility of establishing and maintaining the gaze. Here, visual acuity is disrupted because of the inconsistent presence of light. Further, the phrase "great character" refers to Madison Washington, the subject of the tale, but it likewise refers to any figure historical discourse would seek to enshrine in textual terms. However, as Douglass portrays the process, the "partial satisfaction" signals a constant disruption of what would seem to be spectatorial pleasure. Indeed, the historical figure always "disappears, covered with mystery." That mystery, Douglass suggests, has more to do with the "how" than the "what." But this is intended to remind the reader that it is not spectatorship, but narratorship that is at issue here—and thus Douglass insists that the gaze is not an instrument of narrative. Hence, we might read the passage as one which describes the particularities of one instance of misplacement in the historical record; it is also descriptive of the generic, and indeed arbitrary, nature of historical discourse and national identity itself.

But this sets up the final paragraph in the prologue section of "The Heroic Slave," where the narrator conflates the difficulty of historical discourse with the necessity of telling:

> Curiously, earnestly, anxiously, we peer into the dark and wish even for the *blinding flash,* or the light of *northern skies* to reveal him. But alas! he is still enveloped in darkness, and we return from the pursuit like a wearied and disheartened mother (after a tedious and unsuccessful search for a lost child) who returns weighted down with disappointment and sorrow. *Speaking of marks, traces, possibles, and probabilities, we come before our readers.* (Douglass, 26; my emphasis)

"Blinding flash" is juxtaposed against "northern skies," which infers that a sudden burst of light is not necessary for the purpose of interpretation. The "marks, traces, possibles, and probabilities" the narrator brings before the reader, then, are all that is needed. But the task requires an alternative system to make sense of, to order and interpret, this disparate grouping of signs. The project is not constructive, but *reconstructive.* Since the question is one of refuting Virginia's chattel records, the challenge before the narrator is one of demonstrating an alternative interpretive system that can relocate the figure in question without employing the racial gaze. That system, as Douglass would have it, is not visual, but aural. Like Melville, who envisioned a way to activate a metaphor capable of disconnecting the racial gaze from the dictates of law, Douglass recognized that the racial gaze needed to give way to acts of listening. This is important, especially when we consider that Douglass felt himself to be an eloquent spokesman for the abolition of slavery. But more than this, he felt himself capable of articulating in no uncertain terms the humanity and worth of the slave.

What makes a comparison to "Benito Cereno" appropriate here is that both fictions posit the racial gaze as a faulty system of interpretation, grounded as it is in notions of white supremacy. Cereno's "shadow" and Douglass's "marks, traces, possibles, and probabilities," suggest the manner in which alternative methods of interpretation threaten to disrupt conventional sign systems, and it is upon this issue that the plots of both novellas establish narrative pivots. Delano's inability to grasp the concept of metaphor is analogous to Douglass's act of assigning a heroic figure to an inappropriate textual setting on the basis of race.

Recalling George Fredrickson's treatment of the 1840s and '50s in his book *The Black Image in the White Mind,* I want to locate both Douglass's and

Melville's attempts to establish an alternative point of view.[12] Both authors were aware of the manner in which rhetorical constructions of the period emphasized much of what Johns described in American genre painting, namely that blacks did not have lives that could be considered apart from those of whites. Douglass's response is to subvert this circumstance by de-emphasizing the importance of the visual sphere and working to shift attention to information received aurally. I have discussed elsewhere the ways Douglass's first autobiography resists attempts to make the black male body a wholly public site, a form of narrative currency for white abolitionists.[13] Douglass accomplishes this by creating a hero who, in addition to his skill as an orator, accomplishes physical deeds which make him the subject of oral discourse. As Douglass suggests at the outset of "The Heroic Slave," Madison Washington's importance lies in the fact that, first, his entry into the public sphere is restricted to that afforded by visual activity, and second his place in history is mishandled once he is located there because blackness is a visual sign of erasure rather than achievement. Melville, on the other hand, uses Amasa Delano as a vehicle intended to locate the eye as the source of interpretive activity. Of course, Delano's "vision," shaped as it is by New World ideology, fails him at every turn.

These strategies need to be considered alongside both Douglass's, and Melville's use of slave rebellions as the basis for their fictions. As Frederickson takes care to point out, the romantic racialism of the 1840s and 50s

> would have been impossible if the slaves had risen up in large numbers and rebelled against their masters. Romantic racialism was facilitated by the fact that no massive insurrections took place in the South after the Nat Turner rebellion of 1831. This apparent quiescence was widely interpreted in the North as reflecting a natural black docility.[14]

As early as Kinmont, there was the view that blacks were "more feminine and tenderminded" than whites, a view which, by the 1850s, became justification for denying blacks a place in an emancipated society. Their "femininity," the argument ran, marked them as passive figures incapable of formulating and bringing to fruition a viable plan for their own liberation. This, coupled with their docility and benevolence, marked them as figures who lacked a sensibility devoted to deception or guile.[15] This attitude was often conflated with femininity, suggesting that blacks and women shared important qualities, being almost interchangeable in their signal virtues.[16]

However, the 1850s saw a dearth of individuals willing to argue the contrary, for to do so would be to imply that blacks could be as relentless as whites in a struggle for their freedom. Given this, it is odd that neither Melville's nor Douglass's fiction is set in the 1850s. Why, one might ask, does each author backdate these fictional events, given the necessity to refute the mischaracterization of African-American masculinity?[17] Douglass may have chosen 1835 because it was four years after the Nat Turner rebellion in Virginia (1831) and four years before the Amistad rebellion in 1839. Placing the narrative in the midst of these events is at once to recall a period when the fear of rebellion was running high and also to graft such fear onto the discussions taking place at the moment he composed the novella. Melville's decision to set "Benito Cereno" in 1799 is no less controversial, because the events in the story coincide with the Haitian revolution of that year. The 1850s were the beginning of what Eric Sundquist refers to as a "climactic phase," and Melville's "politically volatile tale . . . brings into view the convulsive history of the entire region and epoch—from the Colombian discovery of the Americas, through the democratic revolutions in the United States, Haiti, and Latin America, to the contemporary crisis over the expansion of the 'Slave Power' in the United States."[18] After the brutality of the Vesey and Turner rebellions in the U.S. and the revolution in Haiti, Southerners propagated the stereotype of the docile, happy slave who had been civilized by the domesticating forces of bondage.[19] However, as Fredrickson points out, the Southern imagination harbored fears of rebellion long after the affair had passed:

> Insurrection panics were frequent after 1830, and for men who supposedly ruled over a docile population, Southern slave owners were extraordinarily careful to maintain absolute control over their "people" and quarantine them from any kind of outside influence that might inspire dissatisfaction with their condition. In moments of candor, Southerners admitted their suspicion that duplicity, opportunism, and potential rebelliousness lurked behind the mask of Negro affability.[20]

This is an important consideration: it illuminates the disingenuousness of Southern plantation rhetoric, and it suggests the extent to which Northerners's romantic racialism was as much a foreclosure on African-American social possibility as an insistence upon black exclusion. The act of equating their fictions with moments of black unrest allowed Douglass and Melville to destabilize the stereotypes held by a Northern, white readership. But, more importantly, it challenged the terms upon which Northern readers attempted to refute Southern justifications of slavery. Indeed, as Allan Moore Emery has argued, this is most certainly the case with Melville's novella, which he argues "serves to demolish the notion of black amiability."[21] But Douglass and Melville work to very different ends, because, as I will demonstrate below, Madison Washington possesses heroic traits that make him the subject of verbal exchange between whites, unlike Babo, who upon being captured silences himself and Cereno as well. As both Stepto and McFeeley have observed, part of the reason for this is that Douglass saw himself on a par with Washington;[22] in many ways he felt the novella to be the "fantasy of his own heroism." But this makes the racial gaze all the more important to his task, for it allowed him to step back from his own story and, by focusing it upon Madison Washington, to achieve the dual purpose of inserting the African-American subject within the field of romantic narrative while refuting the dominant stereotypes of the day.

As Douglass's novella begins, we find that Mr. Listwell, a Northern traveler "through the state of Virginia," happens upon the hero of the tale, Madison Washington. Interestingly, it is Washington's voice—not the visual manifestation of his physical presence—which "arrests [Listwell's] attention." Moreover, Douglass allows Listwell to follow the sound of Washington's voice till he finds him, though he chooses to remain concealed from Washington's view. What comes next is a "soliloquy" from Madison Washington which describes the evils of slavery and, more importantly, his own virtues and ambitions. As Robert Stepto has argued, one is struck by the overwrought nature of the passage and the manner in which Madison presents himself in the "high mode" of human endeavor. Here we have an individual who articulates his ideas and emotions, eschewing the dialect that we find being used by slaves in Stowe's *Uncle Tom's Cabin.*

Though I am in complete agreement with Stepto's reading of Madison Washington's presentation as a figure who is "literate, revolutionary, and quintessentially American," I would add that Douglass's strategy, upon introducing us to Madison, is one of subverting racial stereotypes that issue from the visual sphere.[23] Thus, the soliloquy takes place without any narrative comment on the appearance of the speaker. Indeed, the narrator withholds the visual details by which we might connect voice and body and thus create a mental image of the speaker— and more importantly assign social value, credible weight, to his speech. Also, it must be remembered that Madison is a Virginian. To tell his story is to revise the "American annals" that document the exploits of his fellow Virginians, but serve, because they rely on the visual sign of race, to exclude him.

The reason for this, of course, is that Douglass wishes to subvert the propensity on the part of his reading audience to deny the slave's ability to formulate resistant agency. Interestingly, Douglass accomplishes this by including Madison's self-doubt, his ambivalence about his ability to free himself from bondage:

> I neither run nor fight, but do meanly stand, answering each heavy blow of a cruel master with doleful wails and piteous cries. I am galled with irons; but even these are more tolerable than the consciousness, the galling consciousness of cowardice and indecision. Can it be that I dare not run away? Perish the thought, I dare do any thing which may be done by another. When that young man struggled with the waves for life, and others stood back appalled in helpless horror, did I not plunge in, forgetful of life, to save his? The raging bull from whom all others fled, pale with fright, did I not keep at bay with a single pitchfork? Could a coward do that? No,—no,—I wrong myself,—I am no coward. Liberty I will have, or die in the attempt to gain it. (Douglass, 27)

This passage accomplishes several things. First, it demonstrates Madison's predisposition toward action. Second, we see Madison working to redefine his bondage; he moves away from the impulse to equate his bondage with a lack of courage, citing instances where, as a slave, he acted quickly and selflessly. Though we see traces of the service impulse at work here, what is more important is that these acts of selflessness are "marks" that must be installed in a new context to have utility. In an alternative system of signs, these actions are the basis for resistance. Third, Douglass posits Madison as a man who can "make a way out of no way"; he is a figure of improvisation, standing his ground even when others are *"pale with fright."* Here Douglass signifies on the racial gaze by referring to an interpretive practice grounded in racial essentialism, where whiteness is linked with fear. But what is more important is Madison's assertion of an alternative history, an unwritten history which can only be accessed in the service of a subjectivity whites cannot recognize. For while the conventional history would construe such exploits as the acts of a brute, Madison acts without direction from whites: he acts on an impulse that originates in his own being.

It is this activity which Listwell witnesses—and he does so, significantly, before he gains a full view of Madison's physical features. Douglass's use of language here, his decision to delay description of Washington for a brief moment more, underscores what is perhaps the most essential detail in Listwell's initial encounter with the hero:

> Madison was standing erect, a smile of satisfaction rippled upon his expressive countenance, *like that which plays upon the face of one who has but just solved a difficult problem or vanquished a malignant foe; for at that moment he was free, at least in spirit.* (Douglass, 28; my emphasis)

Listwell gazes upon the presumably incongruous image of a slave engaged in deductive reasoning. It is the act of problem-solving he witnesses, and not merely Madison's verbal dexterity, that has such transformative force. Further, in keeping with his first autobiography, Douglass refuses to accede to the Northern insistence that the slave is incapable of achieving and sustaining human agency without the benefit of contact with benevolent whites. Though Madison is only free "in spirit," Douglass sees the importance of positing freedom in a conceptual, purely subjective, frame. The broken fetters at Madison's feet are as non-existent as the galling irons in the earlier passage, but in shifting attention away from the literal, they likewise assert Madison's ability to transform—and inhabit—symbolic space. This move also enacts Douglass's insistence that blackness, though a cipher in the white world, is actually a sign lacking the proper contextual frame.

When the reader is finally given a description of Madison's physical appearance, Douglass can use it to challenge further the prevailing constructions of black masculinity:

> Madison was of manly form. Tall, symmetrical, round, and strong. In his movements he seemed to combine with the strength of the lion, a lion's elasticity. His torn sleeves disclosed arms like polished iron. His face was "black, but comely." His eye, lit with emotion, kept guard under a brow as dark as and as glossy as the raven's wing. His whole appearance betokened Herculean strength; yet there was nothing savage or forbidding in his aspect. (Douglass, 28)

Clearly this passage responds to the issues that would have pertained to the construction of black subjectivity in the 1850s. Madison Washington is neither childlike, nor feminine, and he is imbued with both physical strength and intellectual vigor. In particular here, note the manner in which it is the eye, not the heart, which serves as the seat of emotion. This would seem an especially ironic move, in light of Douglass's subversion of the visual. But if we consider the linkage of the visual with the emotional, the passage suggests that what makes the eye an ineffective source of objective reportage is the fact that it is vulnerable to emotional suasion. This displacement precedes an especially subtle move, namely, Douglass's separation of Herculean strength from that which is "savage or forbidding." Invoking the Greek hero allows Douglass to split off all the negative connotations that arise when black masculinity and physical strength are conjoined, and attach Madison's physique to the ultimate symbol of Western masculine power. The passage concludes:

> A child might play in his arms, or dance on his shoulders. A giant's strength, but not a giant's heart was in him. His broad mouth and nose spoke only of good nature and kindness. *But his voice, that unfailing index of the soul, though full and melodious, had that in it which could terrify as well as charm.* He was just the man you would choose when hardships were to be endured, or danger to be encountered,—intelligent and brave. He had the head to conceive, and the hand to execute. In a word, he was one to be sought as a friend, but to be dreaded as an enemy. (Douglass, 28; my emphasis)

While Douglass clearly embraces some aspects of romantic racialism, he pushes past its limitations by imbuing Madison Washington with a sufficient range of skills that he can in no wise be characterized as docile, passive, or indecisive. Of greatest importance is Madison's voice, which expresses command and expertise, but most of all provides a definitive interpretive site. Douglass's experiences with the Garrisonians had taught him that the problem for him, no less than for the slave, was one of voicelessness, an inability to refute visually determined stereotypes. Hence the move to equate voice and spirit elevates aurality over visual systems of interpretation. Madison Washington works as a fictional character, then, because he works to resist what Douglass would surely have thought to be a distortion of African-American male subjectivity.[24]

Melville enacts the racialized gaze in ways very different from Douglass. Unlike Listwell, Delano utilizes the eye to divergent ends. This is signaled almost immediately, when, upon seeing the *San Dominick* through the spyglass, and seeing that it "showed no colors," Delano resists the impulse to see danger. The "colorless" nature of the vessel should signal the possibility of foul play, yet Delano prides himself on his "singularly undistrustful good nature," and thus his desire is to eschew any indulgence in "personal alarm, any way involving the malign evil in man." We can also read the *San Dominick's* "colorlessness" in several other ways. It could recall the manner in which the Haitian revolution signals a new epoch in the New World and therefore a moment to be wary; a black world would, in a white supremacist gaze, either be invisible or irrelevant. Or it could mean the ship is a *tabula rasa*, a cipher in need of Delano to imbue it with meaning, to provide "color" through an act of interpretation.

Though Delano's obtuse response has been the subject of a great many scholarly responses to "Benito Cereno," I would submit that Melville intends Delano's gaze to be one which is committed to an almost singular need for normalcy, for neat categories. Repeatedly, his gaze seeks to restore, to rationalize, that which is out of order. Though we discern that Delano fails to discover the plot aboard the *San Dominick* until it is nearly too late, he should not be dismissed as a failed agent of the status quo. As Trinh T. Minh-ha observes:

> The inability to think symbolically or to apprehend language in its very symbolic nature is commonly validated as an attribute of "realistic," clear, and accomplished thinking. The cards are readily shifted so as to turn a limit, if not an impoverishment

of dominant thinking, into a virtue. . . . therefore a tool for political demagogy to appeal to widely naturalized prejudices.[25]

As a fictional character who demonstrates Northern racism, Delano is first and foremost a man rooted in the "natural" order of things, as long as that order retains its hierarchical character. This is by no means a revelation; my interest lies in the manner in which Delano works out, with such care, Melville's critique of white supremacy, in which blackness is a cipher lacking meaning, save in a white supremacist visually constructed context.[26] Outside of that context, it cannot generate meaning, and thus the interpretive energy it would require to fuel an alternative reading cannot be sustained.

We can see this when, upon boarding the *San Dominick*, Delano views the matter at hand. When black and white alike greet the ship captain as a "clamorous throng" in "one language and, as with one voice," Delano becomes "the mark of all eager tongues" (Melville, 2501). This suggests the manner in which the construction of whiteness leads to the essentialized notion that whites, specifically those born in the United States, are imbued with the mandate to create unity and cooperative action, the foundation of American republican ideals.[27] This is confirmed by Delano's "eager glance" which takes in "all the faces, with every other object about him." Delano's is an all-consuming glance, a glance which seeks to order all it takes in. But more than this, it is a democratizing glance; Delano wants to respond to each and every voice beseeching him to act on its behalf. This is underscored when the water arrives from his own ship to be distributed among the blacks and Spaniards.[28] Here, we find that Delano complies "with republican impartiality as to this republican element, which always seeks one level, serving the oldest white no better than the youngest black" (Melville, 2525).

Delano seeks to assuage his fears by making constant appeals to the visual realm and to democratic procedures in order to interpret events on Cereno's ship. While many scholars have focused on Delano's brand of racial chauvinism, what is equally important is his constant application of techniques meant to settle his uneasiness with an unfamiliar racial dynamic. Indeed, his wariness of Cereno's motives is based on the failure of the latter to enact a discernible procedurality. That sensibility begins with himself; the Spaniard is, at one point, dismissed by the narrator (and thus Delano) as a "hypochondriac," as if his sensitivity and morbidity indicate his inability to enforce legal order. For Delano, procedure moves outward from the body: hence, he expects that the Spaniard will master, first, his own body (which explains Delano's fixation on codes of behavior) and then the bodies of those under his command. At the same time, the American captain's fears are assuaged by the sight of the Ashanti warriors polishing their hatchets, because Cereno tells him that they have set to work by his order. When Delano declares to himself that Cereno "was not fit to be entrusted with [his] ship," and thinks to put his second mate in command, he reassures himself that Cereno will be "restored to health," and finds these thoughts "tranquilizing." What is most reassuring, of course, is that some semblance of procedure will be restored to the *San Dominick*.

As an exemplar of New England liberalism, and more importantly, of the predominating characteristics of a white man in the New World, Delano's first and best wish is that the democratic possibilities of any situation be achieved. This is not to suggest that he fails to embrace racial hierarchy, but rather that his liberalism leads him to believe that blacks can contribute to his idea of polity by virtue of their subservient nature. Hence his fascination with Babo issues from his feeling that the Negro is more "symbol than human being." What signals this is Delano's interest in Babo's deployment of a racial gaze; he is most interested in Babo when he catches Babo looking at Cereno.

This triangular gaze is established early in the narrative, for when Delano sees Cereno for the first time, he also sees Babo nearby. Taking in Babo's "devoted service" to Cereno, Delano's gaze immediately sets to the task of categorizing what he sees. Thus Babo's behavior confirms Delano's vision of blacks when he performs those duties that demonstrate black loyalty. But note the language Melville uses to categorize the insurrectionist's piety:

> Sometimes the negro gave his master his arm, or took his handkerchief out of his pocket for him; performing these and similar offices with that affectionate zeal which transmutes into something filial or fraternal acts in themselves but menial; and which has gained for the negro the repute of making the *most pleasing* body servant in the world. (Melville, 2503; my emphasis)

Not only does the language of the passage echo proslavery discourse, but Delano's propensity to disrupt his own suspicious inklings indicates that the act of deciphering visual signs has political implications. Melville's use of visual details is precisely the ground upon which Babo creates the procedural illusion in which Delano becomes trapped. For it is Babo's orchestration of bodies, his placement of blacks in key areas, and in particular his use of Atufal to create the illusion of Cereno's adherence to procedure (however tenuous), that displaces the racial gaze altogether. But what this also means is that we need to understand the role of pleasure, the manner in which it prevents the American from gaining the "objectivity" necessary to create a chain of operative signifiers.

Babo remains positioned in the former's view as a sign which not only confirms his world view, but also functions as a source of pleasure, preventing Delano from discerning the plot on board the *San Dominick*. The importance of pleasure is intimated by the name of Delano's ship: *Bachelor's Delight*.[29] Though Delano is a "bachelor" in terms of his naiveté and almost virginal innocence, the name of the ship provides us with yet another way to tease out Melville's interest in the politics of the visual sphere.[30] The ship's name seems to refer to a male gaze. But in my view it more accurately refers to the *female response* to the male gaze. The name of his ship refers to the pleasure derived from the sight of a woman who, upon realizing that she has arrested the male gaze, encourages further contact with a look of her own, which both acknowledges masculine power, confirms its effect, and, most importantly, acquiesces to its demands. Given the conflation of blackness and femininity in the 1850s, this is an important consideration, for it suggests that at least a portion of Melville's intent was to challenge the desire on the part of "well-meaning" whites for black affection.

Thus we have to note all those instances where Delano's fears are assuaged by looking at Babo looking at Cereno, or by looking at other acts of black solicitude. For brevity's sake, I will limit my examination to three occurrences. First, after Delano witnesses the beatings of several of the white sailors, including the cabin-boy, he is so agitated that he turns to Cereno and says, "Don Benito . . . do you see what is going on there? Look!" But just then, the Spaniard begins to cough and later he is supported by Babo and restored by a cordial applied by the slave. What interests me here is the manner in which Delano's interpretive energy is so completely disrupted by the sight of Babo's "caretaking." As Melville's language suggests, the moment erases "any blemish of impropriety" in Delano's eyes regarding Babo's involvement in the fray. In other words, Babo expresses such loyalty that he nullifies the "indecorous conferences" taking place around them. When the slave steps away from Cereno, Delano abandons his curiosity and offers the Spanish ship captain money for Babo instead:

> His glance thus called away from the spectacle of disorder to the more pleasing one before him, Captain Delano could not avoid congratulating his host upon possessing such a servant, who, though perhaps a little too forward now and then, must upon the whole be invaluable to one in the invalid's situation. (Melville, 2517)

The offer is prompted, of course, by the prospect of receiving such treatment, the desire to be the object of black affection, which is why the narrator uses the pronoun "one" instead of "Don Benito"; Melville's decision not to render Delano's remarks as conventional dialogue suggests that the spoken and the observed are in close relation. The gaze in this instance catalyzes an act of reverie on Delano's part, and hence he offers, not only to purchase Babo, but also to redirect that gaze upon himself. Because he considers himself a man who could neither buy nor own a slave, Delano's "paltry" offer (to which Babo responds, "Master wouldn't part with Babo for a thousand doubloons") must be seen as Melville's inference that, while Northerners place a value on black docility and service, that value has to do with the desire to use such a commodity as a source of pleasure rather than labor.

When Don Benito removes himself from this scene, Delano notices that the Spanish sailors return his glance "with a sort of meaning." But when he sees the sailor with his hand in the tar-pot, again he misreads the circumstance, attributing any possibility of foul play (which Melville reinforces by the use of the visual pun of the sailor's hand in the pitch pot) to the whites. But this view is vanquished again when Delano spies the negress and her child. The very act of gazing upon black maternal affection collapses the ship captain's inquisitory posture. Thus, the signs he accumulates to produce any kind of interpretation—even an incorrect one—of events taking place before him become useless, forcing him to start afresh each time. This is underscored by the pleasure Delano finds in gazing upon the African woman's "naked nature." Again, the black body is viewed in the context of the public; it is a "natural sight" which Delano uses as a resource for his own pleasure.

Though Delano attempts to readjust his eyes to more effectively perform the task of interpretation, a gesture intimated by the act of rubbing his eyes, he cannot sustain this posture because he cannot situate anomaly into a viable interpretive procedure. And by a viable procedure I mean a matrix that resists rupture on the one hand, but which is flexible and supple enough to manage the anomalous. When he sees the Spanish sailors, he cannot equate their "strange" behavior with the "normal" behavior of the blacks except by attributing an "evil design" to the whites. Melville's language also suggests, however, that Delano cannot—as a man who is a product of his times—attribute individual or collective agency to blacks. Using a language that reflects the discourse of scientific racism, he concludes:

> The whites, too, by nature, were the shrewder race. A man with some evil design, would he not be likely to speak well of that stupidity which was blind to his depravity, and malign that intelligence from which it might not be hidden? Not unlikely, perhaps. But if the whites had dark secrets concerning Don Benito, could then Don Benito be any way in complicity with the blacks? But they were too stupid. Besides, who ever heard of a white so far a renegade as to apostatize from his very species almost, by leaguing in against it with negroes? (Melville, 2521)

Because his gaze is so vulnerable to assertions of the conventional, Delano cannot breach the illusion before him.

This helps us to understand the significance of the third and final moment I want to discuss, namely the old sailor and his knot. When Delano's attention turns to the scene, his interpretive process is displaced. He refocuses his attention on the knot, but that attention does not attune itself to the metaphorical; it remains fixed in literal space:

> Captain Delano crossed over to him, and stood in silence surveying the knot; his mind, by a not uncongenial transition, passing from its own entanglements to those of the hemp. For intricacy such a knot he had never seen in an American ship, or indeed any other. The old man looked like an Egyptian priest, making Gordian knots for the temple of Ammon. The knot seemed a combination of double-bowline-knot, treble-crown-knot, back-handed-well-knot, knot-in-and-knot-out and jamming-knot. (Melville, 2522)

When he inquires as to the old man's intentions, the old man says the knot is for "someone else to undo." When he throws the knot toward Delano and demands in English ("the first heard in the ship") that the American "Undo it, cut it, quick," he offers a solution to Delano's quandary. For he has suggested an amendment to critical practice: rather than attempting to unravel the mystery via analysis, he insists the best way is to disrupt it by discarding his old interpretive system and moving, perhaps violently, towards another interpretive gesture that, even in its excess, is likely to produce meaning.

But Delano, "knot in hand, knot in head," is driven into a state of interpretive stalemate, which can only be resolved by his reliance on the visual realm and the assumption of black inferiority. The "elderly negro" who accosts Delano and takes the knot away, dismisses the knot as the sign of the old sailor's insanity. But Delano's failure here is one of applying his adherence to procedure, which the knots would symbolize in another context, to the situation at hand. Indeed, the old sailor's insistence that Delano cut the knot invokes emergency procedure. Unlike Alexander, who cut the Gordian knot and assumed control of Persia, Delano's inability to shift to a metaphorical posture is affirmed, all hint of "emergency" obscured. Melville's narrator again mutes the exchange by playing the role of interpreter (since the exchange between Delano and the African is in Spanish). This is crucial because when coupled with the "conge" or ceremonial bow, the African returns Delano to that state of reverie where he experiences, for but a moment, the consummation of his desire to be served.

Melville's use of the racial gaze works out the spectatorial nature of Northern interest in an essentialized African presence. That presence was constructed as one which could improve the white man's prospects, joining the African's "tenderminded[ness]" to the white man's impulse to explore and democratize his surroundings. While they could denigrate the South as a place that dehumanized blacks by exploiting them for labor and leading them to depravity, Northern liberals could revel in racial difference and claim that the "affection" blacks demonstrated toward their antislavery sentiments likewise signaled a lack of Northern culpability. This was the case, even as they utilized the racial gaze to undermine black agency. Melville's task is one of subverting this tendency by showing the interpretive limitations of the visual sphere.

Douglass's "The Heroic Slave" attempts to redress these limitations, using the conventions to be found in middle-class definitions of masculinity and thus challenging the construction of African Americans as a "feminized" race. Madison Washington represents, following Richard Yarborough's observation, nobility, intelligence, strength, articulateness, loyalty, virtue, rationality, courage, self-control, courtliness, honesty, and physical attractiveness.[31] But Douglass reinforces these traits, not because we see Madison Washington enact them throughout the narrative, but rather because other individuals witness them and engage in acts of storytelling which articulate them as myth.

Thus, after Listwell encounters Madison Washington, he is so thoroughly transformed that he asserts, "From this hour I am an abolitionist. I have seen enough and heard enough and I shall go to my home in Ohio resolved to atone for my indifference to this ill-starred race . . ." (Douglass, 30). Washington's speech serves the function of transforming blacks from an "ill-starred race" in the racialized sign system Listwell discards, into a new interpretive matrix. Here, we should remember that it is Listwell who tells Madison when they finally meet that "your face seemed to be daguerrotyped on my memory" (Douglass, 35). Douglass references the relatively new science of photography, where light could be put to new uses in the enactment of a new kind of social gaze: namely, the act of "writing with light." Thus, the image of an "ill-starred" race suggests that the African-American speaking subject has not received adequate light. For Douglass's purposes, photography and the camera, even in their nascent stages, offerred a technology that, as John Tagg has observed, brought "instruments of evidence" to the fore.[32] Remembering that African-American freedom often depended on production of authorized documents, Douglass's emphasis on the aural over the visual sphere articulates his belief that the African-American voice offered documentation of the slave's humanity. Douglass grafts the significance of the photographic process, which was coming to be understood as a way to correlate image-making and history, to the particularities of the voice.[33] It is Madison's voice, not his visage, that creates this effect, as if to argue that escaped slaves, could they speak on their own behalf, would create a lasting image in the minds of their audience.[34]

This resource is urgently needed because, as Douglass suggests, the site of cultural production where the system of signs is generated is itself on the verge of collapse. Consider his description of the tavern that appears in Part III of the novella:

> Its fine old portico looks well at a distance, and gives the building an air of grandeur. A nearer view, however, does little to sustain this pretension. The house is large, and its style imposing, but time and dissipation, unfailing in their results, have made ineffaceable marks upon it, and it must, in the common course of events, soon be numbered with the things that were. The gloomy mantle of ruin is, already, out-spread to envelope it, and its remains, even but now remind one of a human skull, after the flesh has mingled with the earth. (Douglass, 47)

One can take this image to be the visual representation of slavery's impact on American democracy. As the passage insists, democracy is a house about to be overcome by moral decay. The skull image signals the imminent demise of the United States as a slaveholding democracy. But I also want to call attention to the image because it prefigures Aranda's skeleton. What joins these images is the fact that they generate a representative strategy which signals the danger of white supremacy. If we move further into this section of the novella, we see again that the other part of Douglass's critique requires him to utilize Mr. Listwell as the paradigmatic abolitionist. As Stepto suggests, Listwell's greatest gift is that he listens well. But more than this, upon listening to black voices, he acts on their behalf. Given Douglass's difficulties with the Garrisonians, his inability to exercise the full range of his intellectual and critical gifts among them, the relationship between Washington and Listwell is as much an attempt to depict white men who act on black men's word and allow them to take their rightful place in the antislavery struggle as leaders in that movement, as it is a refashioning of a racist sign system.

This is further evidenced in the novella's final section. Having escaped from a slave coffle using the files provided by Listwell, Washington sails from slavery into the realm of narrative. His failure to appear in Part IV of the novella does not mean he has exited the story; rather, he has moved out of the visual realm and into an aural, photographic, or narrative space which does not utilize the racial gaze to accomplish its ends. When he hears Jack Williams's thoughts on how to quell a slave rebellion, Grant is compelled to relate the narrative of the events leading up to the rebellion. What is clear is that Grant resists Williams's interpretation of the scenario, based as it is on his conclusion that the crew of the *Creole* demonstrated their "ignorance of the real character of *darkies* in general" (Douglass, 61). In a tone characterized as much by its machismo as its racism, Williams intones:

> With half a dozen *resolute* white men . . . I could have had the rascals in irons in ten minutes, not because I'm so strong, but I know how to manage 'em. With my back against the *caboose* I could, myself, have flogged a dozen of them; and had I been on board . . . every black devil of 'em all would have had his neck stretched from the yard-arm. Ye made a mistake in yer manner of fighting 'em. All that is needed in dealing with a set of rebellious *darkies,* is to show that yer not afraid of 'em. (Douglass, 61)

The simple-mindedness of Williams's claim notwithstanding, what is striking here is how he constructs blackness as a symbol of ineffectual energy, evidenced by the fact that the management of slaves is an emotional matter. But because blackness and femininity are so closely aligned, he can also implement the language of masculine endurance and potency.

Douglass uses Tom Grant's response to counter this feminization of the black male body. The first mate's tale is meant to suggest the manner in which he has been divested of the ability to participate in a system which locates black inferiority in nature. But this strategy, emblematic of the novella's romantic antecedents, rests upon Madison Washington's ability to show himself to be the equal of nature. The result is that Tom Grant's interpretive system is nullified. This is signaled by Madison's first words after the hurricane, which Grant describes as "characteristic" of his eloquence: "Mr. Mate, you cannot write the bloody laws of slavery on those restless billows. The ocean, if not the land, is free." What this suggests is that nature is not a site of inscription, but a site of erasure. Indeed, it erases, if not the stigma of racial difference, then its interpretive assumptions foregrounded by the racial gaze.

But Douglass is mindful of the fact that interactions between black and white do not take place in nature, but in social configurations. Hence, Tom Grant stops short of complete hero-worship:

> I confess, gentlemen, I felt myself in the presence of a superior man; one who, had he been a white man, I would have followed willingly and gladly in any honorable enterprise. Our difference of color was the only ground for difference of action. It was not that his principles were wrong in the abstract; for they are the principles of 1776. But I could not bring myself to recognize their application to one whom I deemed my inferior. (Douglass, 68)

It is indeed a matter of application. The codes exist, via the documents that create American citizenship (the product, the reader may remember, of Virginian labor), for black men to be free; however, the problem arises because the racial gaze inhibits the ability to link a revisionary posture to interpretive practice. Tom Grant serves the function, then, of articulating the blind spot Douglass found among his Northern counterparts. For while we might assign his refusal to acknowledge the legitimacy of Madison's purpose to the realm of Southern resistance, Grant's reticence symbolizes primarily the ineffectuality of Northern rhetoric.

The novella's final paragraph works this out quite effectively. When the *Creole* lands in Nassau and the slaves go free, a collision of interpretive systems ensues. The black soldiers sent to the ship to guard its property inform Tom Grant that "they [do] not recognize persons as property." The intention of this statement, if one were to consider Southern readers, is obvious, but for the Northern reader this passage argues that black bodies cannot remain the symbolic property of romantic racialism. Douglass could easily have ended Tom Grant's tale in the previous paragraph, but his decision to allow Tom Grant to shift back to chronological narrative, and thus end his tale, rests upon a profound reversal. The blacks who refuse to see "persons as property," because they are soldiers, possess the force necessary to sanction a new interpretive system. In the New World—in ways that reference Haiti as a symbol—they represent a new form of power.

In closing, it could be that the best way to verify the pairing of Frederick Douglass and Herman Melville is to look to the acceptance speech Ralph Ellison gave on receipt of the National Book Award, which appears under the title, "Brave Words for a Startling Occasion" (another veiled reference to Delano perhaps?), where he aligns his novelistic intent with that of nineteenth-century novelists like Melville and Twain (and, one might also conjecture, Douglass as well). Ellison turns to the nineteenth-century and remarks:

> I came to believe that the writers of that period took a much greater responsibility for the condition of democracy and, indeed, their works were imaginative projections of the conflicts within the human heart which arose when the sacred principles of the Constitution and the Bill of Rights clashed with the practical exigencies of human greed and fear, hate and love.[35]

Ellison's observations lead us back to where we began, namely to the task both Frederick Douglass and Herman Melville set for themselves when they endeavored to alter the course of the antislavery discussion. Douglass would go on to a life lived in the public eye: Melville would continue to write fiction that was neither well-paying nor well-received and pass for a time into literary oblivion. But their importance to Ellison's novel suggests the manner in which "Benito Cereno" and "The Heroic Slave" work out a custodial relationship to democratic practice. Melville's role would seem to be simple: Delano's final words ("You are saved! . . . you are saved; what has cast such a shadow upon you?") are used as one of *Invisible Man*'s two epigraphs. Here, Melville remains in symbolic space; as epigraph, Delano's question forces the reader to contend with the inadequacy of racial discourse.[36] Indeed, Melville's concern with shadow plays off the claim Ellison's invisible hero makes in the Prologue of *Invisible Man*, where he asserts, "Light confirms my reality, gives birth to my form." This resonates in a reading of "Benito Cereno" because it forces us to reflect for a moment on the nature of light and darkness, the manner in which light produces shadow. Douglass's role in the novel asserts his importance as both a spiritual presence and the material enactment of American citizenship. He appears as a portrait hanging on the wall of the hero's office in Brotherhood headquarters. Later, he receives a chain link from Brother Tarp where the old man tells him, "I don't think of it but in terms of but two words, *yes* and *no*, but it signifies a whole heap more." Ellison's use of the chain link invokes "The Heroic Slave," if only because it recalls Madison Washington's escape from the slave coffle. And though Brother Tarp's chain link is similar to the one the hero remembers on Dr. Bledsoe's desk at the college, the difference between the two is that Bledsoe's link is "smooth," while the other bears the "mark of haste and violence." The former speaks to the power of illusion, the latter to the kind of commitment required to break out of bondage.

My point here is not only that Ellison's novel results from the use of Melville and Douglass as literary resources, both of whom anticipate Ellison's claim that America is only "a partially achieved nation." But also that both writers believed that an American democracy unwilling to institute radical acts of interpretation and revision was doomed to fail. Their literary kinship is manifest in their respective subversions of the racial gaze, which denote the inadequacy of anti-slavery rhetoric: so dependent on the visual sphere, so unwilling to redress voicelessness or acts of erasure. Each insists, in ways Ellison takes seriously, that democracy was and is a protean enterprise, in which the greatest challenge is to ascertain more than what the eye can see.

## Notes

I wish to thank Henry Wonham, Carolyn Karcher, and Dana Nelson for their useful comments on an earlier draft of this essay. I would also like to thank my colleague Nancy Bentley for her suggestions.

1. My definition of the "racial gaze" owes its origins to Norman Bryson and his assertion that, "Western painting is predicated on the disavowal of the deictic reference, on the disappearance of the body as the site of the image; and this twice over, for the painter, and the viewing subject." Bryson's assertion can be contrasted to the aeoristic, where [visual representation] "describes [an] action without involvement or engagement on the part of the [subject responsible for representing] the action." See Bryson, *Vision and Painting: The Logic of the Gaze*, esp. Chap. 5, "The Gaze and the Glance," (New Haven: Yale University Press, 1983) 88. However, the definition also proceeds from Paul Virilio's contention in Chapter 3 of *The Vision Machine* (Bloomington: Indiana University Press, 1994), 33–34, that the public gaze originates after the French Revolution when the idea of "illumination" takes on meaning beyond the mere shedding of light onto objects and becomes the connotation for an all-encompassing public discourse.

2. Peter Brooks, *Body Work: Objects of Desire in Modern Narrative* (Cambridge: Harvard University Press, 1993), 88.

3. Elizabeth Johns, *American Genre Painting: The Politics of Everyday Life* (New Haven: Yale University Press, 1991), 102.

4. Ibid., 131.

5. Ibid.

6. Herman Melville, "Benito Cereno," in *The Heath Anthology of American Literature* (Lexington, Mass.: D.C. Heath and Company, 1990), 2254. All further reference to the story are from this edition.

7. Ibid.

8. Dana D. Nelson's work offers a useful way to think about this moment. She argues that Babo's death "becomes the emblem of white guiltlessness" and that his head on the pole suggests the merging of two distinct discourses: the legal and the aesthetic. "The two types of discourse," she insists, "exist in a symbiotic relation; legal discourse sanctions power for an elect group, while aesthetic discourse defines pleasure." In her view, "Babo's head as a legally produced artistic object both symbolizes this power and provides its viewers a pleasurable sensation of power." While I agree with Nelson's assessment, my argument rests on the notion that death does not diminish Babo's symbolic power as a site of resistance. For even as he represents closure, Babo likewise represents the possibility that rebellion can recur. So that even as the act of gazing upon his severed head is a "pleasurable" moment, it is a pleasure mediated by conceptual slippage. See "The Crisis of the Subject in 'Benito Cereno,' " in Nelson's *The Word in Black and White: Reading Race in American Literature, 1638–1867* (New York: Oxford University Press, 1993), 109–130.

9. But to say that Babo "looks" at the site of Aranda's remains with anything resembling "pleasure" would be, in my estimation, a distortion. For such an assertion would mean that Babo's propensity for violence was greater than his desire to be free.

10. John Hauss, "Masquerades of Language in Melville's *Benito Cereno,*" *Arizona Quarterly* 44 (Summer, 1988): 18.

11. Frederick Douglass, "The Heroic Slave" (1853; rpt., New York: Mentor Books, 1990). All further references are to this edition.

12. George M. Fredrickson, *The Black Image in the White Mind* (Middletown, Conn.: Wesleyan University Press, 1971), esp. Chaps. 3 and 4.

13. Herman Beavers, "Aural Reconfigurations of Frederick Douglass's *Narrative of the Life of Frederick Douglass, an American Slave,*" presentation given at Duke University, January, 1992.

14. Fredrickson, *Black Image,* 109. As Charles Sumner observed, proponents of slavery were wrong to assume that emancipation, which he was spearheading in 1862, would lead unequivocally to a race war between owner and former slave. "The African," he told an audience in Boston, "is not cruel, vindictive, or harsh, but gentle, forgiving and kind."

15. These scholars' works alone make a very strong case that whatever Northerners in the 1850s thought they were viewing on the parts of African-American slaves was nothing more, in most cases, than the slaves' ability to manipulate reality. In Lawrence Levine's *Black Culture and Black Consciousness* (New York: Oxford, 1977), Roger Abraham's *Singing the Master* (New York: Pantheon, 1992), Henry Louis Gates's *The Signifying Monkey* (New York: Oxford, 1988), and Houston A. Baker's *Blues, Ideology, and Afro-American Literature* (Chicago: Univ. Of Chicago Press, 1984), these scholars repeatedly assert the slave's ability to use language as a site of subterfuge and agency. Moreover, in the collected folktales of Harold Courlander, Abrahams, and William Bascom, we have textual proof that slaves were far from passive, either about their desire to be free, or their ability to comment upon their collective plight.

16. Frederickson, *Black Image,* 112.

17. In the case of "Benito Cereno," 1799, and 1835 in "The Heroic Slave." In the former, 1799 coincides with the slave revolt on the island of Haiti, the Santo Domingo uprising led by Toussaint L'Overture in that year. In the case of the latter, the actual basis for the novella is the revolt on board the *Creole,* a slave-trading brig overrun in 1841.

18. Eric J. Sundquist, "Benito Cereno and New World Slavery," in *Reconstructing American Literary History,* ed. Sacvan Bercovitch (Cambridge: Harvard University Press, 1986). 94.

19. Fredrickson, *Black Image,* 52.

20. Ibid., 53.

21. Allan Moore Emery, "The Topicality of Depravity in 'Benito Cereno,' " *American Literature* 55 (October 1983): 318.

22. Robert B. Stepto "Storytelling: Douglass's 'The Heroic Slave,' " in Henry Louis Gates, ed., *Black Literature and Literary Theory* (New York: Methuen, 1984), 178 and William McFeeley, *Frederick Douglass* (New York: Norton, 1991), 175.

23. Robert B. Stepto, "Sharing the Thunder: The Literary Exchanges of Harriet Beecher Stowe, Henry Bibb and Frederick Douglass," in *New Essays on Uncle Tom's Cabin*, ed. Eric Sundquist (New York: Oxford University Press, 1986), 145.

24. I am in agreement with Robert Stepto's assessment of Madison Washington as a mirror image of Douglass himself. In "Storytelling," Stepto relates: "Washington and Douglass began their escape attempts in 1835, and both gained public attention as free men in the fall of 1841. However, while Douglass caulked ships in Baltimore (including, perhaps a slaver or two such as the *Creole*), Washington led black slaves in a ship's revolt. Similarly, while Douglass escaped from slavery wearing a sailor's suit, Washington was, in both a literal and a figurative sense, a truer and more heroic sailor: Douglass was a good man, and it would be wrong to suggest that he thought that Washington was a better man than himself, or that Washington's story was altogether better than his own," 178.

25. Trinh T. Min-ha, "All-Owning Spectatorship," *Quarterly Review of Film & Video*, 13, 191.

26. This is also a point Sterling Stuckey and Joshua Leslie make in "The Death of Benito Cereno," chap. 9 in Stuckey's *Going Through the Storm: The Influence of African American Art in History* (New York: Oxford University Press, 1994) 158–159. Stuckey and Leslie argue that Melville had "contempt for Delano who is fooled by any and everything because of his underestimation of Negro intelligence." They continue by arguing that Delano's thoughts are a "conglomeration of mid-nineteenth century American racist views—from the romantic racialism that dominated a certain sector of the liberal New England consciousness."

27. Fredrickson, *The Black Image*, 99.

28. My point here is not that white males are, in any way, a homogenous group. Rather, I merely wish to suggest that romantic racialism essentialized the intersection of race and masculinity which came to be characterized as white male identity.

29. As Sundquist observes, Melville changed the name of Cereno's ship from the *Tryal* to the *San Dominick* and thus, one wonders why he did not do the same for Delano's ship.

30. The significance of the "Bachelor's Delight" is illuminated by another Melville story, "The Paradise of Bachelors and the Tarturus of Maids," where the narrator asserts, "but little have you seen, just nothing do you know, not the sweet kernel have you tasted, till you dine among the banded Bachelors, and see their convivial eyes and glasses sparkle." What interests me about this passage is that it works out a double enactment of the gaze: the narrator's investment in looking coupled with, indeed sanctioned by, the gaze of the Bachelors. The "convivial eyes" and glasses, together with their "sparkle," suggest a homoerotic subtext which, for my purposes, substantiates my claim that it is the act of *ascertaining* the arrested gaze that is important, not the unrequited gaze.

31. Richard Yarborough, "The Masculine Ideal: Race, Violence, and Manhood in Frederick Douglass's 'The Heroic Slave,' " in *Frederick Douglass: New Literary and Historical Essays*, ed. Eric Sundquist (Cambridge and New York: Cambridge University Press, 1990), 168.

32. John Tagg, *The Burden of Representation: Essays on Photographies and Histories*

(Minneapolis: University of Minnesota Press, 1988), 3. This helps us to understand the prologue of the novella, where Douglass refers to "quivering flashes of angry lightning" and "blinding" flashes of light, which point to the manner in which light harnessed by technological means, rather than the arbitrary, faulty strategies that arise from the racial gaze, permits the black body to be fixed into its proper place. The daguerreotype, when connected to the voice, represents an irrefutable piece of evidence.

33. Alan Trachtenberg, *Reading American Photographs: Images as History, Matthew Brady to Walker Evans* (New York: Hill and Wang, Noonday Press, 1989), 6.

34. This is an interesting reference, furthermore, because Douglass becomes one of the most photographed African Americans of the century; as a political figure he moves in the civic eye, and thus as he moves in the public sphere, he is fixed there by both artistic and photographic processes.

35. Ralph Ellison, "Brave Worlds for a Startling Occasion," *Shadow and Act* (1964; rpt. New York: Vintage, 1972), 104.

36. That Ellison does not use Cereno's reply suggests the manner in which "the shadow and the act" play an important role in the novel's workings.

# The Ghost of Race:
# Edgar Allan Poe and the Southern Gothic

Monk Lewis once was asked how he came, in one of his acted plays, to introduce *black* banditti, when, in the country where the scene was laid, black people were quite unknown. His answer was: "I introduced them because I truly anticipated that blacks would have more *effect* on my audience than whites—and if I had taken it into my head that, by making them sky-blue the effect would have been greater, why sky-blue they should have been."

—Letter from Edgar Allan Poe to a friend (June 26, 1849)[1]

Poe's reiteration of Monk Lewis's disingenuous remarks about the source of his banditti's "blackness," which claims that the gothic's hauntings are merely a formalistic effect, foregrounds the need to locate the gothic's effects in history. Monk Lewis might claim that his choice of "black" banditti arose from an innate understanding of his audience, but his own history tells a different story. As the son of a slaveholder with two plantations in Jamaica and some seven hundred slaves, Lewis could not help but be cognizant of the cultural context of his aesthetic choice.[2] Even if the scene he depicts in *The Monk* (1796) (Spain during the time of the Inquisition) might not be familiar with blacks, the world of England's slaveholding society, which he inhabited, was. Indeed, the gothic's "blackness" has strong historical connections to slavery: not only did many male gothicists support slavery, but the rise of the gothic novel in England (1790–1830) occurred during a period of increased debate over slavery.[3] As Kari Winter has shown in her important study, *Subjects of Slavery/Agents of Change* (1992), gothic novels actively engaged issues of slavery.[4] The terror of possession, the iconography of entrapment and imprisonment, and the familial transgressions found in the gothic novel were also present in the slave system. Given the historical context of the gothic novel ("le roman noir"), the "blackness" of the gothic needs to be examined in terms of slavery and, more generally, ideologies of race.

Like Monk Lewis, who denied the racial referents of his gothic effects, criticism on the gothic has often failed to view the gothic's most striking and constant symbolic opposition—black/white—in racial terms. It has taken critics of Afri-can-American literature to point out, as Robert Hemenway does in an article on Charles Chesnutt's ghost stories, *The Conjure Woman* (1899), that the gothic's oppositional symbolism carries "a sociological burden even when there is no conscious intention of racial statement."[5] Since the gothic's "color imagery . . . coincides with the mythology of race prevalent in Western culture," Hemenway argues, it leaves "racial fantasies to reverberate in the Gothic effect."[6] According to Hemenway, the gothic's supernatural effects are recurringly haunted by fantasies of race.

In both Toni Morrison's gothic novel, *Beloved* (1987), and her critical works, *Playing in the Dark: Whiteness and the Literary Imagination* (1992) and "Unspeakable Things Unspoken: The Afro-American Presence in American Literature" (1989), she argues further that the *realities* as well as the fantasies of race inform American literature as a whole and, more specifically, its gothic romances. Insisting that the "blackness, ten times black" in American literature does not "derive its force from its appeals to that Calvinistic sense of Innate Depravity and Original sin," as Melville famously stated, but from its social context, Morrison calls for race to be restored to American literature.[7] She insists that we reinterpret the founding nineteenth-century works of the American canon for the "unspeakable things unspoken" by looking "for the ways in which the presence of Afro-Americans has shaped the choices, the language, the structure—the meaning of so much American literature. A search, in other words, for the ghost in the machine."[8] Morrison's revisioning of American literature anchors it securely in the context of slavery and the imaginative (re)production of race:

> Black slavery enriched the country's creative possibilities. For in that construction of blackness *and* enslavement could be found not only the not-free but also, with dramatic polarity created by skin color, the projection of the not-me. The result was a playground for the imagination. What rose up out of collective needs to allay internal fears and to rationalize external exploitation was an American Africanism—-a fabricated brew of darkness, otherness, alarm, and desire that is uniquely American.[9]

By making visible the ghost of race that runs the machinery of American literature, Morrison shows that the American gothic's "blackness" needs to be historicized not only in terms of slavery but, more importantly, in terms of the racial fantasies that haunt it. Moreover, in showing how race is largely a construct of the white imagination, she insists that the gothic's "whiteness" be historicized as well: for the shadow is also a surrogate, a projection of whiteness in black face.[10]

This study takes up Morrison's call not only by placing the gothic's "blackness" in historical context but also by refusing to let the ghost of "whiteness" disappear through reification. Focusing on the figure who Morrison argues is the most important writer of American Africanism, Edgar Allan Poe, it explores the connections between the American gothic and race, while also discussing how these two terms become inextricably linked through a regional identification with the South. Once the gothic gets located in the South, its connection to race becomes suddenly apparent. As the canonical representative of the South and the gothic, Poe becomes the figure through whom romance and race get linked.[11]

Harry Levin might argue in *The Power of Blackness* (1958) that the "blackness" of American literature is symbolic rather than social and that our "greatest" authors were "visionaries rather than materialists, rather symbolists than realists," but the symbolic takes on a specific social inflection in Poe.[12] Levin writes that while "for Hawthorne black and white more or less conventionally symbolize theological and moral values, for Poe, whose symbols claim to be actualities,

they are charged with basic associations which are psychological and social."[13]
It is "the continual presence of darkness in human shape, as a tangible reminder
of the fears and impulsions that it has come to symbolize," that creates in Poe
"a sensibility which seems distinctively Southern."[14] Whereas the "blackness" of
Melville's and Hawthorne's gothic romances is about Calvinistic depravity, the
proper subject for the Southern writer and the Southern gothic, Levin argues, is
slavery. In *Love and Death in the American Novel* (1960), Leslie Fiedler also
locates the gothic's "blackness" in the South: "It is, indeed, to be expected that
our first eminent Southern author discovered that the proper subject for American
gothic is the black man, from whose shadow we have not yet emerged."[15] While
Fiedler implies that the American gothic is about race, he carefully identifies the
gothic's racial "blackness" with a Southern author. Race only becomes central
in the gothic tales of the Southern, not Northern, writer: Melville, who shares
"the bafflement of his American protagonist, a Northerner like Captain Delano,"
and who "finds the problem of slavery and the Negro a little exotic, a gothic
horror in an almost theatrical sense of the word," is "quite unlike Poe who found
this particular theme at the very center of his own experience."[16] Ironically, Poe,
who is rarely historicized in any other terms, is made to take up the burden of
race.

When Richard Gray states that "when Poe tries to describe his vision of evil,
the darkness at the heart of things . . . it is noticeable that he sometimes adopts
the familiar Southern strategy of associating that vision with black people," he
shows how the gothic's blackness becomes noticeable as a Southern strategy.[17]
The gothic, like race, seems to become most visible in a Southern locale. Indeed,
the South's "peculiar" identity has not only been associated with its particular
racial history, but it has also often been depicted in gothic terms: the South is a
benighted landscape, heavy with history, and haunted by the ghosts of slavery.[18]
The South's oppositional image—its gothic excesses and social transgressions—
has served as the nation's safety valve. As the repository for everything the
nation is *not*, the South purges the nation of its contrary impulses. More perceived
idea than social reality, the imaginary South functions as the nation's "dark"
other. By so closely associating the South with the gothic, the American literary
tradition neutralizes the gothic's threat to national identity. Once the gothic is
seen merely as a Southern strategy, then its horrifying hauntings, especially those
dealing with race, can be contained. It is necessary, then, not only to unveil the
complex intertwinings of romance and race, but also to explore how these discourses get regionally inflected.

Since it is through Edgar Allan Poe that the South and the gothic become
inextricably linked and that race most often enters our classic readings of nineteenth-century American literature, I will use Poe's problematic status within the
American literary canon to explore how the Southern gothic and its "blackness"
are demonized and domesticated. Instead of reducing Poe's gothic tales to Southern stories or his meditations on the problem of racial identity to a racial phobia,
this study shows how the gothic offers Poe a complex and complementary notation
to explore the racial discourse of his period, a discourse concerned as much with

perfect "whiteness" as with terrifying "blackness." By exploring the parameters
of Poe's (de)canonization, I examine how race and the gothic come to be identified
as merely Southern problems and argue for a counter *American* gothic tradition
which refuses race a premature burial in the South.

## Placing Poe

The problem of Poe, fascinating as it is, lies quite outside the main current of American
thought, and it may be left with the psychologist and the belletrist with whom it belongs.
            —Vernon Parrington, *Main Currents in American Thought* (1927)[19]

Poe's problematic position within the American literary canon reveals his
complex connections to region and race. As an absent presence, Poe functions
as a ghost in the critical machinery of canon-formation, becoming a figure through
which much cultural work gets done. Poe most often functions as the demonized
"other" who must be exorcised from the "mainstream" of our "classic" American
literature: "It is to save our faces that we've given him a crazy reputation,"
William Carlos Williams writes, "a writer from whose classic accuracies we have
not known how else to escape."[20] While Poe, it would seem, can have no place
in the canon, he constantly poses a problem to it.

Five months after his death, the *Southern Literary Messenger* captured the
problem of Poe when it memorialized him as follows: "Edgar Allan Poe . . . the
true head of American literature—it is the verdict of other nations and after times
that we speak here—died of drink, friendless and alone, in the common wards
of a Baltimore hospital."[21] Poe's position in the corpus of American literature—
let alone his status as its head—has, from the beginning, been problematized by
the mythography of his own drunken corpse and by the diseased bodies and
living dead that haunt his stories. In both his life and his work, Poe would seem
to lie far outside the American mainstream. If he represents anything at all, it is
not American literature's head, but its irrational bodily impulses. The "after
times" have judged Poe harshly; he remains relegated to the "common wards"
and alienated from the community of American literature's founding fathers:
Emerson, Thoreau, Hawthorne, Melville, Whitman. In *The American Renaissance*
(1941), which places these authors at the center of a newly consolidated American
literature, F. O. Matthiessen buries Poe in a footnote. He explains Poe's exclusion
from his "group" as follows: "The reason is more fundamental than that his work
fell mainly in the decade of 1835–45; for it relates at very few points to the
main assumptions about literature that were held by any of my group. Poe was
bitterly hostile to democracy, and in that respect could serve as a revelatory
contrast."[22] As the exception to the rule—the embodiment of everything American
literature was *not*—Poe reveals the parameters of a more "authentic" American
literature. Acting as a ghost who haunts the American literary canon, Poe becomes
a necessary—and useful—evil. Harold Bloom sums up Poe's paradoxical position
when he writes, "I can think of no American writer, down to this moment, at
once so inevitable and so dubious."[23]

Poe's dubiousness, I would argue, is the very reason for his inevitability. For, it is through Poe that a number of "dubious" aspects of American literature get demonized and then exorcised from the mainstream American literary canon. As an excused aberration, Poe becomes the representative for a number of "problems" that the American literary tradition recognizes but refuses to claim. For instance, through Poe, popular literature can enter the canon without threatening the hard won highbrow status of our "classic" American literature. As Harold Bloom argues, "Poe's survival raises perpetually the issue as to whether literary merit and canonical status necessarily go together."[24] Through Poe, as well, a darker, more gothic vision of America comes into view. However, in reading Poe's gothic tales as the projections of Poe's own peculiar psychology instead of as a comment on his wider culture, critics easily contain his disturbing vision of American society. If Poe is merely a case for psychologists, as Parrington argues, or if "he gazed in fascinated reverie upon objects that seemed to swim in 'an atmosphere peculiar to themselves,' " as Charles Fiedelson states, then his particular perspective is not troubling.[25] For, as Levin claims, "Poe came by his own strangeness naturally."[26]

Even when Poe's diseased vision is read as a symptom of a larger cultural malaise, it remains quarantined from "mainstream" America because it comes to be identified with another "problem"—the South. Indeed, his strangeness seems to arise from his placement in the alienated space of the South. When Matthiessen claims that Poe was "bitterly hostile to democracy," he implies a connection between Poe's particular politics and his regional identification. After all, Melville was no less hostile to democracy than Poe. This connection is made explicit in Matthiessen's entry on Poe in Spiller's *Literary History of the United States* (1946). "He was so eager to prove himself a Virginian," Matthiessen writes, "that he followed Allan's tradition, which was that of Marshall and not that of Jefferson. Poe went so far as to deplore the French Revolution, to defend slavery as 'the basis of all our institutions,' and to assume the scorn held by the propertied class for the democratic 'mob.' "[27] Poe's politics, especially his racial politics, is an obsessive theme of much Poe criticism, and critics continually look to his politics to read the racial images in his work.[28] For instance, despite his arguments against authorial intention, John Carlos Rowe states, "My argument is on the face of it simple: Poe was a proslavery Southerner and should be reassessed as such in whatever approach we take to his life and writings."[29] After discussing Poe's "deliberate sectional prejudice," Harold Beaver can state in his introduction to the Penguin edition of *Pym*: "The conscious political intent—of this there can be no doubt—was to forestall the degree zero, the South Pole itself, of racial prejudice."[30] This critical intentionality stems partially from Poe's compelling biography (as Levin argues, "If Hawthorne is the man to whom nothing whatsoever has happened, Poe is the man to whom nearly everything happens"[31]), but more fully from a desire to place Poe in an identifiable position. If Poe's "blackness" can be positioned in the proslavery South, then his "racial phobia," as Levin calls it, can be limited to that region. Once placed in "this world," Poe's peculiar history has only to do with the South, not with the nation.

If Poe must be securely located in the South and politically "pinned down" in order to be accepted as the crazy cousin of the American literary tradition, he must be historically evacuated and regionally disassociated to become a charter member of this group. In order to claim Poe for a national tradition, as G. R. Thompson wants to do in *The Columbia Literary History of the United States* (1988), Poe must be stripped of his Southern associations and turned into an "antiregionalist."[32] Instead of addressing the South, Thompson argues that "Poe focuses on the integrity of the work of art in terms of the ideal—a metaphysical ideal of 'pure' poetry, an aesthetic ideal of total unity of effect in both poetry and fiction."[33] Through form, Poe transcends his region and its politics.

Focussing on his art instead of his relationship to his social setting is also the tactic the Southern literary establishment takes in its effort to claim Poe and his national status for the Southern literary tradition. While Poe is canonized as a Southerner in virtually all of the major Southern anthologies, his lack of specifiable regional identification is constantly remarked upon. In *The Mind of the South* (1941), W. J. Cash calls Poe "only half a Southerner," and Allen Tate states that while he is "a gentleman and a Southerner, he was not quite, perhaps, a Southern gentleman."[34] In a literary tradition that claims distinctiveness based on its unique social conditions, Poe, who spent much of his life outside of the South and who sets few of his stories in a Southern locale, never quite fits the profile of the Southern writer. As Montrose Moses's chapter heading for Poe in *The Literature of the South* (1910), "A Southern Mystery: An Author With and Without a Country—Poe," suggests, Poe's Southernness remains suspect.[35]

However, despite his suspicious Southern roots, Poe becomes the necessary cornerstone of a Southern literary tradition precisely because of his national status. As "one of the chief glories of the literature of our nation and our race," he becomes the "greatest ornament of Southern literature."[36] Louis Rubin explains Poe's paradoxical position as follows: "We confront the obvious fact that of all the antebellum Southern authors it is Poe whose writings are *least* grounded in the particularities, settings and issues of the place he grew up in, and equally *most* lastingly a part of world literature."[37] Ironically, it is the Southern literary establishment that has so much difficulty placing Poe in the South: Rubin, for instance, insists "Poe wrote almost *nothing* about the South, or about living there, or about Southern history and Southern society, or for that matter about any kind of history whatever."[38] If Poe becomes the voice of proslavery from a non-Southern perspective, he must be evacuated from that history by the Southern literary establishment. This move can be traced to the argument, popularized by Allan Tate, that art and politics are not only separate spheres in the South, but that politics hindered the growth of art. Rubin sums up the argument as follows: "The presence of African slavery was incompatible with the growth of an important literature in the Old South."[39] As the only producer of "art" during that period, Poe could not have derived his "blackness" from his cultural context.

Displaced from his social context, Poe is southernized by his art. As Ellen Glasgow argues in *A Certain Measure* (1943), Poe's literary techniques are identifiably Southern. "Poe is, to a large extent, a distillation of the Southerner," she writes. "The formalism of his tone, the classical element in his poetry and in many of his stories, the drift toward rhetoric, the aloof and elusive intensity,—

all these qualities are Southern."[40] Poe could also be saved through his criticism, much of which was published in an identifiable locale, the *Southern Literary Messenger*. Edwin Mims and Bruce Payne state in their *Southern Prose and Poetry for Schools* (1910), that "it is in his critical writing that Poe's Southern bent of mind was most notably evinced."[41] Moreover, Poe's gothic form could make him a forerunner to the Southern Renaissance, and, hence, make him the ancestor of Southern literature's "true" flowering. It is the ahistorical, symbolist, and more respectable Poe, finally, who is adopted into the Southern literary tradition.

Poe, then, poses a problem for both the Southern and national literary traditions. From the national perspective, the problem of Poe can be solved either by defining him in oppositional terms and identifying him with slavery and the South or by evacuating him of history and regional identification entirely; from the Southern perspective, Poe's peculiar place can be addressed by claiming his art for Southern literature while displacing him—along with the rest of Southern literature–from Southern history. In both cases, Poe's regional identification is deployed to read his gothic romances in relation to race. Instead of trying to solve the problem of Poe or locating him in any single place, I will argue that it is in Poe's regional (mis)placement and (dis)location that he becomes significant. By reading him as William Carlos Williams would have us do, as a "genius intimately shaped by his locality and time," I will look at how his gothic tales are engaged with a national, as opposed to regional, discourse on race.[42]

## The Voyage South: *The Narrative of Arthur Gordon Pym*

". . . a geometry of conflict written in gothic notation."
                                        —Kenneth Dauber, "The Problem of Poe"[43]

At the end of *The Narrative of Arthur Gordon Pym* (1838), the editor's note interprets the hieroglyphic chasms that Pym encounters on the island of Tsalal as "to be shady," "to be white," and "the region of the south." This code then gets critically read as an indicator of Poe's prowhite racism. My contention is that *Pym*'s racial codings—as well as the critical deciphering of these codes— have much to tell us about nineteenth-century racial discourse and our own readings of it. As the most frequently historicized of Poe's works, *Pym* reveals how a racial reading of Poe depends upon the cipher of the South. For when *Pym* is not universalized as a psychological voyage into the maelstrom of the mind, it is historicized as a social voyage with a very particular destination, the American South; like Poe's position in the canon, *Pym* either transcends its social context or gets mired in a regional reading. As Harry Levin writes, "The 'constant tendency to the south' in *The Narrative of Arthur Gordon Pym* takes on a special inflection, when we are mindful of the Southern self-consciousness of the author."[44] Once viewed through the regional marker of the South, *Pym*'s obsession with "whiteness" and "blackness" turns into a straightforward allegory of proslavery. Hence, John Carlos Rowe can argue: "I make no claim for originality here; the interpretation of *Pym* as a thinly disguised allegory of Poe's manifesto 'Keep the South White' belongs to others."[45] This critical consensus, however, relies upon a circular argument: *Pym* is at once the sign and the signifier of Poe's Southern racism. That is, critics read *Pym* as a projection of its author's Southernness and they use *Pym* as evidence for Poe's Southern racist position. Because Poe's authorial position on race is a silent absence in most of his critical and personal writing, *Pym* often gets critically projected as the articulation of that silence. In an attempt to "turn up a surer meaning at the level of Poe's intention" after his own reading of *Pym*'s allegory as racist, for instance, Sidney Kaplan asks: "Does all this seem improbable? Is it possible that the critic who flayed allegory as used by Hawthorne because the technique was too artificial and transparent could himself be guilty of the heresy of an allegorical and didactic damning of the Negro from the beginning to the end of time? I will not labor the point that Poe, as critic and fictionist, was no friend of the Negro. This is common knowledge."[46] Kaplan's attempt to reconcile his own allegorical reading of *Pym* with Poe's critical resistance to such a reading is solved by the "common knowledge" of Poe's Southern positioning. Poe's racism as well as his text's, it would seem, can be assumed once they are located in the South.

*Pym*, I would argue, resists such an allegorical reading. For even as the editor's note deciphers the narrative code, it also insists that any such reading is a function of critical desire. While the note claims that "conclusions such as these open a wide field for speculation and exciting conjecture," it also cautions that "in no visible manner is the chain of connection complete."[47] By obsessively locating *Pym* in a regional reading, critics attempt to make the chain of connection complete and, in so doing, reduce Poe's complex meditation on race to proslavery cant. While I do not intend to deny Poe's regional identification or his politics, I do want to complicate them by reading them in the context of a national discourse on race. I am *not* arguing that Poe should be dehistoricized or absolved of his proslavery sentiments; rather I am taking issue with how this historicization occurs. The implicit equation between Poe's Southernness and his proslavery politics belies the complex investments that critics have in a national discourse of racial purity. As Larry Tise argues, proslavery is not in itself a Southern position; it is merely canonized as one: "The ready ascription of proslavery writings and, as a consequence, proslavery ideas to Southernness and particularly to southern sectionalists," he writes, "has blinded historians to the actualities of proslavery history."[48] Reading proslavery or Poe only in terms of a regional, not national, discourse might raise critical comfort levels, but it does little to explain how discourses of race operate in Poe's tales. Moreover, to historicize *Pym* merely in terms of slavery is to miss its larger engagement with nineteenth-century racial ideologies. The debate over Poe's racialism needs to be reconstructed along less oppositional lines so that critics, who attempt to historicize Poe in terms other than a proslavery Southern identity, are not accused of being apologists for that vision. To quote Hazel Carby, I would suggest "that instead of searching for cultural purity we acknowledge cultural complexity."[49] Instead of setting up superficial dichotomies, we need to historicize Poe within a network of multiple discourses on race—regional, national—while also noting how these discourses intersect with and are influenced by other discourses, such as gender and class.[50] Rather than demonizing Poe's reflections on race or quarantining them to the South, I will argue that *Pym* records a complex and often contradictory vision of race and sets into play a national, not just a regional, racial discourse.

That national discourse is evident even in *Pym*'s Southern publication. In the same edition of *The Southern Literary Messenger* (January, 1837) which published the first installment of *The Narrative of Arthur Gordon Pym*, there was also a review of Jeremiah Reynolds's address to Congress arguing for a South Sea Exploring Expedition. Stating that, "the public mind is at length thoroughly alive on the subject," the review summed up the history of Reynolds's endeavors (he had petitioned Congress in 1828 only to be turned down) and the reasons for such a voyage: commercial expansion and patriotic duty.[51] While the initial impetus for the voyage had its origins in a theory put forward by John Symmes in 1818—that the earth was hollow, made up of a number of concentric spheres and accessed by openings at the poles—by the 1830s, Reynolds, Symmes's protegé, had refashioned Symmes's theory to more pragmatic ends: "Indeed, while there remains a spot of untrodden earth accessible to man," Reynolds states in his address, "no enlightened, and especially commercial and free people, should withhold its contributions for exploring it, wherever that spot may be found on the earth, from the equator to the poles."[52] Supported by Northern, Southern and Western states alike, the voyage was seen to be a national endeavor: "The enterprise should be national in its object, and sustained by the national means,—belongs of right to no individual, or set of individuals, but the country and the whole country."[53]

Arising out of this voyage—which aimed "to study man in his physical and mental powers, in his manners, habits, disposition, and social and political relations; and above all, in the philosophy of his language, in order to trace his origin from the early families of the old world"—and others like it during the period, which trafficked in information instead of bodies, was a new theory of race.[54] From the eighteenth century through the 1830s, monogenism, the belief in the original sameness of men, was the dominant racial ideology. Dr. Samuel Stanhope Smith, whose *Essays on the Causes of the Variety of Complexion and Figure in the Human Species* (1787, 1810) established the unity of human species and attributed the differences between races to environmental causes, was the central spokesperson for this theory. Echoing Smith's claims for the superficiality of racial difference, John Drayton, the governor of South Carolina, wrote in his 1802 *A View of South-Carolina* "that all mankind have originally descended from one pair; and that a difference of complexion is only produced by a change of situation, and a combination of other circumstances."[55] Though there were dissenter's from the theory of monogenism as early as 1784 (for instance, John Pinkton's *Dissertation on the Origin of the Scythians or Goths* [1787]), the theory held its ground well into the 1830s and 40s. However, with the publication of Dr. Samuel George Morton's *Crania Americana* (1839) and *Crania Aegyptiaca* (1844), the notion of polygenism, the belief in the innate difference between the races, began to be taken seriously. As Reginald Horsman points out, by the 1850s an inherent inequality between the races was accepted as scientific fact.[56] Moreover, this acceptance was not regionally based: "The overt intellectual argument for innate black inferiority," Horsman states, "was being developed in America before the full surge of abolitionism, it was not restricted to the South in the 1830s and 1840s, and it was not peculiar to those who wished to defend slavery."[57] While Morton's work sold especially well in the South, and while the cause of polygenism was taken up by a Southern physician, Josiah C. Nott, to defend slavery and to prove that physical causes cannot change a white man into a Negro, much of the South resisted the new theory since it directly contradicted biblical knowledge. Indeed, there was a strong national resistance to the notion of polygenism well into the 1840s. Charles Pickering, the chief naturalist of the U.S. Exploring Expedition and a close friend of Morton's, was censored in his 1845 report to Congress when he attempted to argue that races had different origins. Congress responded to his report by stating that it was "extremely necessary to be cautious in publishing any new philosophical inquiries relative to the History of man," in order to avoid "anything that might shock the public mind."[58]

This gradual shift from monogenism to polygenism or, as Nancy Stepan summarizes it, from a "sense of man as primarily a social being, governed by social laws and standing apart from nature, to a sense of man as primarily a biological being, embedded in nature and governed by biological laws," was occurring on the national level as Poe wrote *Pym*.[59] To read *Pym* as merely a Southern manifesto is to misread its national implications; moreover, to read it as an allegory of racial difference is to project upon it an 1850s discourse of polygenism. *Pym*'s narrative of racial convertibility, I would argue, more fully engages the earlier discourse of monogenism. As it insists that identities are fluid (Pym says to Augustus for example, "It is probable, indeed, that our intimate communion had resulted in a partial interchange of character" [*Pym*, 57]), as it claims that character can change according to environment (the white crew turns to cannibalism when the ship becomes disabled), as it constantly inverts and collapses the poles of "black" and "white" (Peters is first demon, then savior), *Pym* registers the fear that the self can easily become the other.

Indeed, as Joan Dayan puts it, the "story depends upon a crisis of color."[60] In its striking reversals and exaggerated racial taxonomies, *Pym* constantly crosses the color line. Death, the ultimate moment of boundary collapse, serves as the central metaphor for this crisis. Characters are described paradoxically as being paler than death, and once white bodies turn black in death. Augustus's corpse, for instance, is not only characterized as a "mass of putrefaction" (155) so without definition and boundaries that his limbs fall off at a simple grasp, but his arm is also described as turning "completely black from the wrist to the shoulder" (154) as he dies. Later, when the surviving castaways spot what they first assume is a rescue ship only to realize that it is a ghost ship piloted by corpses, each corpse is described as having "very dark skin" and a set of the most "brilliantly white teeth" (131). In death, even the most "brilliantly white" can turn "very dark." What happens to the body in death exemplifies the crisis of color inherent in the racial philosophy of monogenism. Dr. John Mitchell of Virginia makes this connection explicit when he observes that "where any Body loses its White colour, it of course turns black, without any other Cause concurring, but a bare loss of its Whiteness. . . . From whence we may justly infer 1. That there is not so great, unnatural, and unaccountable a Difference between Negroes and White People, as to make it impossible for both ever to have been descended from the same Stock."[61] Mitchell's conclusion—that "however different, and opposite to one another, these two colors of Black and White may appear to be to the unskillful, yet they will be found to differ from one another only in Degree"—is similar to *Pym*'s.[62] For even as *Pym*'s color symbolism seems constantly to create difference, it elides that difference by articulating a discourse of racial identity that is constructed and, hence, vulnerable to change.

The novel's insistence on the constructed nature of race is especially evident in Pym's attempt to "represent the corpse of Rogers" in order to trick the mutineers (112). Pym dresses himself in Rogers's shirt, which "was of a singular form and character, and easily recognizable," equips himself with a false stomach "in imitation of the horrible deformity of the swollen corpse," and then "gave the same appearance to [his] hands by drawing on a pair of white woolen mittens" (112). Peters finishes off the simulacrum by "arrang[ing] [Pym's] face," rubbing it with white chalk and splotching it with blood in order to imitate the "chalky whiteness" of Rogers's corpse (111). Made up in "white face," Pym views himself in a mirror and states: "I was so impressed with a sense of vague awe at my appearance, and at the recollection of the terrific reality which I was thus representing, that I was seized with a violent tremor, and could scarcely summon resolution to go on with my part" (113). Unable to recognize himself, shocked by his own "otherness," the actor becomes as frightened of his transformation as his audience will soon be. Pym's gothic trick re-presents reality so terrifically that it threatens to challenge that reality. Described as a matter of appearance, or a role one plays, racial identity becomes performative. Poe's readers, who were themselves audiences to such racial transformations in the minstrel shows, might be similarly disturbed by the way race, as only a function of make-up, could be made-up. As Eric Lott writes in his study of blackface minstrelsy, "The blackface phenomenon was virtually constituted by such slippages, positives turning to negatives, selves into others, and back again."[63] Like one of its sources, Benjamin Morrell's *Four Voyages* (1832), which recounts a scene in which a native has to satisfy himself that the white narrator is also "constructed of bones and flesh, like his own race, and that the white paint could not be rubbed off [his] ebony skin," *Pym* shows that whiteness is as much a construct as blackness and, in doing so, registers a fear that racial identity is fluid, not fixed.[64]

The reproduction of race in this episode highlights the production of race more generally in the text, and the episode's focus on imitation and appearance is central from the very opening of the story. *Pym*'s preface, which is obsessed with how to give his account the "*appearance* of that truth it would really possess," problematizes notions of truth and reality (43). In *Pym*, truth must be produced; reality is only an effect. Similarly, race is only a representation. This is evident the discussions of both "blackness" and "whiteness" in the text. The stereotypical images of "blackness" can be read, as Joan Dayan argues, as exaggerations that dramatize "the fact of appropriation, and thereby undefine the definitions that mattered to civilized society"[65] As the preface points out, excess undermines authenticity: it is the wild and marvelous nature of Pym's story that makes him fear that readers will see it as an "ingenious fiction" (43). If exaggeration has the effect of artifice instead of truth, then the novel's stereotypical descriptions of the natives of Tsalal, its insistence on their total blackness, could actually work to expose the artifice of race instead of merely reinforcing racial difference. Just as the happy, minstrel image of the natives proves false when their plot to kill the crew is revealed, so too might all racial images be a "put on."

This reading, of course, does not take into account the many ways in which the novel deploys and reinforces racial stereotypes, even as it reveals race to be a social invention. *Pym* reproduces racial fantasy even as it points out that such fantasy is merely a representation. This contradictory position is more evident in *Pym*'s depiction of "whiteness." On the one hand, as in the episode with Rogers's corpse, whiteness is terrifying and all-powerful. Its effect allows Pym to reverse positions, turning his non-white captors into "the most pitiable objects of horror and utter despair" (117). Whiteness's terrifying power is most strikingly evident in the final scene of the novel, a point to which I will return. On the other hand, despite its reinforcing of the power of whiteness, the story registers a fear of losing one's whiteness and becoming, as Pym says of the black corpses on the ghost ship, like those "silent and disgusting images" (132). The novel's insistence on the difference between the "very dark" corpses and their "brilliantly white teeth" reinforces its contradictory stance. Its meditation on difference paradoxically registers a fear of racial identity: black skin might harbor the vestiges of a white identity. Instead of policing the color line, *Pym* transgresses it, and in so doing exploits the fears of its readers rather than allaying them.

The ghost story Pym tells echoes the effects of Poe's own gothic tale, *Pym*. In order to set the stage for the "terrific appearance of Roger's corpse," Peters and Augustus tell ghost stories which "wound up [their audience] to the highest pitch of nervous excitement" (115). After Pym makes his grand entrance, dressed as Rogers and "without uttering a syllable," he reflects upon the effect of his appearance:

> The intense effect produced by this sudden apparition is not at all to be wondered at when the various circumstances are taken into consideration. Usually, in cases of a similar nature, there is left in the mind of the spectator some glimmering of doubt as to the reality of the vision before his eyes; a degree of hope, however feeble, that he is the victim of chicanery, and that the apparition is not actually a visitant from the world of shadows. It is not too much to say that such remnants of doubt have been at the bottom of almost every such visitation, and that the appalling horror which has sometimes been brought about, is to be attributed, even in the cases most in point, and where most suffering has been experienced, more to a kind of anticipative horror, lest the apparition *might possibly be real*, than to an unwavering belief in

its reality. But, in the present instance, it will be seen immediately, that in the minds of the mutineers there was not even the shadow of a basis upon which to rest a doubt that the apparition of Rogers was indeed a revivification of his disgusting corpse, or at least its spiritual image. (115–116)

This passage, which is a treatise on the gothic's intense effects, foregrounds the difficulty of explaining away the gothic's appalling horror. By substituting an analysis of the effect for the effect itself, the scientific discourse of this passage attempts to inflect the supernatural event with a rational explanation. However, this metonymic substitution fails: the excessive explanation cannot completely cover over the gap of doubt which always remains. Like Monk Lewis's rationale for his gothic's effect, Pym's explanation is unable to capture fully his haunting impression. It is in this gap—this schism between the scientific and supernatural—that *Pym* gains its effect. For the "vision" before its spectators' eyes is not only the revivification of a corpse but also a "visitant from the world of shadows"—the ghost of race. *Pym*'s gothic effects are always haunted by race. Its scientific discourse might attempt to make sense of race by creating safely segregated categories and by rationalizing its actualities, but its gothic effects reveal science's failure to account fully for its haunting visitations. The hope that this tale of racial convertibility is only chicanery is modulated by the fear that it might be all too true.

## Perfect Whiteness

If we follow through on the self-reflexive nature of these encounters with Africanism, it falls clear: images of blackness can be evil *and* protective, rebellious *and* forgiving, fearful *and* desirable—all of the self-contradictory features of the self. Whiteness, alone, is mute, meaningless, unfathomable, pointless, frozen, veiled, curtained, dreaded, senseless, implacable. Or so our writers seem to say.

—Toni Morrison, *Playing in the Dark*[66]

*Pym* has often been read as a patchwork text, made up of many different narrative modes. Indeed, the book seems to break in half, moving from the gothic tale of sea voyaging horrors to a scientific account of the South Seas once Pym is picked up by the *Jane Guy*. If the gothic tale collapses the boundaries between appearance and reality, death and life, desire and terror, black and white, the second half of the story seems more interested in re-establishing stable categories and reinforcing a straightforward allegory of racial difference. The gothic tale of racial convertibility seems to turn into a sociological study of slavery, replete with its model of racial segregation and polarization. For example, Pym observes as the ship travels south that the variation of the sea "uniformly decreased," and he describes the water as being made up of a "number of distinct veins" that do "not commingle" (186, 194). The allegory of segregation is made clear in the conclusion, which states: "Nothing *white* was to he found at Tsalal, and nothing otherwise in the subsequent voyage to the region beyond" (242). Intent on the "purest white imaginable" and the most "brilliant black," this section of the story seems to reassert the color line that the previous section collapsed (166). On Tsalal the natives' insides match their outsides: their teeth are black like their jet black skin. The signs seem excessively clear.

Yet, as we have seen, such excess can actually create an opposite effect, collapsing instead of creating difference. Indeed, the natives are not what they appear to be. Their exaggerated childlike innocence—"Upon getting alongside the chief evinced symptoms of extreme surprise and delight, clapping his hands, slapping his thighs and breast, and laughing obstreperously"—turns out to be a mask (190). Another insurrection occurs, this time on the island instead of on the ship, which once again destabilizes the poles of black and white. The dark chasm in which Pym becomes buried alive along with Peters on the island of Tsalal represents the color line that is constantly being crossed in the novel. The same fissure that marks difference also threatens to collapse that difference. Pym might believe that through scientific and commercial expertise the proper hierarchy between white and black has been reestablished, but once again the gothic returns when he finds himself entombed in blackness. Pym, like the book's audience, keeps confronting the fact that he cannot escape "blackness."

The extent to which *Pym* continues to collapse the poles of black and white in this section of the story is made clearer by an understanding of how Poe rewrites one of his sources, *Symzonia*. Written by John Cleves Symmes in 1820, *Symzonia* is Symmes's imaginative projection of his hollow-earth theory. Like Pym's voyage South, *Symzonia* is concerned with commercial imperialism and its attendant racial taxonomies. Captain Seaborn, the protagonist of the novel, states: "I felt perfectly satisfied that I had only to find an opening in the 'icy hoop' through which I could dash with my vessel, to discover a region where seals could be taken as fast as they could be stripped and cured."[67] The novel traces Captain Seaborn's voyage to the inside of the earth where he encounters a race of perfectly white beings, whom he calls the internals. In a reversal of the usual colonial contact, Captain Seaborn bows to the natives and remarks upon his own inferiority: "I am considered fair for an American, and my skin was always in my own country thought to be one of the finest and whitest. But when one of the internals placed his arm, always exposed to the weather, by the side of mine, the difference was truly mortifying. I was not a white man, compared to him" (*Symzonia*, 110). Stating that "the sootiest African does not differ more from us in darkness of skin and grossness of features, than this man did from me in fairness of complexion and delicacy of form," Captain Seaborn registers his fear that he may be more black than white (108).

While *Symzonia* adheres to racist stereotypes (Seaborn claims that "it was [his] dark and hideous appearance that created so much distrust amongst these beautiful natives" [107]), it also claims that those stereotypes are not fixed. Indeed, even as it argues that external signs are signifiers of internal behavior (the "gross sensuality, intemperate passions and beastly habits of the externals" are seen in their darker skin; while the "appearance, manners, conduct and expression of countenance of [the internals]" perfectly accorded with his "ideas of purity and goodness" [134, 117]), the novel shows just how changeable these signs are. Moreover, in its description of the outcast tribesmen who are relegated, because of their participation in the "contaminating intercourse" of trade, to a land in the north where the intense heat has turned them dark, *Symzonia* argues that any race—even the most perfectly white—can degenerate into brutes: "The influence of their gross appetites and of the climate," Seaborn explains, "causes them to lose their fairness of complexion and beauty of form and feature. They become dark coloured, ill favoured, and mis-shapen men, not much superior to brute creation" (167, 132). The seafaring life, which also darkens Seaborn's skin, threatens a similar fate for him; for it is Seaborn's addiction to trade that makes him assume that the externals are descended from this exiled tribe. Judged by the Symzonians to be contaminated, the externals are another fallen race turned "black" from the crime of trade, specifically slavery. Seaborn states that "it appeared that we were of a race that had either wholly fallen from virtue, or was at least very much under the influence of the worst passions of our nature [since] . . . we were guilty of enslaving our fellow-men for the purpose of procuring the means of satisfying our sensual appetites" (196).

In preaching an anti-slavery message even as it enforces racist stereotypes, *Symzonia* reflects the contradictory positions that a single text can hold. While on the one hand it claims that slavery is contaminating and argues for the fluidity of racial identity, on the other hand it reinforces racial hierarchies: races might be socially constructed, it argues, but the more advanced and developed race is always the whiter one. Monogenism, it turns out, is potentially no less racist a philosophy than polygenism. Like *Pym*, then, *Symzonia* reinforces racial stereotyping even as it argues for the constructed nature of identity; moreover, like *Pym*, its obsession with "perfect" whiteness underscores its fear that one might not after all be perfectly white.

But it is *Pym*'s difference from *Symzonia* that is more telling. Against the hierarchical philosophy of *Symzonia*'s monogenism, *Pym* insists that "whiteness" is only the obverse of "blackness." For instance, when *Pym* replays the scene of Seaborn's first contact with the internals by making the natives recoil from Pym and his crew with the same horror as the internals do from the externals, *Pym* places whites in the position of the "other": "It was quite evident that they had never before seen any of the white race—from whose complexion, indeed, they appeared to recoil" (190). More importantly, by refiguring the voyage to the center of the earth as a journey into blackness, not whiteness, the novel argues that Pym's search for selfhood has more to do with discovering how "whiteness" relates to "blackness" than with how he reflects an ideal of "perfect whiteness."

Journeying to the center of the island, Pym and Peters, his half-breed companion, get literally buried alive in the black granite caverns of Tsalal. Here, Seaborn's and his crew's fear of plunging through the earth's hole into "total darkness," "never [to] be able to find their way out again," becomes a reality for Pym (*Symzonia*, 91). When Pym awakens, he finds himself "enveloped" in a "blackness of darkness" among a "quantity of loose earth, which was threatening to bury [him] entirely" (208). By deciding to pause at this moment of dissolution (Pym states that he thought "the whole foundations of the solid globe were suddenly rent asunder, and that the day of universal dissolution was at hand" [207]), *Pym* takes *Symzonia*'s fears to their nightmarish ends. Moreover, when Pym finally plunges through the hole into the abyss, it is into the saving arms of his alter-ego, the "dusky, fiendish" Peters (229). Coming out the other side feeling a new being, Pym discovers himself through "blackness," not "whiteness." Indeed as Toni Morrison has recently argued, the black shadow often becomes the reflexive surrogate through which whites meditate upon the self.[68] *Pym*, then, not only points out how "whiteness" gets constructed in relation "blackness," as *Symzonia* does, but also shows how white identity is mediated through a desire for, yet dread of "blackness." Pym's fear of falling into the abyss is matched only by his longing for this plunge: "my whole soul was pervaded with *a longing to fall*; a desire, a yearning, a passion utterly uncontrollable" (229). Inside the world there exists not a more perfect version of the white self, but the black self that Pym must come to terms with—a self he both loathes and desires.

The novel's ending, where Pym is drawn into another abyss, this time to be met by the arms of a shrouded figure of "perfect whiteness," seems to retreat from the more complicated notion of racial identity that the rest of the book sets forth. For instance, Sidney Kaplan reads the ending as Pym's rushing "away from the Black into the embracing arms of the comforting White."[69] I would argue, however, that the ending is less an evasion than a repeat engagement with the issues of the previous scene of live burial and, indeed, of the novel as a whole. The ending not only echoes the events of Pym's plunge into the arms of the "filmy figure" of Peters, but it also reiterates the same complexity of fear and desire: the figure of "perfect whiteness" both blocks and embraces (229, 239). Like the shrouded figure, the ending embraces the comforting illusion of a perfect whiteness while it reveals the limitations of this embrace. The ending reaffirms that race is merely a fantasy, a projection, an illu-sion—a white curtain, a shrouded figure.

The complex production of "whiteness," not its self-evident nature, is the focus of the ending. An external projection instead of an internal identification—everything is described as white but Pym himself—"whiteness" is less a fact of Pym's self-identity than an imaginative wish-fulfillment. In his descriptions of Nu-Nu's strange response to the whiteness that surrounds him, Pym not only denies his own terror ("The Polar winter appeared to be coming on–but coming without its terrors," he claims [237]) by projecting it onto Nu-Nu's black body, but he also reaffirms the power of whiteness by reading terror as its by-product. However, Pym's fantasy of "perfect whiteness" continues to be mediated through "blackness." First, his white imaginary is only visible in relation to the dark: "The darkness had materially increased, relieved only by the glare of the water thrown back from the white curtain before us" (238–239). Second, Nu-Nu's black body regulates the terms of his engagement with this projection: "Here-upon Nu-Nu stirred in the bottom of the boat; but upon touching him, we found his spirit departed. And now we rushed into the embraces of the cataract, where a chasm threw itself open to receive us. But there arose in our pathway a shrouded human figure, very far larger in its proportions than any dweller among men. And the hue of the skin of the figure was of the perfect whiteness of the snow"

(239). In its conclusion, *Pym* seems to argue that blackness blocks whiteness, since Pym cannot rush into the embracing arms of perfect whiteness as long as Nu-Nu is alive. As a result, it would seem to be reinstituting the color line by exorcising blackness in order to embrace whiteness. However, it is also possible to read the ending in precisely the opposite way: whiteness can only be embraced through blackness. Given the timing of Nu-Nu's death, it is possible to see the shrouded figure at the end as the spiritual revivification of Nu-Nu. Pym might be embracing precisely what he hopes to evade.

The difficulty of "pining down" a reading of *Pym*'s ending reflects the contradictory impulses of the novel as a whole. The ending, like the tale itself, desires "perfect whiteness" even as it reveals its impossibility. While the ending makes clear the costs of such an illusion—the terror for blacks, the numbness for whites—it still finds comfort in the hollow reflection of "whiteness." Pym's position as the living dead throughout the story exemplifies the novel's position as well: like Pym who keeps hoping for a rebirth even as he continues to be buried alive, *Pym* keeps trying to resolve the issue of race. The conclusion's final words—"*I have graven it within the hills, and my vengeance upon the dust within the rock*"—however, warn that the ghost of race will continue to return (242).

I want to suggest, then, that *Pym*'s obsession with "whiteness" has less to do with a simple message of white supremacy than with a complex and even at times contradictory claim that, while white might be "right," it is neither perfect nor pure. I also want to suggest that readings of *Pym*'s racial discourse are often the projection of our most comforting critical illusions: that the terror of race exists only in the South. We need to ask how regional stereotypes allow a particular racial discourse to be canonized, a discourse that allows race to be recognized regionally while exorcised nationally. We need to be able to articulate regional difference across the color line while also recognizing the pervasiveness of white racism. Poe's (mis)placement is useful for precisely this reason: his ghostly position can dislocate traditional critical paradigms. We must, then, as Morrison argues, recognize the ghost of race in all of its haunts: "All of us, readers and writers, are bereft when criticism remains too polite or too fearful to notice a disrupting darkness before its eyes."[70] Instead of sleeping with the comforting illusions that race is only a regional spectre, we must remain wakeful to the racial nightmares that haunt our national literature.

## Notes

I would like to thank Michael Kreyling, Cecelia Tichi, Mark Schoenfield, Joyce Chaplin, Harry Wonham, and Jay Grossman for their helpful comments. I am also grateful to the members of the 1991–1992 Faculty Seminar at the Robert Penn Warren Center for the Humanities at Vanderbilt for their encouragement and expertise. The Robert Penn Warren Center and the Vanderbilt University Research Council provided funds to support this work.

1. James Harrison, *Life and Letters of Edgar Allan Poe* (New York: Thomas Y. Crowell, 1902), 361.

2. Lewis himself became a slaveholder upon his father's death in 1812. See Lewis's *Journal of a West India Proprietor* (London: John Murray, 1834) for an account of his life in Jamaica.

3. See Moira Ferguson, *Subject to Others: British Women Writers and Colonial Slavery, 1670–1834* (London: Routledge, 1992). Ferguson traces the intensification of the anti-slavery debate in England to 1791 and the San Domingo revolution; she locates the end of that debate in the Emancipation Bill of 1833. These dates roughly coincide with the rise of the gothic novel in England.

4. Winter, *Subjects of Slavery, Agents of Change: Women and Power in Gothic Novels and Slave Narratives, 1790–1865* (Athens: University of Georgia Press, 1992).

5. Robert Hemenway, "Gothic Sociology: Charles Chesnutt and the Gothic Mode," *Studies in the Literary Imagination* 7 (Spring 1974): 106.

6. Ibid., 101.

7. Herman Melville, "Hawthorne and His Mosses" in *The Piazza Tales and Other Prose Pieces 1839–1860* (Evanston: Northwestern University Press, 1987), 243.

8. Toni Morrison, "Unspeakable Things Unspoken: The Afro-American Presence in American Literature," *Michigan Quarterly Review* 28 (Winter 1989): 11. Reprinted, in part, in this volume.

9. Morrison, *Playing in the Dark: Whiteness and the Literary Imagination* (Cambridge, Harvard University Press, 1992), 38.

10. In making this argument for viewing "whiteness" as a racial category, Morrison adds her voice to a growing number of critics who are demanding that "whiteness" be recognized. See Hazel Carby, "The Canon: Civil War and Reconstruction," *Michigan Quarterly Review* 28 (Winter 1989): 35–43; bell hooks, "Representing Whiteness in the Black Imagination" in *Cultural Studies*, ed. Lawrence Grossberg, Cary Nelson, Paula Treichler (New York: Routledge, 1992), 338–346; Richard Dyer, "White," *Screen* 29 (Autumn 1988): 44–65; Dana Nelson, *The Word in Black and White* (New York: Oxford, 1992); Ruth Frankenberg, *White Women, Race Matters: The Social Construction of Whiteness* (Minneapolis: University of Minnesota Press, 1993); David Roediger, *The Wages of Whiteness* (London: Verso, 1991).

11. See, for example, *The Columbia History of the American Novel*, ed. Emory Elliott (New York: Columbia University Press, 1991) where the connections between romance and race are discussed only in relation to Poe.

12. Harry Levin, *The Power of Blackness* (New York: Knopf, 1970), 35.

13. Ibid., 120.

14. Ibid., 233.

15. Leslie Fiedler, *Love and Death in the American Novel* (New York: Stein and Day, 1966), 397.

16. Ibid., 401.

17. Richard Gray, "Edgar Allan Poe and the Problem of Regionalism" in *The United States South: Regionalism and Identity*, ed. Valeria Gennaro Lerda and Tjebbe Westendorp (Rome: Bulzoni Editore, 1991), 83.

18. There is some debate about when the South actually became a "problem" for the nation. Most historians, however, agree that it was during the 1830s that the South's problematic status became solidified. During this period there was also a rise in the use of gothic rhetoric, especially by abolitionists, to describe and demonize the South. For examples of this gothic rhetoric see Ronald Walters, *The Antislavery Appeal* (Baltimore: Johns Hopkins University Press, 1976). The most famous spokespersons for the South's oppositional identity are C. Vann Woodward, *The Burden of Southern History* (Baton Rouge: Louisiana State University Press, 1960) and W. J. Cash, *The Mind of the South*

(New York: Knopf, 1941). For examinations of the South as an idea rather than a fact, see Richard Gray, *Writing the South: Ideas of an American Region* (New York: Cambridge University Press, 1986); Michael O'Brien, *The Idea of the American South, 1920–1941* (Baltimore: Johns Hopkins University Press, 1979).

19. Vernon Parrington, *Main Currents in American Thought*, vol. 2 (New York: Harcourt, Brace and World, 1927), 58.

20. William Carlos Williams, *In the American Grain* (New York: New Directions, 1956), 216.

21. *The Southern Literary Messenger* 16 (March, 1850): 178.

22. F. O. Matthiessen, *The American Renaissance* (London: Oxford University Press, 1941), xii.

23. Harold Bloom, "Introduction" in *Modern Critical Views: Edgar Allan Poe*, ed. Harold Bloom (New York: Chelsea House, 1985), 3.

24. Ibid. It is interesting to note that Poe remains an outsider even in Leslie Fiedler's gothic reading of American literature for this very reason. According to Fiedler, Poe fails to "transform the gothic into the tragic" and to "raise his characters to the Faustian level which alone dignifies gothic fiction" (*Love and Death*, 430, 428).

25. Charles Feidelson, *Symbolism and American Literature* (Chicago: Chicago University Press, 1953), 2.

26. Levin, *Power of Blackness*, 102.

27. F. O. Matthiessen, "Edgar Allan Poe" in *Literary History of the United States*, ed. Spiller (New York: Macmillan, 1946), 328.

28. Note, for instance, the on-going debate about the authorship of an anonymous review published in the *Southern Literary Messenger* in 1836, known as the "Paulding-Drayton Review." The pro-slavery views of this review have alternately been attributed to Beverly Tucker and to Edgar Allan Poe. In his article, "Poe, Slavery, and the *Southern Literary Messenger*: A Reexamination" *Poe Studies* 7 (1974): 29–38, Bernard Rosenthal attributes the article to Poe and states: "it is hard to believe that any serious scholar could still doubt that Poe supported the institution of slavery" (29). See Nelson, *The Word in Black and White*, pp. 90–92, for a fuller history of this debate. Given the disproportionate amount of critical energy spent on the relatively few documentary sources that reveal Poe's attitude toward race, I would argue that the debate has mainly to do with a critical desire to pin Poe down in terms of his views on slavery so that these views can then be read into his texts. While there is more evidence about Hawthorne's conservative position on the question of slavery, critics seem less interested in exploring these views in connection to the "blackness" in his texts. One notable exception is Jay Grossman's "Race, Authorship, *The Scarlet Letter*," *Textual Practice* 7 (Spring 1993): 1–36.

29. John Carlos Rowe, "Poe, Antebellum Slavery, and Modern Criticism" in *Poe's Pym: Critical Explorations*, ed. Richard Kopley (Durham: Duke University Press, 1992), 117.

30. Harold Beaver, "Introduction" in *The Narrative of Arthur Gordon Pym of Nantucket*, ed. Harold Beaver (London: Penguin, 1975), 25.

31. Levin, *Power of Blackness*, 102.

32. G. R. Thompson, "Edgar Allan Poe and the Writers of the Old South" in *Columbia Literary History of the United States* (New York: Columbia University Press, 1988), 262–277.

33. Ibid., 277.

34. Cash, *Mind of the South*, 94; Allen Tate, "Our Cousin, Mr. Poe" in *Poe: A Collection of Critical Essays*, ed. Robert Regan (New York: Prentice-Hall, 1967), 41.

35. Montrose J. Moses, *The Literature of the South* (New York: Thomas Y. Crowell and Co., 1910).

36. *The Library of Southern Literature* 9, ed. Edwin Anderson Alderman, Joel Chandler Harris, Charles William Kent (New Orleans: The Martin and Hoyt Co., 1907), 4089.

37. Louis Rubin, *The Edge of the Swamp* (Baton Rouge: Louisiana State University Press, 1989), 147.

38. Ibid., 152.

39. Ibid., 17.

40. Quoted in Jay Hubbell, *The South in American Literature* (Durham: Duke University Press, 1954), 542. Note also Carl Holliday's Southernization of Poe: "Perhaps, after all, this sense of the artistic effect of sound—this seeking for perfection in harmony, is the best evidence of the influence of Poe's Southern environment" in *A History of Southern Literature* (New York: The Neale Publishing Company, 1906), 237.

41. Edwin Mims and Bruce R. Payne, *Southern Prose and Poetry for Schools* (New York: Charles Scribner's Sons, 1910), 6.

42. Williams, *In the American Grain*, 216.

43. Kenneth Dauber, "The Problem of Poe," *Georgia Review* 32 (1978): 647.

44. Levin, *The Power of Blackness*, 120.

45. Rowe, "Poe, Slavery, and Modern Criticism," 126.

46. Sidney Kaplan, "Introduction" in *The Narrative of Arthur Gordon Pym* (New York: Hill and Wang, 1960), xvi, xxiii.

47. Edgar Allan Poe, *The Narrative of Arthur Gordon Pym*, ed. Harold Beaver (London: Penguin, 1975), 242. Subsequent page references are to this edition and are given in the text.

48. Larry Tise, *Proslavery: A History of the Defense of Slavery in America. 1701–1840* (Athens: University of Georgia Press, 1987), 3.

49. Hazel Carby, "The Canon: Civil War and Reconstruction," 42.

50. The two critics who have done the most to set Poe within a complex set of interlocked discourses are Dana Nelson and Joan Dayan. Nelson argues "that while on one level *Pym* is a racist text, on another the text provides a reading that counters racist colonial ideology and the racialist, scientific knowledge structure" (*The Word in Black and White*, 92). Dayan not only historicizes Poe in terms of race, but she also discusses how his racial vision intersects with his contradictory discourse on womanhood. She also points to a class reading of Poe. See Joan Dayan, "Romance and Race" in *The Columbia History of the American Novel*, 89–109 and "Amorous Bondage: Poe, Ladies and Slaves," *American Literature* 66 (June 1994): 239–273.

51. *Southern Literary Messenger* 3 (Jan. 1837), 68.

52. Ibid., 70.

53. Ibid., 72.

54. Ibid., 71.

55. Quoted in Reginald Horsman, *Race and Manifest Destiny: The Origins of American Anglo-Saxonism* (Cambridge: Harvard University Press, 1981), 99.

56. Horseman, *Race and Manifest Destiny*, 134.

57. Ibid., 122.

58. William Stanton, *The Great United States Exploring Expedition of 1838–1842* (Berkeley: University of California Press, 1975), 343.

59. Nancy Stepan, *The Idea of Race in Science: Great Britain 1800–1960* (Hamden, Connecticut: Archon Books, 1982), 4.

60. Dayan, "Romance and Race," 108.

61. Quoted in Winthrop D. Jordon, *White Over Black: American Attitudes Toward the Negro, 1550–1812* (New York: W. W. Norton and Co., 1968), 247.

62. Ibid., 247.

63. Eric Lott, *Love and Theft: Blackface Minstrelsy and the American Working Class* (New York: Oxford University Press, 1993), 124.

64. Benjamin Morrell, *Narrative of Four Voyages* (New York: J. and J. Harper, 1832), 397.

65. Dayan, "Amourous Bondage," 250.

66. Morrison, *Playing in the Dark*, 59.

67. John Cleves Symmes, *Symzonia, A Voyage of Discovery* (Gainesville, Florida, 1965), 30. Subsequent page references are given in the text.

68. Morrison, *Playing in the Dark*, 17.

69. Kaplan, "Introduction," xxii.

70. Morrison, *Playing in the Dark*, 91.

# Interrogating "Whiteness,"
# Complicating "Blackness":
# Remapping American Culture

February 1992. I hadn't spoken with him in years, but I knew David Bradley would share my excitement, so I dialed his number.[1] "This may sound crazy," I remember saying, "but I think I've figured out—and can prove—that black speakers and oral traditions played an absolutely central role in the genesis of *Huckleberry Finn*. Twain couldn't have *written* the book without them. And hey, if Hemingway's right about all modern American literature coming from *Huck Finn*, then all modern American literature comes from those black voices as well. And as Ralph Ellison said when I interviewed him last summer, it all comes full circle because *Huck Finn* helps spark so much work by black writers in the twentieth century."

I stopped to catch my breath. There was a pause on the other end of the line. Then a question:

"Shelley, tell me one thing. Do you have tenure?"

"Yes, but what does that have to do with anything?" I asked.

"Thank God." he said. "Look, this stuff has been sitting there for a hundred years but nobody noticed because it didn't fit the paradigm. Whether they wanted to expand the canon or not, they all agreed that canonical American literature was 'white.' And whether they wanted black studies in the curriculum or not, they all agreed that African-American literature was 'black.' Now they'll have to start all over. Think about it."

I did.

In 1993, a year after that conversation, when my book *Was Huck Black? Mark Twain and African-American Voices* came out, I was aware of two or three books published that same year in the U.S. that tilled adjacent fields. The kinds of deep-going changes for which Bradley had argued seemed to be starting to happen. I sensed that my work might be part of a growing trend. But how many isolated academic forays add up to a "trend?" Ten? Twenty? Thirty?

In this essay I will provide a brief overview of over a hundred books and articles from fields including literary criticism, history, cultural studies, anthropology, popular culture, communication studies, music history, art history, dance history, humor studies, philosophy, linguistics and folklore, all published between 1990 and 1995 or forthcoming shortly. Taken together I believe that they mark the early 1990s as a defining moment in the study of American culture.

In the early 1990s, our ideas of "whiteness" were interrogated, our ideas of "blackness" were complicated, and the terrain we call "American culture" began to be remapped.[2]

## Interrogating "Whiteness"

If you white, you all right . . . But if you black, get back.
                    —African-American folk saying, later incorporated into a song[3]

To be white in America is to be very black. If you don't know how black you are, you don't know how American you are.
                    —Robert Farris Thompson[4]

Combatants in the canon wars of the 1980s argued that writing by African Americans had been previously unjustly excluded from the curriculum. New courses proliferated. But, as Dean Flower observed in the *Hudson Review* in 1994,

> the definition of "American" literature did not change. In the college classroom American literature was, and still mainly is, defined by the so-called "classic" texts and "major figures"—as if black writers had really made no difference in our literary history until, say, *Native Son*. Look in any publisher's college catalogue. The canonized (white) writers, who represent "the American tradition," are listed in one place, the African Americans appear in another. Students take courses on "Afro-American" writers or "Black Studies," almost always taught by persons of color, and they take courses in American literature, almost always taught by white persons in departments of English. The segregation could not be more emphatic.[5]

A study published in January 1990 found that college courses with such titles as "The Modern Novel" or "Modern Poetry" continued to be dominated by "works almost exclusively by elite white men."[6] Nonetheless, calling attention to the "whiteness" of the curriculum was still considered bizarre and provocative behavior. A professor who called the standard American literature survey she taught "White Male Writers" was held up to ridicule by *Time* magazine.[7] Evidently the editors subscribed to the idea (as George Lipsitz recently put it) that "whiteness never has to speak its name, never has to acknowledge its role as an organizing principle in social and cultural relations."[8] *Time*'s behavior reflected the widely-held assumptions that American culture is obviously white culture, and that stating the obvious is superfluous, irritating and perverse.

While the idea of the social construction of "blackness" was increasingly discussed in the 1980s, the idea of "whiteness" as a construct did not receive widespread attention until the 1990s. In the 1990s, scholars asked with increased frequency how the imaginative construction of "whiteness" had shaped American literature and American history. Some of our culture's most familiar (and canonical) texts and artifacts turned out to be less "white" on closer look than we may have thought; and the "whiteness" that had previously been largely invisible in the stories we told about who we were suddenly took center stage as the site where power and privilege converged and conspired to sabotage ideals of justice, equality and democracy.

With the 1992 publication of her book *Playing in the Dark: Whiteness and the Literary Imagination*, Toni Morrison launched an eloquent and provocative challenge to the privileged, naturalized "whiteness" of American literature. Expanding on her earlier groundbreaking *Michigan Quarterly* article, Morrison rejected the assumption that "traditional, canonical American literature is free of, uninformed, and unshaped by the four-hundred-year-old presence of, first, Africans and then African-Americans in the United States."[9] She made explicit that which had been implicit in American literary study from the start. "There seems to be a more or less tacit agreement among literary scholars," Morrison wrote, that, because American literature has been clearly the preserve "of white male views, genius, and power, those views, genius and power are without relationship to and are removed from the overwhelming presence of black people in the United States."[10] "The contemplation of this black presence," Morrison argues, "is central to any understanding of our national literature and should not be permitted to hover at the margins of the literary imagination."[11] Analyzing works by Poe, Hawthorne, Melville, Twain, Cather, and Hemingway, among others, *Playing in the Dark* challenged scholars to examine whiteness as an imaginative, social, and literary construction, to explore the ways in which "embedded assumptions of racial (not racist) language work in the literary enter- prise that hopes and sometimes claims to be 'humanistic.' "[12] *Playing in the Dark* put the construction of "whiteness" on the table to be investigated, analyzed, punctured and probed. Morrison's book offered a set of questions and an agenda for research that resonated with a number of projects already under way (including my own)[13] and that also helped spark myriad new publications—including the volume at hand, Henry Wonham's *Criticism and the Color Line*.

The importance of this approach, however, was far from universally recognized. As Eric J. Sundquist observed in 1993 in *To Wake the Nations: Race in the Making of American Literature*, "it remains difficult for many readers to overcome their fundamental conception of 'American' literature as solely Anglo-European in inspiration and authorship, to which may then be added an appropriate number of valuable 'ethnic' or 'minority' texts."[14] Morrison, Sundquist, and I were sug- gesting that these divisions failed to do justice to the complex roots of American culture.

This argument did not burst onto the scene full-blown in the 1990s. Indeed, as early as 1970 Ralph Ellison had commented on white Americans' absurd self- delusions "over the true interrelatedess of blackness and whiteness."[15] In 1987, as I have noted, Toni Morrison laid important groundwork in "Unspeakable Things Unspoken" (reprinted, in part, in this volume) and Sundquist prepared the way as well in the late 1980s both with his own publications on Twain and Faulkner, and the essay collection on Stowe that he edited.[16] In a 1986 essay (in Sundquist's Stowe anthology) entitled "Sharing the Thunder: The Literary Exchanges of Harriet Beecher Stowe, Henry Bibb, and Frederick Douglass," Robert Stepto demonstrated the importance of investigating the African-American roots of canonical American fiction, a move that scholars would soon make with increasing frequency.[17]

Two other American critics pursued some preliminary explorations of this territory in the late 1980s as well. In his final chapter of *The Unusable Past: Theory and the Study of American Literature* (1986), for example, Russell Reising asked how the American Renaissance would look if we posited Frederick Douglass as central to it. In his imaginative juxtaposition of analyses of passages from Douglass and Thoreau in which both writers explore "America's blindness to its own darker truths,"[18] Reising demonstrates affinities and intersections previously missing, for the most part, from discussions of either writer. Reising argues that Douglass's life, his works, the institution of slavery and "the struggle against slavery waged by black and white alike are the material, social, and political basis on which the works of other major writers of the American Renaissance are founded. The dynamics of slavery made [their works] possible."[19] Aldon Lynn Nielson's 1988 book, *Reading Race: White American Poets and Racial Discourse in the Twentieth Century*, was another early study that argued that ideas about race played an important role in shaping canonical American literature, and a vein mined as well by several of the contributors to the 1989 volume *Slavery and the Literary Imagination*, edited by Deborah E. McDowell and Arnold Rampersad.[20] But if the 1980s brought a handful of essays and books, the early 1990s positively exploded with literary studies in this mode.

In the early 1990s a number of critics in addition to myself took up Morrison's challenge to examine mainstream American "literature for the impact Afro-American presence has had on the structure of the work, the linguistic practice, and fictional enterprise in which it is engaged."[21] Dana Nelson's *The Word in Black and White: Reading 'Race' in American Literature 1638–1867* (1992) examined the ways in which seventeenth-, eighteenth- and early nineteenth-century white writers constructed versions of their own identity (and of American identity) by defining themselves as unlike various racial and ethnic "others"; Nelson offered fresh insight into familiar writers such as Cotton Mather, James Fenimore Cooper, William Gilmore Simms, and Catharine Maria Sedgwick.[22] Sterling Stuckey in *Going Through the Storm: The Influence of African American Art in History* (1994), Eric Sundquist in *To Wake the Nations* (1993), and Viola Sachs in *L'Imaginaire Melville* (1992) demonstrated Herman Melville's deep interest in African customs, myth, languages and traditions, and pointed out the African influences on works such as *Moby-Dick* and the short story "Benito Cereno."[23] (Sachs, for example, has uncovered numerous references to the Yoruba god Lebga in *Moby-Dick*. Stuckey and Sundquist have examined the use of Ashanti drumming and treatment of the dead in "Benito Cereno," suggesting that the treatment of the corpse of the rich slaveholder Aranda in "Benito Cereno" was not a racist allusion to African savagery, as critics have argued, but rather, evidence of Melville's insight into Ashanti rituals and the shrewd political use his characters made of those traditions.) And in "*Moby-Dick* and American Slave Narrative" (1994), Michael Berthold argued for the centrality of African-American traditions to Melville's art.[24] While my own work explored the ways in which African-American voices and oral traditions shaped *Huckleberry Finn*, the 1990s brought essays on Twain by Werner Sollors and by Lawrence Howe which examined the influence of slave narratives on *Connecticut Yankee* and *Life on the Mississippi*.[25] And in *Black and White Strangers: Race and American Literary Realism* (1993) Kenneth W. Warren examined the way implicit assumptions about race illuminate the work of Henry James and William Dean Howells.[26]

Warren (like Nelson, Sundquist, Stuckey and Sachs) argued for the importance of investigating "the mutually constitutive construction of 'black' and 'white' texts in American literature."[27] "Concerns about 'race' may structure our American texts, even when those texts are not 'about' race in any substantive way," Warren maintains. "For James," he observes, "the art of fiction is always a reflection on the social conditions necessary for sustaining fiction as high art."[28] Warren's book sheds new light on both the fiction of James and Howells and the society that shaped it and that it helped shape. Along the way he generates some intriguing insights into turn-of-the-century culture—such as the "inadvertent alliance between Northern realism and Southern romance in an assault on the political idealism of the New England tradition."[29]

In recent studies of canonical white twentieth-century figures, as well, unexpected links to African and African-American culture are being explored. While Robert Fleissner examined the influence of African myths on T. S. Eliot, David Chinitz demonstrated intriguing connections between Eliot's poetry and jazz.[30] The construction of whiteness on the part of Eliot as well as other canonical white writers in the twentieth-century was examined by Michael North in *The Dialect of Modernism: Race, Language & Twentieth-Century Literature* (1994). North explores the role of "racial masquerade" and "linguistic imitation" in the works of modernists including Gertrude Stein, T. S. Eliot, Ezra Pound and William Carlos Williams.[31] The course of modernist writing in America, North demonstrates, was shaped indelibly by the linguistic racial impersonations in which these writers engaged. Probing, for example, Pound's and Eliot's excursions into what they thought of as black dialect (lifted from "the world of Uncle Remus"), North observes that "preemptive mimicry of blacks is a traditional American device allowing whites to rebel against English culture and simultaneously use it to solidify their domination at home."[32] North also addresses the dynamics of William Carlos Williams's complicated attraction to African-American language and literature, as does Aldon L. Nielsen, in *Writing Between the Lines: Race and Intertextuality* (1994).[33] And in a series of articles culled from a longer work on the discourse of race in poetry, Rachel Blau DuPlessis examines some related issues not only in the work of Eliot, Pound and Williams, but also in the poetry of Vachel Lindsay, Wallace Stevens, Marianne Moore, Mina Loy, and Gertrude Stein.[34]

While Nielson, North and DuPlessis explore the complex relationship that white modernist poets like Pound, Eliot and Williams had to race-inflected language, Laura Doyle's *Bordering on the Body: The Race Mother in Modern Fiction* (1994) explores the centrality for white modernist novelists on both sides of the Atlantic—including James Joyce, Virginia Woolf and William Faulkner—

of what Doyle refers to as the concept of the "race mother."[35] Ideas of "racial patriarchy," according to Doyle, play a key role in shaping the cultural matrix of high modernism. As Carla Peterson's essay on Gertrude Stein in this volume demonstrates, discussions of white modernists can be enriched by examinations of the role played by ideas of blackness—on both the linguistic and thematic levels—in the genesis of their work.[36]

The whiteness of several forms of popular culture, as well as high culture, was similarly interrogated in the early 1990s, as familiar artifacts generally understood as white were shown to have roots more complicated than previously recognized. Joe Adamson and David Roediger, for example, explored the African roots of Bugs Bunny.[37] As Roediger puts it in a 1994 essay (building on Adamson's extended treatment of the subject in his 1990 book on Bugs Bunny),

> Bugs' heritage is anything but white. The verb "bugs" [as in] "annoys" or "vexes," helps name the cartoon hero. Its roots, like those of "hip," lie partly in Wolof speech.
>
> Moreover, the fantastic idea that a vulnerable and weak rabbit could be tough and tricky enough to menace those who menace him enters American culture, as the historian Franklin Rosemont observes, largely via Br'er Rabbit tales.
>
> These stories were told among various ethnic groups in West Africa, and further developed by American slaves before being popularized and bastardized by white collectors like Joel Chandler Harris. They were available both as literature and folklore to the white Southerner Tex Avery whose genius so helped to give us Bugs.[38]

And Howard L. Sacks and Judith Rose Sacks argued convincingly that a nineteenth-century black family in Ohio wrote "Dixie," the song that became known as the anthem of the Confederacy. Building their case from family records, public documents, and oral histories, the Sacks' *Way Up North in Dixie: A Black Family's Claim to the Confederate Anthem* (1993), detailed the history of the Snowdens, a farming family who performed banjo and fiddle tunes and popular songs for black and white audiences throughout rural central Ohio from the 1850s through the turn-of-the-century. The song's reputed white composer, Dan Emmett, heard the Snowdens sing the song and appropriated it as part of his minstrel show repertoire, bringing it to a wide and receptive public.[39]

The complex blend of appreciation and appropriation of black culture that the minstrel show represented was the subject of Eric Lott's *Love and Theft: Blackface Minstrelsy and the American Working Class* (1994), in which the role of the minstrel show in the construction of working-class white identity in nineteenth-century America receives the attention it has long deserved. Lott takes as his starting point the conventional view of the minstrel show: "While it was organized around the quite explicit 'borrowing' of black cultural materials for white dissemination, a borrowing that ultimately depended on the material relations of slavery, the minstrel show obscured these relations by pretending that slavery was amusing, right, and natural."[40] But, he continues, "I am not so sure that this is the end of the story."[41] In addition to being all of the above, Lott explains, "blackface performance, the first public acknowledgment by whites of black culture," required "small but significant crimes against settled ideas of racial demarcation" that have been little noticed before. Lott's larger concern is "how precariously nineteenth-century white working people lived their whiteness."[42]

Lott's stimulating study resonates with work in the field of history by David Roediger, whose important books *The Wages of Whiteness: Race and the Making of the American Working Class* (1991) and *Towards the Abolition of Whiteness* (1994) helped foreground whiteness on historians' agendas in 1990s.[43] As Roediger observes in the latter volume:

> When residents of the US talk about race, they too often talk only about African Americans, Native Americans, Hispanic Americans, and Asian Americans. If whites come into the discussion, it is only because they have "attitudes" towards nonwhites. Whites are assumed not to "have race," though they might be racists.[44]

But "the whiteness of white workers," Roediger demonstrates, "far from being natural and unchallengeable, is highly conflicted, burdensome, and even inhuman."[45] Roediger offers these essays—which investigate the construction of whiteness at various points in American labor history—as "political, as well as historical, interventions" designed to explode, as he puts it, "the idea that it is desirable or unavoidable to be white."[46] Roediger believes that "making whiteness, rather than simply white racism, the focus of study has had the effect of throwing into sharp relief the impact that the dominant racial identity in the US has had not only on the treatment of racial 'others' but also on the ways that whites think of themselves, of power, of pleasure, and of gender."[47]

Both whiteness as a social and political construct in Roediger's terms, and the kind of complex cultural exchange to which Lott paid such close attention, figure in the work of scholars from the humanities and the social sciences in the early 1990s who, in a variety of ways, asked the question, "Are Jews 'white'?" Eric Cheyfitz, for example, begins the introduction to his 1991 book, *The Poetics of Imperialism*, with the following story:

> When I was twenty, I went out for a while with a black woman, who lived with her mother and sisters in a housing project in Washington, D.C. One night, after I had been seeing her for a while, her mother asked me if I was Jewish. I said, simply, that I was. Her mother replied: I knew you weren't white.[48]

Cheyfitz both suggests "an identity between Afro-Americans, Jews, and Native Americans," and disrupts it "without disrupting it entirely," observing, that in "a book about the origins of imperialism in the Americas," it is worth noting that 1492 not only was the year of Columbus's voyage into the Caribbean but also of the defeat of the Moors in Spain and the expulsion of the Jews. "This conjunction of European violence against Indians, blacks, and Jews is, I assume, not a coincidence."[49]

While Cheyfitz leaves the question of the "whiteness" of Jews after the first few pages of his introduction, this issue is central to Sander Gilman's 1991 book, *The Jew's Body*. "For the eighteenth- and nineteenth-century scientist," Gilman writes, " 'the blackness' of the Jews" was assumed.[50] Gilman notes that the author of an 1850 tract that became "one of the most widely cited and republished

studies on race, for example, referred to "the African character of the Jew, his
muzzle-shaped mouth and face."[51] Both the color of their skin and the shape of
their nose resulted in Jews being "quite literally seen as black."[52] In his final
chapter, Gilman examines the genesis of the 1927 film *The Jazz Singer,* and the
image of Al Jolson playing a cantor's son at the film's close "on bended knee,
[singing] Mammy in black-face for his hugely successful Broadway opening."[53]
Gilman refers to "the long vaudeville tradition of white performers putting on
black-face," and then returns to the question he asked in his chapter on the nose
job:

> Are Jews white? Or do they become white when they . . . acculturate into American
> society, so identifying with the ideals of "American" life, with all its evocation of
> race, that they—at least in their own mind's eye—become white? Does blackface
> make everyone who puts it on white?[54]

In his 1992 article, "Blackface, White Noise: The Jewish Jazz Singer Finds His
Voice," Michael Rogin further explores the complex matrix involving whiteness,
blackness and Jewishness in *The Jazz Singer,* a film which, Rogin observes,
"appropriated an imaginary blackness to Americanize the immigrant son."[55] And
in her innovative 1994 essay "How Did Jews Become White Folks?" anthropolo-
gist Karen Brodkin Sacks explores the economic, social, and psychological impact
of post–World War II changes in real estate practices on Jewish and black
Americans.[56]

Historians' interrogation of "whiteness" in the early 1990s took primarily one
of two forms: 1) explorations of the dynamics of the construction of "white"
identity along the lines suggested by Roediger (Alexander Saxton's *The Rise
and Fall of the White Republic: Class Politics and Mass Culture in Nineteenth-
Century America* [1990] is a key work in this vein);[57] and 2) investigations of
African-American roots of mainstream (and supposedly "white") American culture. Studies in this second category built, of course, on the earlier extremely
valuable work of Melville Herskovits and Peter Wood well as on the broad-
ranging investigations of Sidney Kaplan.[58] Herskovits, some fifty years ago, had
argued in *The Myth of the Negro Past* that the brutality of the Atlantic slave
trade and the oppressions of American bondage did not destroy the African
cultural heritage; aspects of African culture (such as language use), Herskovits
argued, both survived in the African-American community in the twentieth-
century, and influenced aspects of mainstream culture as well; Wood, twenty
years ago in *Black Majority: Negroes in Colonial South Carolina from 1670
Through the Stono Rebellion,* demonstrated the large number of African contributions to colonial American agriculture, animal husbandry, and other fields—
including rice cultivation, cattle breeding, open grazing, basketry, medicinal
practices, and, in certain regions (particularly South Carolina), boat building,
fishing, hunting and trapping, while Kaplan (in several books and more than
fifty articles written over the last forty years) explored the African-American
presence in whaling and shoe manufacturing, classical American painting, and
military history. In the 1990s this line of research is being pursued by at least

two historians and a folklorist: John Edward Philips, in his essay, "The African Heritage of White America" in *Africanisms in American Culture*, edited by Joseph E. Holloway (1990); William D. Piersen in *Black Legacy: America's Hidden Heritage* (1993), and Roger Abrahams in *Singing the Master: The Emergence of African-American Culture in the Plantation South* (1992).[59]

Philips's "The African Heritage of White America" provides a useful summary of work on the subject prior to 1990, and a fruitful agenda for future research. Philips makes explicit some of the implications for white culture of research on African retentions in African-American culture undertaken by scholars in the 1970s and 1980s. Scholars who set out to investigate African influences on African-American culture, he notes, may have been less successful in their efforts "to document much that is specifically African about the way black culture in the United States differs today from white culture" than they have been at showing "how African influences are one important way in which American culture differs from European."[60] While he is fully aware of the complex and problematical challenges entailed in researching the subject, Philips believes that "when social scientists and historians begin to investigate systematically the survival of African culture among European-Americans they will discover that as much African culture survives now among whites as among blacks in the United States."[61] "For too long in this country," Philips notes, "whites have denied learning from blacks";[62] In addition, some blacks themselves have often been reluctant to acknowledge any links to Africa.[63] In 1969, in his essay "Clio with Soul," C. Vann Woodward observed, "so far as their culture is concerned, all Americans are part Negro."[64] But Philips maintains that rather than providing an agenda for historians, the comment passed largely unnoticed.

Philips gives a sample of the kinds of interesting links that scholars might pursue in the future, exploring, for example, potential connections between African singing and instrumental styles and bluegrass music.[65] While his method is of necessity conjectural, some of the fruits of it are intriguing, as his discussion of the potentially African roots of Jimmie Rodgers's "yodeling" demonstrates.[66] Philips also urges scholars to probe "white Africanisms" in the fields of religious belief (particularly in Pentecostal churches), traditions of Southern hospitality and courtesy, Southern foodways and cooking techniques, cowboys' cattle-herding techniques and migratory patterns, and language use. Arguing that "pride in their African heritage is something that white children should be taught along with blacks," Philips presses for "a more complex paradigm to explain African cultural retentions than has hitherto been advanced," one which recognizes the constant process of cultural exchange that has continued throughout American history.[67] Philips concludes:

> African culture among whites should not be treated as just an addendum to studies of blacks but must be included in the general curriculum of American studies. Black studies must not be allowed to remain segregated from American studies but must be integrated into our understanding of American society, for our understanding of white American society is incomplete without an understanding of the black, and African, impact on white America.[68]

Historian William D. Piersen's *Black Legacy: America's Hidden Heritage*
(1993) takes up this challenge, assembling an impressive compendium of ways
in which African culture shaped white American culture, particularly in the
South.[69] Culling intriguing examples from a vast range of primary sources to
make his case, Piersen explores cultural phenomena including storytelling, language use, music, manners, etiquette, folk medicine, folk beliefs, cooking styles,
and communal celebrations. Ambitious and boldly synthetic, *Black Legacy* suc-
ceeds in persuading the reader that "the legacy of African culture is important
to the understanding of America."[70]

Pierson documents a range of medical innovations for which slave medical
practitioners were responsible, including inoculation as a method of reducing the
seriousness of smallpox epidemics, and he credits slaves with increasing the
American pharmacopoeia stock with the addition of at least seventeen African
herbal drugs. Drawing on Gwendolyn Midlo Hall's book *Africans in Colonial
Louisiana* (1992),[71] he notes that slave practitioners regularly cured scurvy with
lemon juice thirteen years before European physicians advocated a similar cure.
Piersen also examines briefly the interpenetration of black and white speech
patterns and musical traditions.

In the book's strongest chapter, "A Resistance Too Civilized to Notice," Piersen
tracks the use of satiric traditions from Africa to the new world, pulling together
a dazzling set of specific examples.[72] He provides an overview of the use of
satirical songs (sometimes called "songs of derision" by other scholars) as a
mechanism of social control in eighteenth- and nineteenth-century African societies, noting the ways in which they allowed the weak to voice grievances against
the strong with impunity. Piersen explores the ways in which satirical songs
functioned in colonial African cultures, and then moves to their manifestations
in the antebellum American South. (Piersen's explorations of this subject in an
earlier article provided important background to my work on the African-American roots of Mark Twain's satirical treatment of racism.)

Roger Abrahams also explores the development of satirical performance rituals
in *Singing the Master: The Emergence of African-American Culture in the Plantation South* (1992). As Abrahams observes, we have yet to "describe effectively
the dynamic, expressive interrelations of black and white cultures living side by
side" in antebellum America.[73] His detailed study of antebellum corn-shucking
rituals provides a model of how such interactions might be probed by scholars
in the future. Underlying Abrahams's study is his agreement with W. J. Cash's
famous comment that "Negro entered into white man as profoundly as white
man entered into Negro—subtlely influencing every gesture, every word, every
emotion and idea, every attitude."[74] Building on work by John Szwed and others,
Abrahams suggests, for example, that while the American square dance grew
out of European dances such as the reel and the quadrille, the distinctly American
practice of calling square-dance figures in rhyme has its roots in corn-shucking
customs in the South, where in the plantation yard teams of slaves entertained
themselves and their masters with improvised rhymes as they husked corn.
Abrahams includes many of his primary materials as appendices, allowing the

reader to follow his interpretations from their sources. A great deal of the culture of the South, Abrahams argues, took shape not in the slave quarters or the Big House, but "in the yard between" the two, "in contested areas betwixt and between the two worlds."[75]

Abrahams's careful reexamination of the intercultural dynamics of slave holidays in the antebellum South, combined with Lott's reconsideration of the role of minstrelsy in the antebellum North, lays the groundwork for new understandings of mainstream American culture from the early nineteenth century to the present. For the traces left by slave holidays on American life, Abrahams observes, were far-reaching. The Beatles, he notes, "began their career as an English skiffle band" indebted to traditions of "the black skiffle and jug bands of the early twentieth century," which "were descendants of minstrel music. And the mountain string band emerged from the blackface stage, and in its wake, the bluegrass band: making them white imitations of a blackface imitation of a plantation musical group."[76] Other elements of popular culture Abrahams sees as coming out of the tradition shaped by the territory between the slave quarters and the big house include the "Grand Ole Opry," the "Ed Sullivan Show," and "Hee-Haw."

Some of the ironies and intricacies of this process of imitation and exchange are probed by David Roediger in his illuminating article, " 'Guineas,' 'Wiggers,' and the Dramas of Racialized Culture."[77] Roediger frames his discussion with the question Ralph Ellison asked two decades ago: "What, by the way, is one to make of a white youngster who, with a transistor radio, screaming a Stevie Wonder tune, glued to his ear, shouts racial epithets at black youngsters trying to swim at a public beach?" Roediger writes,

> The "Ellison question" humanizes key contradictions in white consciousness in the late twentieth century. We might wish to update the images: racist skinheads dancing to ska music; bluesman and Willie Horton advertisement promoter Lee Atwater; the white kid with an X hat and a rebel flag belt buckle; the precise coincidence of a national outpouring of love and sympathy for Magic Johnson with majority white support for David Duke in Louisiana elections.

What, Roediger asks, can be made of the impulses which at once and often in the same person lead to tremendous attraction toward 'nonwhite' cultures and toward hideous reassertions of whiteness as what the theorist and activist A. Sivanandan has called 'apolitical color'?"[78] The "tragic and dramatic complexities of the Ellison Question," Roediger notes, come to the fore when one examines the relatively recent coinage "wigger," meaning "white niggers" or "whites acting 'too black.' " Roediger tracks recent use of this term as "a slur against whites by whites" in Detroit, Michigan; Madison, Wisconsin; Warren, Ohio; Buffalo, New York, "and, most dramatically, in Morocco, Indiana, where the hiphop fashions and musical tastes of the young, rural white women recently resulted in their being called 'wiggers,' suspended from school, spat upon and threatened with death by white male students who demanded that they 'dress white.' "[79] The term has also been used affectionately by African Americans to "name whites seriously embracing African-American cultural forms and values, in contrast to 'wannabe' dabblers in the externalities of rap."[80] "The dynamics of cultural hybridity," Roediger notes, "have long featured much that is deeply problematic on the white side."[81] Roediger applauds the "highly concrete and historicized analyses" of the subject by scholars such as Eric Lott, bell hooks, Michael Rogin, and George Lipsitz.[82] While Roediger makes clear the difficulty of determining the ultimate social consequences of contemporary white youth's attraction to African-American popular culture, his discussion of white hiphop consumers makes the point that "to an unprecedented extent white youth are listening to an explicit critique, often an unsparing critique, of 'white' society."[83]

Like Piersen, Philips, and Abrahams, Roediger takes pains to trace the African roots of cultural phenomena recognized throughout the world as "modern U.S. culture."[84] When they identify with hip hop, Roediger writes, white rap fans are drawing unconsciously on an African heritage:

> The *hip* in hiphop, and in so much else in modern U.S. culture, was put there by Africans. As the extraordinary research of David Dalby and others has shown, enslaved Wolof speakers, from what is now Senegal, probably carried "hipi" meaning "to open ones eyes, to be aware of what is going on" to the New World, as early as the late 1600s. In the melting pot of African ethnicities which slavery and black creativity melded into African American culture, hip survived and prospered.
>
> Nearly three centuries later, it was still there, for whites to discover from jazz musicians. Even the beatnik ideal of the "hepcat" echoed the Wolof *hipi-kat* meaning "someone with eyes open." The millions of white 1960s Americans who searched out eye-opening experiences as "hippies" adopted that name because they grew up in a culture permeated with African influences, although they didn't know it.[85]

While Roediger explored the African roots of what is known throughout the world as "modern U.S. culture," scholars such as Josef Jarab and Renée Kemp-Rotan examined the African-American roots of what is known in the U.S. as "modern European culture"—phenomena including Czech poetry and French architecture. A major strand of twentieth-century Czech poetry, Jarab maintains, grew out of Czech responses to blues and jazz recordings by African Americans.[86] And Renée Kemp-Rotan has explored the influence of Josephine Baker on European architecture, planning, interior design, fashion, sculpture, graphic arts, painting, and photography.[87] Paul Gilroy's felicitous "image of ships in motion across the spaces between Europe, America, Africa, and the Caribbean as a central organizing symbol" for his important book, *The Black Atlantic: Modernity and Double Consciousness*,[88] suggests the continuous process of movement and cultural exchange that scholars are coming to understand as central not only to modern American culture, but to modern European culture as well. The roots of modern Czech poetry and of Le Corbusier's architectural plans turn out to be, like *Huck Finn* and the song "Dixie," less "white" than we thought they were.

Whiteness was interrogated in the early 1990s in fields as diverse as humor studies, linguistics, art history, material culture, rhetoric and communications, dance, and architecture. "Humorists" for example—at least as represented in anthologies of American humor—were assumed to be white: not a single black writer is represented in any of three major anthologies of American humor published in the first half of the twentieth century, each of which is between five hundred and eight hundred pages long.[89] If "humorists" were by definition white, the idea of a "Southern writer" clearly conjured up a white writer, as well.[90] The presumed whiteness of both "humorists" and "Southern writers" is challenged by *Roy Blount's Book of Southern Humor* (1994). "One thing we need to get straight about Southern humor—Southern culture generally," Blount ventures, "is that it is Africo-Celtic, or Celtico-African."[91] (Gene Lees made a similar observation in his 1994 book, *Cats of Any Color: Jazz in Black and White*. Lees believes that what he calls "the inherent poeticism of the South" is "the consequence of the marvelous and mad love of language of the Irish and a decorative, allusive indirection of expression that is a heritage of Africa.")[92] "The ferment that produced Southern culture," Blount continues,

> has been a profoundly confused struggle to determine who is less like New England— Sut Lovingood or Mudbone, Jerry Lee Lewis or Little Richard. . . . What it came down to was that blacks, after all the exploitation and co-optation they had submitted to, proved in the crunch to be *more Southern.*[93]

Blount points to "orality" as something that "black Southerners and white Southerners always had in common," in addition to things like "the soil and the sweet potatoes and the heat and the possums,"[94] noting the role of oral traditions in both the Celtic and African cultures that fed the culture of the South.

Blount says he wishes he could "pull leprechauns and Yoruba tricksters, Brother Dave Gardner and Zora Neale Hurston, George Wallace and Stokely Carmichael together into one unified theory of Crackro-African or Africo-Cracker mischief and indirection, but I'm not exegetical enough."[95] Here he is signifying slyly on the famous exchange he cited on the previous page: " 'Nigger, your breed ain't metaphysical,' wrote Robert Penn Warren in a 1945 poem—to which Sterling A. Brown riposted, 'Cracker, your breed ain't exegetical.' "[96] Blount's subtle move resonates nicely with his subsequent comment on the theory of "signifying" itself:

> I read *The Signifying Monkey,* Henry Louis Gates, Jr.'s book about African-American vernacular irony—which Gates with linguistic nicety calls "Signifyin(g)"—and its traditional uses in fostering tough intimacy among blacks and protecting slaves' pride against white violence. And I kept thinking it was a lot like Southern white irony and its traditional uses in fostering tough intimacy among whites and protecting them against each other and the overbearing North. (To the extent that Southern white irony is a defense against blacks, on the other hand, it is Br'er Bear trying to position himself against Br'er Rabbit.) "Cracking" is a Scots and Irish term for pointed boastful joshing and also an African-American synonym for "Signifyin(g)." One thing I hope this anthology bears out is the kinship, grossly abused but persistent, between the humor of the crackers and the humor of the brothers. Without gainsaying that "lynch" comes from a Virginia Irishman's name.[97]

The impact of African-American humor upon mainstream "white" American sensibilities was also explored by Mel Watkins in *On the Real Side: Laughing,*

*Lying and Signifying—the Underground Tradition of African-American Humor that Transformed American Culture from Slavery to Richard Pryor* (1994).[98] Watkins, for example, notes that many popular jokes and stage routines of white comics in the 1940s and 1950s were pirated from black performers.

> Comedians from downtown reportedly visited Apollo midnight shows regularly, accompanied by secretaries with steno pads . . . Pigmeat Markham insisted that he remembered Milton Berle as "this little white cat hardly out of knee pants" who "showed up with his scratch pad and pencil and started copying down every word I said." He also claimed that Joey Adams once met him downtown and told a bystander, "Here's a man I ought to give half my salary to. I stole my first act from him at the Apollo." And, according to Stump and Stumpy, Dean Martin and Jerry Lewis borrowed freely from their act and once actually offered to pay them for the material.[99]

Watkins offers a lucid and insightful analysis of the role black expressive culture played in shaping the fifties satire of Lenny Bruce (and, by extension, the subsequent forms of satire that developed out of it, including, as Watkins notes, the comedy of "Saturday Night Live"):

> His comic assault on the intrinsic absurdity of race relations, religious practices, police tyranny, and hypocrisy concerning sex and drugs cut to the core of America's social contradictions. Moreover, he delivered his satirical thrusts in a hip, impious style that was clearly removed from polite middle-class society. Mirroring the street wit of the black musicians and night people with whom he associated, it smacked of a profane contempt that was both alien and frightening to mainstream America. . . .
>
> The changes Bruce affected in mainstream comedy—without diminishing the overriding uniqueness or "genius" that even his critics acknowledged—parallel Elvis Presley's impact on popular music. Just as Presley, whom the critic Nelson George has called a "symbol of white Negroism," took on the phrasing and performance style of black R & B gospel singers, Bruce adopted aspects of the style and language of black hipsters and musicians. . . . He adopted the swagger and assertive impiety of the black Hipster in many of his routines and, more than any previous comedian on the mainstream stage, he evoked an iconoclasm and irreverence that mirrored the tempo and thrust of black street humor.[100]

Watkins' descriptions of the African-American roots of Bruce's twentieth-century satire resonate with my own research into the African-American roots of Mark Twain's nineteenth-century satire: clearly African-American traditions of irreverent, satirical social criticism have been leaving indelible marks on American humor for the last two hundred years.

African-American elements in "white" speech and language use were increasingly probed in the 1990s in the fields of linguistics and communications. J.L. Dillard's chapter on "The Development of Southern" in his 1992 book *A History of American English*, is a case in point. Expanding on his earlier influential study of "black English," here Dillard collates additional lively and compelling evidence from primary and secondary sources that affirm the ways in which African Americans influenced what has come to be thought of as Southern speech. Dillard summarizes linguists' research, for example, on the potential "Black influence" in the formation of *you all* (*y'all*), the most frequently cited indicator of Southern dialect.[101] He also makes the case for our conceiving "provisionally of a Black English-influenced 'early Southern', from approximately 1750–1830."[102] Although this book scales down some of the claims that made Dillard's earlier work so dramatic and controversial, its judicious tone and somewhat pedantic erudition amplify and solidify his arguments.

Other work in linguistics which charted adjacent territory includes *The African Heritage of American English* by Joseph E. Holloway and Winifred K. Vass (1993), and *Language Variation in North American English*, edited by A. Wayne Glowka and Donald M. Lance (1993). *The African Heritage of American English* builds on Lorenzo Dow Turner's important early work in this field, as well as on previous work by Dillard, Geneva Smitherman, and Vass. The book's objective is "to make available comprehensive lists of linguistic Africanisms drawn from a wide range of domains, including personal names, place names, language usage, foods, folklore, aesthetics and music."[103] The book's long list of "Africanisms in Contemporary American English" and their derivations includes bad-mouth, banana, banjo, "be with it," bogus, booboo, bronco, bug (as in to annoy, offend), coffee, cola, cool, "do one's thing," guff, gumbo, guy, honkie, hulla-balloo, jam (as in music), jazz, jiffy, jive, kooky, okay, okra, phony, rap, ruckus, tote, uh-huh, mhm, uuh-uh, yam, yackety-yak, and you all.[104] The jambalaya (another Africanism) that Holloway and Vass serve up includes such tasty tidbits as "bambi: Bantu *mumbambi*, one who lies down in order to hide; position of antelope fawn for concealment (cf. Walt Disney, *Bambi*)."[105] Noting the role of black cowboys in shaping American cattle culture and cowboy lore, they observe that the cowboy word "dogies" for cattle, "originated from Kimbundu, *kidogo*, a little something, and *dodo*, small. After the Civil War, when great cattle roundups began, black cowboys introduced such Africanisms to cowboy language and songs."[106]

Like many of the books discussed in this essay, *Language Variation in North American English: Research and Teaching* (edited by A. Wayne Glowka and Donald M. Lance, published by the MLA in 1993) was the fruit of initiatives in the scholarship and teaching of dialect that were launched throughout the preceding decade (as well as earlier). This volume is very much a 1990s artifact, however, in its readiness to foreground an increasingly sophisticated awareness of how black contributions to white American speech have changed the field of linguistics itself and what transpires in linguistics classrooms. Harold B. Allen, in "American English Enters Academe," describes some of his early efforts to get students to recognize the "various linguistic and cultural influences"—including what has become known as "Black vernacular English"—that helped make the American language "a variety of English distinct from British English."[107] Walt Wolfram observes, in his essay "Teaching the Grammar of Vernacular English," that "many of the students who previously abhorred the study of grammar have found genuine enthusiasm for examining the structures of vernacular dialects. In a real sense, studying the patterns of vernacular dialects has opened up a new life for the study of grammar."[108]

In the field of speech communication as well, "whiteness" and "white" American identity were foregrounded in the 1990s. Kathleen Hall Jamieson, for example, in *Dirty Politics: Deception, Distraction, and Democracy* (1992), masterfully examined the veiled racist verbal cues and visual subtexts designed to affect white voters' identification with particular candidates in political campaigns in the 1980s.[109] And Celeste Michelle Condit and John Louis Lucaites, in *Crafting Equality: America's Anglo-African Word* (1993), explored the ways in which the word "equality," an important "rhetorical foundation of the American national identity," has drawn its meaning since the 1760s from the interplay of black and white constructions of the term.[110]

The 1990s also brought new awareness of African-American influences on mainstream "white" American culture, fine arts, and classical dance, as well as foregrounding of the idea of "whiteness" itself in the arts. In the *Models in the Mind: African Prototypes in American Patchwork* (1992), Eli Leon argued that African motifs, organizational principles, and aesthetic values may shave shaped traditions of patchwork quilting in America that we have previously discussed solely in terms of their white antecedents.[111] The decade opened with the publication of two seminal volumes exploring the role of African Americans in shaping mainstream "white" American painting: Guy C. McElroy's *Facing History: The Black Image in American Art, 1710–1940* (1990) and Albert Boime's *The Art of Exclusion: Representing Blacks in the Nineteenth Century* (1990), and with the republication (in 1991) of the introduction to Sidney Kaplan's pioneering 1964 exhibition catalogue, *The Portrayal of the Negro in American Painting*.[112] All of these discussions examined African-American images in the work of canonical and popular (primarily white) American artists, a field which was enriched and expanded by the 1992 publication in this country of Jan Nederveen Pieterse's *White on Black: Images of Africa and Blacks in Western Popular Culture*.[113] In 1992 the concept of "whiteness" was interrogated in innovative ways by contemporary New York artists Kara Lynch, William Easton, Curlee Holton, Johan Grimonprez, and Ayisha Abraham in a show curated by Todd Ayoung entitled "The Perverse Double: Or, a *Cure* for the Discourse of Whiteness."[114] The early 1990s also brought Brenda Dixon-Gottschild's explorations of the role of African dance in shaping George Balanchine's American classical ballet.[115]

The move to recover and value the black influences on so-called white American culture was paralleled by a move to foreground the nature of white privilege and racism in American society. The early 1990s brought stimulating new work on this subject by scholars including Theodore Allen, Neil Foley, George Lipsitz, Jane Marcus, Vron Ware, Ruth Frankenberg, and bell hooks.

Theodore W. Allen, for example, in the first volume of *The Invention of the White Race* (1994), addressed the process by which the Irish "became white" in the United States and became enlisted as intermediaries in and supporters of the dominant culture's system of racial oppression and class privilege.[116] Neil Foley, in a study of the racial politics of the socialist organizers in central Texas in the early twentieth century, explored a chapter of Texas history in which Mexican-Americans found themselves constructed by Anglos as "almost white."[117]

George Lipsitz aptly observed in "The Possessive Investment in Whiteness: Racialized Social Democracy and the 'White' Problem in American Studies" (1995) that

> More than the product of private prejudices, whiteness emerged as a relevant category in American life largely because of realities created by slavery and segregation, by immigration restriction and Indian policy, by conquest and colonialism. A fictive identity of "whiteness" appeared in law as an abstraction, and it became actualized in everyday life in many ways. American economic and political life gave different racial groups unequal access to citizenship and property, while cultural practices including wild west shows, minstrel shows, racist images in advertising, and Hollywood films institutionalized racism by uniting ethnically diverse European-American audiences into an imagined community—one called into being through inscribed appeals to the solidarity of white supremacy.[118]

Lipsitz recognizes the crucial role cultural practices have often played "in prefiguring, presenting, and preserving political coalitions based on identification with the fiction of 'whiteness,' " helping "people who left Europe as Calabrians or Bohemians become something called 'whites' when they got to America, and how that designation made all the difference in the world."[119] But he cautions scholars against allowing a focus on "cultural stories" to mask the legal, social, political and economic "efforts from colonial times to the present to create a possessive investment in whiteness for European Americans."[120] Brilliantly synthetic and carefully researched, Lipsitz's ambitious exploration of the public policy that shaped the "racialization of experience, opportunities, and rewards in the U.S." offers scholars a challenging agenda for further research.

The early 1990s also brought several examinations of whiteness in a particularly gendered context, including two studies of the ways in which a series of upper-class and middle-class English women in the late 19th- and early 20th-centuries deconstructed and reshaped their sense of whiteness as a result of their contact with African Americans. Jane Marcus's engaging article, "Bonding and Bondage: Nancy Cunard and the Making of the *Negro Anthology*," raises these provocative questions:

> What does it mean when Nancy Cunard switches roles and performs "the white woman being lynched" when in reality black men were being lynched in the name of revenge for white woman's lost honor? Can the figure of the "white woman hanged, bound, mandacled, enslaved," ever disrupt in performance the racial fears of sexual mixing she wants to explode? Or is she unaware of the act she is putting on? . . . can she enact the erotics of the white slave along with the politics of the protest against racism?[121]

And Vron Ware, in *Beyond the Pale: White Women, Racism and History*, explores the role that Ida B. Wells and her attention to racial violence in turn-of-the-century America played in English reformers' constructions of their own identities as white women.[122]

The cognitive and emotional dimensions of American women's constructions of whiteness are the subjects of Ruth Frankenberg's "Whiteness and American-

ness: Explaining the Constructions of Race, Culture and Nation in White Women's
Life Narratives" (1994), and of Frankenberg's *White Women, Race Matters: The
Social Construction of Whiteness* (1993).[123] Frankenberg believes that

> the tasks of redefining and rehistoricizing "whiteness" are . . . vital concomitants of
> politicocultural struggles around race, from curriculum and canon transformation to
> the defense and extension of civil rights and racial equality. In other words, I would
> argue that critical engagements with the racial order must deconstruct and rearticulate
> whiteness at the same time as recentering the "others" upon whose existence the
> notion of whiteness depends.

Probing "the complex formation of white women's constructions of racialized
selves," Frankenberg tries to rehistoricize the categories of race and culture
insisting on antiessentialist conceptions of race, ethnicity, and culture, while at
the same time emphasizing that these categories are made materially 'real' within
matrices of power relations."[124] "It is critical to think clearly and carefully about
the parts white people play in the maintenance of the racial order," Frankenberg
believes, "and to ask how our locations in it—and our complicity with it—are
marked by other dimensions of our privilege and oppression, including class,
gender, and sexuality."[125]

As bell hooks notes in *Black Looks: Race and Representation* (1992):

> Whether they are able to enact it as a lived practice or not, many white folks active
> in anti-racist struggle today are able to acknowledge that all whites (as well as
> everyone else within white supremacist culture) have learned to overvalue "white-
> ness" even as they simultaneously learn to devalue blackness. They understand the
> need, at least intellectually, to alter their thinking. Central to this process of unlearning
> white supremacist attitudes and values is the destruction of the category of "white-
> ness."[126]

This goal is articulated with particular forthrightness in the inaugural 1993 issue
of the Cambridge-based journal *Race Traitor*:

> The white race consists of those who partake of the privileges of the white skin in
> this society. Its most wretched members share, in certain respects, a status higher
> than that of the most exalted persons excluded from it, in return for which they give
> their support to the system that degrades them. The key to solving the social problems
> of our age is to abolish the white race. Until that task is accomplished, there can
> be no universal reform, and even partial reform will prove elusive, because white
> influence permeates every issue in U.S. society, whether domestic or foreign. . . .
> So long as the white race exists, all movements against racism are doomed to failure.
> . . .The white race is a club, which enrolls certain people at birth, without their
> consent, and brings them up according to its rules. For the most part the members
> go through life accepting the benefits of membership without thinking about the
> costs. . . .*Race Traitor* seeks to dissolve the club, to break it apart, to explode it.[127]

The journal takes as its motto, *"Treason to whiteness is loyalty to humanity."*[128]

## Complicating "Blackness"

"I sit with Shakespeare and he winces not. Across the color line I move arm in arm with Balzac and Dumas. . . . I summon Aristotle and Aurelius and with what soul I will, and they come."

—W.E.B. Du Bois[129]

It wasn't unusual to be called "oreo" and "nigger" on the same day.

—Trey Ellis[130]

If the whiteness of mainstream American culture was axiomatic in the decades preceding the 1990s, the blackness of African-American culture was axiomatic as well. Courses and programs in black studies or Afro-American studies during this period played a crucial role in exposing a generation of students and future teachers to writers and texts previously excluded from the curriculum. Since American literature was defined, for the most part, as white literature, black writers were often taught in black studies courses, or not at all.[131] In these black studies courses, white writers and the literary conventions they employed were not considered crucial to the discussion; neither were white philosophical or spiritual traditions. (The white side of the family of black writers who were the children of interracial unions was generally an embarrassment, and was ignored as much as possible.)

The essentialist paradigms that accompanied the move to recover and value black writers and black texts in the 70s and 80s began to give way in the early 1990s to a more complex view of African-American culture.[132] Scholars increasingly analyzed the interpenetration of black and white culture in African-American letters and life. They examined more carefully the white roots of black American culture, and gave more careful scrutiny to the black roots of African-American culture, as well, replacing a vague homogenized idea of Africa with sensitivity to specific African cultures and peoples.

As Henry Louis Gates, Jr., observed in 1984,

In the case of the writer of African descent, his or her texts occupy spaces in at least two traditions: a European or American literary tradition, and one of the several related but distinct black traditions. The "heritage" of each black text written in a Western language is, then, a double heritage, two-toned, as it were. Its visual tones are white and black, and its aural tones are standard and vernacular.[133]

But Gates was relatively isolated in this position when he first voiced it. When his fellow scholars referred to "white" influences on "black" culture, they usually did so to condemn them. The 1990s, however, brought a new willingness to acknowledge and understand the interplay of traditions and voices that made African-American letters what they were. Often this involved re-evaluating the role that so-called "white" elements played in shaping "black" culture, as well as attending to dimensions of black culture previously ignored.

The historically Jim Crow nature of the curriculum had helped prompt scholars and teachers of black studies to emphasize the texts, writers and chapters of history that struck them as being the "most black" and the "least white." Understandably, certain categories of people and certain forms of writing were privileged as implicitly more authentic and therefore more worthy of study. In antebellum America it was the slave and slave narratives. In the early twentieth-century it was Southern, rural, working-class, vernacular speaking "folk" and fiction written about them (like Zora Neale Hurston's *Their Eyes Were Watching God*); or it was blues singers and the blues. (I might add that Franklin Frazier's devastating and depressing critique of black middle-class life in 1957 in *Black Bourgeoisie* may well have reinforced an already-in-place tendency on the part of scholars to avoid attending to black middle-class experience). Nevertheless, scholars of African-American culture in the early 1990s are increasingly asking, both directly and by implication, whether practices such as the ones I just described promoted a brand of essentialism that had the effect of redlining as subjects worthy of study writers, texts, ideas and communities that failed to fit the mold.

Ann duCille, for example, in *The Coupling Convention: Sex, Text and Black Women's Fiction*, observes that black women writers missed out on being in the earliest canon of American women writers because of their alleged preoccupation with race, and were excluded from the earliest canon of Afro-American writers because of their alleged preoccupation with gender. By the time scholars were ready to construct a canon of African-American women writers, many of the women and texts in duCille's study lost out a third time around because of the class of their protagonists (middle), their language (standard English, not earthy vernacular), their skin color (light or white) and, as duCille put it, the "so-called white" values, subjects, plots, and conventions (involving domesticity, marriage, and courtship) that were central to their fiction.[134] (It is also interesting that novels by black writers that feature only white characters—books which have long been largely ignored by critics—are now receiving attention. DuCille's extended discussion of Zora Neale Hurston's novel *Seraph on the Suwanee* in *The Coupling Convention* comes to mind, for example, as does the 1994 republication of Richard Wright's 1954 novel *Savage Holiday*, with an introduction by Gerald Early.)[135]

In the 1990s, the validation of the "folk" as the only "authentic" Africans Americans gave way to interest in middle-class blacks and middle-class black communities throughout history. Works in this vein include, in addition to du-Cille's book, impressive literary studies like Carla Peterson's *"Doers of the Word": African-American Women Writers and Speakers in the North, 1830–1880*, Claudia Tate's *Domestic Allegories of Political Desire*, Frances Foster's *Written by Herself*, as well as biographies of Nella Larsen, Frances Harper and Archibald Grimké by Thadious Davis, Melba Boyd, and Dickson Bruce, all of which were published within the last three years.[136] From historians, we have Adelaide Cromwell's 1994 book, *The Other Brahmins: Boston's Black Upper Class*,

*1750–1950*, and Willard B. Gatewood's 1990 book *Aristocrats of Color: The Black Elite, 1880–1920*, among others, and numerous recent studies of middle-class black professionals, including a history of black lawyers and studies of black men who work for IBM, of black women in academia, of black corporate executives, and of the challenges of black middle-class family life.[137]

And Trey Ellis, in a stimulating and controversial essay in *Callaloo* entitled "The New Black Aesthetic," explored the middle-class backgrounds of many of the most prominent black rappers, artists whose cultivation of underclass personae masks their own decidedly non-underclass roots.[138] He writes:

> One categorical mistake many make is thinking that rap is only created by the hard-core children of the slums; that the black middle-class is too busy buying Polo shirts and branding their arms with fraternity emblems to care about black street culture and politics. In fact, most of the big-name rappers are middle-class black kids. Mr. Simmon's father is a former professor of black history at Pace College and his mother a school teacher. His brother is Run of Run D.M.C.; L.L. Cool J grew up around the corner. Public Enemy, Bill Stephney, 27, vice-president of DefJam records, and *Village Voice* rap critic Harry Allen, 27, all met in an Afro-American studies course at Adelphi University on Long Island where they grew up. In fact, Public Enemy's chief, Chuck D., 28, is from Roosevelt, Long Island, sharing the suburban hometown with Eddie Murphy. Nevertheless, his group slugs out the hardest, most militant rap around. . . . They make you realize that you don't have to be black and poor to be black and angry.[139]

(This sentiment is supported by many of the black executives whose comments Ellis Cose recorded in his 1993 book, *The Rage of a Privileged Class.*) "We no longer need to deny or suppress any part of our complicated and sometimes contradictory cultural baggage to please either white people or black," Trey Ellis asserts. "The culturally mulatto *Cosby* girls are equally as black as a black teenage welfare mother. Neither side of the tracks should forget that."[140]

The paradigm that made the "slave narrative" the most truly "authentic" document of antebellum black America was challenged in the early 1990s, not only by the important work of scholars including Carla Peterson and Frances Foster, but also by the republication in 1993 (with a new introduction by William Andrews) of the diary of William Johnson, a free black in antebellum Natchez who became a successful businessman, and by books like Adele Logan Alexander's 1991 study, *Ambiguous Lives: Free Women of Color in Rural Georgia, 1789–1879*.[141] James O. Horton in *Free People of Color: Inside the African American Community* (1993) urged scholars to address "the complexity of black life" by paying greater attention to diversity within the black community than was paid in the past.[142] To this end, Horton addressed at length debates within the black community over how to negotiate the multiple identities imposed by gender, color, and nationality, and how blacks and various immigrant groups in Northern cities constructed each other and their world.

Our understanding of diversity within African-American culture was enriched as well in the 1990s by research on Afro-Dutch communities in New York and New Jersey in the seventeenth, eighteen and nineteenth centuries, and by the publication of autobiographical and analytical narratives of African-American Jews.[143]

In the 1990s, scholars became increasingly interested in the interplay of intellectual traditions and voices that shaped African-American letters. Often this involved reevaluating the role that so-called "white" elements played in shaping "black" culture. Michel Fabre's 1990 study, *Richard Wright: Books and Writers*, a fascinating examination of Richard Wright's reading, for example, documented Wright's response to a wide range of white writers from the U.S. and abroad, including Dostoevsky, Theodore Dreiser and Mark Twain.[144] Interviews I conducted in the early 1990s tracked Mark Twain's influence on black writers including Ralph Ellison, Toni Morrison, and David Bradley.[145] The influence of Herman Melville on Bradley's fiction and on fiction by other contemporary black writers is the subject of his essay, "Our Crowd, Their Crowd, and *Moby-Dick*."[146] David Levering Lewis, in his magisterial biography of W.E.B. Du Bois, added depth and texture to our understanding of the role of such figures as William James, George Santayanna, Josiah Royce, and Nathaniel Shaler on Du Bois's intellectual development.[147] Richard Yarborough demonstrated that *Uncle Tom's Cabin* influenced fiction by African Americans.[148] Ann duCille suggested that William Wells Brown's novel *Clotel* "talked back" to the sentimental fiction of Catharine Maria Sedgwick and Lydia Maria Child.[149] And in work published in the last two years, Phillip Richards and Carla Peterson join duCille in arguing that traditions of white evangelical writing are crucial to understanding the work of black writers Phillis Wheatley, Frances Harper, Emma Dunham Kelley, Amelia Johnson, and others.[150]

"In some cases, the cross-race influence is direct and easily traced," Ann Douglas observes in *Terrible Honesty: Mongrel Manhattan in the 1920s* after commenting that "the perfectly scanned and passionate poems of Countee Cullen sometimes read like companion pieces to the metaphorical, emotion-drenched, highly crafted poetry of Edna St. Vincent Millay."

> Cullen wrote his master's thesis at New York University on Millay, and attended her poetry readings; Millay shared with him a lifelong commitment to the Romantic poets, who had been banished from favor by the white male literary elite. . . . Hart Crane and Jean Toomer were friends who read each other's work, and McKay was conversant with Eliot's poetry.[151]

"Black and white metropolitans," Douglas concludes, "stood on shared ground."[152]

Michael Eric Dyson reminds us that "Ellison owed the habit of a critical style of reading, and the title of his first book of essays, to T. S. Eliot," and that "Baldwin's essays draw equally from the gospel sensibilities and moral trajectory of the black sermon and the elegant expression of the King James Bible."[153] Dyson himself, a dynamic critic of contemporary African-American culture, tracks his own sensitivity to the nuances of language, literature, and learning to a neighbor's unexpected gift of the Harvard Classics when Dyson was in his early teens, making him "the only boy on my block, and undoubtedly in my entire ghetto neighborhood, who simultaneously devoured Motown's music and Dana's *Two Years Before the Mast*."[154] As Dyson comments in his book *Reflecting Black* (1993):

> As mature African-American scholars, teachers, students and citizens, we must embrace the rich and varied racial past that has contributed to our making. We must also acknowledge the profound degree to which we have alternately enjoyed and endured a terrible but sometimes fruitful symbiosis with European-American culture, how we have helped shape many of its cultural gifts to the world, even against its will, and how those expressions emerged in the crucible and turmoil of our uniquely African-American experience.[155]

If white *literary* and *spiritual* foremothers and forefathers of black writers received more attention from scholars, actual white ancestors and the often complicated responses they evoked from offspring defined as "black" by the pervasive "one-drop rule" received more attention as well. Adrian Piper, for example, in her incisive and creative 1992 essay, "Passing for White, Passing for Black," fore-grounded the complexities of owning a dual heritage, as did Maureen T. Reddy in *Crossing the Color Line: Race, Parenting and Culture* (1994), Lise Funderburg in *Black, White, Other: Biracial Americans Talk about Race and Identity* (1994), Naomi Zack in *Race and Mixed Race* (1994), Shirlee Taylor Haizlipp in *The Sweeter the Juice* (1994), and many of the contributors to Gerald Early's stimulat-ing 1993 anthology, *Lure and Loathing: Essays on Race, Identity, and the Ambiva-lence of Assimilation*.[156] A related issue—the ironies, absurdities, and unreal realities of the racial classification system of the United States—was the subject of F. James Davis's 1991 book, *Who is Black? One Nation's Definition*.[157]

A number of books published during the last few years point to an increasingly sophisticated awareness of the multiplicity of specific African cultures that helped shape African-American and American life. The essays in Joseph Holloway's important edited volume, *Africanisms in American Culture*, Holloway's subse-quent book, *The African Heritage of American English* (co-authored by Winifred Vass), John Thornton's book *Africa and Africans in the Making of the Atlantic World*, Salikoko Mufwene and Nancy Condon's book, *Africanisms in Afro-American Language Variations*, and many of the essays in Sterling Stuckey's *Going Through the Storm* explore in all their specificity the distinct and differenti-ated African ethnic, linguistic and religious traditions that shaped African-Ameri-can and American life.[158] Scholars' understanding of the complexities of African cultures and their relationship to African-American history and thought was also increased in the late 1980s and early 1990s by Kwame Anthony Appiah's *In My Father's House: Africa in the Philosophy of Culture*, V.Y. Mudimbe's *The Invention of Africa* and *The Idea of Africa*, and Bernard Makhosezwe Magubane's *The Ties that Bind: African-American Consciousness of Africa*.[159]

The 1990s also brought new attention to dimensions of black expressive culture previously neglected as subjects for serious study. Rap, for example, was exam-ined by Houston Baker in *Black Studies, Rap and the Academy*, by Tricia Rose in *Black Noise*, and by Gregory Stephens in "Interracial Dialogue in Rap

Music."[160] The politics of black hair was among the subjects that Kobena Mercer explored in his 1994 book *Welcome to the Jungle: New Positions in Black Cultural Studies*, and the topic was addressed as well in 1994 by scholars including Tricia Rose, Elizabeth Alexander, Farrah Griffin and Robin D. G. Kelley.[161] Other innovative discussions of black expressive culture in the 1990s include Farrah Jasmine Griffin's *"Who Set You Flowin?" The African-American Migration Narrative* and Glen Alyn's *I Say Me For a Parable: The Oral Autobiography of Mance Lipscomb, Texas Bluesman*.[162] Given the world-wide popularity among young people of rap, braids, and the blues, scholars' insights into these forms of African-American expressive culture may help elucidate the dynamics of international youth culture in the future.

And finally, for some scholars the process of complicating "blackness" in the 1990s occasionally entailed being provocative and "impertinent."[163] "What is black culture?" asked David L. Smith in 1994:

> When Wynton Marsalis plays a Haydn concerto or Leontyne Price sings a Verdi opera, is that black culture? Similarly, when Dr. John plays the blues or Travis Tritt sings soul, is that black culture? In all these cases our answer is probably no. Yet black people relish a game invented by James Naismith, a white man. Don't we commonly accept basketball as part of black culture? . . . .Is participation in black culture a biological privilege, or can anybody join? Conversely, is black culture obligatory for black people, and does blackness preclude them from mastering non-black cultural modes? Such questions are impertinent, because in the absence of fundamental definitions, they cannot be answered.[164]

Building on the "pragmatist spirit" articulated by Cornel West in *The American Evasion of Philosophy*, Smith argues that "we ought to abandon attempts to understand race and blackness in terms of foundations and definitional certainty. Instead, we should take our actual experience of race and blackness as our starting point."[165] Acknowledging "openly the arbitrariness of racial categories will be an important, though not sufficient, step toward the demystification of America's exploitative racial culture."[166] The challenge, Smith writes, "is to understand what race is, how it functions, and ultimately to theorize how we might endeavor within a culture bound by race to subvert the subordinating strictures that race was designed to perpetuate."[167] Or, as West put it in 1993:

> New World African modernity radically interrogates and creatively appropriates Euro-American modernity by examining how "race" and "Africa"—themselves modern European constructs—yield insights and blindnesses, springboards and road-blocks for our understanding of multivarious and multileveled modernities.[168]

## Remapping American Culture

The American synthesis has an inevitable Anglo-Saxon coloration.

—Arthur Schlesinger, Jr.[169]

The monolith is a myth; the "white man's land" even more mythical, and the multicultural nature of America is a fact from its very inception.

—Maghan Keita[170]

"Staring at one another across the void of American identity," Ken Warren wrote in *Black and White Strangers,* "African and European Americans have been constructing themselves and each other, each side trying to lay claim to an unchallenged cultural legacy and each failing (to paraphrase Twain) to prove unambiguous title. As each side strives to construct a *sui generis* account of its own heritage, the Other insists upon emerging in unexpected and embarrassing places."[171] Clearly American culture always was, and continues to be, in Albert Murray's phrase, "incontestably mulatto."[172]

But the "incontestably mulatto" nature of American culture continues to be resisted in some quarters. "The WASP character is the American character," trumpeted Richard Brookhiser in his 1991 book, *The Way of the WASP.*[173] "The U.S. has always been an Anglo-Saxon civilization," declared Laurence Auster in his apocalyptic 1990 book, *The Path of National Suicide: An Essay on Immigration and Multiculturalism.*[174] Auster and Brookhiser fail to understand that what they refer to as the white Anglo-Saxon Protestant civilization of the U.S. was itself shaped from the start by people and traditions who were not white, nor Anglo-Saxon, nor Protestant. American culture has always been multicultural, and rather than some newfangled plot by "tenured radicals," as some have charged, the effort to move the stories we tell about who we are closer to the realities of who we are and who we've been is fueled more by a desire for truth and accuracy than it is fueled by any political agenda.

If we apply to our culture the "one drop" rule that in the United States has long classified anyone with one drop of black blood as black, then all of American culture is black. But well into the twentieth century, as James Horton notes, "white Americans continued to deny, yet exhibit, the complexity of their cultural heritage."[175] The racism and myopia that have allowed this denial to continue should be examined not just in black-studies courses but throughout the curriculum. The influence of white figures and texts on African-American writers and thinkers should be examined throughout the curriculum as well. We need to formulate new ways of addressing such issues as influence, exchange, appropriation, "hommage," intertextual dialogue, "signifying," "capping," borrowing, theft, synergy and cross-fertilization.[176] "Rather than mourning the loss of some putative ancestral purity," Henry Louis Gates, Jr., writes in *Loose Canons: Notes on the Culture Wars,* "we can recognize what's valuable, resilient, even cohesive in the hybrid and variegated nature of our modernity. . . . For whatever the outcome of the culture wars in the academy, the world we live in is multicultural already. Mixing and hybridity are the rule, not the exception."[177] This is a fact that we can no longer bury or dismiss. It is by understanding and celebrating the hybridity of mainstream American culture, and acknowledging the multicultural tributaries that have fed that mainstream, that we can collectively forge what Gates refers to as "a new, and vital, common American culture in the twenty-first century."

We must learn to reclaim our complex roots while not ignoring the history of racism that allowed us, for over two hundred years, to ignore and deny who and what we really were all along. We must learn to appreciate the distinctive blend of cultural traditions that shaped us while simultaneously working to dismantle the paradigms that prevented (and continue to prevent) so many African Americans from receiving credit and respect for all they did (and do) to create that common culture known as "American" throughout the world.

We need to come to terms with how the racism that denied African-Americans respect, rights, and agency for hundreds of years deformed scholars' understanding of the dynamics of twentieth-century life and thought, not only in the U.S. but throughout the world. How, for example, did Europeans as well as Americans disengage themselves from the nineteenth-century values of the Victorian era? Susan Curtis's 1994 cultural biography of Scott Joplin leaves the reader with the sense that any explanation that leaves out the effects of ragtime is of necessity partial and incomplete.[178] And how has our understanding of "modernity" been hobbled by our failure to understand the transatlantic exchanges so lucidly explored in 1993 by Paul Gilroy? Modernity, like the musical transformations Gilroy tracks around the globe, is the product of "untidy elements in a story of hybridisation and intermixture that inevitably disappoints the desire for cultural and therefore racial purity, whatever its source."[179]

The first years of the last decade of the twentieth century may have brought the withering away of simplistic essentialist notions of racial identity as well as increasingly sophisticated understandings of how power relations built on antiquated, discredited assumptions of racial difference sustain and perpetuate themselves. As the twentieth century draws to a close, however, scholars may find their work increasingly at odds with the vision of America's past and present promoted by popular demagogues nostalgic for a time when the "whiteness" of American culture was assumed, and when white privilege went unnamed, unexamined, unchallenged. In such an atmosphere, in which overt and coded racist policies are routinely sanctioned, and in which truth and justice are dismissed for political ends, scholars' efforts to revise the stories we tell about who we are to reflect what we've learned about where we've been are all the more important. We are now and have always been a culture in which a vast range of voices and traditions have constantly shaped each other in profound ways. Our teaching and our scholarship must take into account our increasingly complex understanding of what our common culture is and how it evolved. Doing so will force us to examine how an unequal distribution not of talent, but of power allowed a patently false monocultural myth to mask and distort a multicultural reality. The new vision of our culture will be truer than any we've had before—and more interesting. It will also be a healthier base on which to build our society's future. Forging such a vision may not be easy, but it is a challenge we should be eager to embrace.[180]

## Notes

Portions of this essay were presented between September 1994 and April 1995 as the Butler Lecture sponsored by the Bertrand Library, Bucknell University; at a conference on "The Question of Race in the Americas" sponsored by the Women's Studies Program, University of Pennsylvania; as the keynote talk at a conference on "Multiculturalism in Modern America" sponsored by the U.S.I.S. and the Turkish American Studies Association, in Çesme, Turkey;

at the Annenberg School of Communications at the University of Pennsylvania, and as the Richardson Lecture sponsored by the American Studies Program of Georgetown University. I am grateful to scholars at all of these venues for their invaluable comments and criticisms. I also want to thank David Bradley, Emily Budick, Evan Carton, Robert Crunden, Joel Dinerstein, Michael Dyson, Milton Fisher, Neil Foley, Skip Gates, Ted Gordon, Betti-Sue Hertz, Jim Horton, Kathleen Hall Jamieson, Maghan Keita, George Lipsitz, Elizabeth Maguire, Jim Miller, Leslie Mitchner, Carla Peterson, Lillian Robinson, David Roediger, Arnold Rampersad, Jeffrey Rubin-Dorsky, David L. Smith, Danille Taylor-Guthrie, Karen Winkler, and Harry Wonham, for having shared their thoughts, their libraries, and their work-in-progress with me as generously as they did.

1. As I have acknowledged elsewhere, I track my awareness of the kinds of questions that indelibly shaped my research to a talk Bradley gave on *Huck Finn* in Hartford in 1985 that he titled "The First 'Nigger' Novel," in which he credited Twain with having written a seminal work of African-American literature. See Shelley Fisher Fishkin, *Was Huck Black? Mark Twain and African-American Voices* (New York: Oxford University Press, 1993) vii, 137.

2. The push toward multicultural education in the 1980s and 1990s sparked increased awareness of the interactions and interpenetration of a number of cultural traditions in addition to African-American, Anglo-American, and Euro-American: Latino, Asian-American, and Native American, to name a few. I would not want my decision to frame this essay in "black" and "white" terms to be interpreted as a denial of the importance of these other groups and traditions in our efforts to reformulate and reconfigure our cultural narratives; I am simply choosing to focus, at this time, on one particular aspect of a complex set of issues. Indeed, perhaps the most apt term for describing the new perspectives on American identity that current research requires is Gloria Anzaldúa's concept of "mestiza consciousness," an idea that came from Anzaldúa's efforts to describe an identity that blended Anglo, Spanish, Mexican and Indian cultures, languages and gene pools. See Gloria Anzaldúa, *Borderlands: La Frontera/The New Mestiza* (San Francisco: Spinsters/Aunt Lute, 1987). My own thoughts about the construction of cultural narratives have been deeply influenced by Anzaldúa's work and by the numerous conversations we have had on the subject over the last six years. My first public presentation of the ideas contained in this essay was in a paper entitled "America's Fear of her *Mestisaje*" that I delivered at a faculty colloquium (in which Anzaldúa also participated) at the Universidad Nacional Autónoma de México in Mexico City, June, 1992. My talk addressed, in part, the differences between a society like that of the U.S. that denied the "*mestisaje*" at its core, and a society like that of Mexico that made the idea of "*mestisaje*" central to its official cultural narratives.

3. LeRoi Jones (Amiri Baraka), *Blues People* (New York: William Morrow, 1963), 185.

4. Robert Farris Thompson, Lecture on "The Kongo Atlantic Tradition," University of Texas, Austin, 28 February 1992.

5. Dean Flower, "Desegregating the Syllabus," *Hudson Review* (Winter 1994): 683–684.

6. Lee Katterman, "In Search of an 'American' Literature: UM Scholar Argues that Emphasis on the British Tradition Creates Damaging Myths," *Research News* (University of Michigan) 41 (January–February 1990), 14–15. David Bradley described a similar phenomenon in "Black and American, 1982," *Esquire*, May 1982. Rpt. in William Vesterman, ed., *Essays for the '80s* (New York: Random House, 1987), 397–413. Also of

interest is the Modern Language Association survey released in December, 1994, "What's Being Taught in Survey Courses?: Findings from a 1990–1991 MLA Survey of English Departments," which generated widespread media attention for its finding that, as the *Los Angeles Times* put it, "Dead white men are alive and well and being widely taught in college English courses." (Amy Wallace, "Defenders of Shakespeare Do Protest Too Much, Study Finds," *Los Angeles Times*, 29 December 1994).

7. William A. Henry III, "Upside Down in the Groves of Academe," *Time* (1 April 1991): 66–69. The professor was Valerie Babb of Georgetown University.

8. George Lipsitz, "The Possessive Investment in Whiteness: Racialized Social Democracy and the 'White' Problem in American Studies," *American Quarterly* 47 (September 1995):1–2. As Richard Dyer observes, "white power secures its dominance by seeming not to be anything in particular" (quoted in Lipsitz, "The Possessive Investment in Whiteness," 7).

9. Toni Morrison, *Playing in the Dark: Whiteness and the Literary Imagination* (Cambridge: Harvard University Press, 1992), 4–5.

10. Ibid., 5.

11. Ibid.

12. Ibid., xii–xiii.

13. In December 1991, I presented some of my preliminary research on the role African-American voices had played in shaping Mark Twain's art at an English department colloquium at Princeton University, which Toni Morrison attended. It was the first time I had presented any of this material in public. Toni Morrison's strong encouragement—immediately after my talk, at the dinner which followed, and in subsequent correspondance and conversations—helped prompt me to shelve other projects and devote all of my time to this one. At dinner I remember her describing the ways in which my research resonated with arguments she made in her forthcoming book, *Playing in the Dark*. By the time *Playing in the Dark* came out in the spring of 1992, I had progressed sufficiently on my own research to have sent off the manuscript to Oxford. That summer I was able to insert references to relevant passages from *Playing in the Dark* into *Was Huck Black? Mark Twain and African-American Voices* before it went into production.

14. Eric Sundquist, *To Wake the Nations: Race in the Making of American Literature* (Cambridge: Harvard University Press, 1993), 7.

15. Ellison wrote, "The Negro looks at the white man and finds it difficult to believe that the 'grays'—a negro term for white people—can be so absurdly self-deluded over the true interrelatedness of blackness and whiteness." "Change the Joke and Slip the Yoke," *Partisan Review* 25 (Spring 1958): 212–222. Rpt. in Ralph Ellison, *Shadow and Act* (New York: Random House, 1964), 55. Another critic who attended to the "interrelatedness of blackness and whiteness" early in the game was French scholar Viola Sachs, who asked questions in this vein in works including *Le Blanc et le Noir Chez Melville et Faulkner* (Paris and the Hague: Mouton, 1974); *La Contre-Bible de Melville: Moby-Dick dechiffre* (Paris and the Hague: Mouton, 1975), *The Game of Creation: The Primeval Unlettered Language of Moby-Dick; or The Whale* (Paris: Edition de la Maison des Sciences de l'Homme, 1982), and *The Myth of America: Essays in the Structures of Literary Imagination* (Paris and the Hague: Mouton, 1973). See also Sachs, ed., *L'Imaginaire-Melville: A French Point of View* (Saint-Denis, France: University Press of Vincennes, 1992).

16. Toni Morrison, "Unspeakable Things Unspoken: The Afro-American Presence in American Literature," *Michigan Quarterly Review* 28 (Winter 1989): 1–34; Eric Sundquist, "Mark Twain and Homer Plessy," *Representations* 24 (Fall 1988). Rpt. in Susan Gillman and Forrest G. Robinson, eds., *Mark Twain's 'Pudd'nhead Wilson'* (Durham, N.C: Duke

University Press, 1990), 46–72; Eric Sundquist, "Faulkner, Race, and the Forms of American Fiction," in *Faulkner and Race: Faulkner and Yoknapatawpha*, ed. Doreen Fowler and Ann J. Abadie (Jackson: University Press of Mississippi, 1987), 1–34; Eric Sundquist, ed., *New Essays on 'Uncle Tom's Cabin'* (Cambridge and New York: Cambridge University Press, 1986). Other early studies which reflect aspects of the kind of approach Morrison urges include Sterling Brown's *The Negro in American Fiction* (Port Washington, N.Y.: Kennikat Press, 1937); Seymour Gross and John Edward Hardy, eds., *Images of the Negro in American Literature* (Chicago: University of Chicago Press, 1966); Jean Fagan Yellin's *The Intricate Knot: Black Figures in American Literature, 1776–1863* (New York: New York University Press, 1972); Carolyn Karcher's *Shadow over the Promised Land: Slavery, Race, and Violence in Melville's America* (Baton Rouge: Louisiana State University Press, 1980); and Michael Rogin's *Subversive Genealogies: The Politics and Art of Herman Melville* (Berkeley: University of California Press, 1985). Werner Sollors's pioneering book *Beyond Ethnicity: Consent and Descent in American Culture* (New York: Oxford University Press, 1986), as well as his edited collection, *The Invention of Ethnicity* (New York: Oxford University Press, 1989) must also be credited with helping to place on the agenda of contemporary scholars an issue that implicitly informs the studies discussed throughout this essay: the "constructed" nature of race and identity.

17. Robert Stepto, "Sharing the Thunder: The Literary Exchanges of Harriet Beecher Stowe, Henry Bibb, and Frederick Douglass," in Eric Sundquist, ed., *New Essays*, 135–154.

18. Russell Reising, *The Unusable Past: Theory and the Study of American Literature* (New York and London: Methuen, 1986), 267.

19. Ibid., 271.

20. Aldon Lynn Nielson, *Reading Race: White American Poets and Racial Discourse in the Twentieth Century* (Athens: University of Georgia Press, 1988); Deborah E. McDowell and Arnold Rampersad, eds., *Slavery and the Literary Imagination* (Baltimore: Johns Hopkins University Press, 1989).

21. Toni Morrison, "Unspeakable Things Unspoken," 19.

22. Dana Nelson, *The Word in Black and White: Reading 'Race' in American Literature, 1638–1867* (New York: Oxford University Press, 1992).

23. Sterling Stuckey, " 'Follow Your Leader': The Theme of Cannibalism in Melville's *Benito Cereno*," (1992) in *Going Through the Storm: The Influence of African American Art in History* (New York: Oxford University Press, 1994), 171–184; Eric Sundquist, "Melville, Delany, and New World Slavery," in *To Wake the Nations*, 135–221; Sachs, *L'Imaginaire-Melville*. Also relevant is the unpublished paper Sachs presented in Paris at an international meeting sponsored by the Laboratoire de Recherche sur L'Imaginaire Americain in the spring of 1993; the paper focused particularly on Legba allusions in *Moby-Dick*. Carolyn Karcher also offers some preliminary examinations of the role of issues of race in Melville's work in *Shadow over the Promised Land*, as does Michael Rogin in *Subversive Genealogies*.

24. Michael Berthold, "*Moby-Dick* and American Slave Narrative," *The Massachusetts Review* (Spring 1994): 135–148.

25. Werner Sollors, "Ethnicity," in *Critical Terms for Literary Study*, ed. Frank Lentricchia and Thomas McLaughlin (Chicago: University of Chicago Press, 1990), 288–305; Lawrence Howe, "Transcending the Limits of Experience: Mark Twain's *Life on the Mississippi*," *American Literature* 63 (September 1991): 420–439.

26. Kenneth W. Warren, *Black and White Strangers: Race and American Literary Realism* (Chicago: University of Chicago Press, 1993).

27. Ibid., 9.

28. Ibid., 10, 31.

29. Ibid., 15.

30. See Robert F. Fleissner, *T. S. Eliot and the Heritage of Africa* (New York: Peter Lang, 1992), and David Chinitz, "T. S. Eliot and the Cultural Divide," *PMLA* 110 (March 1995): 236–247, particularly 244–246.

31. Michael North, *The Dialect of Modernism: Race, Language & Twentieth-Century Literature* (New York: Oxford University Press, 1994), 3.

32. Ibid., 81.

33. Aldon L. Nielson, *Writing Between the Lines: Race and Intertextuality* (Athens: University of Georgia Press, 1994).

34. For discussions of Vachel Lindsay, T. S. Eliot, and Wallace Stevens, see Rachel Blau DuPlessis, " 'HOO, HOO, HOO': Some Episodes in the Construction of Modern Whiteness," *American Literature* 67 (December 1995). For discussions of Wallace Stevens, Marianne Moore, William Carlos Williams, Mina Loy, Gertrude Stein and Ezra Pound, see DuPlessis, " 'Darken Your Speech': Racialized Cultural Work in Stevens, Moore, Williams, Loy, Stein and Pound," in Aldon L. Nielsen, ed., *An Area of Act: Race and American Poetries and Poetics* (Urbana: University of Illinois Press, 1995). See also Charles Bernstein, "Professing Stein/Stein Professing," *Poetics Journal* 9 (1991): 44–50.

35. Doyle also examines treatment of the "race mother" figure by black novelists including Jean Toomer, Ralph Ellison and Toni Morrison. Laura Doyle, *Bordering on the Body: The Race Mother in Modern Fiction* (New York: Oxford University Press, 1994).

36. Carla Peterson, "The Remaking of Americans: Gertrude Stein and African-American Musical Traditions," in this volume.

37. Joe Adamson, *Bugs Bunny: Fifty Years and Only One Gray Hare*, prefaces by Friz Freleng and Chuck Jones (New York: Holt, 1990); David Roediger, "A Long Journey to the Hip Hop Nation," *St. Louis Post-Dispatch*, 18 March 1994.

38. Ibid.

39. Howard I. Sacks and Judith Rose Sacks, *Way up North in Dixie: A Black Family's Claim to the Confederate Anthem* (Washington, D.C.: Smithsonian Institution Press, 1993).

40. Eric Lott, *Love and Theft: Blackface Minstrelsy and the American Working Class* (New York: Oxford University Press, 1993), 3.

41. Ibid., 3–4.

42. Ibid., 4. Some similarly complex approaches to the minstrel show in American popular culture emerge in Saidya Hartman's book, *Performing Blackness* (forthcoming, Oxford University Press). Among the many interesting offshoots of Lott's central discussion is his suggestion that many chapters of "white" cultural history usually written without reference to race—such as the history of cultural styles among whites known generally as "bohemianism"—must take into account an ever-present racial subtext. (Lott, *Love and Theft*, 50–51).

43. David R. Roediger, *The Wages of Whiteness: Race and the Making of the American Working Class* (London and New York: Verso, 1991); David R. Roediger, *Towards the Abolition of Whiteness* (London and New York: Verso, 1994).

44. Roediger, *Towards the Abolition of Whiteness*, 12.

45. Ibid.

46. Ibid.

47. Ibid., 75. Roediger provides a useful overview of labor historians' responses to the issue of race in chapter 6 of *Towards the Abolition of Whiteness*, "The Crisis in Labor History: Race, Gender and the Replotting of the Working Class Past in the United States,"

69–81. Roediger notes that "the recent outpouring of work on African-American, Asian-American and Latino labor history further signals the possibility that a consideration of race will structure, and not just appear episodically in, new attempts at synthesis in US working class history" (75). Some of the works Roediger credits with moving the field in this direction that appeared in the early 1990s are: Rick Halpern, "Race, Ethnicity and the Union in the Chicago Stockyards, 1917–1922," *International Review of Social History* 37 (1992): 25–58; Iver Bernstein, *The New York City Draft Riots: Their Significance for American Society and Politics in the Age of the Civil War* (1990), Eric Arnesen, *Waterfront Workers of New Orleans, Race, Class and Politics* (1990), Eric Arnesen, "Rethinking the Historical Relationship between Black Workers and the Labor Movement," *Radical History Review* (1993); Wayne Durrill, *War of Another Kind: A Southern Community in the Great Rebellion* (1990), Nancy Quann Wickham, "Who Controls the Hiring Hall? The Struggle for Job Control in the ILWU during World War II," and Bruce Nelson, "Class and Race in the Crescent City: The ILWU from San Francisco to New Orleans," both in Steven Russwurm, ed., *The CIO's Left-Led Unions* (1992), 19–68; the essays in Robert Zieger, ed., *Organized Labor in the Twentieth Century South* (1991); Earl Lewis, *In Their Own Interest: Race, Class, and Power in Twentieth-Century Norfolk, Virginia* (1991); Joe William Trotter, *Coal, Class and Color: Blacks in Southern West Virginia, 1915–32* (1990); Robin D.G. Kelley, *Hammer and Hoe: Alabama Communists during the Great Depression* (1990) and " 'We Are Not What We Seem': Rethinking Black Working-Class Opposition in the Jim Crow South," *Journal of American History* 80 (June 1993): 75–113; Mario T. Garcia, "Border Proletarians: Mexican-Americans and the International Union of Mine, Mill and Smelter Workers, 1939–1946," in Robin Asher and Charles Stephenson, eds., *Labor Divided: Race and Ethnicity in United States Labor Struggles,* (1990), 83–104. (See Roediger, *Towards the Abolition of Whiteness,* 80–81).

48. Eric Cheyfitz, *The Poetics of Imperialism: Translation and Colonization from The Tempest to Tarzan* (New York: Oxford University Press, 1991), xii.

49. Ibid., xiii.

50. Sander Gilman, "The Jewish Nose: Are Jews White? or, The History of the Nose Job," in Gilman, *The Jew's Body* (New York and London: Routledge, 1991), 172.

51. Ibid., 204, 174. Gilman is quoting Robert Knox's *The Races of Men: A Fragment* (Philadelphia: Lea and Blanchard, 1850), 134.

52. Gilman, *The Jew's Body,* 174.

53. Ibid., 238.

54. Ibid.

55. Michael Rogin, "Blackface, White Noise: The Jewish Jazz Singer Finds his Voice," *Critical Inquiry* 18 (Spring 1992): 421. See also Rogin, " 'Democracy and Burnt Cork': The End of Blackface, the Beginning of Civil Rights," *Representations* 46 (Spring 1994): 1–34, and Rogin, "Making America Home: Racial Masquerade and Ethnic Assimilation in the Transition to Talking Pictures," *Journal of American History* 79 (December 1992): 1050–1077.

56. Karen Brodkin Sacks, "How Did Jews Become White Folks?" in Steven Gregory and Roger Sanjek, eds., *Race* (New Brunswick: Rutgers University Press, 1994).

57. Alexander Saxton, *The Rise and Fall of the White Republic: Class Politics and Mass Culture in Nineteenth-Century America* (London and New York: Verso, 1991).

58. Melville J. Herskovits, *The Myth of the Negro Past* (1941; rpt. Boston: Beacon Press, 1958); Peter Wood, *Black Majority: Negroes in Colonial South Carolina from 1670 through the Stono Rebellion* (New York: Alfred A. Knopf, 1974); Sidney Kaplan,

*American Studies in Black and White: Selected Essays, 1949–1989,* ed. Allan D. Austin (Amherst: University of Massachusetts Press, 1991). See also Mechal Sobel, *The World They Made Together: Black and White Values in Eighteenth-Century Virginia* (Princeton: Princeton University Press, 1987).

59. The publication of Kaplan's collected essays is further testimony to the renewed interest in this kind of research. See *American Studies in Black and White.*

60. John Edward Philips, "The African Heritage of White America," *Africanisms in American Culture* ed. Joseph E. Holloway (Bloomington: Indiana University Press, 1990), 226. Referring to studies like that which Winifred Vass pursued on place names, or that which Dena J. Epstein conducted on the history of the banjo, Philips observes, "Although their approach has done much to document the survival of African culture in the United States, it has ultimately documented as much African culture among whites as among blacks" (226).

61. Ibid., 227.

62. Ibid., 227–228.

63. The only articles from an earlier era that Philips recognizes as directly addressing this issue are Melville Herskovits's 1935 essay, "What Has Africa Given America?" and John A. Davis's 1964 article, "The Influence of Africans on American Culture." Summarizing the key points of these early forays into the subject, Philips notes that Herskovits mentioned areas of cultural influence including music (spirituals and jazz), speech (Southern dialect), Southern etiquette, cuisine and religious behavior (229). John A. Davis mentioned "the formal politeness and courtesy of the South" in passing but, "like most investigators he was concerned primarily with the influence of America on blacks" (229).

64. C. Vann Woodward, "Clio with Soul," *Journal of American History* 1 (June 1969): 17.

65. Philips, "The African Heritage of White America," 230.

66. "Yodeling is known to be common in many areas of Africa in addition to being similar to the 'field hollers' of African-American folk tradition. Thus we can postulate a partially African origin for Jimmie Rodgers's 'blues yodel' style of singing, so important in the development of country music. Rodgers grew up where blacks were in the majority, and his singing shows profound black influences in other respects as well as his yodeling. Although some musicologists try to draw a distinction between the 'true' yodel (found among whites and of European origin) and the falsetto leap (found only among blacks and from Africa), the use of falsetto leaps by such white country musicians as Jimmy Martin and of true yodels in Africa and among African-American singers shows that the distinction, if valid at all, is not relevant to race" (Philips, "The African Heritage of White America," 230).

67. Ibid., 236.

68. Ibid., 237.

69. William D. Piersen, *Black Legacy: America's Hidden Heritage* (Amherst: University of Massachusetts Press, 1993). Portions of my discussion of Piersen's book first appeared in my review of the book in *American Literature* 66 (September 1994): 616–617.

70. Piersen, *Black Legacy,* xv.

71. Gwendolyn Midlo Hall, *Africanisms in Colonial Louisiana* (Baton Rouge: Louisiana State University Press, 1992).

72. Piersen's pathbreaking 1977 article, "Puttin' On Ole Massa," first appeared in *African Folklore in the New World,* ed. Daniel J. Crowley (Austin: University of Texas Press, 1977). In *Black Legacy* Piersen expands on this earlier material in fascinating ways, and provides a real contribution to our understanding of the history of satire in America.

73. Roger Abrahams, *Singing the Master: The Emergence of African-American Culture in the Plantation South* (New York: Pantheon, 1992), xvii.

74. W. J. Cash, *The Mind of the South* (1942; rpt. New York: Vintage, 1963), ix.

75. Abrahams, *Singing the Master*, xxiii.

76. Ibid., 131–132. As Abrahams reminds us, it was Constance Rourke who first pointed out the central place of minstrelsy in American popular culture. See Rourke, *American Humor: A Study of National Character* (New York: Doubleday, 1931).

77. David Roediger, " 'Guineas,' 'Wiggers,' and the Dramas of Racialized Culture," forthcoming in *American Literary History*.

78. Ibid., 8–9. Roediger cites Ellison, "Little Man at Chehaw Station," *Going to the Territory* (New York: Random House, 1987, essay from 1977), 21 and A. Sivanandan, "Challenging Racism," in *Communities of Resistance: Writings on Black Struggles for Socialism* (London, 1990), 66.

79. Roediger, "Guineas, Wiggers," 10.

80. Ibid., 11.

81. Ibid., 14.

82. See Lott, *Love and Theft*, and "White Like Me: Imperial Whiteness and Racial Cross-Dressing" in Donald Pease and Amy Kaplan, eds., *Cultures of U.S. Imperialism* (Durham, N.C.: Duke University Press, 1993); Rogin, "Blackface, White Noise"; hooks, *Black Looks: Race and Representation* (Boston: South End Press, 1992); and Lipsitz, *Dangerous Crossroads: Popular Music, Postmodernism, and the Poetics of Place* (London: Verso, 1994).

83. Roediger, *Guineas, Wiggers*, 16. Interestingly, Mark Twain's earliest exposure to a scathing satirical critique of white society also came from a black performer, the slave named "Jerry" whom Twain called "the greatest orator in the country" in his essay, "Corn-Pone Opinions." See Shelley Fisher Fishkin, *Was Huck Black? Mark Twain and African-American Voices*, 53–76.

84. David Roediger, "A Long Journey to the Hip Hop Nation."

85. Ibid.

86. Josef Jarab, "Black Stars, Red Star, an the Blues" (Paper presented at the European Association for American Studies Conference, 6 April 1992); Seville, *The Black Columbiad: Defining Moments in African-American Literature and Culture*, ed. Werner Sollors and Maria Diedrich (Cambridge: Harvard University Press, 1994), 167–173.

87. Kemp Rotan's research for a forthcoming book is described in Mary Ann French's article, "A Hurting on the Soul," *The Washington Post*, 17 November 1944, Home Section, 14.

88. Paul Gilroy, *The Black Atlantic: Modernity and Double Consciousness* (Cambridge: Harvard University Press, 1993), 4.

89. All of the humorists in *Gems of Modern Wit and Humor*, with stories and an introduction by Robert J. Burdette (n.p.: 1903, L. G. Stahl) (514 pages); E. B. White and Katharine S. White, eds., *A Subtreasury of American Humor* (New York: Coward-McCann, Inc., 1941) (814 pages); and Louis Untermeyer, ed., *A Treasury of Laughter* (New York: Simon and Schuster, 1946) (712 pages) are white.

90. William Andrews observes that until relatively recently, "the history and criticism of southern literature in America proceeded from the unwritten assumption that the literature of the South was the product of white, predominantly male southerners. Black writers from the South belonged to a separate province of letters that was reconstructed into Negro American literature mainly by the literary historians and critics who taught in black colleges of the South." William Andrews, "Mark Twain, William Wells Brown, and the Problem of Authority in New South Writing," in *Southern Literature and Literary Theory*,

ed. Josephine Humphries (Athens: University of Georgia Press, 1990) 1. Andrews' current project, a boldly synthetic book entitled *Junctions on the Color Line: Interracial Dialogue in First-Person Southern Literature*, (forthcoming, Oxford University Press) promises to help reconfigure the field of Southern Studies by making African-American writers integral to that subset of American literature we call "Southern literature."

91. Roy Blount, Jr., *Roy Blount's Book of Southern Humor* (New York: Norton 1994), 27. Blount continues,

> According to the scholarly work *Cracker Culture: Celtic Ways in the Old South*, by Grady McWhiney, (which I believe in absolutely because it makes me feel less pale), the South was originally settled not predominantly by Anglo-Saxons (as was the North) but by wild, oral, whiskey-loving, unfastidious, tribal, horse-racing, government-hating, Wasp-scorned Irish and Welsh and Presbyterian Scotts. Who then brought in Africans. The ferment that produced Southern culture has not been a matter of Wasp civilization guiltily but angrily at odds with (while depending upon) enforced black labor. It has been a profoundly confused struggle to determine who was less like New England— Sut Lovingood or Mudbone, Jerry Lee Lewis or Little Richard. Crackers never did admit that they were oppressors. They could always put that off on Washington. (The fact that Washington, outside the embassies, is in most respects a Southern town, organized around the government instead of, say, sawmills, is something that I suppose Northerners might call an irony.) What it came down to was that blacks, after all the exploitation and co-optation they had submitted to, proved in the crunch to be *more Southern*.

92. Gene Lees, *Cats of Any Color: Jazz in Black and White* (New York: Oxford University Press, 1994), 13.

93. Roy Blount, Jr., *Roy Blount's Book of Southern Humor*, 27. Blount adds, "When Rob Slater's class of high school students in Winston-Salem, North Carolina, rebelled against a Northern-devised intelligence test by making up their own 'In Your Face Test of No Certain Skills' and sent it up to the testers, who scored C's and D's on it, I counted it as not just a racial but also a regional victory. One question was 'Who is buried in Grant's Tomb?' The correct answer was 'Your mama.' "

94. Ibid., 28.

95. Ibid., 29.

96. Ibid., 28.

97. Ibid., 29. Roger Abrahams has commented on the possible Celtic roots of the word "signifying" as Gates uses it and as it has been used in African-American oral tradition (Abrahams, personal communication, November 1994). Blount expands on common dimensions of Southern, African and Irish culture in the following passage: "To Southerners (as to Africans and Irishmen I have sat at tables with), language is the sound of the tongue and the mind clapping, with an understandable tendency to lose the beat, especially in print" (29).

98. Mel Watkins, *On the Real Side: Laughing, Lying and Signifying—the Underground Tradition of African-American Humor that Transformed American Culture from Slavery to Richard Pryor* (New York: Simon and Schuster, 1994). The complex racial exchange involved in the humor of the "Amos 'n' Andy" show, a topic that Watkins raises, was examined by other scholars in the 1990s as well. See Melvin Patrick Ely's *The Adventures of Amos 'n' Andy: A Social History of an American Phenomenon* (New York: The Free Press, 1991) and George Lipsitz's *Time Passages: Collective Memory and American Popular Culture* (Minneapolis: University of Minnesota Press, 1994), chapter 3, "The Meaning of Memory: Family, Class, and Ethnicity in Early Network Television," 39–75.

99. Mel Watkins, *On the Real Side*, 396.

100. Ibid., 485–486.

101. J. L. Dillard, "The Development of Southern," in Dillard, *A History of American English* (London: Longman, 1992), 93–96.

102. Ibid., 101.

103. Joseph Holloway and Winifred Vass, *The African Heritage of American English* (Bloomington: Indiana University Press, 1993) xiii.

104. Holloway and Vass also list "Africanisms in the Gullah dialect, Africanisms in American names, and words borrowed from African languages found in . . . non-Standard English" (xiii).

105. *The African Heritage of American English*, 137.

106. Ibid., 154.

107. Wayne A. Glowka and Donald M. Lance, eds, *Language Variation in North American English: Research and Teaching* (New York: Modern Language Association, 1993), 14.

108. Walt Wolfram, "Teaching the Grammar of Vernacular English," in *Language Variation*, 27.

109. Kathleen Hall Jamieson, *Dirty Politics: Deception, Distraction, and Democracy* (New York: Oxford University Press, 1992).

110. Celeste Michelle Condit and John Louis Lucaites, *Crafting Equality: America's Anglo-African Word* (Chicago: University of Chicago Press, 1993), xviii.

111. Eli Leon's *Models in the Mind: African Prototypes in American Patchwork* was the exhibition catalogue for an exhibit at the Diggs Gallery at Winston-Salem State University, Winston-Salem, North Carolina, in 1992.

112. Guy C. McElroy, *Facing History: The Black Image in American Art, 1710–1940* (San Franciso: Bedford Arts; Washington, DC: Corcoran Gallery of Art, 1990. Catalogue of Exhibition at Corcoran, 13 January–25 March 1990); Albert Boime, *The Art of Exclusion: Representing Blacks in the Nineteenth Century* (Washington: Smithsonian Institution Press, 1990), and Sidney Kaplan, *American Studies in Black and White* (1991). The recent volumes built, of course, on Hugh Honour's magisterial four-volume study, *The Image of the Black in Western Art*, originally published in 1976 (New York: William Morrow, foreword by Amadou Mahtar M'Bow.)

113. Jan Nederveen Pieterse's *White on Black: Images of Africa and Blacks in Western Popular Culture* (New Haven: Yale University Press, 1992).

114. "The Perverse Double: Or, a *Cure* for the Discourse of Whiteness" (Exhibition curated by Todd Ayoung, January 9–February 27, 1992, Longwood Arts Gallery, Bronx, New York. Sponsored by the Bronx Council on the Arts). I am grateful to Betti-Sue Hertz for making me aware of this exhibit and providing me with materials about it.

115. Brenda Dixon-Gottschild, "Stripping the Emperor: Africanisms in American Concert Dance." Paper presented at the American Studies Association Convention, 28 October 1994, Nashville) A version of this paper will appear in the forthcoming volume, *Looking Out: Perspectives on Dance and Criticism in a Multicultural World*, David Gere, Lewis Segal, Patrice Koelsch and Elizabeh Zimmer, eds. (Pennington, NJ: A Capella Books). See also John Szwed and Morton Marks, "The Afro-American Transformation of European Set Dances and Dance Suites," *Dance Research Journal* (Summer 1988): 29–36.

116. Theodore W. Allen, *The Invention of the White Race, Volume One. Racial Oppression and Social Control* (London and New York: Verso, 1994).

117. Neil Foley, " 'Almost White': Mexican Tenant Farmers and the Politics of Race in Socialist Central Texas, 1911–1917" (Unpublished paper presented at the Southern Historical Association, Louisville, Kentucky, 11 November 1994).

118. George Lipsitz, "The Possessive Investment in Whiteness," 370.

119. Ibid.

120. Ibid., 372.

121. Jane Marcus, "Bonding and Bondage: Nancy Cunard and the Making of the Negro Anthology" in *Border, Boundaries & Frames: Cultural Criticism and Cultural Studies*, Mae Henderson, ed. (New York: Routledge, 1994), 44–45.

122. Vron Ware, *Beyond the Pale: White Women, Racism and History* (London and New York: Verso, 1994).

123. Ruth Frankenberg, "Whiteness and Americanness: Explaining Constructions of Race, Culture and Nation in White Women's Life Narratives," in Gregory and Sanjek, *Race*, 62-77. See also Ruth Frankenberg, *White Women, Race Matters: The Social Construction of Whiteness* (Minneapolis: University of Minnesota Press, 1993).

124. Frankenberg, "Whiteness and Americanness," 66, 74.

125. Ibid., 75.

126. bell hooks, *Black Looks*, 12.

127. Editorial: "Abolish the White Race—By Any Means Necessary," *Race Traitor* (Winter 1993): 1–2.

128. *Race Traitor* Winter 1993 and Spring 1993 front covers and inside front covers. The inside back cover of the first issue reproduces a portion of a May 1992 issue of the journal, *Racial Loyalty*, whose motto is "its great to be white!" and which calls itself "Spearhead of the White Racial Holy War." The seal that appears between the two words of the publication's title bears the inscription, "White people awake. Save the White Race." Across this page the editors of *Race Traitor* have written the words (in thick magic marker lettering), "we prefer *treason*."

129. W.E.B. Du Bois, *The Souls of Black Folk*, 76.

130. Trey Ellis, "The New Black Aesthetic," *Callaloo* 12 (1989): 235.

131. Signs that this practice is eroding in the 1990s include the publication of groundbreaking volumes like the *Heath Anthology of American Literature*, General Editor Paul Lauter, 2nd ed. (Lexington, Mass.: D.C. Heath, 1994), and its widespread adoption in courses, and *The Columbia History of the American Novel*, General Editor, Emory Eliot (New York: Columbia University Press, 1991), both of which pioneered in remapping the terrain we call "American literature." Critical studies that resist the notion of segregated canons by exploring parallel issues in works by black and white writers include Werner Sollors's *Beyond Ethnicity*, Peter Messent's *New Readings in the American Novel* (London and New York: Macmillan, St. Martin's Press, 1990); Elizabeth Ammons's *Conflicting Stories: American Women Writers at the Turn into the Twentieth Century* (New York: Oxford Univesity Press, 1992); Allessandro Portelli's *Il Testo e la Voce. Oralita. Lettera- tura. e Democrazia in America* (Rome: Manifestolibro, 1992); trans. *The Text and the Voice: Writing, Speaking, and Democracy in American Literature* (New York: Columbia University Press, 1995); and Eric Sundquist's *To Wake the Nations* (1993).

132. Elliott Butler-Evans examined some related issues in "Beyond Essentialism: Rethinking Afro-American Cultural Theory," in *Inscriptions 5: Traveling Theories: Trav- eling Theorists*, ed. James Clifford and Vivek Dhareshwar (1989), 121–135.

133. Henry Louis Gates, Jr., "Criticism in the Jungle," in *Black Literature and Literary Theory*, ed. Gates (New York: Methuen, 1984), 4.

134. Ann duCille, *The Coupling Convention. Sex, Text, and Tradition in Black Women's Fiction* (New York: Oxford University Press, 1993).

135. Richard Wright, *Savage Holiday*, Introduction by Gerald Early (1954; rpt. Jackson, Miss.: University Press of Mississippi, 1994).

136. Carla Peterson, *"Doers of the Word": African-American Women Writers and*

*Speakers in the North, 1830–1880* (New York: Oxford University Press, 1995); Claudia Tate, *Domestic Allegories of Political Desire: The Black Heroine's Text at the Turn of the Century* (New York: Oxford University Press, 1992); Francis Smith Foster, *Written by Herself: Literary Production by African American Women, 1746–1892* (Bloomington: Indiana University Press, 1993); Thadious Davis, *Nella Larsen: Novelist of the Harlem Renaissance: A Woman's Life Unveiled* (Baton Rouge: Louisiana State University Press, 1994); Melba Joyce Boyd, *Discarded Legacy: Politics and Poetics in the Life of Frances E.W. Harper, 1825–1911* (Detroit: Wayne State University Press, 1994); Dickson D. Bruce, Jr., *Archibald Grimké: Portrait of a Black Independent* (Baton Rouge: Lousiana State University Press, 1994).

137. Adelaide Cromwell, *The Other Brahmins: Boston's Black Upper Class 1850–1950* (Fayetteville: University of Arkansas Press, 1994); Willard B. Gatewood, *Aristocrats of Color: The Black Elite, 1880–1920* (Bloomington: Indiana University Press, 1990); J. Clay Smith, Jr., *Emancipation: The Making of the Black Lawyer, 1844–1944*, Foreword by Justice Thurgood Marshall (Philadelphia: University of Pennsylvania Press, 1993); Charles Thomas, *Black and Blue: Profiles of Blacks in IBM* (Atlanta: Aaron Press, 1993); James Joy and Ruth Farmer, eds., *Spirit, Space & Survival: African American Women in White Academe* (New York: Routledge, 1993); Ellis Cose, *The Rage of a Privileged Class* (New York: Harper Collins, 1993); Sara Lawrence-Lightfoot, *I've Known Rivers: Lives of Loss and Liberation* (Reading, Mass: Addison-Wesley, Solidas, Merloyd Lawrence, 1994). See also Ann Morris and Henrietta Ambrose, Photographic Restoration by James Nagel, *North Webster: A Photographic History of a Black Community* (Bloomington: Indiana University Press, 1993); Charles T. Banner-Haley, *The Fruits of Integration: Black Middle-Class Ideology and Culture, 1960–1990* (Jackson: University Press of Mississippi, 1994); and Carla L. Peterson, " 'Further Liftings of the Veil': Gender, Class, and Labor in Frances E. W. Harper's *Iola Leroy*," in *Listening to Silences: New Essays in Feminist Criticism*, ed. Elaine Hedges and Shelley Fisher Fishkin (New York: Oxford University Press, 1994).

138. Trey Ellis, "The New Black Aesthetic," 233–243.

139. Ibid., 241.

140. Ibid., 235.

141. *William Johnson's Natchez: The Ante-bellum Diary of a Free Negro*, William Ransom Hogan and Edwin Adams Davis, eds., with a new Introduction by William L. Andrews (Baton Rouge: Louisiana State University Press, 1993); Adele Logan Alexander, *Ambiguous Lives: Free Women of Color in Rural Georgia, 1789-1879* (Fayetteville: University of Arkansas Press, 1991).

142. James O. Horton, *Free People of Color: Inside the African American Community* (Washington, D.C.: Smithsonian Institution Press, 1993), 14. Horton partly endorses Clarence Walker's provocative call—in *Deromanticizing Black History: Critical Essays and Reappraisals* (Knoxville: University of Tennessee Press, 1991)—that scholars not paper over or ignore divisions, disunity and tensions in black communities over time. Horton's study builds on earlier work by Leon Litwack, Benjamin Quarles, Theodore Hershberg, Jane and William Pease, Floyd J. Miller, Ira Berlin, Gary Nash, and others, as Horton acknowledges in his first chapter, "Northern Free Blacks."

143. See David Steven Cohen, "Afro-Dutch Folklore and Folklife," in Cohen, *Folk Legacies Revisited* (New Brunswick, NJ: Rutgers University Press, 1995), 31–45; Allison Blakely, *Blacks in the Dutch World: The Evolution of Racial Imagery in a Modern Society* (Bloomington: Indiana University Press, 1993); Laurence Mordekhai Thomas, "The Soul of Identity: Jews and Blacks," forthcoming in *People of the Book: Thirty Scholars Reflect on Their Jewish Identity*, ed. Jeffrey Rubin-Dorsky and Shelley Fisher Fishkin (Madison:

University of Wisconsin Press, 1996); and Oliver W. Holmes, "Perceptions of 'Otherness': A Personal Interpretation of Jewish Experience," also in *People of the Book*. See also Laurence Mordekhai Thomas, *Vessels of Evil: American Slavery and the Holocaust* (Philadelphia: Temple University Press, 1993).

144. Michel Fabre, *Richard Wright: Books and Writers* (Jackson: University of Mississippi Press, 1990).

145. See Fishkin, *Was Huck Black?* For further comments on Mark Twain by Bradley and by Morrison, see also David Bradley, "Preface to *How to Tell a Story and Other Essays*" and Toni Morrison, "Preface to *Adventures of Huckleberry Finn*," forthcoming in *The Oxford Mark Twain*, ed. Shelley Fisher Fishkin, 29 vols. (New York: Oxford University Press, 1996). See also Prefaces in *The Oxford Mark Twain* by Charles Johnson, Walter Mosley and Sherley Anne Williams.

146. David Bradley, "Our Crowd, Their Crowd, and *Moby-Dick*," forthcoming in *The Ever Moving Dawn: Essay in Celebration of the Melville Centennial*, ed. John Bryant and Robert Milder (Kent, Ohio: Kent State University Press, 1996).

147. David Levering Lewis, *W.E.B. Du Bois: Biography of a Race 1868–1919* (New York: Henry Holt and Co., 1993). Lewis's access to Du Bois's papers allowed him to extend and amplify a number of issues first raised in Arnold Rampersad's early groundbreaking study, *The Art and Imagination of W.E.B. Du Bois* (New York: Cambridge University Press, 1976).

148. Richard Yarborough, "Strategies of Characterization in *Uncle Tom's Cabin* and the Early Afro-American Novels," in Eric Sundquist, ed., *New Essays on* Uncle Tom's Cabin (New York: Cambridge University Press, 1986).

149. Du Cille, *The Coupling Convention* 24.

150. Philip M. Richards, "Phillis Wheatley and Literary Americanization," *American Quarterly* 44 (June 1992): 163–191; Carla Peterson, *Doers of the Word*; and Ann du Cille, *The Coupling Convention*.

151. Ann Douglas, *Terrible Honesty: Mongrel Manhattan in the 1920s* (New York: Farrar, Straus and Giroux, 1995), 82. See also Tracy Mishkin, ed., *Literary Influence and African-American Writers* (New York: Garland, 1995).

152. Douglas, *Terrible Honesty*, 82.

153. Michael Eric Dyson, "Language, Race and Identity," (paper presented at "The Power of Language," Mark Twain Memorial Fall Symposium, 1 October 1994, Hartford), 4.

154. Dyson, "Language, Race and Identity," 5.

155. Michael Eric Dyson, *Reflecting Black: African-American Cultural Criticis* (Minneapolis: University of Minnesota Press, 1993) 162–163.

156. Adrian Piper, "Passing for White, Passing for Black," *Transition* 58 (1990): 14–32; Maureen T. Reddy, *Crossing the Color Line: Race, Parenting and Culture* (New Brunswick, NJ: Rutgers University Press, 1994); Lise Funderburg, *Black, White, Other: Biracial Americans Talk about Race and Identity* (New York: William Morrow, 1994); Naomi Zack, *Race and Mixed Race* (Philadelphia: Temple University Press, 1994); Shirlee Taylor Haizlip, *The Sweeter the Juice: A Family Memoir in Black and White* (New York: Simon and Schuster, 1994); Gerald Early, ed., *Lure and Loathing: Essays on Race, Identity, and the Ambivalence of Assimilation* (New York: Penguin Books, 1994).

157. F. James Davis, *Who is Black? One Nation's Definition* (University Park: Penn State University Press, 1991).

158. Holloway, *Africanisms in American Culture*; Holloway and Vass, *The African Heritage of American English*; John Thornton, *Africa and Africans in the Making of the Atlantic World, 1400–1680* (Cambridge: Cambridge University Press, 1992); Saltkoko S.

Mufwene and Nancy Condon, eds., *Africanisms in Afro-American Language Variations* (Athens: Georgia University Press, 1993); Sterling Stuckey, *Going through the Storm: The Influence of African-American Art in History* (New York: Oxford University Press, 1994).

159. Kwame Anthony Appiah, *In My Father's House: Africa in the Philosophy of Culture* (New York: Oxford University Press, 1992); V. Y. Mudimbe, *The Invention of Africa* (Bloomington: Indiana University Press, 1988) and *The Idea of Africa* (Bloomington: Indiana University Press, 1994); Bernard Makhosezwe Magubane, *The Ties that Bind: African-American Consciousness of Africa* (Trenton, NJ: Africa World Press, 1987).

160. Houston Baker, *Black Studies, Rap and the Academy* (Chicago: University of Chicago Press, 1993); Tricia Rose, *Black Noise* (Hanover, NH: Wesleyan University Press/University Press of New England, 1994); Gregory Stephens, "Interracial Dialogue in Rap Music: Call-and-Response in a Multicultural Style," *New Formation* 16 (Spring 1992): 62–79.

161. Kobena Mercer, *Welcome to the Jungle: New Positions in Black Cultural Studies* (New York and London: Routledge, 1994); Tricia Rose, Elizabeth Alexander, Farrah Griffin, and Robin D.G. Kelley all participated in the lively roundtable discussion, " 'Hair-piece'—The Culture and Politics of Black Hair," at the American Studies Association Conference in Nashville, 28 October 1994.

162. Farrah Jasmine Griffin, *"Who Set You Flowin?" The African-American Migration Narrative* (New York: Oxford University Press, 1995); Glen Alyn, *I Say Me For a Parable: The Oral Autobiography of Mance Lipscomb, Texas Bluesman* (New York: Norton, 1993).

163. D. L. Smith, "What is Black Culture?" (Paper presented at Princeton University Conference on "Race Matters: Black Americans/U.S. Terrain," April 30, 1994) 4. Forthcoming in *The House that Race Built: Black Americans, U.S. Terrain,* ed. Wahneema Lubiano (New York: Pantheon, 1996).

164. Ibid., 4.

165. Ibid., 12. See also Cornel West, *The American Evasion of Philosophy* (Madision: University of Wisconsin Press, 1989), 213.

166. Smith, "What is Black Culture?" 12.

167. Ibid., 5.

168. Cornel West, *Keeping Faith: Philosoohy and Race in America* (New York and London: Routledge, 1993), xii.

169. Arthur Schlesinger, Jr., *The Disuniting of America: Reflections on a Multicultural Society* (New York: Norton, 1992), 118.

170. Maghan Keita, "Multiculturalism: The Mandate for the Nineties—The Myth of the American Monolith," *Journal of Multicultural Studies* (Spring 1991): 22–23. Keita also sketches a number of intriguing examples of the multicultural dimensions of European culture through the fifteenth century, of the Ottoman Ernpire, and of pre-Columbian societies in Meso-America.

171. Warren, *Black and White Strangers*, 10.

172. Albert Murray, *The Omni-Americans* (New York: Vintage, 1983), 22.

173. Richard Brookhiser, quoted in Stanley Fish, *There's No Such Thing as Free Speech . . . and it's a good thing too* (New York: Oxford University Press, 1994), 84.

174. Laurence Auster, quoted in Stanley Fish, *There's No Such Thin as Free Speech*, 83–84.

175. James O. Horton, "Race, Nationality and Cultural Identity: Free Blacks in the Age of Jackson" (paper presented at the Organization of American Historians Convention, Atlanta, April 1994), 33–34.

176. Ann DuCille's recent critique of Afrocentrism makes a related point: "While the empowering premise of an 'unembarassingly black' Afrocentric methodology offers an essential challenge to the assumed universality of European paradigms, it does not, to my mind, sufficiently address the question of cultural mediation that is the consequence of centuries of appropriation and cross-fertilization. Although it acknowledges blacks in the Americas as an Africa-derived people with a cultural legacy different from that of Euro-Americans, it does not adequately consider the degree to which that culture is necessarily intertwined with others around it." DuCille, "Postcolonialism and Afrocentricity: Discourse and Dat Course," in *The Black Columbiad: Defining Moments in African American Literature and Culture*, ed. Werner Sollors and Maria Diedrich (Cambridge: Harvard University Press, 1994).

177. Henry Louis Gates, Jr., *Loose Canons: Notes on the Culture Wars* (New York: Oxford University Press, 1992), xvi.

178. Susan Curtis, *Dancing to a Black Man's Tune: A Life of Scott Joplin* (Columbia: University of Missouri Press, 1994). See especially chapter 6, "The Legacy of Scott Joplin," 161–189.

179. Gilroy, *The Black Atlantic: Modernity and Double Consciousness* (Cambridge: Harvard University Press, 1993), 199.

180. See Shelley Fisher Fishkin, "The Multiculturalism of 'Traditional' Culture," *The Chronicle of Higher Education*, 10 March 1995, A48, for further discussion of the ideas in this section.

# Notes on Contributors

*Herman Beavers* is an assistant professor of English at the University of Pennsylvania. He is the author of *Wrestling Angels into Song: The Fictions of Ernest J. Gaines and Alan McPherson* (1995), as well as essays on Eddie Murphy, Charles Johnson, and Langston Hughes. Beavers is currently at work on a study of the immune system and African-American masculine identity in literature and film.

*Dickson D. Bruce, Jr.,* is professor of History at the University of California, Irvine. Among his books are *Black American Writing from the Nadir: The Evolution of a Literary Tradition, 1877–1915* (LSU, 1989) and *Archibald Grimké: Portrait of a Black Independent* (LSU, 1993). His current research focuses on concepts of race in the early American republic.

*Peter Carafiol's* most recent book is *The American Ideal: Literary History as a Worldly Activity,* published by Oxford University Press in 1991. His essay in this volume, written with the support of a Guggenheim Fellowship, is taken from his next book, *UnAmerican Literature,* a pragmatist effort to bring the words "literary" and "history" into closer acquaintance.

*Shelley Fisher Fishkin* is a professor of American Studies at the University of Texas. Her books include *Was Huck Black? Mark Twain and African-American Voices* (Oxford, 1993) and two co-edited volumes, *Listening to Silences: New Essays in Feminist Criticism* (Oxford, 1994) and a collection of essays on Jewish identity in the academy (Wisconsin, 1996). She is also editor of the 29–volume *Oxford Mark Twain* (1996) and co-editor of the "Race and American Culture" book series published by Oxford University Press.

*P. Gabrielle Foreman* teaches African-American and nineteenth-century American literature at Occidental College. She has contributed essays to numerous journals, including *Black American Literature Forum, Feminist Studies,* and *Representations,* and is currently at work on two book manuscripts, *Sentimental Subversions: Reading Acts and African-American Women's Writing (1859–1909)* and *The Charge of Erotics: Interracial Desire in the Nineteenth Century.*

*Teresa Goddu* teaches American and African-American literature at Vanderbilt University and is currently completing a book on the American gothic, entitled *Haunted by History: The American Gothic, 1780–1870.* She has also published articles on Frederick Douglass, Nathaniel Hawthorne, Gloria Naylor, and country music.

**Robert S. Levine,** an associate professor of English at the University of Maryland, College Park, is the author of *Conspiracy and Romance: Studies in Brockden Brown, Cooper, Hawthorne, and Melville* (Cambridge, 1989). He is currently editing a Martin R. Delany reader and has recently completed a book-length study of Delany and Frederick Douglass.

**Eric Lott** teaches American Studies at the University of Virginia. He is the author of *Love and Theft: Blackface Minstrelsy and the American Working Class* (Oxford, 1993), and his work on the racial politics of culture has appeared in *The Nation, The Village Voice, Social Text, Representations, American Quarterly,* and other journals.

**Toni Morrison** is a Nobel laureate and the author of many prize-winning works of fiction, in addition to the recent critical study, *Playing in the Dark: Whiteness and the Literary Imagination* (Harvard, 1992). She is Robert F. Goheen Professor in the Council of the Humanities at Princeton University.

**Carla L. Peterson** is a professor in the Department of English and the Comparative Literature Program at the University of Maryland, College Park. She has published articles on writers including Frances E. W. Harper, Pauline Hopkins, and Frederick Douglass, and she is the author of *"Doers of the Word": African-American Women Speakers and Writers in the North (1830–1880),* published by Oxford University Press in 1995.

**Ashraf H. A. Rushdy** is an associate professor of English and African-American Studies at Wesleyan University. In addition to numerous articles on literature and literary theory, he is the author of *The Empty Garden: The Subject of Late Milton* (1992) and is currently working on a book-length study of African-American modes of representation in contemporary narratives of slavery, to be entitled *NeoSlave Narratives: Studies in the Social Logic of a Contemporary African American Literary Form.*

**Jeffrey Steele** is a professor of English at the University of Wisconsin, Madison. He is the author of *The Representation of the Self in the American Renaissance* (1987) and *The Essential Margaret Fuller* (1992), as well as a recent essay on representations of American Indians in nineteenth-century advertising.

**Todd Vogel** is a doctoral student in the American Civilization program at the University of Texas at Austin. Since 1984, his work as a journalist has appeared in *Business Week, The Washington Post, The Boston Globe,* and *The Dallas Morning News.*

**Henry B. Wonham**, an assistant professor of English at the University of Oregon, is the author of *Mark Twain and the Art of the Tall Tale,* published by Oxford University Press in 1993. He is currently writing a book on Charles W. Chesnutt.

# Index

Bryson, Norman, 226n1
Butler, Octavia, 66

Cable, George Washington, 34
Calhoun, John, 26
Campbell, James Edwin, 121
Campbell, Karlyn Kohrs, 162
Cantor, Eddie, 154
Canzoneri, Robert, 71, 73, 77
Carafiol, Peter, 7, 43–61
Carby, Hazel V., 103–104, 158, 164,
    237–238
Cary, Mary Shadd, 183
Cash, W. J., 235, 260
Cather, Willa, 3, 29, 253
Cézanne, Paul, 140, 144–145
Chase, Richard, 5
Chase-Riboud, Barbara, 66, 89
Chesnutt, Charles W., 4, 15n15, 135–136,
    230
Cheyfitz, Eric, 257
Child, Lydia Maria, 272
Chinitz, David, 255
Christy's Minstrels, 30
Clarke, John Henrik, 64, 81; *William
    Styron's Nat Turner: Ten Black Writers
    Respond*, 65–67, 70, 78–82, 85–90
Clarke, Lewis, 171, 173
Cold War criticism, 1–2
Cole, Bob, 147
Condit, Celeste Michelle, 266
Condon, Nancy, 273
Cone, James, 82
Conrad, Joseph, 22
coon songs, 10, 145–148
Cooper, Anna Julia, 10–11, 126–127, 129;
    *A Voice from the South*, 158–168
Cooper, J. California, 66
Cooper, James Fenimore, 254
Core, George, 79
Cornish, William, 114
Cose, Ellis, 271
Cox, James M., 44, 188n24
Craft, Ellen, 172
Craft, William, 172
Cromwell, Adelaide, 270
Crozier, Alice C., 177, 183
Crummell, Alexander, 159
Cuffe, Paul, 112
Cullen, Countee, 272
Curtis, Susan, 276

D'Aguiar, Fred, 66
Dauber, Kenneth, 236

Davis, F. James, 273
Davis, Thadious, 270
Dayan, Joan, 239, 241, 249n50
Deaver, James, 114
DeKoven, Marianne, 148, 149
Delany, Martin, 11, 172, 183
Deval, Patrick, 43
Dew, Thomas, 67, 68–70, 71, 76, 80–81,
    89
Dickinson, Emily, 18
Dillard, J. L., 264–265
Dinesen, Isak, 22
Dixon-Gottschild, Brenda, 266
Dostoyevsky, Fyodor, 272
double consciousness, 10, 127–129,
    135–137
Douglas, Ann, 272
Douglass, Frederick, 4, 5, 8, 11, 15n15, 84,
    96, 99, 102, 105, 108, 109, 159,
    171–175, 178, 180–181, 183–184,
    205–206, 253, 254; "The Heroic
    Slave," 11–12, 191–201, 210–226; *My
    Bondage and My Freedom*, 11–12, 97,
    191–201; *Narrative of the Life of
    Frederick Douglass*, 97, 100–101
Douglass, H. Ford, 84
Doyle, Laura, 255–256
Drayton, John, 238
Dreiser, Theodore, 51, 272
Drewry, William, 72, 84
Duberman, Martin, 65, 82, 86
Du Bois, W.E.B., 2, 6, 9–10, 126–129,
    170n33, 269, 272; *The Souls of Black
    Folk*, 10, 127–129, 135–137
duCille, Ann, 270, 272, 289–290n176
Duff, John, 83
Dunbar, Paul Laurence, 121
DuPlessis, Rachel Blau, 255
Dyson, Michael Eric, 272–273

Early, Gerald, 270, 273
Easton, William, 266
Eco, Umberto, 46
Edmundson, Milly, 172, 175
Elgin Community, 183
Elkins, Stanley, 79–80
Eliot, George, 128
Eliot, T. S., 255, 272
Ellis, Trey, 269, 271
Ellison, Ralph, 1–4, 5, 14, 32, 33, 85, 89,
    98, 225–226, 253, 261, 272
Emerson, Ralph Waldo, 128, 233
Emery, Allan Moore, 214
Emmett, Dan, 256

Equiano, Olaudah, 5
ethnic criticism, 43–47, 58–61, 53–54
ethnocentrism, see literary ethnocentrism

Fabre, Michel, 272
Farrison, William, Jr., 95
Faulkner, William, 15n15, 19, 29, 97, 253, 255
Fern, Fanny, 8, 9, 109; *Ruth Hall*, 107–108
Fiedelson, Charles, 234
Fiedler, Leslie, 37, 232
Finley, Robert, 120
Fish, Stanley, 59
Fishkin, Shelley Fisher, 13–14, 36, 63, 200, 251–276
Fitzgerald, F. Scott, 29, 122
Flaubert, Gustave, 140, 144–145
Fleissner, Robert, 255
Flower, Dean, 252
Foley, Neil, 266–267
Foner, Eric, 83, 84
Foreman, P. Gabrielle, 11–12, 191–201
Forkner, Ben, 71
Foster, Frances Smith, 197, 270, 271
Foster, Stephen, 37
Frankenberg, Ruth, 266, 267–268
Franklin, Benjamin, 5, 43, 47, 52
Frazier, E. Franklin, 270
*Frederick Douglass' Paper*, 172, 193–194
Fredrickson, George, 34, 212–213, 214
Fremont-Smith, Eliot, 85–86
Freud, Sigmund, 99
Friedman, Melvin, 83
Fry, Gladys-Marie, 36
Fugitive Slave Law, 26, 194
Fuller, Margaret, 9, 99, 109
Funderburg, Lise, 273

Gaines, Ernest, 8, 66, 89
Garnet, Henry Highland, 84
Garrison, William Lloyd, 12, 97, 191–195, 217, 223
Gates, Henry Louis, Jr., 13–14, 269, 275
Gatewood, Willard B., 271
Genovese, Eugene, 65, 82, 84, 87
Gilbert, Sandra, 159
Gilly, Annie, 148
Gilman, Charlotte Perkins, 107
Gilman, Sander, 153, 257–258
Gilroy, Paul, 262, 276
Glasgow, Ellen, 235
Gloucester, Jeremiah, 115
Glowka, A. Wayne, 265
Goddu, Teresa, 12–13, 230–246

Goethe, Wolfgang von, 128
Gramsci, Antonio, 40
Gray, Richard, 232
Gray, Thomas, 8, 67–90, 174, 185
Greenfeld, Alfred, 148
Greenfield, Elizabeth, 172
Griffin, Farrah, 274
Grimké, Archibald, 270
Grimonprez, Johan, 266
Gross, Seymour, 65
Gubar, Susan, 159

Hairston, Loyle, 65
Haizlipp, Shirlee Taylor, 273
Haley, Alex, 66
Hall, Gwendolyn Midlo, 260
Hamilton, Charles, 81
Harding, Vincent, 79, 84–85, 89
Harper, Charles C., 115–116, 117
Harper, Frances, 127, 270, 272
Harris, Joel Chandler, 34, 256
Harris, Susan K., 111n53
Harvey, Remus, 114
Hauss, Jon, 210
Hawthorne, Nathaniel, 3, 19, 29, 231–232, 233, 234, 237, 253
Hayden, Lewis, 171
Haynes, Mabel, 142, 151
Hedrick, Joan, 189n29
Hemenway, Robert, 230–231
Hemingway, Ernest, 5, 29, 122, 253
Henderson, Stephen, 5
Henson, Josiah, 171, 173, 175, 183, 194
Herskovits, Melville, 258
Hogan, Ernest, 147
Holliday, Carl, 249n40
Holloway, Joseph E., 259, 265, 273
Holton, Curlee, 266
hooks, bell, 109, 262, 266, 268
Hopkins, Pauline, 9, 66, 100, 167–168
Horsman, Reginald, 239
Horton, James O., 271, 275
Howe, Lawrence, 255
Howells, William Dean, 18, 34, 126–129, 133, 255; *An Imperative Duty*, 9–10, 129–137
Hurston, Zora Neale, 270

Irigaray, Luce, 99

Jacobs, Harriet, 4, 8, 96, 107, 108, 109, 172, 173, 175, 200; *Incidents in the Life of a Slave Girl*, 102–105
James, Henry, 19, 128, 255